Feminisms with Chinese Characteristics

Gender and Globalization
Susan S. Wadley, *Series Editor*

Select Titles in Gender and Globalization

For a full list of titles in this series,
visit https://press.syr.edu/supressbook-series
/gender-and-globalization/.

Feminisms with
Chinese Characteristics

Edited by Ping Zhu and Hui Faye Xiao

Syracuse University Press

For a listing of books published and distributed by Syracuse University Press,
visit https://press.syr.edu.

ISBN: 978-0-8156-3739-4 (hardcover)
       978-0-8156-3725-7 (paperback)
       978-0-8156-5526-8 (e-book)

Library of Congress Cataloging-in-Publication Data

Names: Zhu, Ping (Professor of Chinese literature) editor. | Xiao, Hui Faye, editor.
Title: Feminisms with Chinese characteristics / edited by Ping Zhu and Hui Faye Xiao.
Description: First Edition. | Syracuse : Syracuse University Press, 2021. | Series: Gender
    and globalization | Includes bibliographical references and index. | Summary:
    "This volume offers a timely examination of the special characteristics of different,
    sometimes clashing, Chinese feminisms when the "#METOO" movement sweeps
    over the world under the mantle of global capitalism"— Provided by publisher.
Identifiers: LCCN 2021013207 | ISBN 9780815637394 (hardcover) |
    ISBN 9780815637257 (paperback) | ISBN 9780815655268 (ebook)
Subjects: LCSH: Feminism—China—History—21st century. | Sex role—China—
    History—21st century. | MeToo movement—China. | Feminism in literature.
Classification: LCC HQ1767 .F456 2021 | DDC 305.42095109/05—dc23
LC record available at https://lccn.loc.gov/2021013207

Contents

Illustrations

Acknowledgments

The inception of this volume can be traced to the American Comparative Literature Association (ACLA) conference in Utrecht, Netherlands, in 2017. That year we co-organized the seminar "Feminism with Chinese Characteristics," which attracted ten other scholars. During the intense three days of intellectual exchange it became clear that the singular *feminism* must be replaced by its plural form, *feminisms*. One-third of the ACLA seminar presentations were developed and collected in this volume. We sincerely thank the other participants in the seminar, Dusica Ristivojevic, Bingchun Meng, Weiling Deng, Geraldine Fiss, Sarah Woodland, Kun Qian, and Xi Liu, for their early participation, which led to the fruition of this project. We are also grateful for our seminar audiences' invaluable comments, questions, and suggestions. Our special thanks go to Tani E. Barlow, who provided extremely helpful comments on the two editors' chapters during the 2020 Association for Asian Studies panel "Rearticulating Gender and Class in Postsocialist China: Women's Literature as Method" (which was moved online due to Covid-19), and also read and commented on the introduction of this volume to make it better.

The editors' home institutions offered various forms of support for this project: the University of Oklahoma funded an undergraduate student, Tera Mills, in fall 2018 and spring 2019, so she could work closely with Ping Zhu and Hui Faye Xiao to cotranslate four pieces in the volume; the University of Kansas Research Excellence Initiative offered one course release to Xiao for her editorial work in fall 2018. In addition, an American Philosophical Society Franklin Research Grant, University of Kansas International Affairs, and the

Center for East Asian Studies funded Xiao's field research conducted in summer 2019.

Two chapters in this volume are reprints of previous publications in English. Chapter 1, Nicola Spakowski's "'Gender' Trouble: Feminism in China under the Impact of Western Theory and the Spatialization of Identity" is a reprint of the author's article of the same name published in *positions: east asia cultures critique* 19, no. 1 (2011). Chapter 5, Wang Zheng's "Feminist Struggles in a Changing China" is a reprint of her chapter by that title in *Women's Movements in the Global Era: The Power of Local Feminisms* (edited by Armrita Basu, Westview, 2017), with slight modifications. Duke University Press and Westview Press have respectively permitted us to reprint the pieces in the current volume for free, and we would like to take this opportunity to express our gratitude for their generous support.

We thank the Chinese artist Jiang Jie for allowing us to use an image of her 2014 sculpture installation *Over 1.5 Tons* as the cover art of this book. This detail of her artwork vividly illustrates the plurality of Chinese feminisms.

Finally, it was a pleasure to work with the acquisitions editor Peggy Solic and the production team of Syracuse University Press. Meg Wallace has done a fabulous job in copyediting the manuscript. We give warm thanks to everyone at Syracuse University Press who helped to bring this book to life.

Feminisms with Chinese Characteristics

Feminisms with Chinese Characteristics

An Introduction

Ping Zhu and Hui Faye Xiao

The two key terms of this volume are "feminisms" and "Chinese characteristics." "Feminisms" can be translated as *nüquan zhuyi* 女权主义 (women's-rights-ism) or *nüxing zhuyi* 女性主义 (womanism) in Chinese, but the two are not interchangeable.[1] Following the conceptual framework proposed by Dai Jinhua, we view *nüxing zhuyi* as a broader category that can incorporate *nüquan zhuyi*.[2] It is under this umbrella term of the plural *nüxing zhuyi* that we set out to examine and theorize the multifarious feminisms in contemporary China.

Chinese feminisms must remain plural because those concepts represent the changing practical consciousness in response to historical and social developments. Plurality is an effective strategy for

---

1. As the following genealogy of Chinese feminisms shows, the terms *nüquan zhuyi* and *nüxing zhuyi* have been rendered under different historical conditions by different feminist groups and therefore carry different sociopolitical connotations. Neither of these terms was used during the socialist period, when *funü jiefang* (women's liberation) and *nannü pingdeng* (equality between men and women) were preferred.

2. Dai Jinhua, *After the Post-Cold War: The Future of Chinese History* (Durham, NC: Duke Univ. Press, 2018), 163.

1

subverting the systematic oppressions that often exercise their power by creating, maintaining, and consolidating binary structures. According to Lisa Rofel, the problem faced by Chinese feminists lies "in the binary divisions we utilized to forge a singular feminism: socialism versus capitalism, Chinese traditions versus Chinese socialism, and Chinese feminism versus western feminism."[3] The imperative for Chinese women, as Rofel puts it, is that they need to rise "above the generalizations about them to become subjects of a counterhistory."[4] Plurality, on the other hand, does not mean replacing the critique of the systematic problems with fragmented strategies; rather, it invites pluralistic, systematic thinking. For example, Dai Jinhua has proposed a broader definition of "feminism" as "the search for different worlds and alternative possibilities other than global capitalism"; such explorations, "through women's, especially Third-World women's thinking of nationalism, reveal the plurality of historical processes, so as to open broader space for thoughts, criticisms, and social practices."[5]

The other key term, "Chinese characteristics," is a neologism invented by Westerners in the late nineteenth century, when Chineseness was racialized, oftentimes in a negative way, as a result of the colonial encounter.[6] The New Culture reformers and the later socialist revolutionaries both set out to reform Chinese tradition, which can be regarded as another form of "Chinese characteristics," following the Western model and the Marxist paradigm, respectively. Since 1984

3. Lisa Rofel, *Other Modernities: Gendered Yearnings in China after Socialism* (Berkeley: Univ. of California Press, 1999), 51.

4. Rofel, *Other Modernities*.

5. Dai Jinhua, "Liangnan Zhijian Huo Tuwei Keneng?" 两难之间或突围可能? (A Dilemma or a Breakout?), in *Funü, Minzu yu Nüxing Zhuyi* (Women, Nation, and Feminism), ed. Chen Shunxin 陈顺馨 and Dai Jinhua 戴锦华 (Beijing: Zhongyang bianyi chubanshe, 2002), 29.

6. For example, English political economist John Bowring's "Chinese Characteristics" was published in the *Fortnightly Review* on July 15, 1865. American missionary Arthur Henderson Smith's *Chinese Characteristics* was published by North China Herald in Shanghai in 1890 and was widely circulated in China and East Asia; the first edition sold out in less than three years.

the phrase "Chinese characteristics" has become the official translation of *zhongguo tese* 中国特色 as it appeared in the epithet "zhongguo
tese shehui zhuyi" 中国特色社会主义 ("socialism with Chinese characteristics"), proposed by Deng Xiaoping.[7] This epithet justifies China's
integration into the world capitalist system in the postsocialist period
under the premise that the Chinese Communist Party (CCP) remains
the sole ruling party of China, which "signals the state's insistence on
its monopoly on explaining and defining Chinese society."[8] Whether
as a racialized term or as a political guideline, "Chinese characteristics" presupposed a binary structure, be it East and West, traditional
and modern, or socialist and capitalist. From a grand perspective, the
history of twentieth-century China is a history when the binary structures and patriarchal hierarchies embedded in the epithet "Chinese
characteristics" were challenged, dismantled, and replaced by constantly renewed feminist ideas and practices across "multiple centers
and peripheries."[9] To continue the liberating potential of Chinese
feminisms, therefore, we must keep identifying and problematizing
multifarious contemporary figurations of patriarchal power.

Therefore, by juxtaposing the plural "feminisms" to "Chinese
characteristics," we intend to deconstruct the binary structures and patriarchal hierarchies embedded in history, language, race, culture, and
politics. We propose a broader use of "feminisms" in this volume to
contest and open up "Chinese characteristics" as a notion constrained
by racism, traditionalism, nationalism, or hierarchical spatialization

---

7. The term *zhongguo tese de shehui zhuyi* was proposed by Deng Xiaoping in a
talk when he met a Japanese delegation in 1984. Deng emphasized in the talk that
Marxism must be integrated with reality in China, and socialism must be geared to
the Chinese reality too.

8. Nicola Spakowski, "Socialist Feminism in Postsocialist China," *positions: east
asia cultures critique* 26, no. 4 (2018): 570.

9. Inderpal Grewal and Caren Kaplan, "Introduction: Transnational Feminist
Practices and Questions of Postmodernity," in *Scattered Hegemonies: Postmodernity
and Transnational Feminist Practices*, ed. Inderpal Grewal and Caren Kaplan (Minneapolis: Univ. of Minnesota Press, 1994), 19.

and biopoliticization in different historical periods—and at the same time, we propose to view the ensemble of Chinese feminisms as a transnational product that seeks to situate the imaginary notion of Chineseness in the global context. In this way, feminisms with Chinese characteristics can denote "the circulation of feminist discourses across various kinds of difference without reinscribing national(ist) boundaries or invoking a global-to-local hierarchy."[10] We argue that the strength of Chinese feminisms lies precisely in their plurality and in the plural Chinese characteristics that they simultaneously challenge and redefine.

With this mission in mind, in this introduction we first provide a brief genealogy of the fraught history of feminisms in China since the early twentieth century, then offer a critical survey of the contested terrain of Chinese feminisms in the contemporary period, especially after the 1995 World Conference on Women in Beijing. After laying out the historical context, opportunities, and challenges of Chinese feminisms, we discuss different forms of feminisms with Chinese characteristics that have emerged as counterdiscourses to masculinist populism, nationalism, and neoliberalism in twenty-first-century China and beyond. Here Chinese feminisms are regarded not as ersatz counterparts of Western feminisms, but as an active component of transnational feminisms in the age of globalization.[11]

This volume features a hybrid selection of scholarly articles, interviews, and talks from a representative group of women's and gender

10. Janet M. Conway, "Troubling Transnational Feminism(s): Theorising Activist Praxis," *Feminist Theory* 18, no. 2 (2017): 208.

11. The notion of transnational feminism is proposed by Inderpal Grewal and Caren Kaplan in their introduction to their volume *Scattered Hegemonies*. It is a more inclusive notion of feminism, with which questions such as "the place of women in the nation-state, resistance to revivals of 'tradition,' the complex issue of fundamentalism, the situation of workers in multinational corporations, and the relationship between gender, the nation-state, and mobile, transnational capital" (22) can be addressed.

studies scholars, women writers, and activists in mainland China, Hong Kong, the United States, and Europe. Their contributions to the discussion of feminisms with Chinese characteristics range from historical reflections, theoretical ruminations, and accounts of lived experiences, to cultural studies and social critiques, painting a panoramic picture of Chinese feminisms in the age of globalization. The plural Chinese feminisms negotiate and contend with one another, exhibiting the unstable and fractured terrain of feminist ideas and practices in contemporary China. This hybrid model allows us to pinpoint the multifaceted and dynamic contentions and representations of contemporary Chinese feminisms in a single volume—one that does not intend to present an authorial voice of any singular form of Chinese feminism, but instead sets a stage for multiple voices, analyses, and interpretations of contemporary Chinese feminisms, which constantly substantiate, underlie, supplement, contradict, offset, and dialogue with one another. It is our hope that these plural feminisms with Chinese characteristics can open up more possibilities of both action and imagination in history.

Genealogy of Chinese Feminisms

In order to understand the contested terrain and plurality of contemporary Chinese feminisms, it is necessary to look at the genealogy of Chinese feminisms as situated in history. The purpose of providing this genealogy is not to emphasize the particularity of Chinese feminisms, but to continually question the narratives in which Chinese feminisms are embedded, as Kumkum Sangari and Sudesh Vaid suggest:

> If feminism is to be different, it must acknowledge the ideological and problematic significance of its own past. Instead of creating yet another grand tradition or a cumulative history of emancipation, neither of which can deal with our present problems, we need to be attentive to how the past enters differently into the consciousness of

other historical periods and is further subdivided by a host of other factors including gender, caste, and class.[12]

The birth of Chinese feminisms can be traced back to the turn of the twentieth century, when China was plagued with a series of military defeats, foreign invasions, and economic crises. In the face of a crumbling Qing empire, Chinese elites were seeking new ways to stall China's sinking into a backwater colony in the imperialist-capitalist world system. Lamenting the inferior position of China (and Chinese men) in a world dominated by Euro-America, some progressive Chinese male intellectuals and political activists turned to a nationalist-feminist agenda. They advocated for female education, abolition of the centuries-old foot-binding practice, free love, free marriage, a new sexual morality, and even gynocentrism in the hope that women could live a healthier and happier life and actively contribute to the birth of a modern nation-state and its younger and, ideally, stronger citizens. As Tani E. Barlow asserts, the core of progressive modern Chinese feminism was eugenics,[13] which can be directly translated into national rejuvenation. For many early male feminists, "women's emancipation was part of a larger project of enlightenment and national self-strengthening, coded either 'male' or 'patriarchal.'"[14] In this historical context, early Chinese feminists were not in direct opposition to the patriarchal society or to men; instead, they "proved the value of their existence through negotiations with, or making concessions to, the society, the government, the nation, or even men."[15]

12. Kumkum Sangari and Sudesh Vaid, "Recasting Women: An Introduction," in *Recasting Women: Essays in Colonial History*, ed. Kumkum Sangari and Sudesh Vaid (New Brunswick, NJ: Rutgers Univ. Press, 1989), 18.

13. Tani E. Barlow, *The Question of Women in Chinese Feminism* (Durham, NC: Duke Univ. Press, 2004), 10.

14. Lydia H. Liu, Rebecca Karl, and Dorothy Ko, eds., *The Birth of Chinese Feminism: Essential Texts in Transnational Theory* (New York: Columbia Univ. Press, 2013), 7.

15. Dong Limin 董丽敏, "Xingbie Yanjiu: Wenti, Ziyuan he Fangfa; Dui Zhong-guo Xingbie Yanjiu Xianzhuang de Fansi" 性别研究: 问题、资源和方法: 对中国性别研

Dorothy Ko and Wang Zheng assert that Chinese feminism "is always already a global discourse, and the history of its local reception is a history of the politics of translation."[16] In modern China, male-authored discourse on women's liberation and female empowerment emerged as a counterdiscourse to the Western gaze, which perpetuated the image of "China as woman".[17] As Ping Zhu's study shows, modern Chinese intellectuals in the early twentieth century sought to challenge the naturalized view of gender hierarchy in order to alter the power structure embedded in the heterosexual dichotomy in the Western gaze, and to reject the "bio-destiny" of the Chinese race.[18] Some women writers, activists, and revolutionaries had joined their male peers to publish feminist writings advocating women's rights and gender equity largely within the nationalist-feminist framework, while others criticized their androcentric and often male-chauvinist views of gender, history, and modern nationhood. The booming publication industry at the time, including the rise of women's journals, provided an essential venue for the articulation and circulation of early feminist ideas and words.[19]

From its very origination Chinese feminism could not be understood as singular. Under the umbrella term of *nüquan* (women's rights), "anarchist, socialist, liberal, evolutionary, eugenic, and nationalist positions shaped various feminist articulations" and cultural imaginations for a modern China.[20] From the first Chinese feminist

究现状的反思 (Gender Studies: Problems, Resources and Methods; Rethinking the Current Situation of China's Gender Studies) *Shehui kexue*, no. 12 (2009): 168.

16. Dorothy Ko and Wang Zheng, "Introduction: Translating Feminisms in China," *Gender & History* 18, no. 3 (2006): 463.

17. Rey Chow, *Woman and Chinese Modernity: The Politics of Reading between West and East* (Minneapolis: Univ. of Minnesota Press, 1991), 9; Shu-Mei Shih, *The Lure of the Modern: Writing Modernism in Semi-Colonial China, 1917–1937* (Berkeley: Univ. of California Press, 2001), 8.

18. Ping Zhu, *Gender and Subjectivities in Early Twentieth-Century Chinese Literature and Culture* (New York: Palgrave, 2015), 19.

19. Liu, Karl, and Ko, *Birth of Chinese Feminism*, 43.

20. See Wang Zheng's "Feminist Struggles in a Changing China" in this volume.

martyr Qiu Jin 秋瑾 (1875–1907) to the first Chinese feminist theorist He-Yin Zhen (1884–ca. 1920)[21], from the "new woman" (*xin nüxing* 新女性) to "the modern girl" (*modeng nülang* 摩登女郎), from "mothers of national citizens" (*guomin zhimu* 国民之母) to avatars of sexual love, Chinese women were endowed with different identities and agencies despite the overarching nationalist agenda and the persisting patriarchal system.[22] A cohort of women writers, including Ding Ling 丁玲, Lu Yin 庐隐, Xiao Hong 萧红, Zhang Ailing 张爱玲 (aka Eileen Chang), Ling Shuhua 凌叔华, and Xie Bingying 谢冰莹, also contributed to literary feminisms in the early twentieth century by composing numerous narratives portraying Chinese women's everyday lives, dilemmas, struggles, and revolutionary aspirations and practices.[23] Many radical May Fourth feminists, such as Ding Ling and Chen Xuezhao 陈学昭, later joined the CCP during the Yan'an Period (1935–48) and brought their feminist agenda into the core of the Party.

Women's liberation was a significant part of the Chinese socialist revolution after the Yan'an period. As Wang Zheng has observed,

21. The first Chinese translation of *The Communist Manifesto* appeared in *Natural Justice*, a Chinese feminist journal edited by He-Yin Zhen. See Liu, Karl, and Ko, *Birth of Chinese Feminism*, 5.

22. Earlier scholarly works tend to contend that the early Chinese feminisms were subsumed under the masculinist nationalism. Joan Judge, "Talent, Virtue, and the Nation: Chinese Nationalisms and Female Subjectivities in the Early Twentieth Century," *American Historical Review* 106, no. 2 (2001): 765–803; Charlotte L. Beahan, "Feminism and Nationalism in the Chinese Women's Press," *Modern China* 1, no. 4 (1975): 379–416. While it is true that nationalism is masculine in nature and early Chinese feminist moments were largely part of the nationalist agenda, national liberation and women's liberation are dependent on each other in Third World countries, and the former lays the foundation for the diversification and deepening of feminist movements, while also giving rise to ideological and institutional tensions, constraints, and conflicts.

23. Detailed discussions of literary feminism in China can be found in Amy Dooling, *Women's Literary Feminism in Twentieth-Century China* (New York: Palgrave, 2005), and Haiping Yan, *Chinese Women Writers and the Feminist Imagination, 1905–1948* (New York: Routledge, 2006).

the term "feminism" (*nüquan zhuyi*) was deemed "bourgeois" during this period.[24] Hence the slogans *funü jiefang* 妇女解放 (women's liberation) and *nannü pingdeng* 男女平等 (equality between men and women) were more favored by the CCP and were listed on the official political agenda. The subject of the socialist women's policies was *funü*, a national woman who was "intertwined directly in state processes over the period of social revolution and socialist modernization who, because of her achievements as a state subject, would modernize family practices."[25] Socialist state feminism aimed to situate women first in the state and then in the family. As Cai Xiang points out, socialist state feminists did not adopt a radical stance by breaking with men; instead, "liberation" meant "reconciliation between sexes" on the premise that sexism was no longer in the way, so men and women could be equal socialist subjects.[26]

As early as 1939, the Yan'an government passed the first marriage law that endowed women with the freedom of free marriage and certain financial support after divorce.[27] According to Dong Limin, women's work during the Yan'an period was led by the government and carried out by women, and showed a conspicuous pro-women tendency.[28] In 1949 the All-China Democratic Women's Federation (renamed in 1957 the All-China Women's Federation, *Zhonghua quanguo funü lianhe hui* 中华全国妇女联合会, or *fulian* 妇联) was established. With its

24. See Wang, "Feminist Struggles."

25. Barlow, *Question of Women*, 38.

26. Cai Xiang 蔡翔. *Geming/Xushu: Zhongguo Shehui Zhuyi Wenxue-Wenhua Xiangxiang, 1949–1966* 革命/叙述: 中国社会主义文学-文化想象, 1949–1966 (Revolution and Its Narratives: China's Socialist Literary and Cultural Imaginations [1949–1966]) (Beijing: Beijing daxue chubanshe, 2010), 270.

27. See Dong Limin, "Yan'an Jingyan: Cong 'Funü Zhuyi' dao 'Jiating Tongyi Zhanxian'—Jian Lun 'Geming Zhongguo' Funü Jiefang Lilun de Shengcheng Wenti" 延安经验: 从"妇女主义"到"家庭统一战线"—兼论"革命中国"妇女解放理论的生成问题 (The Yan'an Path: From "Feminism" to the "United Family Front"—The Rise of a Theory of Women's Liberation in "Revolutionary China"), *Funü yanjiu luncong*, no. 6 (2016): 23.

28. Dong, "Yan'an Jingyan."

local branches reaching all the way to the neighborhood level all over China, *fulian*, under the leadership of senior women cadres within the CCP, promoted a series of national policies aiming for gender equity.[29] Between 1949 and 1978, *fulian* was the biggest and the sole legalized women's organization in China.[30]

As a result of the state feminism that was spearheaded as a formally institutionalized top-down campaign, women's social status, literacy rate, educational level, and workforce participation have all been enormously improved. The employment rate among Chinese women age sixteen to sixty-four is not only the highest in East Asia but stays in the top tier of employment rates for women in the entire world.[31] Although women in the workplace still face the challenges of sexist discrimination in its various forms, China's gender pay gap (the percentage by which average male pay exceeds average female pay) is, at 7.5 percent in 2009, the narrowest in East Asia and smaller than that of some developed countries, including the United States (19.8 percent in 2009).[32]

The remarkable practices and ideas of socialist feminism were gradually encroached on, however, when China embraced a market economy in the postsocialist period. The nascent yet robust women's studies (*funü yanjiu* 妇女研究) that emerged in the 1980s in China tacitly participated in and advocated the drastic economic and ideological turn toward markets and globalization.[33] The first generation

29. For a more detailed discussion on *fulian*, see Wang, "Feminist Struggles."

30. Gao Xiaoxian 高小贤, ""Zhongguo Minjian Funü Zuzhi de Kongjian he Celüe" 中国民间妇女组织的空间和策略, in *Shen Lin "Qi" Jing—Xingbie, Xuewen, Rensheng* 身临"奇"境: 性别、学问、人生 (Being in Wonderland: Gender, Knowledge, and Life), ed. Li Xiaojiang (Nanjing: Jiangsu renmin chubanshe, 2000), 234.

31. W. Lawrence Newman, *East Asian Societies* (Ann Arbor, MI: Association for Asian Studies, 2014), 46.

32. Newman, *East Asian*, 73.

33. In 1984, the All-China Women's Federation organized the First National Conference on Theoretical Studies of Women (*Funü lilun yantaohui* 妇女理论研讨会). Since 1985, with the aid of the Women's Federation, Women's Studies Councils have been established at the municipal and provincial level all over China. Meanwhile,

of women's studies scholars in postsocialist China, such as Li Xiaojiang and Du Fangqin, bid farewell to the era of revolutions in their own ways. Li advocated restoring the "sex gap" (*xinggou* 性沟) between men and women so women could reclaim their feminine space and feminine nature.[34] She argues that her proposition is not to go back to presocialist gender relations, but to awaken women's consciousness to supplement the already achieved socialist style of gender equality. Du, by contrast, is more interested in the notion of gender (*shehui xingbie* 社会性别) as a social construct and promotes "Asian women's studies" (*Yazhou funü yanjiu* 亚洲妇女研究) as a way of connecting the regional with the global.[35]

Overall, postsocialist Chinese feminist discourse deliberately kept its distance from socialist feminism and Marxist social theories that upheld the ideal of gender equity. As Rofel puts it, renaturalized gender is regarded as part of "an emancipatory story, holding out the promise that people can unshackle their innate human selves by emancipating themselves from the socialist state."[36] Intellectuals in the postsocialist period emphasize rediscovering and restoring "women's real, natural, feminine, singularity," which is often materialized through market-oriented consumer practices and commodified ways of self-expression in post-Mao China.[37] Along these lines the socialist

---

women's civic associations and societies were also founded, mainly by female intellectuals and scholars working at research institutes and universities. Over forty journals on women's studies were published in 1980s. In 1987 the first program of women's studies (*funü yanjiu*) was established by Li Xiaojiang at Zhengzhou University. See Tan Shen 谭深, "Funü Yanjiu de Xin Jinzhan" 妇女研究的新进展 (The New Developments of Women's Studies), *Shehuixue yanjiu*, no. 5 (1995): 68. In postsocialist China women's studies was by no means a marginalized discipline.

34. See Li Xiaojaing, *Xinggou* 性沟 (Sex Gap) (Beijing: Sanlian shudian, 1989). For a detailed discussion of Li Xiaojiang's feminism, see Tani Barlow, "Socialist Modernization and the Market Feminism of Li Xiaojiang," in *The Question of Women in Chinese Feminism*, 253–300.

35. For a detailed discussion of Du's works, see chapter 1 of this volume.

36. Rofel, *Other Modernities*, 218.

37. Barlow, *Question of Women*, 253.

party-state's emancipatory discourse has often been criticized for sub-suming women under a nationalist agenda and proletarian class revo-lution.[38] Further appropriating a market-individualism discourse, a backlash of patriarchal conservatism devalued the socialist feminist legacy by condemning Chinese women who grew up in the Maoist era as "over-liberated" and thus unfeminine according to the new gender norms, which place great value on "the formulation of an expressive personal lifestyle and the ability to select the right commodities to attain it."[39] This was a period when "masculinity and power came together" because, on the one hand, "the criticism of Maoism was from a masculinist perspective,"[40] and, on the other hand, issues con-cerning gendered division of labor, women's decreasing level of politi-cal participation, and structural inequalities were considered trivial personal matters and thus systematically neglected.

A similar trend can also be found in the development of wom-en's literature and cinema that have responded to the marketization of cultural production in postsocialist China. Since the 1980s multiple series of women literature were published all over China.[41] Women writers of different generations have profusely published literary works to continue and expand the female literary tradition. In comparison to pioneering figures such as He-Yin Zhen, Qiu Jin, and Ding Ling, post-Mao women writers in general appear to be less committed to master narratives such as nationalism, revolution, modernization, class struggle, and socialist women's liberation, but are more concerned

38. Lydia H. Liu, "Invention and Intervention: The Making of a Female Tradi-tion in Modern Chinese Literature," in *Chinese Femininities/Chinese Masculinities: A Reader*, ed. Susan Brownell and Jeffrey N. Wasserstrom (Berkeley: Univ. of Cali-fornia Press, 2002), 150.

39. Diane Negra, *What a Girl Wants?: Fantasizing the Reclamation of Self in Postfeminism* (New York: Routledge, 2008), 4.

40. Dai, *After the Post–Cold War*, 160.

41. For example, the *Women* series (*Tamen* 她们) is published by Yunnan chu-banshe, the Red Pepper (*Hong lajiao* 红辣椒) series is published by Sichuan renmin chubanshe, and the Red Poppy (*Hong Yinsu* 红罂粟) series is published by Hebei jiaoyu chubanshe.

about women's individual problems and existential angst in their every-day lives, particularly in the domestic realm, as well as about their awakening gender consciousness, sexual desire, and norm-bending self-expressions. While the older generations of women writers, such as Wang Anyi 王安忆, Zhang Jie 张洁, and Zhang Xinxin 张辛欣 paid more critical attention to gendered inequality in family, sexuality, and reproduction, the publication of younger writers' works marked the rising new trend of "private writing" (*si xiezuo* 私写作) in the 1990s.[42]

The literary essentialization of gender differences based on a physiological foundation has been further amplified and capitalized by the accelerating commercialization of women's literature and the marketization of China's publication industry. In a dialogue with Dai Jinhua, Wang Gan, a literary critic, even laments that the only unique contribution women writers can make to Chinese literature is candid descriptions and confessions of their own private lives because women are always positioned as the object of the male gaze.[43] The Cloth Tiger (布老虎 *Bu laohu*) series repackaged women writers' literary explorations of gender consciousness as sensational bestsellers catering to the voyeuristic gaze at woman's body and sexuality on the book market. A series of women writers' "body writing" (*shenti xiezuo* 身体写作), the most (in)famous of which is Zhou Weihui's banned novel *Shanghai Baby* (*Shanghai Baobei* 上海宝贝, 1999), is another salient example of the commodification of woman's body, as well as the blatant exploitation of female authors' creative writings about women's private lives and intimate relationships.

Compared to a blossoming women's literature, women's cinema in the 1990s fell into a lull. Back in the 1980s China still had a large army

---

42. Some examples include Lin Bai's "Yigeren de Zhanzheng" 一个人的战争 (One Person's War, 1994); Xu Xiaobin's 徐晓斌 *Shuangyu Xingzuo* 双鱼星座 (Pisces, 1995); Chen Ran's 陈染 *Siren shenghuo* 私人生活 (Private Life, 1996); and Hai Nan's 海男 *Shengming Shengjing* 生命圣经 (Bible of Reproduction, 1998).

43. Wang Gan 王干 and Dai Jinhua 戴锦华, "Nüxing Wenxue yu Gerenhua Xie-zuo" 女性文学与个人化写作 (Women's Literature and Private Writing), *Dajia*, no. 1 (1996): 197.

of women filmmakers who were working in state film studios, thanks to the political legacy of women's liberation during the socialist era. According to official statistics, fifty-nine women directors produced 182 feature films between 1980 and 1989, which was a rare accomplishment for female filmmakers not only in Chinese film history but in world cinema.[44] This trend did not continue into the 1990s. Due to the domination of imported Hollywood blockbusters in the Chinese film market, as well as the rapid expansion and proliferation of other entertainment venues and platforms, the market for domestic Chinese films was drastically shrinking. Moreover, since the 1990s the "cultural system reform" (*wenhua tizhi gaige* 文化体制改革) has applied market logic to cultural production and distribution. The state subsidy to film studios was radically cut, and as a result the Chinese film industry was hurled into a crisis. In particular, the marketization of the cultural industry and mass media posed serious challenges for women's cinema, as films concerning gender consciousness and gender-specific social issues were hardly competitive with lucrative genre films that emphasized audiovisual spectacles and star images to cater to the mainstream market.

The number of Chinese women filmmakers was dramatically reduced in the 1990s. Ning Ying 宁瀛, Hu Mei 胡玫, Li Shaohong 李少红, Huang Shuqin 黄蜀芹, and Liu Miaomiao 刘苗苗 were a handful of women directors who were still struggling to produce films for the mainstream market. Their works produced in this period were often criticized as either lacking a gendered perspective or falling into the old trap of displaying an overly sexualized female body to appeal to a voyeuristic audience. In other words, these works were shaped more by the combined forces of market rationale and the dominant discourse of male desire than by the critical tradition of feminist women's cinema, both thematically and formalistically.

44. Huang Shuqin 黄蜀芹, "Nüxing, zai Dianyingye de Nanren Shijie li" 女性, 在电影业的男人世界里 (Women, in the Men's World of the Film Industry), *Dangdai dianying*, no. 5 (1995): 71.

This shifting trend in postsocialist cultural production and intellectual discourse on gender can be better understood if we consider that the development of postsocialist market feminism, as Barlow renders it, is an indispensable part of the capitalization and marketization of post-Mao China. In a market-oriented masculinist discourse, "the Maoist image of strong, heroic women was ridiculed as a symbol of backward obstacles to China's modernization" and lent a ready excuse to the massive layoffs of women workers.[45] Discrediting Maoist mass politics and revolutionary modernity, postsocialist Chinese intellectuals engaged in heated debates about individual subjectivity, which complements the reform ideology of promoting personal responsibility and freeing individuals for the market. As a part of the intellectual discourse centered on market individualism, postsocialist Chinese market feminism criticizes allegedly gender-erasing and desexualizing state feminism and affirms the value of asserting individual gendered identity based on anatomical features, which leads to biological determinism and the objectification of the female body and female labor as ready commodities in a new roaring market economy.

Postsocialism, in Xudong Zhang's words, "does not suggest a more advanced, superior—or, for that matter, more backward and inferior—form of socioeconomic and political development. Rather, it is an experimental way to address a bewildering overlap of modes of production, social systems, and symbolic orders, all of which lay claim to a fledging world of life."[46] The revival of new Confucianism in China since the 1990s attests to the postsocialist market's astonishing power to revamp and reintegrate different ideologies and resources, creating new figurations of patriarchal power from the specter of history. Dai's interview "The Specter of Polygamy in Contemporary Chinese Gender Imaginations," presented in the first section of this volume, provides a sobering discussion of the collusion of traditional

45. Jieyu Liu, *Gender and Work in Urban China: Women Workers of the Unlucky Generation* (New York: Routledge, 2007), 143–44.

46. Xudong Zhang, *Postsocialism and Cultural Politics* (Durham, NC: Duke Univ. Press, 2008), 10.

culture and the capitalist narrative. What Chinese feminists currently face is a postmodern landscape where new Confucianism exists side by side with neoliberalism, where socialist aspirations merge with capitalist expansion, and where politics and culture join hands to cement the traditional gender hierarchy.[47]

Not only does postsocialism prove to be heterogeneous terrain that makes the pluralistic mode of thinking and practice imperative, Chinese women in the postsocialist period cannot form a singular and monolithic feminist subject. Catherine Rottenberg has warned us that the "emergent neoliberal order is slowly expunging gender and even sexual differences among a certain strata of subjects while it simultaneously produces new forms of racialized and class-stratified gender exploitation."[48] Marshaled by neoliberal discourse, market feminism in post-Mao China has dismantled the egalitarian legacy of state feminism but fails to address the increasing inequalities between men and women, and between women of different regions, classes, ethnicities, educational levels, and age groups, let alone the differences between Chinese women and women in the First World countries. The return of Hong Kong and Macao to mainland China in 1997 and 1999, respectively, has further diversified this already dynamic and complex terrain of Chinese feminist practices and ideas.[49] Ya-chen Chen proposes in *The Many Dimensions of Chinese Feminism* that we should expand the scope of Chinese feminism to include all histories and

47. Examples include the hypermasculine personality cult around top CCP leaders, which has been revived in recent years, and dozens of popular TV dramas set in imperial harems (*gongdouju* 宫斗剧) that portray how concubines compete for the emperor's favor in the palace in a fantasized dynastic China. For more examples, see Leta Hong Fincher's "China's Patriarchal Authoritarianism" in her *Betraying Big Brother: The Feminist Awakening in China* (New York: Verso, 2018), 159–86.

48. Catherine Rottenberg, "Neoliberal Feminism and the Future of Human Capital," *Signs: Journal of Women in Culture and Society* 42, no. 2 (2017): 332.

49. For a discussion on Hong Kong's feminisms, which have become a unique branch of Chinese feminisms since 1997, see Adelyn Lim, *Transnational Feminism and Women's Movements in Post-1997 Hong Kong: Solidarity beyond the State* (Hong Kong: Hong Kong Univ. Press, 2015).

realities of all Chinese-speaking areas.[50] While this volume cannot be so exhaustive, it uses the plural *feminisms with Chinese characteristics* as a way to summon feminist practices and imaginations from these overlapping modes and intersectional discourses, and to address the heterogeneous feminist subjects in contemporary China.

The 1995 World Conference on Women and the Rise of NGOs in China

The difference between Chinese women and women in First World countries, or the difference between the local and the global, has been at stake in the development of NGOs in China since 1995. In September 1995 the Fourth World Conference on Women, attended by more than 17,000 participants, was held in Beijing.[51] In addition, a parallel NGO forum was opened in Huairou, in the northern suburbs of Beijing. It hosted sixty symposiums and thirty-five exhibitions, and drew over 30,000 attendees.[52] The 1995 conference ushered in a new age for the globalization of Chinese feminisms by bringing transnational capital into Chinese women's studies and Chinese feminist practices both in China and overseas. Thereafter, women's studies projects and feminist NGOs, funded by transnational corporations and organizations such as the Ford Foundation, flourished in China and among expatriate Chinese, fundamentally changing the outlook, agents, and concerns of Chinese feminisms, and further fracturing the already contested terrain.

On the eve of the 1995 World Conference on Women, the All-China Women's Federation (ACWF) characterized itself as an NGO so as to "connect the tracks" with women's movements around the

50. Ya-chen Chen, *The Many Dimensions of Chinese Feminism* (New York: Palgrave, 2011), 5.

51. It was the first World Conference on Women held in Asia.

52. UN Women, "World Conferences on Women," www.unwomen.org/en/how-we-work/intergovernmental-support/world-conferences-on-women (accessed February 15, 2019).

world.[53] In November 1993, a Chinese delegation of forty-three participants attended the Asia-Pacific Women's NGO Forum, held in Manila,
which constituted China's first official encounter with the global NGO
movement. At the Manila Forum, Huang Qizao, vice chair of the
ACWF and director of the NGO subcommittee, called Women's Federation as the biggest NGO in China, which invited questions and
debates in the international community. This controversy revolving
around the nature and organization of the ACWF reveals the Chinese
characteristics of women's NGOs: while functioning largely outside of
the government, they are expected to follow the model of the Wom-
en's Federation to play supplementary rather than oppositional roles
to governmental agencies. In many cases, NGOs and the ACWF have
developed a collaborative relationship to pool resources and carry out
their advocacy projects, which must be aligned with national policy
and official ideology, as Li Jun points out in chapter 6.

This collaboration between NGOs with the Women's Federation
has become a distinctive mode of contemporary Chinese feminisms.[54]
The first-generation organizers of women's NGOs took advantage of
their positions within the Women's Federation or its affiliated institutions and agencies to secure social and financial resources. Their
careful self-positioning as nonpolitical and nonoppositional civic
organizations was determined to be the foremost precondition for the
survival and development of Chinese NGOs, which have been struggling with limited resources and a heavily constrained public space
since their birth.[55]

Following the 1995 World Conference on Women, some of the
earliest women's NGOs got further development through the support

---

53. Liu Bohong 刘伯红, "Zhongguo Funü Fei Zhengfu Zuzhi de Fazhan"
中国妇女非政府组织的发展 (The Development of Chinese Women's NGOs), *Zhejiang
xuekan*, no. 4 (2000): 110.

54. Wang Zheng and Ying Zhang, "Global Concepts, Local Practices: Chinese
Feminism since the Fourth UN Conference on Women," *Feminist Studies* 36, no. 1
(2010): 62.

55. Liu, "Zhongguo Funü Fei Zhengfu Zuzhi de Fazhan," 113.

of transnational funding and increased media visibility.[56] Going along with the global associational revolution, an increasing number of NGOs have been registered all over China to provide institutional support for women's development and gender equity.[57] These NGOs have propagated feminist ideas in China, linked some Chinese women with the world, and at the same time greatly transformed the programs, organizations, languages, and practices of Chinese feminisms. Meanwhile, their unprecedented publicity and transnational networks also alerted the state that the Chinese feminist program might have grown to an extent that "exceeded the capacity of the government to control its agenda or interests."[58]

The tension between feminist NGOs and the state rapidly deepened when the older generation who had worked simultaneously

56. For example, in 1996 the Shaanxi Province Association of Women, Marriage, and Family Studies opened its first women's hotline. In 1998 the Maple Women's Psychological Counseling Center of Beijing established the Ark Family Service Center (*Fangzhou jiating zhongxin* 方舟家庭中心) to provide aid to single-parent families. In 1999 the Shaanxi Province Association of Women, Marriage, and Family Studies established the Women's Legal Studies and Service Center (*Funü falü yanjiu yu fuwu zhongxin* 妇女法律研究与服务中心) and launched a series of projects for rural women's development, such as health education, a women's literacy class, and professional skills training workshops.

57. Examples include the Beijing University Women's Legal Studies and Service Center (*Beijing daxue funü falü yanjiu yu fuwu zhongxin* 北京大学妇女法律研究与服务中心, founded in 1995), the Migrant Women Workers Home (*Dagongmei zhi jia* 打工妹之家, founded in Beijing in 1996, the first NGO providing social services and legal aid to migrant women workers), Xishuangbannan Women and Children's Psychological and Legal Counseling Center (*Xishuangbanna zhou funü ertong xinli falü zixun fuwu zhongxin* 西双版纳州妇女儿童心理法律咨询服务中心, founded in 1997 in Yunnan, a province in southwest China with a high concentration of ethnic minority residents), the Henan Community Education Research Center (*Henan shequ jiaoyu yanjiu zhongxin* 河南社区教育研究中心, founded in 1998), and the Women's Media Monitor Network (*Funü chuanmei jiance wangluo* 妇女传媒监测网络, founded in Beijing in 1999).

58. Gail Hershatter, Emily Honig, and Lisa Rofel, "Reflections on the Fourth World Conference on Women, Beijing and Huairou, 1995," *Social Justice/Global Options* 23, nos. 1/2 (1996): 375.

in NGOs and the Women's Federation retired from their positions within the governmental bureaucracy and the younger generation endeavored to push forward the feminist cause outside of the statist model. With the rise of masculinist nationalism in China in recent years, the feminist NGOs have become targets of state surveillance due to their transnational theoretical framework and activist program. That surveillance led to the detention of the "Feminist Five" in 2015[59] and the permanent ban on Feminist Voice (*nüquan zhisheng* 女权之声), a prominent feminist NGO, on March 8, 2018.[60] Having lost the state's full support and even acquiescent tolerance, the NGO feminists are in urgent need of new strategies of negotiation and new ways of advocacy.

To discuss the transformation of feminist NGOs in the twenty-first century, another paradigm of Chinese characteristics should also be considered and tackled: neoliberalism with Chinese characteristics. In his book *A Brief History of Neoliberalism*, David Harvey portrays the outcome of China's neoliberalization in the postsocialist era as "the construction of a particular kind of market economy that increasingly incorporates neoliberal elements interdigitated with authoritarian centralized control."[61] This shift to neoliberalism with Chinese characteristics represents the latest alliance of economic neoliberalism and ideological neoconservatism: while a neoliberal market rationale shapes the reconfiguration of the economic realm and social institutions, including marriage and family, centralized authoritarian management and containment of public spaces have also been reconsolidated.

59. The five young feminists collectively known as Feminist Five were arrested and detained on the basis of their NGO affiliations when they were planning to hand out stickers against sexual harassment on the eve of International Women's Day, March 8, 2015. See Wang Zheng, "Detention of the Feminist Five in China," *Feminist Studies* 41, no. 2 (2015): 476–82.

60. For more information about Feminist Voice, see Wang Zheng's chapter in this volume.

61. David Harvey, *A Brief History of Neoliberalism* (Oxford, UK: Oxford Univ. Press, 2005), 120.

Along a similar line, Li Jun's chapter in this volume characterizes China's escalating privatization, marketization, and neoliberalization as the recent local manifestation of a global patriarchal capitalism that has exerted enormous influence on Chinese women. Hui Faye Xiao's chapter also examines how China's radical turn to postsocialist patriarchy creates and consolidates various forms and intersections of gender, age, and class-based inequalities in social, economic, and cultural realms. In the wake of the paradigmatic transformation of the state's agenda from equity-centered socialist revolution (including egalitarian women's liberation) toward an efficiency-driven marketization and privatization, women of younger generations found themselves faced with a different set of gender-specific issues and problems.

Like women writers and filmmakers, younger feminist activists now also live with the dilemma of struggling to survive while keeping the feminist cause afloat under adverse sociopolitical conditions. In recent years the radical reduction in state support and social resources allocated to gender programs has led to Chinese feminist NGOs' increasing dependence on international, mainly Western, funds. Further restraints imposed on NGO registration and activities by the 2017 Foreign NGO Law have made it even more challenging for feminists to acquire necessary funds and resources. Hence it has become a new norm for many feminist activists to resort to individual economic capital, media literacy, and social networking for organizing activities and campaigns.[62] Such a binding situation makes massive mobilization and collective action in heavily censored real-life and virtual public spaces difficult to achieve and also causes a highly skewed demographic constitution: younger cohorts of Chinese feminists consist mainly of well-educated and urban-based college students

62. Lü Pin 吕频, "'Nüquan Wu Jiemei' Si Zhounian, Nüquan Hexin Zuzhizhe de Pinkun, yu Pinkun de Nüquan Yundong" "女权五姐妹"四周年, 女权核心组织者的贫困, 与贫困的女权运动 (The Fourth Anniversary of the "Feminist Five": The Poverty of Core Feminist Activists and the Impoverished Feminist Movement), *The Initium*, March 8, 2019, https://theinitium.com/article/20190308-opinion-lvpin-feminist-and-metoo/.

and professionals who have relatively more economic, cultural, technological, and social capital to invest in feminist NGO activism.

As a result, the gender programs championed by these younger feminists are often preoccupied with concerns mainly pertaining to young urban professional women and appear to be less resonant with other women's everyday struggles and problems. Although a growing number of feminists have started paying more attention to the intersection of class and gender, not all transnational NGOs are committed to or successful in connecting with women of lower classes, from different age groups, and in the rural areas, for many of whom the socialist legacy is still at work in their conceptualization of gender, equity, and rights. Hence this younger cohort's NGO-sponsored feminist activities and studies have drifted farther from the legacy of socialist feminism in China, as the latter not only followed a different, Marxist paradigm, but also relied heavily on nuanced negotiations within the state to achieve its feminist agenda and on locally rooted practices to mobilize women.

As Wang Zheng and Ying Zhang point out, the younger and more urban-educated cohort of Chinese feminists in the age of NGOization are more interested in gender equality (*shehui xingbie pingdeng*) than in equality between men and women (*nannü pingdeng*).[63] The term *nannü pingdeng* is associated with the socialist state agenda, while *shehui xingbie pingdeng* suggests that women can claim their rights without subjecting themselves to the patriarchal state.[64] The rights these feminists pursue are "deployed to demand citizens' rights against an authoritarian state,"[65] and thus differ drastically from those pursued by the earlier nationalist-feminists or socialist state feminists. Therefore they are not the most effective in addressing the questions that Dai Jinhua asks: "How to correct this 'visionary error' without losing a female and feminist perspective? How to think about the tension between

63. The Engendering China conference held at Harvard University in 1992 is regarded as the beginning of bringing the notion of gender to China studies.

64. Wang and Zhang, "Global Concepts," 47.

65. Wang and Zhang, "Global Concepts," 47.

contemporary China's historical context and Western theories? How to evaluate the influences of socialist history and practice on today's culture and notion of gender?"[66] The tension between the local and the global, between the rural and the urban, between history and the present, and between academia and activists calls for new theorization of feminisms with Chinese characteristics beyond those binaries.

Toward a Feminist Politics with Chinese Characteristics

Nearly one century ago, He-Yin Zhen conceptualized gender not simply as a form of social identity determined by sexual distinction, but also as a mechanism to "create forms of power and domination based on that distinction" in a structurally unequal society.[67] He-Yin's groundbreaking feminist vision suggests that it is far from enough if women focus only on discovering their "female consciousness," writing about their bodies or narrating their personal histories, because women's "consciousness," "bodies," or "histories" are always already defined by masculinist visions and patriarchal power. However, this problematic "gender consciousness" or "female body" has become the selling point for "women's literature" and "women's cinema" in mainstream discourse. This has led to the denunciation of the feminist label by some women writers, filmmakers, and scholars in contemporary China. Feminists must develop different forms of representation to challenge the social institutions and historical narrative that define men and women unequally. Ding Ling, for examples, had to become a "misogynist" to overcome the feminist impasse in a patriarchal society.[68]

One of the biggest achievements of the socialist state feminists was their redefinition of women and femininity, which allowed women to

66. Dai Jinhua, *Yinheng* 印痕 (Marks), (Shijiazhuang: Hebei jiaoyu chubanshe, 2002), 169.

67. Liu, Karl, and Ko, *Birth of Chinese Feminism*, 21.

68. For a detailed discussion of Ding Ling's "misogynism," see Zhu, *Gender and Subjectivities*, 148–52.

claim equal status with men. It is disheartening that the old gender hierarchy has been restored in the postsocialist period and that the achievements of earlier generations of Chinese feminists have been thrown on the dustheap of history. This is why Dai laments that in the contemporary period while women's writers are starting to move to the cultural center, women in real life are continuously being marginalized.[69] The developments, amnesias, contradictions, and limitations of post-1995 Chinese feminist practices and representations compel us to revisit the ramifications and reinventions of feminist legacies that are firmly grounded in changing historical and social conditions, in order to articulate different forms of feminisms with Chinese characteristics beyond the binary of the local and the global.

To be clear, neither Chinese history nor the 1995 World Conference on Women and the subsequent NGOization of Chinese feminism can serve as a sufficient frame of reference for present-day Chinese feminisms. To understand the contested terrain of Chinese feminisms, we must look at other Chinese feminist imaginations and practices in the age of globalization. Early Chinese feminisms, socialist state feminisms, and new-period feminist recuperations all emerged against a global background; some prominent contentions of post-1995 Chinese feminisms, in particular, register overlapping or contradictory imaginations and practices around the problem of situating Chineseness in the global context.

Nicola Spakowski's 2018 study shows that since around 2010 a new theoretical strand within Chinese feminism has been forming, which she labels "socialist feminism" or "critical socialist feminism."[70] She writes, "Socialism as a historical legacy and memory is indicative of China's postsocialist situation, which . . . has a deep impact on the epistemological, theoretical, and political outlook as well as the

69. Dai Jinhua, *Shedu zhi Zhou: Xinshiqi Zhongguo Nüxing Xiezuo yu Nüxing Wenhua* 涉渡之舟: 新时期中国女性写作与女性文化 (A Boat Crossing the Ocean: New-Period Chinese Women's Literature and Culture). (Beijing: Beijing daxue chubanshe, 2007), 25.

70. Spakowski, "Socialist Feminism," 561.

identity of socialist feminists in today's China."[71] The roots of so-called socialist feminism can be dated back to the New Left thought that emerged in China in the mid-1990s,[72] which coincided with the systematic importation of neoliberal feminisms into China. While socialist feminism is just one of the many feminisms in contemporary China, the rise of socialist feminism indicates the crucial importance of preserving critiques of systemic problems, such as the inequalities perpetuated by the neoliberal world order formed in the post–Cold War era and the specter of patriarchy revived by the victory of capital in various social sectors.

A leading figure of Chinese socialist feminism, Song Shaopeng, writes, "it is possible that the 'female consciousness' released by the enlightenment movement in the 1980s unwittingly matches the neoliberal capitalist ideology in the 1990s."[73] Quite a few socialist feminists, both in the West and in China, have gone one step farther to bombard the complicity between neoliberalism and second-wave feminism. In 2009 the US feminist Nancy Fraser published the famous essay "Feminism, Capitalism, and the Cunning of History" in the *New Left Review*, in which she pinpoints the institutional failure of second-wave feminism despite its cultural success.[74] In the neoliberal age, she writes, "claims for justice were increasingly couched as claims for the recognition of identity and difference" that "dovetailed all too neatly with a rising neoliberalism that wanted nothing more than to repress

71. Spakowski, "Socialist Feminism," 562.

72. In her essay "Socialist Feminism," Spakowski makes a distinction between socialist feminists and New Leftists by saying that the latter continue to be gender-blind by focusing exclusively on the category of class.

73. Song Shaopeng 宋少鹏, "Ziben Zhuyi, Shehui Zhuyi he Funü: Weishenme Zhongguo Xuyao Chongjian Makesi Zhuyi Nüquan Zhuyi Pipan" 资本主义、社会主义和妇女:为什么中国需要重建马克思主义女权主义批判 (Capitalism, Socialism, and Women: Why China Needs to Rebuild a Marxist Feminist Critique), *Kaifang shidai*, no. 12 (2012): 105.

74. Nancy Fraser, "Feminism, Capitalism and the Cunning of History," *New Left Review* 56 (2009): 99.

all memory of social egalitarianism."[75] Fraser's essay was soon translated into Chinese and widely echoed by Chinese socialist feminists.
Song points out that the feminists in China fail to direct their criticism at the injustice caused by capitalism and neoliberalism; instead,
the struggles they address are limited to matters of individual freedom
and rights, and their targets are the state and its policies.[76] Bai Di, a
Chinese feminist scholar working in the United States, points out that
the slogan "the personal is political" has transferred the target of criticism from social power structures and economic institutions to the
individual.[77]

The rise of New Left thinking in mid-1990s China represents
a backlash against the victory lap of neoliberal capitalism, as epito-
mized in Francis Fukuyama's 1989 essay "The End of History?"[78]
After the implosion of the Soviet Union in 1991, China became the
bellwether of world socialism and sometimes the target of animosity
from the capitalist camp led by the United States,[79] which alienated
some Chinese from neoliberal ideology. At the same time, "socialism
with Chinese characteristics" seemed to have helped China withstand
the Asian financial meltdown in 1998 and greatly influenced Chinese
policy makers' confidence in the Chinese model. While in the academic world reflections on the achievements and lessons of socialism
had started in the 1990s, in popular culture there emerged a specific

75. Fraser, "Feminism," 108–9.

76. Song, "Ziben Zhuyi," 105.

77. Bai Di 柏棣, "Lishi Shiming de Zhongjie? Zai Ziben Zhuyi Weiji Zhong
Sikao Nüxing Zhuyi yu Ziben Zhuyi de Guanxi (xia)" 历史使命的终结? 在资本主义危机
中思考女性主义与资本主义的关系(下) (Is It the End of the Historical Mission? A Study
on the Relationship between Feminism and Capitalism in the Capitalist Crisis [Part
Two]), *Shandong nüzi xueyuan xuebao*, no. 4: (2014): 6.

78. Francis Fukuyama, "The End of History?" *The National Interest*, (1989):
1–18.

79. Two prominent examples are Beijing's bid to host the 2000 Summer Olympics, which was frustrated by a US-led campaign in 1993, and the bombing of the
Chinese embassy in Belgrade in 1999.

form of "nostalgia for the egalitarian structures of socialism"[80] amid the increasing social and gender inequality in the postsocialist period.

At the top level, the CCP started to emphasize the "four self-confidences" (*sige zixin* 四个自信) in 2012,[81] which led to a wave of funded studies on socialist literature, culture, politics, and practices. Therefore, although the New Leftists' criticism of neoliberal capitalism is valuable, it must maintain a critical distance from popular nostalgia for socialism and official political discourse that endorses cultural particularism, as both of them, or their subtle collusions, might lead to the hegemony of Chinese characteristics in a singular form. Sharon R. Wesoky has reminded us that male intellectuals' criticism of what it means to be modern and Chinese is "easily colonized by statist factions in a period in which a thin surface of state socialist ideology coexists with an increasingly neoliberal economic core." She also argues that some male intellectuals' "cultural nationalist tendencies enact a post-Mao reform-era gender erasure."[82]

The rise of socialist feminist ideas also coincided with the postmodern turn toward decolonization of knowledge. In this sense socialist feminists can sometimes join hands with earlier Chinese feminists who value local knowledge production.[83] For example, in chapter 1 of this volume Spakowski observes that Li Xiaojiang has

80. Spakowski, "Socialist Feminism," 569.

81. The notion of the "four self-confidences", proposed by Xi Jinping in 2012, refers to the self-confidence in the path, theory, institution, and culture of socialism with Chinese characteristics.

82. Sharon R. Wesoky, "Bringing the *Jia* Back into *Guojia*: Engendering Chinese Intellectual Politics," *Signs: Journal of Women in Culture and Society* 40, no. 3 (2015): 653–54.

83. Spakowski explains that Chinese scholars' defense of the local centers around three points: Marxism-Leninism and the socialist tradition of women's liberation, a tradition of nonantagonistic gender relations, and the particular social constituency of feminism in China. See Spakowski, "'Gender' Trouble: Feminism in China under the Impact of Western Theory and the Spatialization of Identity," *positions: east asia cultures critiques* 19, no. 1 (2011): 38.

been championing the local knowledge and experience of Chinese women in her women's studies work since the 1980s and continues to believe in the necessity of restoring binary sex because it reflects the urgent need of local history to overcome the gender-blindness of socialist ideology.[84] Although Li's advocacy of binary sex has been criticized by many Marxist feminists both in China and abroad, it cannot be denied that her view of Chinese women is deeply rooted in the specific historical conditions and local knowledge production that completed the farewell to socialism in the 1980s. Instead of viewing Li's feminism as an accomplice of the masculinist "capitalism with Chinese characteristics," we propose to view such a feminist voice as an integral part of feminisms with Chinese characteristics that are shaped by and are shaping various sociopolitical matrices at different historic junctures.

In order to counter the postmodern position that tends to domesticate "power differences, transforming systemic projects of resistance into commodified, private acts of rebellion,"[85] some Chinese feminist scholars seek to restore the political potential of feminisms and use it as a revolutionary force to challenge different forms of national and international patriarchies. In 2002, Chen Shunxin and Dai Jinhua coedited the volume *Women, Nation, and Feminism* (*Funü, Minzu yu Nüxing Zhuyi* 妇女、民族与女性主义) to introduce the often repressed tension between women and nation from a wide array of both First World and Third World feminist scholarship. Chen writes in her preface that feminists can choose to either be critical outsiders of nationalist discourse or participate in nationalist discourse by adding a gendered perspective in political and cultural representations

---

84. Li Xiaojiang 李小江, "Funü Yanjiu de Yuanqi, Fazhan ji Xianzhuang" 妇女研究的缘起、发展及现状 (The Origin, Developments, and Current Status of Chinese Women's Studies), *Funü yanjiu*, no. 1 (1999): 132.

85. Chandra Talpade Mohanty, "Transnational Feminist Crossings: On Neoliberalism and Radical Critique," *Signs: Journal of Women in Culture and Society* 38, no. 4 (2013): 968.

of nationalism.[86] The second method has a long and rich tradition in China. For example, through her studies of Chinese history, Dong Limin argues that feminisms can mean negotiations and interactions with existing power structures, social orders, and institutions, and can be accomplished within those structures.[87] With the rise of virulent nationalism in China in recent years, the feminist mission of criticizing and challenging nationalism and patriarchal structures (for example, "socialism with Chinese characteristics") from within still has a long way to go, which means that Chinese feminisms will remain a very useful critical resource.

The contested terrain of Chinese feminisms also poses challenges to Chinese feminists who seek to form alliances and propose concrete agendas of action. After all, what is the rallying point of feminisms with Chinese characteristics when there are multiple centers and peripheries? How to do feminist work across differences embedded in history, race, nationhood, ethnicity, gender, sexuality, class, age, education, religion, location, and personality without falling into unproductive relativism? How to incorporate gender justice into the imagination of Chinese modernity? Dai's proposal of treating feminisms as ways of imagining a different world might be useful here. Dai asserts that feminisms should prove their significance to our current world, which is depleted of critical resources, by providing imaginings of a brand new world of plurality and inclusiveness.[88] Dai's words suggest that today the concern of Chinese feminisms should not be limited to the contentions between the Left and the Right, the First World and the Third World, the global and the local, or socialism and capitalism, although these will remain important

86. Chen Shunxin 陈顺馨, "Nüxing Zhuyi dui Minzu Zhuyi de Jieru" 女性主义对民族主义的介入 (Feminist Intervention of Nationalism), in *Funü, Minzu yu Nüxing Zhuyi* (Women, Nation, and Feminism), ed. Chen Shunxin 陈顺馨 and Dai Jinhua 戴锦华 (Beijing: Zhongyang bianyi chubanshe, 2002), 20.

87. Dong, "Xingbie Yanjiu," 168.

88. Dai, "Liangnan Zhijian Huo Tuwei Keneng?," 37.

feminist contentions for a long time. Perhaps the ultimate product of feminisms should be the utopia that feminists, men and women together, constantly imagine and create for the existing world. This illuminating suggestion is helpful for contemporary Chinese feminists as they form a strategic alliance despite their wide-ranging differences in theories and practices.

In their advocacy of transnational feminism, Inderpal Grewal and Caren Kaplan write that today's feminists require efforts "to compare multiple, overlapping, and discrete oppressions rather than to construct a theory of hegemonic oppression under a unified category of gender."[89] However, the lesson from feminisms with Chinese characteristics is that pluralistic thinking and practices must not reject totalities or exclude concerted actions. The unique vitality of Chinese feminisms is precisely that they continue to address the asymmetrically organized totalities in the notion of Chinese characteristics. While the anti-imperialist and anticapitalist movements in which Chinese women participated in the past century have endowed Chinese feminists with a unique historical legacy and valuable resources, postsocialist conditions have provided a plethora of new urgencies and opportunities for forging a pluralistic feminist politics with Chinese characteristics, which can help us look for an alternative world or a counterhistory.

The history of Chinese feminisms over the past century has proved that the political potential of women can be maximized when the notion of Chinese characteristics can be constantly challenged, reconstructed, and pluralized. This was true when the racialized "Chinese characteristics" were challenged by feminists in the early twentieth century, when socialist feminists challenged the "Chinese characteristics" in traditional Chinese gender ideology, when women's studies scholars challenged the "Chinese characteristics" in Chinese socialist state ideology in the postsocialist period, and when socialist feminists challenged the hegemonic new model of global neoliberalism with

89. Grewal and Kaplan, "Introduction," 17–18.

Chinese characteristics. In all these examples, the main achievements of Chinese feminists were not limited to each individual woman's liberation, but extended to the dismantling of the existing social order of China or even the world that brought about different forms of injustice. In history these pluralistic and shifting positions of Chinese feminisms have helped us challenge hegemonic forms of knowledge production such as Orientalism, racism, nationalism, and socialism. In our current age of neoliberal capitalism this revolutionary power of feminisms may be revived if we place the notion of Chinese characteristics under interrogation and open it up for more pluralistic thinking and practices. We believe that only by challenging and opening up Chinese characteristics can we also challenge and open up possibilities of an alternative world and a counterhistory.

Layout and Chapters

The twelve chapters of this volume are grouped into three sections. The first section, "Chinese Feminisms in the Age of Globalization," consists of four essays that delineate the unique Chinese characteristics of contemporary Chinese feminisms at the interface of the local and the global. This section opens with Nicola Spakowski's examination of articulations of an identity for Chinese feminism as part of a new conceptual grid of global-local interrelations, which demonstrate the variety of ways in which feminists in China have responded to the import of gender and the destabilizing effect of the influx of what is perceived as Western theory. We thus get a glimpse of the dynamic process of theory building in Chinese feminism, which consistently uses the local as its frame of reference to negotiate with different kinds of transnational flows, be they economic, cultural, or theoretical. In Li Xiaojiang's talk, given at a summit forum sponsored by the Women's Institute of Spain in Madrid in 2008, Li examines the notion of gender equality in the historical context of modern China and argues that in China gender equality means not only the sharing of privileges and rights, but also the sharing of hardships between men and women. Therefore, the ethnocentric Western notion of gender equality alone cannot give Chinese women the broader humanistic care they need to live better lives.

Xueping Zhong challenges the binary opposition between class and women's liberation in the postsocialist period by arguing that Chinese modernity has always been classed and gendered. Zhong demonstrates that this feminist tradition with Chinese characteristics, which is displayed through her comparison between two Chinese films (*Stage Sisters* and *Yellow Earth*) with two Indian films (*Charulata* and *Ankur*), still lurks in writings by and about contemporary working-class women. Dai Jinhua's recent interview alerts us to the specter of polygamy resurrected by the formidable alliance of male-dominant power and transnational capital in twenty-first-century China. Dai argues that while capitalist logic transcends national borders and gender divisions, it also dehumanizes men and women alike; it is therefore necessary to reevaluate the legacy of women's liberation in socialist China in the face of global capitalism.

As feminist theories and practices always go hand in hand and fight shoulder to shoulder, the second section centers on feminist struggles on the ground. All three authors in this section are both feminist scholars and activists. Wang Zheng's chapter examines three cohorts of Chinese feminists (socialist state feminists, NGO feminists around 1995, and young feminist activists in recent years) to illustrate the shifting settings of and constant tension over gender equality in China. The first half of Wang's chapter combs through different threads of Chinese feminisms in the early twentieth century and during the socialist period, and the second half offers a comprehensive overview and evaluations of the feminist NGOs and new styles of feminist activism following the 1995 World Conference on Women. Li Jun's chapter starts with the question why mainland Chinese, male-dominant liberals always prioritize human rights over women's rights, and offers detailed, contextualized answers by drawing ample examples from Chinese social media. Li argues that male intellectuals, who are beneficiaries of postsocialist gender division, continue to uphold the patriarchal, heterosexual, and procapitalist class position, and therefore cannot become a strong ally to Chinese feminists.

Using the Chinese adaptations of Eve Ensler's *The Vagina Monologues* as a case study, Ke Qianting's essay discusses creative linguistic strategies in the localization of this feminist play. These multilayered strategies, Ke contends, are effective ways of articulating Chinese women's voices and visions, promulgating locally produced feminist knowledge and advocacy tactics, facilitating women-friendly policies and law, and finally, formulating a new feminist discourse in postsocialist China.

The five essays in the final section cover the literary, artistic, and cinematic creations and representations of contemporary Chinese feminisms. Liu Jindong's 2001 interview of Chinese writer Wang Anyi, "Am I a Feminist?," demonstrates Chinese women's hesitance to identify with Western feminists. According to Wang, her own female-centered works represent her aesthetic rather than political choices, as well as her reflection on Chinese women's situation in the Chinese historical context. In the second essay Ping Zhu draws on Wang Anyi's novel *Fu Ping* as an example to show how Wang uses labor to construct a different kind of feminine Shanghai: not one of markets and commodities, but one of communities and laborers. Zhu argues that the focus on unproductive labor in this story not only is a protest against capitalist consumerism, but also corrects the socialist blind spot for gender.

Hui Faye Xiao's essay takes a close look at the 2017 Fan Yusu phenomenon. By investigating the links of Fan's autobiographical writings with feminist literary traditions, as well as with the local literary practices of her working-class cohorts, Xiao argues that Fan serves as a node in a new literary network that is buttressed by collective efforts in the spirit of an emerging grassroots feminism against the postsocialist patriarchy. Through her psychoanalytical reading Jiang Jie's recent massive sculpture installation *Over 1.5 Tons*, Shuqin Cui addresses the question of how to construct a Chinese feminist identity between the translated vocabulary of Western feminism and China's dynamic economy, which complicates gender politics. Lastly, Gina Marchetti's chapter focuses on the importance of a cosmopolitan vision to the ways in which Hong Kong women filmmakers have depicted feminist movements, women's issues, and sexual politics on screen, as well as their contribution to Chinese-language screen feminism with specifi-cally Hong Kong characteristics since 1997.

The twelve contributors to this volume come from different back-grounds and write in varying styles, demonstrating the pluralistic spirit of feminisms with Chinese characteristics. Moreover, five out of the twelve pieces are translated from Chinese to English because the editors of this volume believe that Chinese feminists are not only cre-ative receivers of feminisms written in other languages, but also active contributors of world feminisms in the age of globalization.

Part One

Chinese Feminisms
in the Age of Globalization

1

"Gender" Trouble

Feminism in China under the Impact of Western Theory and the Spatialization of Identity

Nicola Spakowski

Feminism in China over the past ten to fifteen years has been marked by three related characteristics. The first is the introduction of "Western" feminism, with "gender" as a core theory import.[1] The second is the articulation of the "trouble" this import of Western theory has caused. Chinese feminist texts abound with terms such as *trouble* (*mafan* 麻烦), *difficulty* (*kunjing* 困境, *kunnan* 困难), *predicament* (*kunjing*), *deficiency* (*quexian* 缺陷), and *clash* (*chongtu* 冲突), which are used to express worries about the consequences of this new orientation of feminism in China. They prove that the importation of Western theory and the transition to gender as the basic category of analysis is not the logical development some authors claim it to be.[2] A third characteristic

This chapter was originally published in *positions* 19, no. 1 (2011): 31–54. Copyright © 2011 Duke Univ. Press. All rights reserved. www.dukeupress.edu. We thank Duke University Press for granting us permission to reprint this essay in the current volume.

1. I use the term *Western* here in the way it is used in China, where distinctions among Western feminist theories become secondary to their origin in Western industrialized countries.

2. References to these expressions of trouble will be given throughout the article. For the introduction of gender in China as a logical step, see Du Fangqin

is the search for an identity for Chinese feminism in a global context. Differing from an earlier preoccupation with defining the feminism of the reform period vis-à-vis the Maoist approach to women's liberation, Chinese scholars, under the impact of Western theory, rather turn to spatial definitions of Chinese feminism vis-à-vis international feminism and adopt the notion of the local to define their place in the world.

I have discussed elsewhere the institutional and material side of the import of Western theory to China.[3] In particular, I have highlighted the transnational networks of individuals, institutions, governments, and nongovernmental organizations (NGOs)—both Chinese and non-Chinese—that support this transfer of theory, and the impressive financial support this project receives from Western foundations. Rather than perceiving this transfer as part of quasinatural global flows of culture, unbounded travels of theory, or logical responses to an even more influential external force, global capital, I see it primarily as the product of human action and as part of a deliberate process of standardizing and universalizing theory on a global scale.[4] This process unites "international" (that is, Western) feminism in its efforts to integrate local feminisms as kinds of "local branches" and certain groups of "local" feminists in their efforts to become part of an international network. Still, the material and discursive power that shapes this process primarily lies with actors located in the West.

In this essay I look at the intellectual side of these theory transfers. In particular, I am interested in articulations or rhetorics of a Chinese

---

杜芳琴, "Quanqiu Shiye Zhong de Bentu Funüxue—Zhongguo de Jingyan: Yige Wei Wancheng de Guocheng" 全球视野中的本土妇女学—中国的经验: 一个未完成的过程" (Indigenous Women's Studies in a Global Horizon—the Chinese Experience: A Process that Is Not Yet Completed), *Funü yanjiu*, no. 6 (2001): 33–42.

3. Nicola Spakowski, "The Internationalization of China's Women's Studies," *Berliner China: Hefte/Chinese History and Society* 20 (2001): 79–100.

4. See Tani Barlow on gender as the "unifying element in the ideology of global governance." Tani E. Barlow, "Asian Women in Reregionalization," *positions: east asia cultures critique* 15, no. 2 (2007): 291.

feminist identity as part of a new conceptual grid of global-local inter-relations.[5] To get a comprehensive picture I find it necessary, however, to depart from earlier approaches that examined the relations between Western and Chinese feminism and focused on individual encounters between either persons or theories. These earlier approaches have provided us with very important insights. At the level of personal encounters, Shu-mei Shih has demonstrated how self-definitions and mutual perceptions tend to be simplified in cross-cultural encounters and how scholars tend to align with either universalism or particularism to stabilize troublesome relations.[6] Maria Jaschok and Shui Jingjun, on the other hand, have proposed their own work as a model for a multicultural research team, which leaves the greatest possible room for all the complexities and dynamics of self-positioning and mutual perception.[7] Their concept of constant dialogue, in its deconstructive thrust, leads to continuous instability and thus is the other extreme of how to respond to the challenges of cross-cultural feminist interaction.

At the level of theory, Min Dongchao has used the concept of traveling theory to trace the transfer of terms such as *feminism* and *gender* to China to explore how they are adapted to the Chinese context.[8]

---

5. See Margaret R. Somers, "Narrativity, Narrative Identity, and Social Action: Rethinking English Working-Class Formation," in *The History and Narrative Reader*, ed. Geoffrey Roberts (London: Routledge, 2001), 354–74, on the relational nature of identity constructions, and Shu-mei Shih, "Towards an Ethics of Transnational Encounter, or 'When' Does a 'Chinese' Woman Become a 'Feminist'?," *differences: A Journal of Feminist Cultural Studies* 13, no. 2 (2002): 90–126, especially 120n4, on the strategic articulation of identity. See also Anna Tsing, "The Global Situation," *Cultural Anthropology* 15, no. 3 (August 2000): 327–60, on the global (and, by implication, the local) as claims or rhetoric.

6. Shih, "Towards an Ethics of Transnational Encounter"; like Shih, I use universalism and particularism as epistemological stances and identity claims that see theory as universally applicable or as shaped by and responding to local particularities.

7. Maria Jaschok and Shui Jingjun, "'Outsider Within': Speaking to Excursions across Cultures," *Feminist Theory* 1, no. 1 (2000): 33–58.

8. Min Dongchao 闵冬潮, "Gender (Shehui xingbie) zai Zhongguo de Youxing Pianduan" Gender （社会性别） 在中国的游行片段 (Fragments of the Travel of Gender

Her articles further testify to the trouble these transfers have caused—Min's focus is on the problem of language and translation—and to the negotiations and multiple meanings that are implied in terms that build the core vocabulary of transcultural feminist encounters.[9] The problematic side of the traveling theory or traveling concept approach, however, is that it privileges concepts that originate in the West and leaves obscured whatever lies beyond these concepts. It tries to carve out the shape of the local through the traces it leaves on the global—instead of looking at an entire field of local theory production that might be affected but still not totally absorbed by the global. My discussion here, therefore, takes reflections on gender as a departure to move on to wider discussions of what Chinese feminism is in light of theory importation from the West.

What I want to demonstrate is the variety of ways in which feminists in China have responded to the import of gender and the destabilizing effect of the influx of what is perceived as Western theory in general. The range of responses include the well-known extremes of either universalist or particularistic stances, which still seem to be the two most common ways to restabilize identity in the face of cross-cultural encounters. Between or beyond universalism and particularism,

---

in China), *Funü yanjiu*, no. 1 (2004): 3–19; Min Dongchao, "Awakening Again: Traveling Feminism in China in the 1980s," *Women's Studies International Forum* 28, no. 4 (2005): 274–88; Min Dongchao, "Yige Youxing de Gainian: Gender (Shehui xingbie)—Yi Bei'ou, Dong'ou he Nanmei dui gender de Fanyi wei Li" 一个游行的概念: Gender (社会性别)—以北欧、东欧、和南美对 gender 的翻译为例 (A Traveling Concept: Gender [*Shehui Xingbie*]—A Case Study of Translating Gender in Northern and Eastern Europe and South America), *Zhejiang xuekan*, no. 1 (2005): 209–14; Min Dongchao, "*Duihua* (Dialogue) In-Between: A Process of Translating the Term 'Feminism' in China," *Interventions: International Journal of Postcolonial Studies* 9, no. 2 (2007): 174–93.

9. See also Nicola Spakowski, "The Internationalisation of China's Women's Movement—'Global Sisterhood' between Western Domination and Chinese Self-Definition," in *Negotiating Space for Gender Studies: Disciplinary Frameworks and Applications*, ed. Özen Odag and Alexander Pershai (Hamburg: Peter Lang, 2005), 47–65, on strategies of self-definition in Chinese encounters with Western feminism.

however, we will also find more complex, semi-stable answers to the challenges posed by Western theory—answers that take the multitude of perspectives into account, address the interdependencies and temporary contradictions between approaches, highlight the temporal dynamics and the contextual nature of certain stances, or point out the particular social outlook of their supporters. In light of this plurality of responses to the introduction of gender and the complexity of their interaction, it will become clear that gender is a particular concept that finds support only among particular (though by no means exclusively "Western") groups.

A few qualifications are necessary. Since this essay aims to explore Chinese perspectives, it is impossible to base it on standardized definitions. This holds true in particular for *gender*, which has come to China in various and often intermingled meanings as a category of analysis, a theory of the nature of gender differences, a political approach, and a comprehensive political agenda. I will get back to the problem of the definition of *gender* where it is important. The term *local*, first of all, is an indicator of the spatialization of identity. Chinese feminists use the term with different meanings, each of which implies different relations between China and the rest of the world—a feature that becomes clear over the course of this article and is addressed in the conclusion. This article is structured systematically along basic issues of discussion. This systematic structure, however, should not obscure the fact that theory building in Chinese feminism is a highly dynamic process, and certain stances are to be seen as answers to particular theoretical or practical challenges that occurred at a particular point in time. I will try to point out these dynamics where they matter.

Translating and Defining *Gender*

"Gender" trouble starts where the term *gender* needs to be translated into Chinese, and one of the most salient indicators for the plurality of ways to respond to *gender* is the existence of two competing translations of the term: *shehui xingbie* 社会性别 and *xingbie* 性别. Both strongly reflect the contact of Chinese women's studies with Western feminism and the examination of gender as a theory and an analytical category.[10] In the final analysis, however, *shehui xingbie* and *xingbie* point at two quite distinct (re)interpretations of gender, with *shehui xingbie* supported by a universalist rhetoric and *xingbie* as a truly indigenous concept.[11]

The translation of *gender* as *shehui xingbie* has been most strongly promoted by Wang Zheng, a Chinese diaspora scholar who has played a vital role in disseminating Western feminism in China.[12] *Shehui xingbie*, as Wang explains, is an expression directed against essentialist notions of gender or sex.[13] By adding *shehui* 社会 (social) to *xingbie* (gender/sex), the term emphasizes the social and constructed nature of gender roles. *Shehui xingbie* has come to be favored by those women scholars who confirm the translatability and transferability of West-ern concepts into China. In mainland China, Du Fangqin is central among them, as are younger scholars who have received part of their education in the West do not question *shehui xingbie* as an analytical category. They praise *shehui xingbie* as a breakaway from essentialist definitions of women's roles as they have been displayed in calls for femininity in the feminism of the 1980s or in contemporary commod-ity culture that instrumentalizes a traditional concept of femininity. Gender, in the view of these scholars, is more critical than essential-ist sex or the notion of equality between men and women (*nannü pingdeng* 男女平等) in official Chinese discourse.[14] It is an analytical

10. The two dimensions are closely linked and not clearly differentiated in Chi-nese discussions. Gender relates to theory in its antiessentialist explanation for the differences between men and women. As an analytical category it is able to address the great variety of phenomena where men and women are constructed as different.

11. On the various translations and interpretations of *gender*, see also Min, "Gender (Shehui xingbie)," 5–7.

12. On the role of diaspora scholars in the internationalization of Chinese femi-nism, see Spakowski, "The Internationalization of China's Women's Studies."

13. Wang Zheng, "'Nüxing Yishi,' 'Shehui Xingbie Yishi' Bianyi" 女性意识、"社会性别意识"辨异 (Distinguishing between "Women's Consciousness" and "Gen-der Consciousness"), *Funü yanjiu*, no. 2 (1997): 17–23.

14. Du, "Quanqiu Shiye Zhong," 35–37.

weapon that women can use to fight the myriad manifestations of patriarchy in Chinese society, which provides them with a new perspective and which finally reflects the integration of Chinese women's studies into international feminism. Gender is accepted as a universally valid category, and Chinese feminism is seen as the local variant of a global feminist venture based on the category of gender.[15]

Li Xiaojiang, on the other hand, vehemently rejects the idea of translatability and transferability and explains *xingbie* as an indigenous category, which, in Li's view, also reflects the particularity of Chinese feminism. Li is most articulate among those who claim that concepts and theories are determined by their linguistic and cultural contexts and cannot be transferred to other contexts without distortions or even harm.[16] The introduction of gender as *shehui xingbie*, in her view, is at the heart of the difficulties of contemporary Chinese feminism: "In the 1990s, this word (gender) entered the Chinese mainland and was translated into this category: *shehui xingbie*. Trouble had arrived (*mafan laile* 麻烦来了)!"[17] Li's discussion of gender

15. Du, "Quanqiu Shiye Zhong," 35; Liu Bohong 刘伯红, "95 Shijie Funü Dahui he Zhongguo Funü Yanjiu" 95世界妇女大会和中国妇女研究 (The 1995 World Conference on Women and Chinese Women's Studies), *Funü yanjiu*, no. 2 (1999): 47; Wang Zheng, "Shehui Xingbie Gainian zai Zhongguo de Yunyong" 社会性别概念在中国的运用 (The Application of the Concept of Gender in China), *Funü yanjiu*, no. 2 (2000): 3.

16. Li Xiaojiang 李小江, "With What Discourse Do We Reflect on Chinese Women?: Thoughts on Transnational Feminism in China," in *Spaces of Their Own: Women's Public Sphere in Transnational China*, ed. Mayfair Meihui Yang (Minneapolis: Univ. of Minnesota Press, 1999), 261–77. It is obvious, however, that Li is also influenced by Western feminism. Her own shift from women studies to gender studies must be understood as a reaction to the debate over gender in China.

17. Li Xiaojiang 李小江, "Daoyan: Cong Gender (Xingbie) Zai Yijie Zhong de Qiyixing Tanqi" 导言: 从Gender(性别)在译介过程中的歧义性谈起 (Introduction: On the Ambiguity of Gender in Translation), in Li Xiaojiang et al., *Wenhua, Jiaoyu yu Xingbie: Bentu Jingyan yu Xueke Jianshe* 文化, 教育与性别—本土经验与学科建设 (Culture, Education, and Gender: Local Experiences and the Construction of a Discipline) (Nanjing: Jiangsu renmin chubanshe, 2002), 5.

includes questions of translation and approach. She promotes *xingbie* as a contextualized concept. According to her, the word *xingbie* in Chinese refers to both sex and gender roles. *Shehui xingbie* thus is a redundant term—it adds the social to a concept that is social in the first place—and also one that easily neglects the biological aspects of *xingbie*, which in Li's view are constituent of human nature.[18] To use the term *shehui xingbie* means overemphasizing women's and men's social roles and ignoring the physical differences between the sexes. Thus *shehui xingbie*, to Li, is yet another form of women's self-denial (following the Maoist concept of identical gender roles).[19]

Writing the History of Chinese Feminism in a Global Context

Different notions of gender produce different stories of its career in China and of the origins and characteristics of Chinese women's studies in general. Du Fangqin's *shehui xingbie yanjiu* 社会性别研究 and Li Xiaojiang's *xingbie yanjiu* 性别研究 have become the basis for two of the most systematic and influential outlines of women and gender studies as an academic discipline in China and of its history in a global context. While both Li and Du construct an almost teleological development of Chinese women's studies with the shift to *shehui xingbie* or *xingbie* as an indicator of the establishment of (purely) academic women's studies in the late 1990s, the two authors differ in their constructions of the context and history of Chinese women's studies.[20]

In Du's view, the establishment of women's studies is a universal trend that started in the West in the 1960s and 1970s and spread all over the world.[21] Though Asian women's studies is a latecomer within

18. Li, "Daoyan," 2.
19. Li, "Daoyan," 3.
20. The academic women's studies that evolved in the late 1990s are distinguished from the problem/policy-oriented research of the 1980s and the involvement in development projects of the mid-1990s.
21. Du, "Quanqiu Shiye zhong."

global women's studies, and Chinese women's studies is a latecomer within Asian women's studies, they are still part of women's studies as a universal effort, and their particularities only testify to the local within the global. The global, regional, and local form a logical chain of points of reference at different levels of the research process: "Promoting women and gender studies has become a trend of globalization. To develop Chinese women and gender studies one needs a global perspective, regional comparison, and local action."[22] Du explicitly rejects the view that contemporary Chinese women's studies has strong local roots.[23]

Du concedes that women's studies in China emerged in the mid-1980s, but her emphasis is on the flaws of this earlier Chinese feminism: its focus on practical problems, its use of traditional theories and methods, its lack of a critical attitude, its collaboration with the Women's Federation, and its essentialist stance. The mid-1990s in her history of Chinese feminism appear as a kind of transitional period with the benefits of international exchange but at the same time a focus on project-oriented research. It was not until the late 1990s that women and gender studies (*funü yu shehui xingbiexue* 妇女与社会性别学) emerged as—in her view—the most appropriate approach, which could then become the basis for discipline building within academia as the true place for women's studies. As part of international feminism, Chinese women and gender studies emphasizes the need to introduce and to localize (*bentuhua* 本土化) Western concepts, which are perceived as more advanced than those available in China.[24]

Li Xiaojiang, on the other hand, emphasizes the uniqueness of China, the particular context and historical origin of the emergence

22. Du, "Quanqiu Shiye Zhong," 38.

23. Du, "Quanqiu Shiye Zhong," 8–9.

24. For discussions on the meaning of localization among those who welcome the importation of Western theories, see Chen Fang 陈方, "Xinxing de Xueke, Kaifang de Kecheng" 新兴的学科, 开放的课程 (A New Discipline and an Open Curriculum), *Funü yanjiu luncong*, no. 1 (2003): 61–65.

of Chinese women's studies, and the necessity of its independent development.[25] In Li's account, the 1980s were the peak of a truly local (*bentu* 本土), and at the same time nonstate (*minjian* 民间),[26] feminism in China that expressed a new subjectivity of Chinese women.[27] This positive development of a local nonstate feminism, however, was interrupted in 1993 with the increasing influence of Western feminism that had resulted from the preparations for the World Conference on Women. To be sure, Li is critical of the entire Chinese tradition of women's liberation since the late nineteenth century and also of traditional discourses on women. However, she perceives them as a part of Chinese women's history that cannot simply be denied: "As long as it is still this nation that lives, breathes, and works on this stretch of land, it is impossible to be completely cut off from our history."[28] With regard to socialist-style liberation, Li points out the deficiencies but also concedes that liberation through socialism was the necessary basis for the development of women today.[29]

The concept of particularity makes Li and others much more critical of the importation of Western feminist theory. Their criticism

25. See, in particular, Li, "With What Discourse"; Li Xiaojiang, "Qianyan: 'Qi' zai Nali?" 前言: "奇"在哪里? (Foreword: In What Way Are We "Strange"?), in *Shen Lin "Qi" Jing: Xingbie, Xuewen, Rensheng* 身临"奇"境: 性别、学问、人生 (Being in Wonderland: Gender, Knowledge, and Life), ed. Li Xiaojiang (Nanjing: Jiangsu renmin chubanshe, 2000), 1–6; and Li Xiaojiang and Zhang Xiaodan, "Creating a Space for Women: Women's Studies in China in the 1980s," *Signs: Journal of Women in Culture and Society* 20, no. 1 (1994): 137–51.

26. *Minjian* denotes "being rooted in the people" as opposed to the state (*guanfang* 官方). Independence from both the state and Western feminism has always appeared as a pair in Li Xiaojiang's work.

27. Li, "With What Discourse," 222.

28. Li, "With What Discourse," 264.

29. Li Xiaojiang, "50 Nian, Women Zou dao le Nali?: Zhongguo Funü Jiefang yu Fazhan Licheng Huigu" 50年, 我们走到了哪里?: 中国妇女解放与发展历程回顾 (Fifty Years, Where Have We Reached?: Looking Back onto the Project of Chinese Women's Liberation and Development), *Funü yanjiu*, no. 2 (2000): 58.

is focused on either the harmful role of the West or the unsatisfying role of Chinese scholars themselves. Li called for Chinese independence from Western feminism early on.[30] She bases her argument on epistemological considerations—the differences in language and traditions that easily lead to distortions and detrimental effects in transfers across cultures[31]—and political grounds, namely the imperialist or, more precisely, postcolonial structures underlying these transfers.[32] Postcolonialism, in Li's view, is an approach typical of today's world of foreign aid and cultural exchange.[33] Li is particularly critical of the role of Chinese diaspora scholars and their missionary zeal in instructing mainland Chinese scholars on how to do things in line with Western ways.[34] In an article published in 2000, therefore, she distinguished between "localization" (*bentuhua*) and "local research" (*bentu yanjiu* 本土研究) and made clear that she favored local research—that is, research without any outside interference.[35] In

30. See Nicola Spakowski, "'Ihr hört uns nicht an und verliert dadurch viel': Zum Dialog der chinesischen und der westlichen Frauenforschung und Frauenbewegung" ("You Don't Listen to Us and Thereby Lose a Lot": On the Dialogue between Chinese and Western Women's Studies and Women's Movement). *Newsletter Frauen und China* 2 (1992): 26–29.

31. See especially Li, "With What Discourse."

32. See, for instance, Li Xiaojiang, *Guanyu Nüren de Dawen* 关于女人的答问 (Questions and Answers on Women) (Nanjing: Jiangsu renmin chubanshe, 1997), 56. See also Zhao Xifang 赵稀方, "Zhongguo Nüxing Zhuyi de Kunjing" 中国女性主义的困境 (The Predicament of Chinese Feminism), *Wenyi zhengming*, no. 4 (2001): 74–79, especially 76–78 on the colonial relationship between Western and Chinese feminism and on "the modern East itself participating in the process of orientalization."

33. Li Xiaojiang, "Quanqiuhua Beijing xia Zhongguo Funü Yanjiu yu Guoji Fazhan Xiangmu" 全球化背景下中国妇女研究与国际发展项目 (Chinese Women's Studies and International Development Projects under Globalization), *Funü yanjiu luncong*, no. 3 (2005): 59.

34. Another critique of the role of diaspora scholars is Pan Jintang 潘锦堂, "Wo Kan 'Shehui Xingbie Lilun' ji qi Liuxing" 我看"社会性别理论"及其流行 (My View on 'Gender Theory' and Its Popularity), *Funü yanjiu*, no. 1 (2003): 60.

35. Li, "50 Nian," 62–63.

a recent article, however, she tones down her earlier radical stance by distinguishing between research that addresses practical problems—here she continues to insist on *bentu yanjiu*—and purely academic research, in which knowledge of theoretical developments outside China helps broaden one's horizons.[36] Also she is more self-reflective in pointing out that the nationalist stance of *bentu yanjiu* has to be understood as a conscious political choice made under pressure from outside but bearing the potential of being instrumentalized by one's own government.[37]

Dong Limin also warns against the introduction of Western theory and its localization, but differing from Li, focuses on the role of mainland scholars and—as she puts it—their lack of creativity in theory production as the root of the "difficulties and deficiencies" (*kunjing yu quexian* 困境与缺陷) of contemporary Chinese feminism. She accuses Chinese feminists of departing from Chinese reality and forming a "discursive ivory tower."[38] Western feminism, in Dong's view, is being "mystified"[39] and has become a "system of reference" that reduces Chinese feminism to the role of a student and Chinese society to a mere extension of the West.[40] Chinese feminists have become consumers instead of producers of knowledge, a feature they share with contemporary Chinese academia in general, which Dong sees as being in "a state of 'aphasia' vis-à-vis the indigenous experience."[41] Discursive creativity and ability, in Dong's view, necessarily arise from one's own linguistic and cultural contexts. Chinese feminism, therefore, should

36. Li, "Quanqiuhua Beijing xia," 60.

37. Li Xiaojiang 李小江 and Paek Won-dam 白元淡, "Jieji, Xingbie yu Minzu Guojia" 阶级、性别与民族国家 (Class, Gender, and the Nation State), *Dushu*, no. 10 (2004): 11–12.

38. Dong Limin, "Nüxing Zhuyi: Bentuhua ji qi Weidu" 女性主义：本土化及其维度 (Feminism: Indigenization and Its Purview), *Nankai xuebao*, no. 2 (2005): 7.

39. Dong, "Nüxing Zhuyi," 8.

40. Dong, "Nüxing Zhuyi," 8–9.

41. Dong, "Nüxing Zhuyi," 11.

take Chinese women and China, "this specific cultural space and economic region," as orientation points.[42]

Defining the Local

The growing defense of the local that is expressed in the statements above has also forced scholars to define what in their eyes distinguishes China from the West. Definitions of the local that have been brought up over recent years can broadly be categorized according to the following three concepts, each of which puts emphasis on different political, cultural, and social aspects of the local: Marxism-Leninism and the socialist tradition of women's liberation; a tradition of nonantagonistic gender relations; and the particular social constituency of feminism in China.

A first possible definition of the local is "Marxist women's theory" (*Makesizhuyi funüguan* 马克思主义妇女权), general state policy, and the socialist tradition of women's liberation in China. The fact that Marxism, which had formerly claimed universal significance, is now being discussed under the rubric of the local is one of the most telling indicators of the political maneuvers underlying claims of the local and the reversal of discursive power in Chinese feminism under the impact of Western theory.[43] This particularization of Marxism is best reflected in a report on a conference titled The Localization of Teaching in Women's Studies: Asian Experience, held at China Women's University (*Zhonghua nüzi xueyuan* 中华女子学院) in 2002. While positions on how to handle Marxism as theory and Marxist-oriented state policy varied, this report makes clear that it is only one among many possible choices of theory.[44]

42. Dong, "Nüxing Zhuyi," 12.

43. See also Spakowski, "The Internationalization of China's Women's Studies," 81–82.

44. Chen, "Xinxing de Xueke," 62–64.

With regard to feminist practice, the Chinese socialist tradition of women's liberation has become one of the central suggestions for defining the local. By the 1980s Li Xiaojiang had already claimed a Chinese socialist top-down (*zi shang er xia* 自上而下) approach and a Western bottom-up (*zi xia er shang* 自下而上) approach to be the decisive difference between Chinese and Western feminism.[45] Implied was the notion that China had to break with the concept of state intervention on behalf of women and get on track with a bottom-up feminism as the norm of social development.[46] This oppositional view of Western feminism as a movement from below and Chinese feminism as a movement from above, however, is not uncontested. US-based scholar Zhong Xueping sees it as the key to understanding the failure of Chinese feminists' efforts to localize Western feminism. In her article "Worries about Wrong Positions," published in the Chinese mainland journal *Dushu* 读书 (Reading) in 2003, Zhong points out that localization has so far occurred only unconsciously and problematically.[47] The self-perception of Chinese feminism as a movement from above, in Zhong's view, is not only a definition of the local derived from the West but also a simplification of historical experience. It glosses over the positive sides of women's liberation in China, especially the effect

45. Nicola Spakowski, "'Women Studies with Chinese Characteristics'? On the Origins, Issues, and Theories of Contemporary Feminist Research in China," *Jindai Zhongguo funüshi yanjiu*, no. 2 (1994): 314–15. See also Zhang Liming 章立明, "Quanqiuhua Yujing zhong de Zhongguo Funüxue Jianshe" 全球化语境中的中国妇女学建设 (On the Construction of Women's Studies in China in the Context of Globalization), *Sixiang zhanxian*, no. 4 (2006): 54–60, especially 57 on the "pattern of women's liberation from above."

46. For the liberal trend in Chinese feminism, see Nicola Spakowski, "Von der Befreiung zur Entwicklung. Modernisierungsbegriff und Emanzipationsstrategie im feministischen Diskurs der VR China" (From Liberation to Development: Theories of Modernization and Emancipation in Chinese Feminism), *Berliner ChinaHefte* 10 (1996): 11–47.

47. Zhong Xueping 钟雪萍, "Cuozhi de Jiaolü" 错置的焦虑 (Worries about Wrong Positions), *Dushu*, no. 4 (2003): 47–53.

that state ideology had on women's self-consciousness. Zhong criticizes: "How can this attitude lead to an understanding of the limits of Western feminism and of China's local 'historical resources' as a precondition for truly realizing the 'localization' of feminism?"[48]

Zhong's notion of the local as a historical resource is also at the heart of a second way of defining the local, namely the idea of non-antagonistic and more harmonious gender relations or a more general reference to collectivism.[49] Scholars who emphasize nonantagonistic gender relations as the distinguishing feature of the local usually refer to the Chinese tradition of women's liberation as a concern of both men and women.[50] Those who approve of this tradition of a shared concern for women's issues tend to perceive women's studies as part of a more encompassing "study of humanity" (*renxue* 人学). This trend is well reflected in talks and discussions published by Li Xiaojiang and colleagues in 2002 under the title "Culture, Education, and Gender: Local Experiences and the Construction of a Discipline."[51] Zheng Bijun, a historian of the older generation and former teacher of the history of women in premodern China at Beijing University, pointed out in her talk that women's studies is only a temporary effort to counter the neglect of women in general history. It will be replaced by a discipline that explores "complete human beings" (*wanzheng de ren* 完整的人).[52] Zheng writes, "I think what we have to particularly empha-

48. Zhong, "Cuozhi de Jiaolü," 52.

49. References to collectivism in the sense of a national character (as it is expressed in Zhao, "Zhongguo Nüxingzhuyi de Kunjing") are rare. Rather, scholars stress the need to discuss women's problems as part of overall social problems. See, for instance, Li, "Daoyan," 8–10, and Spakowski, "'Women Studies with Chinese Characteristics'?," 315, for earlier statements to this effect.

50. Collaboration with men as a distinguishing feature of Chinese feminism had already been brought up by Li Xiaojiang in the 1980s (Spakowski, "'Women Studies with Chinese Characteristics'?," 317). See also Li, "*Qianyan*," 1.

51. Li et al., *Wenhua*, 1

52. Zheng Bijun 郑必俊, "Nüxingxue Xueke zai Beijing Daxue de Jianshe Shijian ji Sikao" 女性学学科在北京大学的建设实践及思考 (*Practice of and Reflections on*

size today is to explore the specific characteristics (*teshuxing* 特殊性) of women, starting from the commonality (*gongxing* 共性) of human beings (*ren* 人)."[53]

A most recent trend in the discussion of localization and efforts to define the local is the desire to find labels for what one might call a distinctive Chinese feminism. One such label is "Chinese feminism" (*Zhongguo nüxingzhuyi* 中国女性主义) or, even more precisely, "smiling Chinese feminism" (*weixiao de Zhongguo nüxingzhuyi* 微笑的中国女性主义). The latter was coined by Huang Lin, professor of literature at Capital Normal University in Beijing and editor of the journal *Chinese Feminism* (*Zhongguo nüxingzhuyi*).[54] A blurb for the third issue explains the features of "smiling Chinese feminism": "Chinese feminism is sharp but not aggressive. It explores women's problems; it is concerned with the harmonious development of the two sexes (*liangxing de hexie fazhan* 两性的和谐发展) and eventually pays attention to the eternal topic of 'man' (*ren* 人). This book develops for us a smiling Chinese feminism, combining past and present, translation and localization, theory and practice, scholarly arguing and current

Constructing Women's Studies at Peking University), in Li Xiaojiang et al., *Wenhua, Jiaoyu yu Xingbie: Bentu Jingyan yu Xueke Jianshe* 文化, 教育与性别——本土经验与学科建设 (Culture, Education, and Gender: Local Experiences and the Construction of a Discipline) (Nanjing: Jiangsu renmin chubanshe, 2002), 32.

53. Zheng Bijun, "Nüxingxue Xueke," 22. For a similar position, see Zheng Yongfu 郑永福, "Funüshi yu Da Lishi Jiaoxue zhong de Hudong: Yi Lishi Zhuanye Zhongguo Jindaishi wei Li" 妇女史与大历史教学中的互动: 以历史专业中国近代史为例 (*Interaction between Women's History and the Teaching of Macro History: The Example of Modern Chinese History for History Majors*), in Li Xiaojiang et al., *Wenhua, Jiaoyu yu Xingbie: Bentu Jingyan yu Xueke Jianshe* 文化, 教育与性别——本土经验与学科建设 (Culture, Education, and Gender: Local Experiences and the Construction of a Discipline) (Nanjing: Jiangsu renmin chubanshe, 2002), 131–53.

54. *Chinese Feminism* was founded in 2004. Huang also launched a "cultural salon of Chinese feminism" (*Zhongguo nüxingzhuyi wenhua shalong* 中国女性主义文化沙龙) in Beijing and the website *Field of Vision of the Two Sexes* (*Liangxing shiye* 两性视野). See www.alleyeshot.com.

taste."[55] As one can see from other publications by Huang, and also from the editorial board and authors grouped around Chinese feminism, however, the new label does not necessarily imply an uncritical or anti-Western stance within feminist research.[56] Still, self-definition seems to be a concern for those involved.

Another recent label that is evident in Huang's definition of smiling Chinese feminism is "harmony between the sexes" (*liangxing hexie* 两性和谐). The term is linked to the broader concept of a "harmonious society" (*hexie shehui* 和谐社会), which has been promoted by the Chinese government since 2004 and thus reflects interaction with a local discursive context. Again, however, harmony between the sexes does not refer to one single view on gender issues. Nor does it necessarily reflect closeness to the Chinese government. Some authors claim that it is a solution to the "fierce conflict and collision" evoked by the importation of Western feminism.[57] Others use the term as the starting point for discussing the lack of harmony between the sexes, thus turning it critically against violations of the rhetoric in social

55. From the website of the Guangxi Normal University Press Group (bbtpress .com), accessed September 29, 2006. On smiling Chinese feminism, see also Bao Hong 鲍红, "Weixiao de Zhongguo Nüxingzhuyi" 微笑的中国女性主义 (A Smiling Chinese Feminism) *Chuban cankao*, no. 11 (2004): 14.

56. See, for instance, Huang's discussion of Simone de Beauvoir, Hannah Arendt, and Susan Sontag as examples of "traveling feminist images" in China. Huang Lin 荒林, "Zuowei Nüxing Zhuyi Fuhao de Linglei Changjing: Ximeng Bofuwa, Hanna Alunte, Sushan Sangtage de Zhongguo Yuedu" 作为女性主义符号的另类场景: 西蒙·波伏娃、汉娜·阿伦特、苏珊·桑塔格的中国阅读 (Another Scene of Feminist Symbols: The Reading of Simone de Beauvoir, Hannah Arendt, and Susan Sontag in China), *Zhongguo tushu pinglun*, no. 5 (2006): 78–84.

57. Zhu Yanfang 朱彦芳, "'Liang Xing Hexie': Zhongguo Nüxing Zhuyi de Zhongji Zhuiqiu: Di Qi Jie Zhongguo Nüxing Wenxue Xueshu Yantaohui Zongshu" "两性和谐": 中国女性主义的终极追求——第七届中国女性文学学术研讨会综述 ("Harmony between the Two Sexes": The Ultimate Goal of Chinese Feminism: Report on the Seventh Academic Conference on Chinese Women's Literature), *Luoyang shifan xueyuan xuebao*, no. 6 (2005): 18.

practice. Han Dongping, for instance, employs the term to reveal that gender relations in Chinese society are "not harmonious" (*bu hexie* 不和谐) and to discuss the evidence and reasons for, as well as solutions to this problem.[58] What we can see from the way scholars refer to harmony between the sexes is how feminists in China mediate between discourses of external and internal origin.

A third suggestion on how to define the local is made by Sun Shaoxian in her article "'Aristocratized' Chinese 'Feminism.'"[59] Instead of making culture or history her point of departure, Sun focuses on the social constituency of contemporary Chinese feminism. According to her, the particular class[60] base of Western feminism—the "white middle classes"—can also be found with contemporary (that is, Western-influenced) Chinese feminism, which typically reflects the concerns of "female intellectuals in the humanities" and female students.[61] Whereas in the West, according to Sun, a middle-class horizon represents the majority of women, in China this category is a quite narrow approach supported only by a small minority of women who are privileged in the first place.[62]

True localization, for Sun, means turning to the problems of the majority of Chinese women—that is, female workers and peasants who are at the margins of Chinese society. These include laid-off workers, prostitutes, beggars and homeless persons, school dropouts, women in labor camps, criminal women, drug addicts, and so on.[63] Apart from

58. Han Dongping 韩东屏, "Liangxing Hexie" 两性和谐 (Harmony between the Sexes), *Hunan shehui kexue* 2 (2006): 22–24.

59. Sun Shaoxian 孙绍先, "'Guizuhua' de Zhongguo 'Nüxing Zhuyi'" "贵族化"的中国"女性主义" ("Aristocratized" Chinese "Feminism"), *Tianya*, no. 1 (2005): 23–25.

60. Sun uses the term *class* only with regard to Western "middle-class" feminism.

61. *White middle class* is translated as middle bourgeoisie (*zhongchan jieji* 中产阶级). Sun, "'Guizuhua,'" 23.

62. Sun, "'Guizuhua,'" 23–24. However, Sun also recognizes the efforts of people such as Xie Lihua, Li Xiaojiang, and Pan Suiming (the latter working on prostitution but not under the umbrella of feminism). See Sun, "'Guizuhua,'" 24–25.

63. Sun, "'Guizuhua,'" 24.

accusing contemporary Chinese feminism of being "aristocratized" (*guizuhua* 贵族化), Sun wonders why it does not forge links with the Women's Federation, which—despite its shortcomings—still helps women at the bottom of society. Local feminism thus is something that still waits to be realized and will be situated beyond the two mainstream approaches in Chinese feminism: "On the one hand there is the organization of the Women's Federation dominated by government concerns; on the other hand there is 'aristocratized' feminism.' When will the masses of Chinese working women (*guangda laodong funü* 广大劳动妇女) have their own true representative?"[64]

Going Asian/Northeast Asian

Another quite recent trend in Chinese feminist thought is regionalization (*quyuhua* 区域化) and the pronouncement of Asia and Northeast Asia as new sites of feminist identity formation. The new interest in Asia and East Asia as units of research is not restricted to feminism and can be found in other academic fields as well.[65] In the field of feminism it demonstrates the dynamic and complex nature of theory production in the context of various and shifting discursive influences. Part of the attractiveness of Asia for Chinese feminists lies in the fact that it can be used as a bridge between the local and the global and offers a way out of purely particularistic or universalist stances. This shift toward a middle-ground position is particularly evident in the works of Li Xiaojiang and Du Fangqin, the two pioneers of discipline

64. Sun, "'Guizuhua,'" 25. See also Qu Yajun 屈雅君, "Nüxingzhuyi Wenxue Piping Bentuhua Guocheng zhong Ying Zhuyi de Wenti" 女性主义文学批评本土化过程中应注意的问题 (Issues to Be Noted in the Process of Localizing Feminist Literary Criticism), in Li Xiaojiang et al., *Wenhua, Jiaoyu yu Xingbie: Bentu Jingyan yu Xueke Jianshe* 文化, 教育与性别—本土经验与学科建设 (Culture, Education, and Gender: Local Experiences and the Construction of a Discipline), Nanjing: Jiangsu renmin chubanshe, 2002, 154–78, especially 176.

65. See, for instance, "Dushu" zazhi, ed., *Yazhou de Bingli* 亚洲的病例 (Asia's Pathology) (Beijing: Sanlian shudian, 2007). See also Barlow, "Asian Women."

building in women's studies, who, however, start from very different premises and display quite different understandings of the regional.

Du, who is obviously influenced by the agenda of the Asian Center for Women's Studies at Ewha Womans University in Seoul, promotes the idea of Asian women's studies (*Yazhou funüxue* 亚洲妇女学).[66] Asian women's studies is a regional variant within a culturally pluralistic international feminism. Again, the local is part of the global: Asian women's studies, in Du's view, originated in a global wave that started in the feminism of the 1960s and 1970s.[67] It offers a framework to articulate the "Asian voice" within Western-dominated international feminism.[68] Within the region commonalities and differences form a dialectic relationship of "differences within commonality" (*gongxing zhong de chayi* 共性中的差异) or "commonality of goals and plurality of practical tactics."[69] Regional feminism uses a common grid of topics such as "family, work, sexuality, culture, law, politics, women's studies' knowledge production, women's movement, religion, body and health" to explore Asian women's "lives" and "experiences."[70] Based on this standardized approach, Asian women's history appears as a sequence of (gendered) patriarchal society followed by modernization in its specific manifestations of (semi)colonialism and postcolonialism

---

66. See her explicit reference to the center in Du Fangqin, "Zai Gongxing yu Chayi zhong Fazhan Yazhou Funüxue" 在共性与差异中发展亚洲妇女学 (Developing Asian Women's Studies within Commonalities and Differences), *Funü yanjiu luncong*, no. 1 (2002): 28.

67. Du, "Quanqiu Shiye zhong de Bentu Funüxue."

68. Du, "Zai Gongxing yu Chayi zhong," 32.

69. Du, "Zai Gongxing yu Chayi zhong," 30, 32.

70. These are the topics used in a book series edited by Ewha Womans University that Du reviewed enthusiastically. Du Fangqin, "Lijie, Bijiao yu Fenxiang: Yazhou Funüxue de Jueqi—'Yazhou Funüxue Congshu' Shuping" 理解、比较与分享：亚洲妇女学的崛起—"亚洲妇女学丛书" 书评 (Understanding, Comparing, and Sharing: The Rise of Asian Women's Studies—A Review of the "Book Series on Asian Women's Studies"), *Funü yanjiu luncong*, no. 9 (2005): 77.

and, finally, globalization. Within this scheme of shared experiences, again national variants occur.[71]

Li's project lacks this systematic outline. She articulates the idea of "Northeast Asian research" (*Dongbeiya yanjiu* 东北亚研究) in the transcripts of two conversations she had during a research trip to Japan and Korea in 2004.[72]

These conversations covered a wide range of concerns that were not limited to women's issues.[73] Again, Li's starting point is concrete history, which in the case of Northeast Asia (including China, Japan, and Korea) is a history of a shared cultural heritage (for Li, an "all-Han culture circle" [*fan Han wenhua quan* 泛汉文化圈]), but also, and primarily, one of the wars of modern history that caused hostility and misunderstandings. Looking at Korean and Japanese neighbors reveals first and foremost their differences,[74] and research on Northeast Asia is faced with big challenges and obstacles.[75] Still, Li is convinced that overcoming these obstacles is worth the effort. In explaining the benefits of Northeast Asian research, Li outlines her own position as moving from nationalism as a standpoint produced by pressure from outside, to "transcultural research" (*kua wenhua yanjiu* 跨文化研究) as a method that counterbalances the narrowness of nationalism and the danger of research being utilized by a potentially belligerent nation-state. The final aim of the project of Northeast Asian research is "peace."[76] Northeast Asia thus is a site that is

71. Du, "Zai Gongxing yu Chayi zhong," 30–31.

72. Ueno Chizuko 上野千鹤子 and Li Xiaojiang 李小江, "'Zhuyi' yu Xingbie" "主义"与性别 ("-isms" and Gender), *Dushu*, no. 8 (2004): 39.

73. Li and Paek, "Jieji, Xingbie yu Minzu Guojia," and Ueno and Li, "'Zhuyi' yu Xingbie." The conversations were held with Korean scholar Paek Won-dam and Japanese Marxist-feminist scholar Ueno Chizuko.

74. See Ueno and Li, "'Zhuyi' yu Xingbie," 39, and Li and Paek, "Jieji, Xingbie yu Minzu Guojia."

75. Ueno and Li, "'Zhuyi' yu Xingbie," 13.

76. Li and Paek, "Jieji, Xingbie yu Minzu Guojia," 11–12.

not, as in Du's case, the local within the global but a concrete place of complex interrelations and conflicts. Gender, for Li, is one of the potential categories that can be used to explore history, but, as she seems to agree with her Korean and Japanese counterparts, it is not the only and also not the primary one.[77]

For both Du and Li, regionalism seems to be a way out of the predicaments of universalism versus particularism—epistemological and political standpoints into which they had maneuvered themselves in the course of discussions over the global and the local. While Du counters the accusation of Westernization by promoting Asianization, Li tones down her earlier nationalist stance by looking beyond the borders of China and including two neighboring countries. They meet at the intermediate level of the region but still follow quite different scholarly and political agendas.

Mediating between Perspectives and Preserving Contradictions

Differing from the various attempts at stabilizing the identity of a universal Asian or Chinese feminism, a few authors try to preserve the tensions within Chinese feminism and between Chinese and Western perspectives. In their accounts, various feminist positions appear as answers to concrete historical contexts and problems. These positions form complex interrelations; they may converge on some topics and be irreconcilable on others.

Qu Yajun, in her study of Chinese feminist literary criticism, discerns the coexistence of "three women's voices" in contemporary China whose "complexity and complex interrelation are different from any nation-state in the world and any period in Chinese history."[78] These are, first, the voice of the Women's Federation, which Qu calls

---

77. Li and Paek, "Jieji, Xingbie yu Minzu Guojia," 8–9; Ueno and Li, "'Zhuyi' yu Xingbie," 42–43.

78. Qu, "Nüxingzhuyi Wenxue Piping Bentuhua," 163.

"mainstream women's discourse" (*zhuliu nüxing huayu* 主流女性话语); second, "feminist discourse" (*nüxingzhuyi huayu* 女性主义话语) based on the concepts of human rights and gender; and third, "commercial women's discourse" (*shangyexing de nüxing huayu* 商业性的女性话语) manifested in advertising, television, and film, where women are simply used as a selling point.[79] Each of these discourses, according to Qu, has its positive and negative side; it may converge with certain aspects of one discourse and oppose others. For instance, feminist and commercial discourses have different roots and intentions but still share a focus on the individual, the body, and the private.[80]

The "orthodoxy" of mainstream discourse helps contain the negative sides of commercial discourse, while through its very orthodoxy it easily becoming conservative. Commercial discourse, on the other hand, undermines the authority and monopoly of mainstream discourse while at the same time being part of "liberal capitalist male culture."[81] It becomes clear that in Qu's view the three discourses, in their particular roots and perspectives, might compensate for one another's deficiencies but remain irreconcilable. They cannot be merged into a unified Chinese feminism; nor can any of them claim to represent the true voice of Chinese women.

Xu Ping distinguishes between "mainstream" (*zhuliu* 主流), "academic" (*xueyuan* 学院), and *"minjian"* discourse. While it is quite clear what she means by mainstream discourse (the official stance on women's liberation based on Mao Zedong Theory) and academic discourse (feminism imported from the West), *minjian* is used here in a quite interesting way: it signifies discourse that is both "unofficial" (or not originating from Marxist theory) and local in the sense of being "born and developed in China and [being] authentic, based on experience and concrete."[82]

79. Qu, "Nüxingzhuyi Wenxue Piping Bentuhua," 163–67.
80. Qu, "Nüxingzhuyi Wenxue Piping Bentuhua," 167.
81. Qu, "Nüxingzhuyi Wenxue Piping Bentuhua," 168.
82. Xu Ping 许平, "Yi ge Zhongguo Nanren Tushengtuzhang de Nüxing Zhuyi Guandian" 一个中国男人土生土长的女性主义观点 (A Chinese Man's Local Feminist

Also Xu takes the example of a male *minjian* "feminist" to discuss what she means by "local discourse." In her article "A Chinese Man's Local Feminist Viewpoint," she portrays Deng Dingjie, a male scholar-cum-administrator who works in the field of migrant women and whose practical and theoretical work is based on a mission to help young women out of the oppressive life in poor hinterland villages.[83] Born in 1933, Deng spent his career in various offices of the administration of Zhu county in Sichuan province. Since 1986 he has worked in the field of "labor export" (*laowu shuchu* 劳务输出), which means that he sends young rural (hinterland) Sichuanese women to (coastal) Guangdong province to work in factories owned by international companies. This practice of government-steered migration is based on the principle "We send women where there is capital" (*nali you ziben, women jiu ba funü song wang nali* 哪里有资本, 我们就把妇女送往哪里).

Xu, well versed in Western feminist theories, is quite aware that labeling this Chinese policy as *minjian* feminist is an insult to Western feminist critiques of Third World women's exploitation by international capital.[84] However, in her discussion she demonstrates that the phenomenon is hard to assess. In a first step, she discloses the rationale behind the *minjian* approach by relating Deng's personal, political, and professional background and his perception of the problems young rural Chinese women are facing. Deng obviously

---

Viewpoint), in *Nüxing? Zhuyi: Wenhua Chongtu yu Shenfen Rentong* 女性? 主义: 文化冲突与身份认同 (Femin?ism: The Clash of Cultures and Identity), ed. Li Xiaojiang (Nanjing: Jiangsu renmin chubanshe, 2000), 234.:

83. *Local* here is translated as "born and formed on (native) soil" (*tu sheng tu zhang de* 土生土长的).

84. The phenomenon of Chinese migrant women following international capital as a challenge to feminist criticisms of globalization has also been stated by Li Xiaojiang, "From 'Modernization' to 'Globalization': Where are Chinese Women?," trans. Tani E. Barlow, *Signs: Journal of Women in Culture and Society* 26, no. 4 (2001): 1274–78, and Tani E. Barlow, "Asia, Gender, and Scholarship under Processes of Re-regionalization," *Journal of Gender Studies (Ochanomizu University)* 5 (2002): 11.

considers migration an opportunity for young rural women to acquire skills and earn money, which enhances their status in their places of origin, where they experience severe forms of repression within the family and also general backwardness.[85] It is a path toward liberation relative to the concrete origins of these women: from the "margin of the margin" (as women living in the Chinese rural hinterland) to the "margin" of the center (as women living in China's coastal areas).[86]

In a second step, Xu juxtaposes the various standpoints one could take on the question of migrant women in three "dialogues" (*duihua* 对话): one among Chinese mainstream, *minjian*, and academic discourse; one between China and the West; and one between male and female.[87] These dialogues throw light on the questionable sides of "labor export" in the name of women's liberation. Xu herself seems to sympathize with the propositions of *minjian* discourse on the basis of the concrete circumstances of Chinese reality. However, she also points out the temporary nature of stances such as Deng's and its lack of general validity:

> Deng Dingjie's feminist standpoint is an attitude towards women in the transition phase of Chinese society. . . . These views, just as their background, are also characterized by transition (*zhuanxing* 转型) and mediation (*zhongjie* 中介). They are certainly not the ultimate expression of local Chinese feminism. But through the analysis and critical selection of these views one can get a deeper understanding of the circumstances of the lives of the women of Zhu county. This can help the development of local Chinese feminism.[88]

The local here is not a permeable local, a simple variant of the global, but a concrete answer to a concrete situation, one that is determined by differences within China, shaped by Chinese history, highly

85. Xu, "Yi ge Zhongguo Nanren," 228–33.
86. Xu, "Yi ge Zhongguo Nanren," 237.
87. Xu, "Yi ge Zhongguo Nanren," 234–41.
88. Xu, "Yi ge Zhongguo Nanren," 241.

contradictory in light of various national and international understandings of feminism, and impossible to assess by an absolute and
universal standard of liberation.

Conclusion

I have outlined the various responses feminists in China have encountered with the introduction of gender to China—a process many
authors have found troublesome because of its universalist and inter-
ventionist overtones and the cutting off of indigenous creativity, traditions, and resources. The responses to gender included acceptance
based on universalist assumptions, as well as rejection on the grounds
of a particularistic outlook. Those scholars who found that Western
concepts and theories did not fit the Chinese context defined what they
thought made women's experience and women's liberation in China
a particular case. Another twist in the discussion was the move from
nation to region. Some scholars embraced the concept of Asia or East
Asia—albeit, again, in quite contradictory definitions—as a way out
of earlier extreme stances of particularism or universalism. All of the
responses mentioned so far can be seen as efforts to restabilize feminist theory in China in the face of troublesome intercultural encounters. These attempts at stabilization entailed simplifications and thus
contrasted with the more complex, semi-stable approaches, which I
present in the final part of the essay. The scholars discussed there try
to mediate between perspectives and preserve contradictions. They
point out the frictions between various definitions of the local—their
contextuality and historicity, their irreducibility to a single definition
of a "Chinese feminism," and their complex interaction with international feminism. Altogether, the various responses paint a picture of a
pluralist and complex feminism in China that does not fit the formula
of "differences within commonality" put forth by international feminism, and thus calls for a particularization of gender.[89]

89. Du, "Zai Gongxing yu Chayi zhong," 30. There are a number of varia-
tions on this expression of a unified and inclusive feminism—for example, "unified

In all the discussions of whether and how gender fits the Chinese context, the local is a central notion and indicates the spatialization of a feminist identity in China. This reference to the local, cannot remain uncontested, however, because certain concepts of the local have quite problematic implications. A first concept to be found in the texts I have analyzed is the destination of global cultural flows, or travels, of theory.[90] What is problematic with this concept is that while local scholars might be assigned some agency in terms of selecting or modifying global theory, in the final analysis they are still reduced to occupying the receiving end of transfers from the West and thus to the periphery of global theory production. A second meaning of the local that seems particularly popular among those Chinese and Western scholars who support gender as a universally applicable concept is that of a concrete manifestation of global or universal structures.[91] Here one wonders whether the seeming permeability between the local and the global ("differences within commonality") is not an effect of standardized concepts in the first place. A third notion can be found with those who present the local as a historically and culturally particular place that is isolated from any outside influence—a concept that easily leads to essentialist definitions of what is Chinese.[92] The most sophisticated concept of the local has been developed by the scholars discussed in the last part of this essay. Here the local is a site of complex interactions and contradictions between feminisms of various origins.

Scholars in China obviously insist on using the local as their frame of reference, a space for identity formation, and a site of theory production despite its problematic implications, and even where they are

---

multifaceted strategy." See Brooke A. Ackerly and Bina D'Costa, "Transnational Feminism: Political Strategies and Theoretical Discussions" (working paper 2005/1, Department of International Relations, Australian National University, 2005), 28, who promulgate human rights as the "common ground" of a transnational feminism.

90. Min, "Yige Youxing de Gainian," and Huang, "Zuowei Nüxing Zhuyi Fuhao."

91. Du, "Zai Gongxing yu Chayi zhong."

92. Li, "With What Discourse."

aware of its complexities and transnational dimension. From the texts quoted in this essay, it becomes clear that they have various reasons for doing so. One is the specific (local) nature of certain problems that call for specific (local) solutions. Another is the necessity to engage with local discursive contexts that also have a bearing on feminist theory production. A third is the empowering effect of a long tradition of commitment to women's issues and Chinese (feminist) history as a legacy and resource. Many of the scholars discussed here are wary of cutting ties with pre-reform history, which has left deep imprints on the political life of China. To them, theory imports that fail to address the complex experience of Chinese history seem to be disempowering rather than empowering.

2

Equality and Gender Equality with Chinese Characteristics

Li Xiaojiang
Translated by Tera Mills and Ping Zhu

I would like to thank the Spanish Minister of Equality, Ms. Bibiana Aido Almagro, for her invitation.

Over a month ago, I accepted the invitation for an interview by the Spanish TV channel at the (Beijing) Cervantes Institute, where the keen host asked me three interesting questions. Here, I would like to use them as an introduction to discuss China's equality and gender equality: our experiences and lessons, the problems in our lives, and the challenges we face, which I would like to share with our friends in Spain.

Civilization and Gender Equality

"Gender equality" (*nannü pingdeng* 男女平等) is the common goal of women all over the world.

This is a speech given at the Twenty-First Century: Era of Women, Era of Freedom summit forum, sponsored by the Women's Institute of Spain in Madrid on November 7, 2008. The speech is a succinct reiteration of Li Xiaojiang's feminist ideas contained in her early works, such as *Nüzi yu Jiazheng* (Women and Homemaking 女子与家政, 1986), *Xiawa de Tansuo* (Eve's Exploration 夏娃的探索, 1988), *Nüxing Shenmei Yishi Tanwei* (Inquiry into Women's Aesthetic Consciousness 女性审美意识探微, 1989), *Xinggou* (Sex Gap 性沟, 1989), and *Gaobie Zuotian* (Bidding Farewell to Yesterday 告别昨天, 1995).

However, in the fight for equality, we have had different encounters, and as a result different experiences. Even if we are now facing the same problems, these problems may stem from different causes. Even within the same country, similar problems will still have different origins. For example, the first question the TV host posed to me was: "In the context of globalization, what is the biggest problem that Chinese women face?" I told her that during the thirty years of the Reform of Opening Up, Chinese women became differentiated and are no longer a homogenous group; the problems of rural women and the problems of urban women are completely different. Even among rural women, the situation of those who migrate to the city to work and those who stay in the village are also quite different.

The host asked, "Do they have any common needs?"

I replied: "The problems are different, and so the needs, of course, will not be exactly the same."

She was not satisfied, and pursued the matter further: "Is 'equality' not the common need and pursuit of all women?" This is the second question the host asked me, and although it seems quite ordinary, it is actually very important, as it gets to the heart of issue. I recall that at the time I responded by saying that in China, "equality" (*pingdeng* 平等) is the social background we live in, rather than a political goal in speeches or writings.

Since the founding of the People's Republic of China in 1949 we have lived in a society of gender equality. People all said "the times have changed, men and women are the same" (*shidai butongle, nannü dou yiyang* 时代不同了, 男女都一样), and they all acknowledged that "women hold up half the sky" (*funü nengding banbiantian* 妇女能顶半边天). Gender equality seemed to be a matter of course. Discrimination against women was regarded as a shameful display of political backwardness associated with the remnants of feudalism. In the 1980s came China's Reform and Opening Up. We went to Europe, America, Japan, and Korea, and in these well-off countries we were shocked to see gender discrimination and instances of gender inequality behind the "lady first" slogan. From offices to college classrooms, from gas stations to malls, from social life to romantic relationships, feminists in these well-off countries need to constantly tell people that men and women should be equal.

We did not expect that the common sense of gender equality is a principle that, in many places in the world, takes a lot of effort to explain clearly. Thus it is evident that the advanced level of a society's material culture does not necessarily bring a common understanding of gender equality. This brought me to understand the political mission, historical achievements, and basic position of Western women in terms of rights, and also see why the Spanish TV host would relentlessly inquire about gender equality.

Because of time constraints my answer at the time was simple and only served to confuse her. This event led me to many ideas, and I will take this opportunity to continue my answer to her question.

The History of Gender Equality in China

As I have mentioned on many different occasions, in contrast to the Western feminist movement the liberation of Chinese women was, to a large extent, a result of social support and social participation. Since modern times at least three different factors of different origins transformed the traditional Chinese attitude toward women and have had an enormous influence on the fate of Chinese women.

First of all, in the Chinese enlightenment movement of the early twentieth century it was Chinese men who first called for, and acted on, women's liberation. In contrast, in the West women had to liberate themselves, and it was one of the hardest things to do.

Second, China's civil wars and the War of Resistance against Japan from the 1920s to the 1940s marked the moment when women really started entering society. In fact, it can be said that Chinese women stepped into society in large numbers due to their participation in war. This is very different from Western countries, where middle-class women enter society through education and employment.

Third, after the founding of the People's Republic of China, gender equality acquired an ideological legitimacy. The state mobilized women into participating in all kinds of social work; the related gender policies became an important supportive factor in women's liberation.

In modern China, there have been three major instances for Chinese women's social participation. The first instance is the appearance of female industrial workers beginning at the end of the nineteenth century.[1] They were few in number and mostly found in coastal cities. The second instance is the urban intellectual women of the 1920s and 1930s, who were active in the spheres of culture and education. While few in number too, they had great potential and are the earliest women in Chinese history with a consciousness of independence and self-reliance. The third instance is the women who took part in the wars, which was for the majority of women (and especially rural women) the only way to free themselves from feudal households. My "Twentieth-Century (Chinese) Women's Oral History" (*Ershi shiji zhongguo funü koushushi* 二十世纪中国妇女口述史) project[2] confirmed this. The story of the film *The Red Detachment of Women* (Hongse naingzijun 红色娘子军) is another example. From it we can see that Chinese women's attitudes toward war differ from those of Western women. Behind the Chinese revolution (*geming* 革命) was an endorsement of gender equality, even if that equality meant facing death in every moment.

There is another important reason for Chinese women's social participation: traditional China was an agricultural society where the division between housework and social work was not clear-cut. China's industrialization and urbanization for the most part occurred

1. For more details, see the discussion of women workers by Zheng Yongfu 郑永福 and Lü Meiyi 吕美颐 in *Jindai Zhongguo Funü Shenghuo* 近代中国妇女生活 (The Life of Modern Chinese Women) (Zhengzhou: Henan renmin chubanshe, 1993).

2. Out of the two hundred people interviewed for the "War and Women" section in the "Twentieth-Century (Chinese) Women's Oral History" project, 95 percent of the personal accounts proved this. This project led to Li Xiaojiang's book *Rang Nüren Ziji Shuohua: Qinli Zhanzheng* 让女人自己说话: 亲历战争 (Let Women Speak for Themselves: Experiencing the War First Hand) (Beijing: Sanlian shudian, 2003).

after 1949, coinciding with women's socialization. The change of women's gender roles was on pace with the transformation of many male social identities, which lessened the traditional pressure from men when women "entered society" (*zouxiang shehui* 走向社会).[3] The polarization of rural and urban areas made this last feature even more prominent: working women were mostly found only among urban women; as a result, women's employment and gender equality are two different concepts.

From the beginning of modern times until the mid-1970s, Chinese history was almost entirely a history of wars. For a long time after the end of World War 2 China was in the middle of the Cold War, and the state of war lasted until the end of the Cultural Revolution. Over the course of the last hundred years Chinese women went through the chaos of wars before they could successfully complete the transformation from "members of a household" (*jiatingzhongren* 家庭中人) to "members of society" (*shehuizhongren* 社会中人).

After the People's Republic of China (PRC) was founded, women participated extensively in social production. On the surface this suggests the liberation of women as well as that of productive forces. However, if we investigate deeper, we will discover that this change did not consciously originate in women; nor did it cater to the demands of the market. Rather than saying it reflected the needs of social construction, it is better to say that it was the continuation of war. After the eight-year War of Resistance against Japan were three years of civil war, then the Korean War, the Three-Anti and Five-Anti Campaigns (*Sanfan wufan* 三反五反), the Great Leap Forward, "Cut off the Tail of Capitalism" (*Ge ziben zhuyi weiba* 割资本主义尾巴), and so on. The brutality of political movements was no less than that of war.

The socialist revolution liberated women to the greatest extent it could, thereby breaking out of the old era. However, it did not give

---

3. In industrialized countries when women entered society, resistance mostly came from middle-class families and the labor unions, which were composed mainly of male workers.

women (*funü* 妇女) back to themselves, but rather subjected them to the nation-state. The state gained complete control of women through "liberation" (*jiefang* 解放), and as a direct result transferred the traditional women's reliance on men to women's reliance on and identification with the nation-state. At the same time, through urging women into jobs, the state integrated (urban) women into the job–work unit–nation (*jiuye-danwei-guojia* 就业-单位-国家) structure, thus completing the reform of traditional family relationships, and thereby fully instituting the state's integrated control of the entire society, including everyone within a family.

Was such a move right?

For the moment we will not evaluate whether it was right or wrong; but the indisputable reality is that it did liberate women to a large degree, and advanced women's relationship with the nation-state to a new historical phase. It was also highly effective in transforming the depth and scope of the social structure.

What Exactly is Equality?

With such a background, how should we evaluate "equality"? Is it merely an ideal, a principle, or a standard of progress?

This is where our situation is unique: when Western feminists were still flying the banner of equality to seek equal gender rights in the society, Chinese women had already started to question the meaning of equality.

Equality must face the entire reality provided by the specific era and the specific society. During a time of war, equality means shedding blood together (Chinese women experienced this kind of equality to the full over more than half a century of wars). During a time of famine, equality meant sharing soup from the same "big pot" (*daguo* 大锅) (such as during the Three Years of Natural Disasters between 1959 and 1961). During a time of social turmoil or political movements, like the Cultural Revolution, equality meant wearing the same dunce's cap and having their heads shaved when women's dignity and humans' dignity were equally trampled. Not only in China, but in this entire world full of war, hunger, slavery, and injustice, equality is important, but equality alone is not enough. Chinese women, in a life marked by gender equality, fully experienced the fact that men's world is far from perfect. Because of this, they may have to look to society instead of men before they can rediscover the meaning of equality by comparing the advantages and disadvantages of gender equality.

What exactly is equality?

Equality is a basic human right; it is a problem of "who gives who" or "who should get how much" that should not have emerged. It is only because some groups of people (such as women and slaves) lost equality that it has become a historical objective that must be fought for. Equality is not the ultimate goal, nor is it a means. It cannot become an excuse for parasitism with which individuals make demands from the others or the society, nor can it become an accomplice to a totalitarian society that forces everyone to become exactly the same. Any breach of equality could lead to the deprivation of the human right of freedom. Essentially, equality is only subordinate to the goal of freedom—it is the foundation of free choices. If there are no free choices, equality is meaningless.

Chinese men's deprived state is not a result of the liberation of women: Chinese women were equally "deprived" (*bei boduo* 被剥夺) when they were "bestowed" (*bei fuyu* 被赋予) equal rights. One of the important missions of contemporary Chinese women's studies is to rediscover women's autonomous consciousness that was lost when they were bestowed rights. This perspective makes gender equality a much simpler problem. To Chinese women, no matter in what way, and no matter how many rights are gained, this equality is more precious than gold, because it is the foundation of women's claim to humanity and is part of what forms women's human dignity and honor. Over the last half century one of the most important achievements of Chinese social progress is women's liberation: as a "social legal person" (*shehui faren* 社会法人), a woman shares the same right to education, employment, voting and being elected, choosing a spouse, and inheritance as a man. No matter how many problems there still are, no one can erase this achievement. China progressed from slavery and war toward peace and development in the modern period. In a China in extreme hardship, equality meant no one could be exempt from hardship. Sharing hardship was the price for and meaning of equality in modern China. However, we are not the most miserable generation. Overall women's history has been a history of suffering, and the most painful thing is that there was no choice, no way out, and thus no hope; in comparison, isn't our current situation much better?

Equality: China's Problem

Since the founding of the PRC, gender equality has been protected by legislation, but this does not mean that there are no cases of inequality in China. On the contrary, inequality has likely been concealed by outward appearances and become a deep societal issue about which we must heighten our vigilance and which we must painstakingly strive to unearth.

For example, using gender quality as a basic measure of social progress and women's liberation as a main political accomplishment of the PRC has quite possibly hidden a more important issue—namely, the present structure of urban-rural divide. It has caused farmers, who make up 56 percent of the total population in China, to be reduced to second-class citizens. Millions of rural Chinese women's political privileges, and their social status on the whole, are lower than that of urban women (including female workers and urban unemployed women). Why has the number of Chinese shot up in the increasing wave of overseas immigrants? Of the overseas Chinese who are illegal immigrants, a majority came from the Chinese countryside. Chinese farmers used to hate leaving their home and land, but after being treated as second-class citizens in their own country and suffering a life of poverty for a long time, they were forced to leave their hometowns. Even though they would still be viewed as the inferior group, they would rather make a living in a more advanced country.

Therefore, it is not enough for urban women and especially intellectual women in China to talk about gender equality. They must have a broader humanistic concern, caring not only about women's issues, but also about disadvantaged social groups so they can bring the problems of social equality to the agenda of women and gender studies. We cannot be content with legal provisions and popular support when it comes the problem of gender equality. The government's official performance reports are always touting progress and successes. While there have certainly been enormous successes (as the progress of Chinese women and our personal experiences have proved), this does not mean that there is an absence of women's problems when we have laws that uphold gender equality. Nor does it mean that the acquisition of social rights equates with the liberation of women. If equal rights have not made women happier and healthier, but rather given them even heavier burdens and more pressure, then the so-called equality must be doubted and examined seriously.

If we look deeply into the lives of women from different social statuses, we will discover that those problems that have disappeared from the societal level may well have already transformed into concrete and trivial obstacles that silently but stubbornly exist in women's everyday lives. For example, female college students have difficulty finding jobs, and professional women bear the double burden of work and family. These problems all originate from the same important cause: even though our society is saturated with the ideology of gender equality, there has not been a feminist revolution in the domains of the family and everyday life. Our family relationships, family ideology, and gender roles within the family are still very traditional, and the levels of social productive forces and social welfare are still relatively low. In a society in which the degree of civilization as a whole is limited, the professionalization and social liberation of women does not necessarily bring professional women autonomy, happiness, health, and a high-quality life.

What Is the Price?

If we inspect the countryside, we will discover an even more important issue. For example, the yardstick for gender equality originated with Western educated middle-class women and was popularized after the Industrial Revolution, becoming a universal value. However, if it is applied in an agricultural society still relying on a bartering economy, and in every aspect of women's lives, it may in fact bring various kinds of damage. If women's social labor is built on the foundation of the traditional patriarchal household, it is impossible for women to be independent economically, as they would lose the protections of the traditional family. The problem we are facing is not simply one of putting gender equality into practice; we must examine some important theoretical issues that the mystifying concepts of equality and gender equality themselves imply, such as: Does equality come with a price, such as restrictions on freedom and equity? To what degree is this price acceptable and possible? What is the bottom line? And the question that is more pertinent to our lives: Since equality in the social realm was originally a public political category associated with social class, can it be transferred directly to the personal realm and family life, which encompasses the private life and sexual relationships?

Compared to women in many other places in the world, Chinese women have certainly enjoyed many of the benefits of equal social life, but they have also experienced some of its hardships. No matter if these hardships are large or small, few or many, it is important to talk about them so more people can reflect on them, and they can become a warning to latecomers.

I still remember, during the interview, while I was speaking of the many differences in women's lives, the host was very surprised and asked a third question: "In this case, is there anything Chinese women and Spanish women can learn from each other?" My reply was: Of course, otherwise why would I come to Madrid?

The theme of this conference is Twenty-First Century: Era of Women, Era of Freedom. I agree with the first concept. Indeed, if we say that the twentieth century was the century that women entered society, then in the twenty-first century women gained a broader world and have become more capable of creating a new era. However, I do not believe this will be an era of freedom. Globalization is the prelude to a new century. The problems that liberated women must face are not only those of women themselves; they must also make proper response to the problems in this unrestful world, such as the current problem of immigration.

At this conference scholars and social activists from many different countries have gathered together, each airing their own views, dialoguing with each other. Professor Amelia Sáiz López from the Autonomous University of Barcelona discussed immigration issues, including Chinese-Spanish women's lives, in her presentation, which greatly inspired me. This is actually an extension of the problems of rural Chinese women and migrant workers. Spanish scholars have already started to investigate these problems, and the Spanish government has already launched some concrete responsive measures. At least in this place that we call a foreign country (*waiguo* 外国), there are already people who invest the necessary humanistic concern for female Chinese immigrants. In comparison, Chinese scholars are still insensitive to these issues, and our government has just barely started paying attention to the problems of migrant workers in the cities. Our research perspectives and humanistic concern have not covered the Chinese people who left their homeland. These are things we should learn from the Spanish scholars and for which we should pay respect to the Spanish government. I would like to stay a while longer in Spain this time, even though I cannot speak Spanish. I want to move out of this five-star hotel into a Chinese inn in the Chinese community for the next three days, so I can observe for myself the lives of Chinese immigrants and listen to their stories. It is not a research project yet, but at least it is a beginning.

3

The Class Characteristics of China's Women's Liberation and Twenty-First-Century Feminism

Xueping Zhong

For a few decades now, "gender, race, and class" has been a common mantra, indeed a kind of discursive trinity in US-based feminist discourse. It does not follow, however, that feminist scholarship treats the three categories with an even sense of importance. Ever since the alleged divorce between Marxism and feminism in the late 1970s and early 1980s, class as an analytical category has largely remained a tag-along term whenever the notion is evoked (while its definition not altogether clear). Occasional criticisms notwithstanding, mainstream (American) feminism has tended to approach women's and gender issues through lenses largely premised on a male-female binary complicated mainly by LGBTQ perspectives and race-related critical interventions.[1]

By comparison, studies have shown that when it comes to understanding women's and gender issues and the development of feminism in China, it is not possible to sidestep issues of class.[2] At the same

---

1. For recent critical analysis of US-based feminism and its influence, see Susan Watkins, "Which Feminisms?," *New Left Review* 109, nos. 1–2 (2018): 5–76.

2. In recent years feminist scholarship in English has ventured into issues of women's liberation in relation to the Chinese communist revolution and socialist construction by looking at "state feminism" or "socialist feminists." Many such

time, despite occasional critical interventions, the dominant views continue to treat class as somehow detrimental to the development of Chinese feminism.[3] The operating assumption underlying this view reflects the "postdivorce" feminist tendency that treats class as largely (and sometimes by definition) masculine or male-centric and intrinsically incompatible with feminist concerns over women's and gender issues. When it comes to critically assessing the Chinese revolution–led (that is, Chinese Communist Party–led) women's liberation, this conceptual orientation tends to frame criticisms in a way that reduces the relationship between class and women's liberation in modern Chinese history to a male-female binary opposition and to problems seen through that lens. The key problem underlying this reductionistic approach is by no means a new one, but its ambivalence toward the classed social-revolutionary nature of Chinese women's liberation continues to linger and dominate.

Of course, there have been studies that recognize the social-revolutionary characteristics of China's twentieth-century quest and struggle for women's liberation. Examples include those by Marilyn Young, one of the early pre-divorce-from-Marxism feminist scholars of China;[4] Christina Gilmartin, whose *Engendering Chinese Revolution* addresses some of the central tensions between class and women's work

---

studies highlight issues related to what I discuss in this paper, but with a few exceptions, they do not offer a clear definition of *class* when they evoke the term. In China, on the other hand, the issue of class and women and gender has continued to be revisited by scholars, both men and women. One recent example is Nan Fan 南帆, "Xingbie, Nüquan Zhuyi yu Jieji Huayu" 性别、女权主义与阶级话语 (Gender, Feminism, and Class Discourse) *Dangdai zuojia pinglun*, no. 3 (2017): 4–16.

3. The more sympathetic attention in feminist scholarship tends to be reserved for "women's voices," be they from May Fourth women writers, from women activists or revolutionaries during revolutionary times, or from different kinds of oral histories conducted, interpreted, and reconstructed by feminist scholars at the turn of the twenty-first century. Such studies constitute the majority of feminist scholarship on modern Chinese women and gender issues and are too many to cite here.

4. Marilyn Young, *Women in China: Studies in Social Change and Feminism* (Ann Arbor: University of Michigan Center for Chinese Studies, 1973).

in the early political activities led by the Chinese Communist Party (CCP);[5] Tani Barlow, whose ruminations on "the power of weakness" in her introduction to Lu Xun and Ding Ling's writings within the context of the Chinese revolution recognize these writers' revolutionary consciousness, which was developed in identification with both the nationally and the socially oppressed and downtrodden;[6] and Wang Zheng, whose argument in her interview titled "We Had a Dream that the World Can Be Better than Today" also pertains to the social changes related to women's liberation.[7]

A more recent reconsideration along these lines comes from Lin Chun's studies of the Chinese Communist revolutions. Echoing Rosa Luxemburg and in her own understanding of China as "a class nation," Lin offers illuminating discussions on the classed nature of those revolutions. By way of Ernest Gellner, Lin highlights the historical and political implications of modern China as a class nation within the larger context of capitalist expansion and the imperialist conquests that have been part of that expansion. As Gellner states, "Only when a nation became a class . . . did it become politically conscious and activist . . . [as] a nation-for-itself."[8] Echoing this point in her discussion of "Chinese socialism and global capitalism," Lin goes on to argue that "it was due to China's oppressed 'class' position in global capitalism that the Chinese party emerged as an innovative proletarian organization." "Class," she states, "cannot be a positivist sociological category as its defining identities are rooted in the dominance of global

5. Christina K. Gilmartin, *Engendering the Chinese Revolution: Radical Women, Communist Politics, and Mass Movements in the 1920s* (Berkeley: Univ. of California Press, 1995).

6. Tani E. Barlow, "Introduction," in *The Power of Weakness*, ed. Tani E. Barlow (New York: Feminist Press, 2007), 1–25.

7. Wang Zheng, "We Had a Dream that the World Can Be Better than Today," *Revolution* 59 (2006), accessed March 21, 2019, https://revcom.us/a/059/some-of-us-en.html.

8. Quoted in Lin Chun, "China's Lost World of Internationalism," *Chinese Vision of World Order: Tianxia, Culture, and World Politics*, ed. Ban Wang (Durham, NC: Duke Univ. Press, 2017), 181.

political economy."[9] It was class understood in relation to global capitalism, Lin argues, that conditioned the "social-national character of the communist revolution."[10] And by extension, it also conditioned the social-national character of Chinese revolution–led women's liberation; the social here is always already both classed and gendered.

And so is the political consciousness—the focus of this study—that came to be expressed in this context. Two of the earliest modern Chinese thinkers' voices on issues regarding women's liberation, those of He-Yin Zhen and Lu Xun, manifest the early formation of such consciousness.

As the book *The Birth of Chinese Feminism* makes clear, a complex understanding of the intricate relationship between gender and class already existed in the early twentieth century when He-Yin, one of the few modern female intellectuals in the last years of the Qing Dynasty, pondered the issue of women's liberation. In "On the Question of Women's Liberation" (1907), for example, He-Yin argues that "since the rich control the basic livelihood of the poor, the poor are often compelled to ingratiate themselves to the rich, and this situation prevails among men as well as among women. Moreover, the poor, be they workers or bondservants, make up the majority by far among women; and these women depend on the rich for food and clothing."[11] Given this condition, "How can we be sure," she asks, "that a working class woman would not vote according to the desires of the rich lady on whom she depends for her livelihood?"[12] In another piece from the same year, titled "Economic Revolution and Women's Revolution," He-Yin argues, "If you desire to realize a women's revolution, you must begin with an economic revolution. What is economic

9. Lin Chun, "Chinese Socialism and Global Capitalism," in *China and Global Capitalism: Reflections on Marxism, History, and Contemporary Politics*, ed. Lin Chun (New York: Palgrave, 2013), 44.

10. Li Chun, "China's Lost World," 182.

11. He-Yin Zhen, "On the Question of Women's Liberation," in *The Birth of Chinese Feminism: Essential Texts in Transnational Theory*, ed. Lydia H. Liu, Rebecca E. Karl, and Dorothy Ko (New York: Columbia Univ. Press, 2013), 66.

12. He-Yin, "On the Question," 66.

revolution? It is to overthrow the system of private property and to replace it with communal property, meanwhile abandoning all monies and currencies."[13] The birth of Chinese feminism, we realize, burst into the world with a clear understanding of the tensions between gender and class and the political economy of social-gender relations.

This understanding came not only from a woman critic like He-Yin, but also from many male intellectuals and revolutionaries.[14] Lu Xun, among them, recognized the connection between women's plight and socioeconomic inequality. In addition to such representations as Xianglin's wife in "New Year's Sacrifice," Zijun in "Regret for the Past," the mother figure in one of his prose poems "Tremors of Degradation" (*Tuibaixian de chandong* 颓败线的颤动) in *Wild Grass*, Lu Xun's question "What happens to Nora after she walks out?" points directly at the need for fundamental social change so women can achieve their economic rights and real independence, instead of facing only two choices: either returning home or languishing in destitution. "So for Nora," Lu Xun stipulates, "money (or to put it more elegantly, economic means) is crucial. It is true that freedom cannot be bought, but it can be sold. . . . I have no idea how to obtain these rights, other than that we will have to fight for them, perhaps with even more violence than we have to fight for our political rights."[15] Lu Xun's comments regarding the need to fight for women's economic means "with perhaps even more violence than fighting for political rights," along with his perceptive recognition of the limitations on the part of

13. He-Yin Zhen, "Economic Revolution and Women's Revolution," in *The Birth of Chinese Feminism: Essential Texts in Transnational Theory*, ed. Lydia H. Liu, Rebecca E. Karl, and Dorothy Ko (New York: Columbia Univ. Press, 2013), 83.

14. Male embrace of the "woman question" and male support of China's women's liberation have been a point of contention among feminist scholars. See Gilmartin's *Engendering the Chinese Revolution*, for more examples and arguments. Many of the criticisms are informed by a male-female binary that tends to render criticism in a reductive fashion.

15. Lu Xun, "What Happens to Nora after She Walks Out," in *Jotting under Lamplight*, ed. Eileen Cheng and Kirk Denton (Cambridge, MA: Harvard Univ. Press, 2017): 258–59.

(modern) male intellectuals (found in his often flawed or inadequate male narrators), portended a key characteristic of Chinese women's liberation, namely that such a liberation could be achieved only by way of an actual social revolution participated in by both men and women.

Foregrounding the relationship between class and gender as part of modern Chinese political consciousness, birthed out of the context of capitalist worldwide expansion and China's social and political decay and the struggles within, this discussion explores the fate of this political consciousness in (to borrow a term from Cai Xiang) "after-the-revolution" (*geming hou*革命后) socialist China (1949–78) and in the postrevolution period (since 1978). Essential questions that run through this discussion are: In what ways does class as (part of) political consciousness continue to remain central to women's liberation endeavors in the after-the-revolution socialist period? How can we (re-)assess its cultural manifestations today? In what ways does this "Chinese characteristic" continue to matter in feminist debates in twenty-first-century China and in the world, especially against the backdrop of market reform in China and China's participation in the latest round of globalizing capitalism? I explore these questions by looking at an eclectic group of cultural texts—film and literature— and approaching them in a comparative manner.

Western feminism as scholarship was introduced into China precisely at the start of the reform era (in 1978), so a related question that this paper implicitly addresses is the characteristics of Western feminism itself. In what ways do we understand its relatively successful introduction and spread in reform-era China, as well as pushback and resistance to it, against the backdrop of the decline of political consciousness and the rise of class divides (and to some extent, class struggle) during the same period?

Superimposition of Class Consciousness and Women's Liberation

Periodically I co-teach a course with my colleague Modhumita Roy, of the English department at Tufts University, on Chinese and Indian cinema. When we started to prepare for the course, we noticed that the cinema of both countries had produced countless films that have women as their major leads. The figure of woman, in other words, looms large in the cinematic representations of both China and India. This similarity, we believed, merits a comparative approach.

For meaningful comparisons we decided to focus on films made after 1949 and 1947, the founding of the People's Republic of China (PRC) and the year of India's independence, respectively, one striving for national and social liberation toward the goal of building a socialist country and the other striving for national independence while being (nominally) inspired by socialism.[16] After several rounds of teaching this course, I find such a comparative approach to be particularly generative, especially regarding the need for, as well as the difficulties in, thinking about issues of class and gender. Indeed, while I am not sure how successful we have been in getting students to fully recognize the significance of these issues and to appreciate related implications, I have consistently found the comparisons illuminating.

Scholars, feminist or otherwise, have argued for the need, and many have carried out research, to compare China and India on a range of issues, including women's and gender issues. One of the more recent comparative ruminations appears in the article "Nationalism, Modernity, and the 'Woman Question' in India and China." Author Sanjay Seth examines "how the relations between nationalism and modernity were discursively elaborated and imagined in India and China, with reference to the 'woman question,'" why there was "greater radicalism around the woman question in Chinese nationalism than India," and why "woman became the signifier of national essence and tradition in Indian but not in Chinese nationalism, and hence the different trajectories of the 'woman question' in each country."[17] Seth stipulates that in order to better understand these questions, a bigger question

16. I thank Professor Roy for this and other points and insights related to India's political and social context.

17. Sanjay Seth, "Nationalism, Modernity, and the 'Woman Question' in India and China," *The Journal of Asian Studies* 72, no. 2 (May 2013): 273, 287.

to ask and explore in this comparison is how "colonialism figured in anticolonial thought" differently in India and China and with what consequences.[18]

This bigger question is an important one, but the focus on the two versions of nationalism could be more socially grounded, and the notion of nationalism could be rendered in a less reified but more historically sound fashion. To push the author's question further, one can add even bigger questions: Why, for example, as a completely colonized country, did India not develop the same kind of class-nation-oriented political consciousness as China did? How does this difference explain the fact that India's struggles for national independence did not yield the same kind of national-social revolutionary character and results as the Chinese struggles for national independence did? And for that matter, what would happen if such a national-social revolutionary character were to be betrayed or undone?[19]

In the film course we pair films from China and India for comparison precisely with these bigger questions in mind, and we do so first with films that largely correspond to the socialist period in China and postindependence period in India, and then with those made in postsocialist China and postliberalization India. One of the pairs lines up *Stage Sisters* (*Wutai jiemei* 舞台姐妹) and *Charulata*.[20] Both made in 1964, the former narrates the vicissitudes of two Shaoxing Opera singers' rise and fall in fame, along with the choices they make in their personal and professional lives against the larger historical and political backdrop of China in the 1930s and 1940s. The latter, *Charulata*, is set in mid-to-late-nineteenth-century Calcutta and focuses on the eponymous character's inner struggle as an educated upper-class woman confined in the compounds of her wealthy husband's home. With women as their leads, *Stage Sisters* situates its women characters mainly outside the confines of family and home, while *Charulata* sets

18. Seth, "Nationalism," 276.

19. I would like to thank Professor Roy for her untiring efforts in foregrounding these questions to students every time when we teach the course.

20. *Stage Sisters* (1964), dir. Xie Jin; *Charulata* (1964), dir. Satyajit Ray.

the narrative within a rich (upper-caste) family setting, focusing on the tensions between Charu's role as an idle wife and her desires, talent, and literary inspirations. Predictably, *Charulata's* narrative structure and its focus on the interiority—the inner struggles—of Charu, the main character, would strike a familiar cord in students who have less difficulty in recognizing struggles between tradition (meaning bad) and modernity (meaning good) and between men and women. *Stage Sisters,* by comparison, while more layered and radical in its implications, appears propagandistic to the students, especially with regard to how the film ends.[21]

Based on a story by Rabindranath Tagore titled "Nastanirh" (The Broken Nest), *Charulata* explores the confined life of Charu, wife of a Western-educated and supposedly liberal-minded man named Bhupati, whose interest in current political affairs in Britain in relation to India (of the mid-to-late nineteenth century) is such that he devotes much of his time to the newspaper he is editing and printing.[22] Charu whiles away her time by either playing cards with a female relative, reading fiction, or doing embroidery or other kinds of needle work. When a cousin of her husband comes to stay with them, having newly graduated from college, the cousin encourages her to write—something Charu's husband dismisses as trivial but encourages this cousin to help Charu pursue. As Charu starts to write and eventually publishes her work, she develops a crush on the cousin. The young man is startled by her affection and decides to leave without letting her know

21. This outside-of-family narrative structure has been questioned and criticized by feminist scholars, many arguing that it is an indication of the shortcomings of socialist Chinese women's liberation in that it avoids dealing with gender roles and gender power relations in the family. While such criticisms are worth attending to, they often fail to acknowledge the radical nature of carving out space for laboring women in the public domain and as men's equals in formerly nonfeminine pursuits.

22. Rabindranath Tagore, "Nastanirh" (The Broken Nest), 1901. I thank Professor Roy for the information regarding Tagore's original text and its historical implications.

directly beforehand. Charu feels terribly distraught at his departure, so much so that her emotions surprise her husband, who finally figures out what has happened. The film then shows that the husband taking off in a horse-drawn carriage, presumably to clear his head. He eventually returns to the house.

This is where the film is about to end, with the camera capturing a number of aesthetically interesting shots that obviously invite the viewer to respond. One set of shots shows Charu standing inside the entrance to the living quarters of the house with her hand extending toward her husband, and her husband right outside the entrance with his hand extending toward Charu. And then before their hands touch one another, the shot turns into a still. Intercutting with this scene, in which the couple are presumably about to reconcile, is a shot that shows an old male servant holding a lamp and standing not far from them. Before the camera zooms in on the about-to-touch hands of the couple, it uncharacteristically gives the old servant a full-screen shot by himself. The household's servants had been nowhere to be seen (though they were occasionally heard) until this very last moment. At the end of the film the viewers are left with these two memorable images.

In both Tagore's original text and the film, sympathy is clearly placed on Charu, the female protagonist. At the same time its central theme remains safe, in that it appears to suggest that the best hope for women like Charu is for their educated husbands to become more enlightened in recognizing their wives' intellectual talents and, if possible, their emotional desires. Through such recognition, by extension, men and women have the potential to become equals.

By comparison, *Stage Sisters*, set in an era of wars and revolutions in China, situates the story of the two Shaoxing Opera singers within the context of their lives on and off stage, but outside the familiar narrative structure of family. The two female protagonists, Zhu Chunhua and Xing Yuehong, meet for the first time when Chunhua hides herself in a costume trunk in behind a temporary stage where Yuehong and her traveling Shaoxing Opera troupe are performing. Chunhua is a child bride who is running away from her in-laws. Yuehong's father manages to persuade the troupe's owner to keep Chunhua, suggesting that the latter can be trained into a performer. The film then proceeds to show that while Yuehong plays the *xiaosheng* (young male scholar) role, Chunhua is groomed into the *qingyi* (young female) role.

Much of the first half of the film relates how, as part of the traveling troupe, Chunhua and Yuehong are subject to physical and sexual abuses at the hands of the rich and powerful. The second half of the film shifts the setting from the countryside to Shanghai after Yuehong's father passes away and the cost of his burial forces the two performers into an indentured contract with the troupe's owner. Over time their performance in Shanghai wins them fame and also buys them out of the indentured contract. Also over time Yuehong comes under the spell of their stage manager, who eventually lures her into a marriage with him, while the friendship or sisterhood between the two women frays until it breaks. In contrast to Yuehong, Chunhua resists material lures and becomes increasingly aware of the social ills both back stage and beyond the opera world.

In representing Chunhua's coming into her political consciousness, the film places her in an exhibit that commemorates the tenth anniversary of Lu Xun's death (Lu Xun died in 1936). When Chunhua stands in front of a wood-cut image of Xianglin's wife, the major character in Lu Xun's "New Year's Sacrifice" (1924), we see a shot that superimposes Chunhua's image—one that recalls a past scene in which she was tied to a pole after she tried to fight away the local police when the latter harassed Yuehong on stage—over that of Xianglin's wife and that of a child bride whom Chunhua met in the same village where she was publicly punished and humiliated. (This other child bride is also named Chunhua and was brave enough to offer the older Chunhua some water during her public humiliation.) This moment is narratively important in the film because it is followed by Chunhua's decision to put "New Year's Sacrifice" on stage, the censorship and physical harm that she encounters as a result, and her eventual transformation into a revolutionary opera performer. After the founding of the PRC, Chunhua goes to the countryside to perform, among other things, *The White Hair Girl* (a revolutionary opera), participating in cultural activities that aim at mobilizing peasants for the land reform movement (in the early 1950s).

For further comparison, let us recall the aforementioned ending shots in *Charulata* and the superimposition shots in *Stage Sisters*. Reading these shots in conjunction with the multiple temporalities each film signifies, we see the differences in the dominant (political) consciousness manifested in each of these representations, as well as their implications.

In *Charulata*, the man-woman dichotomy is paired with the tradition-modernity dichotomy in a way that echoes Seth's discussion regarding the role of tradition deployed for an imagined Indian modernity. Charu not only does not choose to leave home (contrary to Nora's decision), she is also shown to be the more enlightened party of the two, ready to receive her husband home, presumably as his equal now. With their hands extending to each other but not touching, however, the film also appears to suggest that more needs to happen before they can be real equals. At the same time, what remains unquestioned by the film is the socioeconomic structure—symbolized by the upper-class household and the hierarchy within, the traditional marriage, the familial structure, and so on—all wrapped in both caste and class prerogatives and privilege. The showing of the male servant seems to disrupt all of this, but the filmmaker obviously remains uncertain about the matter. On the one hand, the filmmaker appears to recognize the old servant's (and other servants') presence, but on the other hand, he does not seem to know where to locate the class/caste hierarchy and the oppression in relation to the upper class/ caste that this couple represents. Therefore, while the singling out of the male servant in a separate shot may indicate a degree of awareness of class difference as a social issue on the part of the filmmaker, it does not necessarily indicate the presence of a political consciousness regarding how to tackle it as a fundamental social issue. It is even less meant to indicate self-awareness on the part of the servant himself.

The superimposition in *Stage Sisters*, by contrast, unabashedly suggests a self-recognition on the part of Chunhua in relation to the socially and economically oppressed poor women, including her own past self. This superimposition condenses multiple temporalities with regard to women's issues and struggles for women's liberation in China throughout the twentieth century, with a linkage through a class and gendered political consciousness fostered and shaped by revolutionary struggles. By evoking Lu Xun, *Stage Sisters* continues what Seth identifies as a greater radicalism in relation to the woman question, and does so by representing a moment of political-consciousness formation. Back to the superimposition scene: in addition to the three poor women superimposed in that shot, Chunhua is also shown standing in front of the woodcut portrait of Xianglin's wife. In relation to the film's story as a whole, the juxtaposition of the superimposition shot and the shot showing Chunhua standing in front of the portrait demonstrates a recognition—indeed, a political consciousness that is both gendered and classed—on the part of Chunhua. They consist of layered references: Xianglin's wife, the younger Chunhua as a child bride, and the older Chunhua persecuted for her resistance, all converging into this moment toward showing the downtrodden state of the poor and the oppressed, laboring-class women. For Chunhua, by now a famous performer, this recognition symbolizes the crescendos of her political consciousness, which eventually turn her into a revolutionary culture worker when, toward the end of the film, her performance of *The White-Haired Girl* connects issues of class and women to the social-revolution tenor of women's liberation.

The temporalities that *Stage Sisters* evokes—the early 1920s (when Lu Xun wrote "New Year's Sacrifice"), the 1930s to early 1950s (when the film's story takes place), and the 1960s (when the film was made)—constitute part of China's revolutionary century and its modern characteristics, which are premised on struggles toward new social and gender relations that are free from class exploitation and class oppression. Compared with the temporalities evoked in *Charulata*—the late nineteenth century (the time frame of the film's story), the early twentieth century (when Tagore wrote the story), and the 1960s (when the film was made), *Stage Sisters* indeed exhibits a greater radicalism in a social revolutionary sense that characterizes China's revolution-led women's liberation and its class consciousness.

Return of the "Repressed"?: Whither Women's Liberation

To be sure, the comparison between *Charulata* and *Stage Sisters* is being made more than fifty years since the two films were produced and, for the Chinese film in particular, forty years since the start of the economic reforms in China. Throughout these years, rapid changes have happened, among them a transition from a discourse oriented around women's liberation to a discourse of feminism oriented around the notion of gender. When one revisits a film like *Stage Sisters* today and the superimposition in question in particular, how does one square its political message with all that has happened in China, especially in relation to the discursive struggles today over how to define notions of woman, gender, female, femininity, and, yes, class and the history of CCP-led women's liberation?

With this question in mind, let us briefly return to *Stage Sisters* one last time. In the second half of the film, when both Chunhua and Yuehong make it in Shanghai and become successful performers of Shaoxing Opera, Chunhua's coming into her political consciousness is contrasted by Yuehong's gradual degeneration into the plaything of their stage manager, whom she eventually marries. In contrast to Chunhua's, Yuehong's story is reminiscent of the familiar "figure of woman," whose life's vicissitudes are represented as a way to criticize the corrupt or oppressive society. She is the usual female victim in that society—having been lured, cheated, bullied, and abandoned by a corrupt man. Hers, in other words, is mainly a cautionary tale regarding the power dynamics between rich men and poor women who are lured by the former's power. But unlike Chunhua's story, Yuehong's victimhood does not translate into, let alone transcend to, a political consciousness that would define her. Although the film shows her eventual "liberation" when Chunhua finds her in the countryside, at which point Yuehong joins the revolutionary performing troupe, nowhere in the film do we find Yuehong's own transformation of consciousness.

This not-so-obvious discrepancy in the film would surface in the reform era, manifested in cultural texts that would render images of the Chunhua type into a literal and metaphorical fade, never to return again. And in their stead, "new" images of women—in many ways reminiscent of Yuehong as someone with individual desires and material aspirations—would turn up in the "new era" (*xin shiqi* 新时期) to contest what it means to be a woman. Indeed, if, as György Lukács puts it, "every form of art is a metaphysical dissonance of life,"[23] the cultural forms of the 1980s—literature, arts, and cinema chief among them—would constitute a dissonance (first with the Cultural Revolution and then with the Chinese revolution as a whole) out of which different (always under the rubric of the word *xin* 新, or *new*) metaphors would be produced to contest Chinese-revolution-related ideas, values, visions, and ideals. Many new-era cultural texts produced in the first half of the 1980s still have women as their leads, but this time with their representations geared towards questioning, or even negating, the accomplishments of the Chinese revolution–led women's liberation.

A brief comparison between another pair of Chinese and Indian films can help segue into the implications of this change: *Yellow Earth* and *Ankur*, two films that we pair up in our course immediately following *Stage Sisters* and *Charulata*, signal in diametrically opposite directions in terms of their underlying political message.[24] In *Ankur* (or The Seedling), an alternative-cinema film made in the 1970s, the question of land ownership, caste, and class comes into sharp focus to confront the still entrenched and systemic class and caste divides, oppression, and exploitation in India. All of this comes to a head at the end of the film, when a child throws a stone at a window of the village landlord's house, and the screen turns completely red in the next shot. The political message seems clear: the oppressed villagers, men and women, must rise up to overthrow the existing oppressive system.

As Modhumita Roy, the colleague who co-teaches the course with me, keeps reminding students, in the 1970s India's alternative cinema made a number of films focusing on class-related oppression

---

23. Quoted in Franco Moretti, "Lukács's Theory of the Novel," *New Left Review* 91 (2015): 42.

24. *Yellow Earth* (1984), dir. Chen Kaige; *Ankur* (1974), dir. Shyam Begegal.

and exploitation, as well as villagers coming into a political awareness about the need to rise up against the ruling landowning class. The fact that India has never had a thoroughgoing social revolution, Professor Roy points out, continues to leave women, especially poor and low-caste women, to shoulder the burden and consequences of entrenched socioeconomic and gender inequalities. And what Chinese-revolution-led women's liberation was able to do in its thoroughgoing social revolution, she argues, is precisely what India has not been able to carry out; this marks the fundamental difference between the paths taken by these two countries.

In contrast to *Ankur*, in its aestheticization of yellow earth (a new metaphor), the film *Yellow Earth* questions human's efforts to change their own fate by specifically rendering the CCP-led social revolution as human folly: ineffective and even detrimental to those who answer its revolutionary mobilization. To do so, this film also resorts to the figure of woman, in this case Cui Qiao, a poor peasant's daughter, suggesting that even though a CCP soldier (symbolizing the revolution) succeeds in raising Cui Qiao's awareness of her position as a suffering woman, he fails to save her from her suffering and may even cause her demise.

At the end of *Yellow Earth*, Hanhan, Cui Qiao's brother, fails to locate the soldier, who is shown to be returning to their village. The very last shot zooms in on the yellow earth, and we hear Cui Qiao's disembodied singing voice still celebrating the Party. The film ends on an ambivalent note, symbolically replacing Chunhua, little Chunhua, and the white-haired girl with Cui Qiao, signifying the "future" (that is, the failure) of the CCP-led revolution and women's liberation. Even though *Yellow Earth* may indicate more ambivalence than outright negation of the revolution, by reducing the revolution to a struggle between human and nature, and by superimposing the revolution onto tenaciously resistant tradition, it signifies a different kind of political (gendered and classed) consciousness that was coming into play in the reform-era China.

Looking back, one can find a long list of cultural texts from the 1980s, authored or produced by men and women, with the figure of woman in their representations expressing similar sentiments. In film alone, these figures range from Jiuer in *Red Sorghum* 红高粱 (1987), to Judou in *Judou* 菊豆 (1990), Si Taiai or the fourth concubine in *Raise the Red Lantern* 大红灯笼高高挂 (1991), the female soldiers in *Army Nurse* 女儿楼 (1984), and Hu Yuyin in *Hibiscus Town* 芙蓉镇 (1984). In literature they are the various female protagonists in stories by such women writers as Zhang Jie, Zhang Xinxin, and Zong Pu, among many others.

Regardless of what historical periods these stories and their women protagonists' lives are set in, they share in common a sense of repression—repression of the female self in particular—by larger forces (often implying Chinese revolution–led social changes), a sentiment that was surfacing on the political horizon of the reform era. This sentiment was accompanied by calls for a "new Enlightenment" in the 1980s that, as in *Yellow Earth*, would turn the women's liberation theme into a narrative in which tradition continues to dominate, essentially rendering after-the-revolution China into a repressive premodern entity still waiting for real modernization to happen. Needless to say, such sentiment portended something quite different from what Lu Xun's comments on Nora walking out had portended.

More than fifty years since *Stage Sisters* was made, when we revisit the last shot of the film, in which the two sisters, reunited, sit side by side on a boat that is moving fast along the river, presumably toward a hopeful socialist future, we cannot but be struck by a huge irony. On the one hand, the superimposition in *Stage Sisters* has but all been dismantled, and along with it, the significance of the figure of Chunhua and all the women superimposed in her identification. On the other hand, the figure of Yuehong, together with the story of Cui Qiao, which questions or even negates women's liberation and its achievements, has returned in their stead, symbolizing the return of the repressed, embodied by the material-desiring female/*nüxing*, or women, still mired in unchanged premodern traditions.

This return of the repressed would come to dominate the new-era cultural discourses on women, replacing the revolutionary discourse of the oppressed—laboring women who are to be or have been liberated—and transforming women's and gender issues from their relation to women's liberation to considerations of feminism (though the term *feminism* itself has constantly been contested and debated).[25] The spread of Western feminism in China has corresponded to this shift and has contributed to the sharpening of the focus on the repressed in their critique of Chinese revolution–led women's liberation. At the same time, this change toward focusing on the repressed female self or individual constitutes a major contradiction in Chinese feminism that has developed since the late twentieth century, a contradiction that continues to inform various debates about women's and gender issues in today's China.

Class and Gender Consciousness in Twenty-First-Century China

Many such cultural expressions of the return of the repressed, which have come to dominate the cultural scene since the 1980s, have been fellow travelers of the biggest return of all, that of capital.[26] And along with the latter, of course, is the return of exploitation and of the exploited. A key point of contention in relation to women's and gender issues in today's China, therefore, continues to pertain to the notion of class, despite the prevalent fear and dismissal of the concept. While the dismantling of classed political consciousness in post-socialist and post–women's liberation China has made the notion of

25. For example, how to translate *feminism* into Chinese (as "nüquan zhuyi" or "nüxing zhuyi), whether someone who self-identifies as a feminist is a real feminist, whether Chinese male intellectuals and revolutionaries who supported women's liberation can be considered feminists, and more.

26. For further discussion along this line, see Nancy Fraser's "Feminism, Capitalism and the Cunning of History," *New Left Review* 56 (2009): 97–117; Bai Di 柏棣, "Cong Makesi Zhuyi de Jiaodu Kan Zhongguo Nüxing Wenhua Sanshinian" 从马克思主义的角度看中国女性文化三十年 (On Chinese Women's Culture of the Last Three Decades from a Marxist Perspective), accessed October 12, 2015, www.wyzxwk.com/Article/lishi/2015/10/352841.html.

class ideologically homeless, the socioeconomic reality has nevertheless resurfaced issues of class into the life politics—that is, social and everyday life—in China.

In the remaining part of this discussion, I will take a brief look at two writings, produced in the second half of the last forty years of economic reforms in China, in whose narratives issues of class and gender are tackled against the changed and changing social context of the reform era. Placing them in conjunction with the texts discussed above, I am mainly interested in the critical consciousness that these new texts manifest and in assessing their implications in relation both to the legacy of Chinese revolution–led women's liberation and to the new challenges, in gender and class terms, facing today's feminists.

The first text in question is the novella "Ni Hong 霓虹," or "Neon Lights," by Cao Zhenglu, author of numerous short stories, novellas, novels, and essays.[27] Elsewhere I have published a piece on Cao's best-known novella, titled "Na'er 那儿," in which I discuss his writings in conjunction with the so-called *diceng wenxue* (底层文学, not so accurately translated as "subaltern literature"), a literary phenomenon that burst onto the scene in China in the early twenty-first century.[28] Without digressing into the debate regarding the notion of *diceng* 底层 and whether or not "subaltern" is an accurate translation, I do argue that "Neon Lights" precisely captures some of the consequences of the *diceng hua* 底层化 or "subalternization" of working class men and women. And as a male writer, Cao Zhenglu produces representations of working women that unabashedly carry on both the modern Chinese (May Fourth) intellectual tradition and the Chinese revolutionary tradition in which women's issues were recognized as an integral

27. Cao Zhenglu 曹征路, "Ni Hong" (Neon Lights), in *Cao Zhenglu Wenji* 曹征路文集 (Collection of Cao Zhenglu's Works), vol. 3 (Shenzhen: Haitian chubanshe, 2014): 55–112. The story was first published in *Dangdai*, no. 5 (2006).

28. Xueping Zhong, "*Internationale* as Specter: Na'er, 'Subaltern Literature,' and Contemporary China's 'Left Bank,'" in *China and New Left Visions: Political and Cultural Interventions*, ed. Ban Wang and Jie Lu (Lanham, MD: Lexington, 2012): 101–20.

part of social and class issues and social change. What is different in Cao's representations is his recognition that working women are subject to the downward social turn, and his surfacing of the postsocialist phenomenon of the exploited—embodied in this case by a laid-off woman worker—within the context of the return of capital.

In "Neon Lights" Ni Hongmei, a laid-off textile mill worker who has become a prostitute, is murdered by a young man. The novella begins like a detective story, with a police officer's notes, but its structure quickly changes to a diary left behind by the deceased Ni Hongmei and discovered at the scene of her death by the police officer. Through her voice via the diary, Ni Hongmei conveys the harsh reality of the state-sponsored collapse of formerly state-owned factories and enterprises—a profound social and economic change in China that was started in earnest in the 1990s and completed in the early twenty-first century. The story reveals how its negative consequences are experienced in laid-off women workers' lives.

More specifically, the protagonist relates the difficulties she faces after her husband dies and although she has been laid-off, she still has to raise her daughter while continuing to support her mother-in-law, who lives with them. She remarries, hoping to secure a stable life, but the second husband is a good-for-nothing who essentially abandons her and her family. With no other means to support her family and especially provide for her daughter's education, she resorts to prostitution, along with some other women she knows. Her diary records her thoughts about having to deal with the nauseating feelings of prostituting herself and about the types of men she encounters. These thoughts are juxtaposed with her occasional ruminations about her recent past when she worked in the state-owned textile mill; about her initial lack of understanding of what was happening to the workers until after their working lives were dismantled; about her late father, who had devoted all his life to the factory without knowing what would happen to it and to all the workers who once worked there; and about her belated realization that as workers they have been sacrificed in the name of economic modernization. The novella reads like a strong indictment of the selling off of the assets built up during the socialist period and the betrayal leveled at the once proud workers, men and women.

Indeed, with traces of previously formed consciousness of what it meant to be a woman, worker, and person mixed with the current sense of despair, hopelessness, and meaninglessness, the story is a sharp critique of the capitalistic nature of the economic reform that, to parody a line in the play *The White-Haired Girl*, has turned human beings (back) into ghosts. Their specter-like presence makes a mockery of the political consciousness that women like Ni Hongmei once took for granted (even if she did not fully intellectually comprehend it), but that now has little social basis for people to even find it wanting. In showing this reversal, the author questions the role of capital in rendering formerly independent and proud women workers into commodities who have to sell either their labor or their bodies in order to survive.

With a touch of didacticism in the writing style, Cao's representation of Ni Hongmei (and of his other women characters who face deterioration of their social and economic positions in reform-era China) is reminiscent of the tradition in modern Chinese literature in which male writer-intellectuals express their sympathy toward oppressed and exploited women. Meanwhile, there are critics of *diceng* literature who argue that intellectuals (in this case mostly male writers), not being subaltern themselves, cannot truly represent the "subalterns." Other critics dismiss *diceng* literature as being low in literary quality and merely imitating writers like Lao She. Still others suggest that in *diceng* literature subalterns are mainly used as conduits for New Left intellectuals to criticize the direction China's market reforms have taken.[29] But what exactly is wrong with recognizing the presence

---

29. For a more systematic analysis of the *diceng* literature phenomenon, see Li Yunlei 李云雷, *Xinshiji Diceng Wenxue yu Zhongguo Gushi* 新世纪底层文学与中国故事 (*Diceng* Literature in the Twenty-First Century and the Stories of China) (Guangzhou: Zhongshan daxue chubanshe, 2014); Liu Xu 刘旭, *Diceng Xushi: Cong Daiyan dao Ziwo Biaoshu* 底层叙事: 从代言到自我表述 (*Diceng* Narratives: From Representation by Others to Self-Representation) (Shanghai: Shanghai renmin chubanshe,

of capitalistic degradation and its negative impact on women's lives, especially when many have lost their dignity and have been subject to blatant exploitation? And furthermore, what exactly is the point of contention for critics to fuss over whether it is realistic that someone like Ni Hongmei would take certain actions or, for that matter, would have the intellectual capacity to write such a diary?

While elites' condescension toward working men and women is nothing new in China, anyone who is familiar with the revolutionary transformation in women's social status and cultural growth in political consciousness during the socialist period and their drastic dismantling in the postsocialist market reform era will find Ni Hongmei's voice compelling. And Cao's representations of Ni Hongmei indicate another coexisting reality in China that often goes unnoticed: that the subalternization of the working class does not entail a corresponding subalternization of their mind, or a lack of intellectual capability to speak. Indeed, increasingly critical voices have emerged directly from working people themselves, so much so that their writings come to be known as *dagong wenxue* 打工文学 ("literature by migrant workers") or *xin gongren wenxue* 新工人文学 ("literature by new workers").[30] One of the most recent voices comes from an essay by Fan Yusu 范雨素, a female migrant worker in Beijing. Hui Faye Xiao's essay in this volume offers a detailed and comprehensive reading of Fan's writings. I evoke

---

2013); and Liu Xu, *Diceng Xushu: Xiandaixing Huayu de Liexi* 底层叙述: 现代性话语的裂隙 (*Diceng* Narration: Fractures in Modernity Discourse) (Shanghai: Shanghai guji chubanshe, 2006).

30. Critics in China differentiate *diceng* literature from *dagong* literature, noting that the former are works by writers who are urban, well-educated, and do not themselves belong to the *diceng* in a sociological sense, and the latter are works written by laboring individuals—migrant workers in particular. The term *xin gongren wenxue*, or new workers' literature, denotes a subjective agency on the part of those who write and is reminiscent of the socialist zeitgeist that promotes the spirit of the working class. The term *dagong* 打工 simply means "working for a boss," with a derogatory designation in reference to migrant workers. *Dagong zhe* 打工者 ("someone working for a boss") does not at all convey the same meaning and implications as *xin gongren* 新工人 ("new worker").

Fan here primarily with regard to the question of the subaltern, or working women's class and gender consciousness of the twenty-first century in relation to the legacy of Chinese revolution–led women's liberation.

In April 2017 an essay titled "I Am Fan Yusu" (*Wo Shi Fan Yusu* 我是范雨素) was widely circulated online.[31] The wide circulation generated unprecedented instant responses to a piece written by a middle-aged female migrant worker. Initially the sensation turned out to be so overwhelming for the author that she reportedly decided to hide away from the media and the people who were interested in knowing more about her. At the same time, Fan's essay generated much debate over the style of her writing, with some marveling at her stylistic sophistication and others dismissing the piece as having been composed by someone selling her personal story. Still others question middle-class netizens' interest in her, seeing the interest as condescension and predicting that it would be short-lived. The controversy over Fan's piece is reminiscent of the dismissive view toward Cao's representation of Ni Hongmei's voice. Both voices were considered too good to be true, and critics concluded that there must therefore be something wrong with what they convey.

Written in six parts and around seven thousand words, "I Am Fan Yusu" is a succinct essay about Fan's own life. She writes about her strong mother and her four siblings; her daughters; her childhood interest in reading; a brief but spectacular episode in which she ran

---

31. Fan Yusu's "Wo Shi Fan Yusu" first appeared on a WeChat public platform called *Zhengwu Gushi*: Fan Yusu 范雨素, "Wo Shi Fan Yusu" 我是范雨素 (I Am Fan Yusu), *Zhengwu Gushi*, April 25, 2007. https://news.qq.com/a/20170425/063100 .htm?fbclid=IwAR0ULJ8wDiukyQ5ASRXicLRWAtl-92lUTQxyMHPTkbkz8PJH ccIZvT5RauU. Many criticisms can be found online, on blogs and elsewhere. For example, see Lu Taiguang 鲁太光, "Sikai Shidai de Chenmo: 'Wo Shi Fan Yusu' Beihou de Shehui Qishi" 撕开时代的沉默："我是范雨素"背后的社会启示 (Tearing apart the Silence: Understanding the Social Implications in "I Am Fan Yusu"), *Honggehui*, December 15, 2017, accessed March 20, 2019, www.szhgh.com/Article/gnzs /worker/2017-12-15/155952.html.

away from home before age twelve, her experience of becoming a temporary elementary school teacher at the age of twelve; her brief marriage, in which she experienced domestic violence and which ended in divorce; her migration to Beijing, where she found work as a maid, mainly taking care of rich people's children; and her finding a place in Picun Village, where she lives and participates in a literature group for migrant workers.[32] Imbricated in her narration are reflections that are conveyed in a humorous, self-deprecating, and poignant fashion, giving Fan Yusu's voice a cognitive power and critical edge seemingly unusual for a middle-aged female migrant worker.

Many readers marvel at Fan's opening line: "My life is like an unreadable book, hard to finish; fate has turned it up terribly bound."[33] In a short passage like the following, she humorously but also poignantly shows the difference between her parents: "Ever since I could remember, my father was like the shadow of a big tree. It was there, but of little use. He did not talk much. Nor did he do any physical labor, due to poor health. The five kids were all my mother's responsibility and hers alone." Under her pen, her mother, "a rural woman who was born in the evil old society," appears as a strong and publicly minded woman who was the "director of the local Women's Federation" for forty years beginning 1950 and who has also lived a difficult life trying to support her five children, all of whom, according to Fan, have had their own share of struggle and have largely remained "ordinary."

Reading through the piece, one realizes that this essay is an ode to her mother and to what her mother has taught her. Toward the end

32. Picun is a formerly rural village on the outskirts of Beijing that is now administratively part of the municipality. Like many similar villages on the outskirts of Beijing, with cheaper rents it attracted migrants who came to find work. Unlike in many of those villages, however, there emerged a few social and cultural organizations that offer services to migrant workers. The best known among them are Gongyou zhi Jia 工友之家 (Workers' Home) and Picun Wenxue Xiaozu 皮村文学小组 (Picun Literature Group). Left-leaning intellectuals support and participate in many of the activities organized by these entities.

33. Unless otherwise noted, translations are mine.

she asks: "What can I do for my mother? She is a kind person. . . . When as an adult I came to make a living in a big city, there I became one of the weakest at the bottom of society. As the daughter of strong country folk, I have often been looked down on and bullied by city folks. At those moments I wonder if it is always the case that people bully those who are weaker than they are. Do they get some kind of sensational pleasure out of doing that? Or is it simply replication of human genes? Those moments gave me the idea that whenever I come across someone who is as weak as I am, I'll let them feel loved and treated with dignity."

In light of the criticisms of *diceng* and migrant workers' literature in general and the way they are articulated in Ni Hongmei's and Fan Yusu's voices in particular, I would like to turn to the classed and gendered consciousness conveyed in them, focusing briefly on Fan's piece by highlighting a few layers. First, there is something compelling in a title that declares "I am Fan Yusu." Unlike Ni Hongmei's voice, which comes through untitled and in a disembodied way because she has died, Fan's directly announces her arrival. Then in telling the reader who she is, Fan offers a complex understanding of the changes that have taken place in her life, and more important, she implicitly raises questions related to the meaning of the vicissitudes of her life. Furthermore, she relates her own intellectual development by self-deprecatingly mentioning that she has been an avid reader from an early age and by stating matter-of-factly that she has been part of a writing group in Picun Village, all the while invoking a collection of cultural texts and individuals from both the socialist and postsocialist periods who have helped shape her mind.

In the end, who is Fan Yusu? A middle-aged migrant woman who works as a maid taking care of other people's children, to be sure. And yet she is also a middle-aged migrant woman who confidently speaks from "the bottom of society." The combination of understanding where she is socially and how she conveys that understanding adds symbolic meaning to her pronouncement "I am Fan Yusu." Hers is both a voice of the exploited and a voice that questions the return of exploitation. The double consciousness that runs through the essay "I Am Fan Yusu" is what proves most compelling and challenging.[34]

In both Ni Hongmei's diary and Fan Yusu's essay the specter of classed consciousness lurks. Although this consciousness no longer comes through via a neatly edited superimposition, it nevertheless harks back to the origin of the Chinese revolutionary consciousness that was aimed at eradicating class and gender oppression and inequality. The specter of this classed consciousness sustains a sense of dignity in the pronouncement of "I Am Fan Yusu" and informs the way she respects herself and the people who are as "weak" as she is.

When it comes to women's and gender issues in twenty-first-century China, issues of class continue to remain central. The legacy of Chinese revolution–led women's liberation is more than just a debate about the past. It is very much part of a debate about the present and future.

Coda

The introduction of Western feminism—primarily US-based feminism—into China during the reform era, especially since the 1990s, has helped spread the notion of gender far and wide. As a key feminist conceptual category, the notion of gender has contributed to the critical understanding of sexism, male-centrism, and even misogyny, which have existed in Chinese revolutions, numerous other political and social movements, and the political, economic, social, and cultural changes in both socialist and postsocialist Chinese society. At the same time, the spread of Western feminism has also encountered gender trouble in China.

The trouble mainly pertains to a reductionistic tendency when it comes to Western feminist–influenced assessment and understanding

---

34. For a while Fan's essay was censored on many online platforms. Although it can be found online now, the sensation over and debates about her piece have long since receded.

of Chinese revolution–led women's liberation.[35] Resistance on the part of the Chinese women intellectuals and feminists is not merely a nativist move (despite use of the term *bentuhua* 本土化, or "localization"). It is a long historical echo of He-Yin Zhen, Lu Xun, and many other early revolutionaries, both men and women, who recognized that if economic inequality is not dismantled, women cannot achieve real equality and freedom. Precisely because of the return of capital and of exploitation in the latest round of global capitalism, the principles found in revolution-led women's liberation become worth remembering and once again invoking. Despite the mistakes, disasters, and even crimes of the socialist period, and despite the seemingly complete fading of images of Zhu Chunhua in identification with the poor and the oppressed, there is still a tenacious residual of the classed political consciousness whose presence, though now lurking in society like a specter, is an important part of political memory and life's politics in today's China.

35. For a recent criticism of such an assessment, see Lingzhen Wang, "Wang Ping and Women's Cinema in Socialist China: Institutional Practice, Feminist Cultures, and Embedded Authorship," especially the section headed "Cold War ideology and Western feminist interpretations of Chinese women and socialist cinema," *Signs: Journal of Women in Culture and Society* 40, no. 3 (2015): 590–93.

4

The Specter of Polygamy in Contemporary Chinese Gender Imaginations

An Interview with Dai Jinhua

Wu Haiyun

Translated by Tera Mills and Ping Zhu

WU HAIYUN. Not long ago, several Chinese representatives of the Chinese "New Confucianism" (*xin rujia* 新儒家) expressed views that were extremely disrespectful of women, such as the idea that "only Confucianism can provide a home for modern women," or that polygamy is "reasonable" in some ways. I am personally both shocked and indignant hearing these views. What are your feelings about them?

DAI JINHUA. I am not shocked when facing these ugly and obsolete, yet familiar arguments because these things have always appeared under different names. I am not indignant either, because indignancy is one of the most powerless emotions.

Actually, I do not like accusation and indignation. Even if I accuse my opponent and denounce the evil patriarchal system, that is not enough to complete my own construction and

This interview was originally conducted for thepaper.cn (澎湃) in 2015. www.thepaper.cn/newsDetail_forward_1409159.

liberation, and it cannot support me in continuing to open new prospects.

WU HAIYUN. Then please rationally and calmly analyze the background and source of those views for us.

DAI JINHUA. Today New Confucianists have resurrected so-called traditional (*chuantong* 传统) views against the background of the rise of China and Chinese cultural consciousness. Everyone can more palpably feel that Western logic, or Western culture and universal values, have been gradually misplaced or invalidated in China. This kind of cultural consciousness permeates our daily lives, and then there appears a succinct response: China has a long and continuous history, and it is that continuous history that formed today's China.

However, when you respond with this kind of "civilization of continuity" argument (*wenming lianxu lun* 文明连续论), or when you make traditional culture the prescription to solve the dilemmas of today's modernization, you may not realize that the so-called tradition has already gone through intense and repeated destructions in the last century. You must know that twentieth-century China experienced all kinds of revolutions in human history, and each revolution was an instance of destruction.

Traditional culture holds rich cultural heritage, but because of the repeated destructions, it is no longer able to reanimate itself. The question of "modernization of tradition" (*chuantong de xiandaihua* 传统的现代化) was raised as early as during the May Fourth Movement (1919–24), but it has never been completed in a century. Why? Because tradition cannot be reanimated; it is no longer living knowledge.

WU HAIYUN. Are you suggesting that the New Confucianists' call to tradition is futile?

DAI JINHUA. Yes, resorting to traditional culture is virtually summoning a specter. So we do not need to be afraid, angry, or worried about this discourse. It is an ineffective narrative that has already been foreclosed.

We refuse to regress into history, but more important, regression is impossible. Modern history has unfolded before us the greatest happiness and sorrow in that it has made any regression a mere daydream.

WU HAIYUN. What you are describing is the ineffectiveness of the kind of narrative in real life, but I still feel indignant that they can so brazenly express such outworn values.

DAI JINHUA. Many people, when they criticize modernity, will emphasize history, tradition, and culture—especially non-Western cultures. However, there are two fundamental realities of premodernity: one is class oppression, and the other is gender oppression. Yet the traditionalists pretend that these two realities did not exist, or perhaps those realities are precisely what they secretly support—like premodern people used to support "the superior and the inferior both know their place, men and women are intrinsically different" (*zunbei you xu, nan nü you bie* 尊卑有序, 男女有别).

WU HAIYUN. I think today there are many people—not just New Confucianists—who still desire that kind of "order and distinction" (*xubie* 序别).

DAI JINHUA. I agree. This is related to another important reason why I am not angry. I have seen clearly that these things have their more variegated and penetrative social reality or cultural reality in our world. Today China's reality is a condensed version of several hundred years of European history: the memories of the premodern era and its historical structure survive in various ways. Even without the call of New Confucianism, the specter of polygamy still exists deep in contemporary Chinese familial and gender imaginations.

Taiwanese scholar Hsiao-Hung Chang once told me that Taiwan's most popular tabloid stories and TV shows are the ones about concubines and mistresses. Is it not the same on the mainland? Is not *Empresses in the Palace* (*Zhenhuan zhuan* 甄嬛传) a classic example? This kind of TV show narrates power struggles

in the imperial harem, and yet attracts the identification and fas-
cination of audiences of various social classes, and most of these
audiences are women. This fully illustrates that the polygamous
structure still exists in the mass psychology.

More important, capital has already summoned and resurrected the specter of polygamy in today's China. How many
women a man owns is proportional to the power and capital he
owns. I want to use a movie as an example: Lou Ye's 娄烨 *Mystery*
(*Fucheng mishi* 浮城谜事). The male protagonist of the movie—a
lower-middle-class man—has a nuclear family sanctioned by a
legal marriage. He also has a "concubine" (*erfang* 二房) approved
by the Chinese blood-relative family and authority, represented
by his mother. At the same time this man would also occasionally call a prostitute, a female college student from a poor family.
I was shocked when I watched this movie. I felt that Lou Ye had
captured the true state of Chinese society: the premodern logic
can summon the authority of the patriarchal specter.

WU HAIYUN. What you are saying is, some narratives that summon
the specter of patriarchy are actually not frightening; what is
truly frightening is capital.

DAI JINHUA. Yes. Compared to the reincarnation of polygamy in
the cultural imagination, the resurrection of polygamy through
capital and power is much more corrupting and frightening. In
reality the structure of capitalism is patriarchal: it is monopoliz-
ing, tyrannical, greedy, pragmatic, and authoritative. As a massive patriarchal endeavor, the process of establishing monopolistic
capital globally is a process of continuous exclusion; all disadvantaged groups, including women, are doomed to a position of
perpetual exile.

WU HAIYUN. However, as soon as the idea of capital is introduced,
the issue of gender becomes more complex. You just said that the
number of women a man owns is proportional to the amount
of capital he has, but the reverse is also true. In our society, if
a woman has a lot of capital or power, she can also own a lot of
men.

DAI JINHUA. Certainly, therefore when we see the patriarchal attribute inherent in capitalism, we should also see that capital surpasses a pure patriarchal system. We can see that there are women who use capital to elevate themselves. Around the world there are more and more female presidents, politicians, and CEOs. Actually, modern Chinese writer Zhang Henshui 张恨水 long ago already insightfully wrote in his novel *The World of Demons and Ghosts* (*Wangliang shijie* 魍魉世界) that the women who hold economic power or have a job are intimidating. This indicates that the internal logic of capital does not care about the distinction between male and female.

WU HAIYUN. Then this naturally leads to a question: has the globalization of capital truly advanced gender liberation?

DAI JINHUA. There is not a simple answer to this question. In my opinion, even though the internal logic of capital includes the overcoming of gender, what it is accomplishing is a process of dehumanization. In the omnipresent logic of capital, the meaning of each of us as human is constantly declining and being degraded as we are becoming links in the chain of capital. Of course, no one cares if you are male or female if your capacity is simply as a link or tool.

WU HAIYUN. After discussing the groups that oppress women, let us talk about those that support feminism—China's current feminist activists. I have found that for today's radical feminists, liberalism and the calls for feminism are always intertwined. Why is that?

DAI JINHUA. First, Western feminist movements were born from liberal movements. There is one sentence I have said repeatedly: if the US Declaration of Independence was signed by white people on the backs of black slaves, then men trampled over women's bodies to sign France's Universal Declaration of Human Rights. The so-called "born equal" and "natural rights" excluded women! Women were not citizens! It can be said that the discriminatory gender structure is itself a structure of modernity.

WU HAIYUN. This is very different from what we have imagined.

DAI JINHUA. Because one of the features of modernization in most non-Western countries is that the national liberation movement and the women's liberation movement happened nearly simultaneously. As a result it is very easy for us to connect modern history with the history of women's liberation. But things were different in the West. The rights of women in the Western world to citizenship, suffrage, and inheritance were won with the blood and lives of feminists over the past two hundred years. Their goal was nothing more than to share the same rights as citizens claimed by white males. When was this process completed? It hasn't been completed yet! When was an important turning point? In 1995, at the time of the UN World Conference on Women. The United Nations added a new clause in that year: women's rights are human rights.

WU HAIYUN. What you are saying is, feminists are at the same time liberals, and this is logical.

DAI JINHUA. Just a moment, I have more to say. In the 1960s, Western feminism experienced an era of explosive progress when Western women, for the first time, truly experienced equal rights. At the time there were many interesting headlines, such as when the Canadian prime minister's wife ran away and joined the hippies.

But this was followed by a more important historical process—namely, the fight of non-Western, nonwhite women. Their revolt against their status quo went beyond the boundaries of liberalism. In other words, from that time forward feminist movements across the world can no longer be encompassed by the logic of liberalism invented by Western white men; instead, feminists have challenged the context and logic of liberalism. Therefore we can say that the high degree of unity between feminism and liberalism in today's China is both logical and outdated.

WU HAIYUN. In my opinion, contemporary Chinese feminist activists are hesitant to face the history of women's liberation in the new People's Republic of China precisely because of the liberal political ideas they hold to.

DAI JINHUA. Of course, because they believe that liberal discourse is a strong weapon for critiquing institutions! But my view has always been that when you simply regard liberal discourse as a force to advance Chinese society, you are letting your opponent define you, because your own logic is not enough to sustain your legitimacy and the effectiveness of your practice.

Has the new People's Republic of China had a deep and widespread women's liberation movement? The answer is obviously yes. In reality, during the Cold War all socialist countries practiced comprehensive women's liberation and gender equality in terms of politics, economy, and legislation, and all were completed through the violent actions of the state—abolition of arranged marriages, abolition of polygamy, gender equality, equal pay for equal work. Back then, people had no choice but to liberate women.

WU HAIYUN. But today's feminists are not willing to admit that. They say that at the time the state just wanted to use women's labor; there was not real liberation for women.

DAI JINHUA. First, this argument certainly touches on one aspect of the issue: at the time, socialist countries were generally less developed countries, and thus in those countries women's liberation was certainly subordinate to the liberation of the female workforce.

However, at the same time we must see that China's New Democratic Revolution included two basic principles throughout, one was to abolish feudalism, the other was women's liberation. They were inherited from the May Fourth Movement and were enacted by the pioneers of China's modern revolutions.

We can also see that during the Mao era, when "women can hold up half the sky" was championed, there indeed appeared many Chinese women who were capable of holding up half the sky. They were so outstanding and held irreplaceable positions, in every field and profession, in a world led by men in every field and profession. You can see in the "fourth generation" (*disidai* 第四代) film directors how many of the leading figures were female directors. Tu Youyou 屠呦呦, who received the Nobel Prize in Medicine in 2015, was also an outstanding woman in the Mao era.

WU HAIYUN. I once saw a news report on Tu Youyou that said at the time she invested completely in her work and did not really take care of her children.

DAI JINHUA. I belong to her generation. You know, if the women from my generation got married or had children, we would feel obligated to explain it to our friends, as we would feel a little ashamed. But today people once again have started to feel that marriage and having children is the self-evident duty of women.

Of course, I have also come to realize that the 1960s is an exception, a special era among several hundred years of modern history. But I still believe that this exceptional era, though it may have failed on the whole as a social experiment, opened a world of possibilities; or we can say it proved to us many possibilities. I am also convinced that this period of history, in which gender equality was institutionalized in politics, economy, and legislation, still remains an extremely valuable legacy to the younger generation.

WU HAIYUN. But recently a new phenomenon has appeared in China: more and more women choose to return to being homemakers, and they view this as a superior lifestyle.

DAI JINHUA. This is true. In the past, we used to encourage women to charge into industries led by men; later, women chose to do so voluntarily. Today's women, however, live within the confines of patriarchal rules. The life plans of more and more women have once again revolved around a plain, everyday feeling: they ask themselves why they should have all these troubles.

Just as your question points out, in recent years supporting a wife at home has become the sign of a successful man; similarly, marrying a husband that can let you stay idle at home has become the mark of a successful woman. I think the values implied by this new view of success are much more corrupting than those values that are blatantly stated from a patriarchal position.

Compared to the views of outright patriarchal chauvinism, what worries me more is the internal transformation that has been thrust upon women throughout history. If it were outright deprivation or oppression, there would certainly be corresponding resistance, or at least rebound. But this kind of internal transformation and brainwashing led to real changes. Women will believe that they do not need a sense of self to be happy, that they do not need to set standards for themselves as social beings. They are completely capable of "choosing" and are happy to "choose" to return to the home, and they even see this kind of "choice" as exercising their freedom. In this sense, I am much more disappointed, because true structural violence is carried out in these ways.

WU HAIYUN. According to my observations, one of the important reasons that women choose to be homemakers is children. I don't know when it started, but all kinds of popular parenting theories about the importance of the mother started circulating, as if mothers would fall short of the standard of mothers if they did not spend a great amount of high-quality time around their children.

DAI JINHUA. My suggestion is: do not have a direct dialogue with these arguments, because if you did you would fall prey to the pitfalls of their presumptions. You should know that these ideas always set up many unwritten presumptions.

For example, a counterexample to this kind of argument is that research has discovered that mothers of children aged one to five are the group with the highest suicide rates in the world. An American female social psychologist describes a mother holding an infant as a kind of socially invisible human. She could be on the verge of a breakdown at any moment, but no one sees her or cares about her. You can imagine if this woman were not only the mother to a newborn, but also had her own profession, how much help that would bring!

WU HAIYUN. But to tell the truth, I am still a little worried. Now China is moving to a two-child policy. Once a family has two children, will it not force a large group of career women to become homemakers in the near future?

DAI JINHUA. I don't think that you need to worry too much about that. Today when people imagine a couple having two children, they use the one-child dynamic to do so. They do not realize that if a family has two or more children, that original one-child dynamic will no longer exist, and the original parenting method and parenting psychology will change completely.

Of course, on the other hand, we should also realize that under the influence of the two-child policy, Chinese society, which has been structured by the one-child policy in the past forty years, must go through enormous adjustments. Once again our values, activities, lifestyles, and daily trivialities will undergo seismic changes. This once again evidences the cruelty of our everyday lives as Chinese. If we can realize this, perhaps the change of fate that may come upon women will not be the only thing we are panicked about.

WU HAIYUN. If in the near future more and more career women choose to become homemakers, what do you want to say to them?

DAI JINHUA. I can only say, be sober-minded. No matter what choice you make, you must have a sober consciousness. We all know that historical heritage is also historical liability. Today you may think you do not want to have to work as hard as your mother, but her situation was a consequence of economic equality. Now young women want more freedom and leisure, but are they aware of the price of economic inequality they will have to pay?

People nowadays only emphasize the price of being a career woman without discussing the price of being a homemaker. Do you know exactly how huge that price is? Without economic independence, do you really think you will have autonomy? Today people like to cite Virginia Woolf's statement that a woman must have "a room of her own," but often overlook that in the next sentence Woolf also writes that a woman must have money. People have further forgotten that in the era in which Woolf lived she could not even walk into a university library to borrow a book.

Yes, today's women all seem to have the right to choose, but when you choose, by no means think that any of the choices is a free lunch.

WU HAIYUN. Because we still live in the social reality of a patriarchal system.

DAI JINHUA. That's right. Society's mainstream logic is always predominant. Thorough change of the gender system is predicated on change of the entire social structure, and it will certainly not be achieved single-handedly. As an individual you can only pursue more wisdom and more awareness; there is no other way.

Part Two

Chinese Feminisms on the Ground

5

Feminist Struggles in a Changing China

Wang Zheng

Embedded in political, social, economic, and cultural transformations, gender has been a highly salient site of contention since the Chinese elite started to search for a modern China in the late nineteenth century. Having risen to become the world's second largest economy in the twenty-first century, China nonetheless witnesses growing conservative social and political forces that have importunately attempted to reinstall and consolidate gender and class hiera^{rchies in the context} of global capitalism. This chapter examines three cohorts of Chinese feminists as a way to illustrate shifting settings and constant contentions over gender equality: state feminists of the socialist period, postsocialist NGO feminists around the Fourth World Conference on Women (FWCW), and young feminist activists ascending the public stage since the second decade of the twenty-first century. Each cohort has adopted distinct strategies for their diverse agendas, conditioned by their particular historical contexts and social and political parameters.

But continuities remain. While the first generation of socialist-period feminists has long left the historical stage, some of its legacies have persisted, especially in terms of its institution building in the form of an official mass organization: the All-China Women's Federation. The relationship between feminism and the state remains central to feminist struggles in China even though state socialism has long evolved into state capitalism, and a rapid privatization of the economy has produced 250 million citizens who do not work in the state sector.[1] And just as Chinese feminism's inception was inseparable from a global context a century ago, today it is as deeply embedded in processes of globalization as ever. Contemporary China is in a time of compressed temporalities in the sense that various contentious discourses over the past century have neither reached closure nor faded out, but have often been reenacted and remobilized simultaneously against a drastically changed historical setting. This chapter traces both continuities and changes in Chinese feminist struggles while critically examining constraints and possibilities for further development.

A Brief Overview of Chinese Feminism in the Early Twentieth Century

Feminism is one of the many ideologies that educated Chinese have embraced in their pursuit of modernity and rejection of an ancient dynastic system underpinned by a hierarchical sex-gender system that held chastity as the supreme value of women in the interest of patrilineal kinship. Just as the imagination of a modern China has never been singular, feminism has also been understood in diverse ways that, nevertheless, express a shared concern with gendered social arrangements.

At the turn of the twentieth century, anarchist, socialist, liberal, evolutionary, eugenic, and nationalist positions shaped various

---

1. Xing Zheng 邢郑, "Geti Siying Jingji Cheng Xina Jiuye 'Xushuichi'" 个体私营经济成纳就业 "蓄水池" (Private Enterprises Have Become the "Reservoir" for Absorbing Labor), People.cn, October 28, 2015, http://finance.people.com.cn/n/2015/1028/c1004-27747492.html.

feminist articulations. In their proposals for changing gender hierarchy, rooted in ancient Chinese philosophy and gender norms based on Confucian ideals of gender differentiation and segregation, feminists expressed different imaginings of a better future: a more humane society that centered on social justice and equality, a modern society that allowed individuals to break away from the constraints of Confucian social norms embedded in kinship relations as well as the control of an imperial polity, and a stronger nation that turned China from being the prey of imperialist powers into a sovereign state. Regardless of their diverse political positions, reformers, revolutionaries, professionals, and educated women and men from elite social backgrounds who embraced various versions of feminism agreed on the necessity of changing gender practices in transforming their ancient civilization, which had fallen into deep crisis in a time of imperialist and colonialist expansion. The confluence of diverse and often contradictory ideas and practices rapidly made a neologism a key phrase in twentieth-century China: *equality between men and women* (*nannü pingdeng* 男女平等), a Chinese rendition of the English phrase *sexual equality*, which had been circulating globally since the late nineteenth century. Signifying a conscious rejection of the foundation of Confucian social order prescribing differentiation between men and women, equality between men and women became a badge of modernity that social groups and political parties adopted to assert a progressive identity.

After the collapse of the Qing dynasty in 1911, educated women from elite families who had joined the revolution against the Qing government launched a women's suffrage movement to demand equal political rights in the new Republican polity. Suppressed by a dictatorial president in 1913, the suffragists turned to women's education and careers to lay a social foundation for women's political rights. Radical male intellectuals launched the New Culture movement in 1915 to challenge the dominant Confucianism, which provided a renewed critical feminist thrust. Gender hierarchy, gender differentiation, gender segregation, double sexual standards that demanded chastity of women while legitimizing polygamy, and cultural practices ritualized in the service of maintaining a deeply entrenched hierarchical society that was fundamentally based on the dominance of men over women were highlighted as quintessential symbols of the backwardness of Confucian culture, defined as feudalist. Feminism was enthusiastically embraced as a powerful weapon to combat the feudalism that had dominated China for millennia.

The small circle of cultural radicals, which included the future founders of the Chinese Communist Party (CCP), rapidly expanded its social and intellectual influence after May 4, 1919, when college and secondary school students spearheaded a nationwide patriotic movement. Incensed by the treaty about to be signed by world powers at the Versailles Conference, which transferred all of Germany's rights in Shandong province to Japan after World War I, the May Fourth Movement, with its vehemently anti-imperialist female and male students as major constituents, became a powerful vehicle that carried the New Culture's advocacy of antifeudalism, including the promotion of feminism, into mainstream urban society. Equal educational and employment opportunities for women, and their freedom to socialize with men, ending centuries of gender segregation, were seen as the foundation for women's liberation. Pursuing equality in all spheres of life and achieving an independent personhood became the hallmarks of May Fourth women's feminist subjectivities. Many May Fourth feminists—by definition, educated women and men—later played important roles in China's political, social, and cultural transformations.[2] From two cohorts, older New Culturalists and younger student participants in the May Fourth Movement, emerged a small group of men and women, disillusioned with the Western liberal but imperialist powers, who in 1921 formed the CCP, modeled after the newly founded Soviet Union, and openly endorsed "equality between men and women" in its platform.[3]

2. For a historical study of May Fourth feminism, see Wang Zheng 王政, *Women in the Chinese Enlightenment: Oral and Textual Histories* (Berkeley: Univ. of California Press, 1999).

3. For a study of radical women's participation in the inception of the CCP, see Christina K. Gilmartin, *Engendering the Chinese Revolution: Radical Women,*

Even though many high-profile May Fourth feminists joined the CCP, the term *feminism* began to lose favor within the Party when CCP feminists came into contact with Western socialists and communists and adopted their view that feminism was bourgeois—a discursive practice that had originated in rivalries between radical suffragists and socialist women in the early twentieth century.[4] Nonetheless, CCP feminists kept alive the May Fourth feminist agenda of women's liberation, simply replacing the discredited word *feminism* with *women's rights* and maintaining pressure on the Party to promote those rights. They mobilized women for the revolution with yet another new term: *women-work*.[5]

Managed by a Women Department or a Women-Work Committee in various periods, women-work was a major platform for CCP feminists engaged in pursuing gendered social justice and equality, especially for lower-class women, as well as an important branch of the CCP specialized in mobilizing women's participation in the Communist Revolution. In urban areas the underground CCP feminists targeted women factory workers as the major constituents of women-work; in the CCP military bases in rural areas, peasant women were the target for feminist organization and mobilization. Running literacy classes and raising both class and gender consciousness were part of the women-work among factory workers; addressing abuse of women in patriarchal families, opposing arranged marriage, and promoting freedom to divorce were issues adopted by CCP feminists in rural base areas,[6] though the focus on the latter item largely shifted

---

Communist Politics, and Mass Movements in the 1920s (Berkeley: Univ. of California Press, 1995).

4. Marilyn J. Boxer, "Rethinking the Socialist Construction and International Career of the Concept 'Bourgeois Feminism,'" *The American Historical Review* 112, no. 1 (2007): 131–58.

5. For an early study on women-work in the CCP, see Delia Davin, *Woman-Work: Women and the Party in Revolutionary China* (Oxford: Clarendon, 1976).

6. For a detailed study of marriage and divorce in the CCP's base areas in Northern China, see Xiaoping Cong, *Marriage, Law, and Gender in Revolutionary China, 1940–1960* (Cambridge, UK: Cambridge Univ. Press, 2016).

to enhancing women's economic status in rural families by encouraging them to participate in gainful productive work in the early 1940s.

The inner logic of the two-pronged agenda of women-work was that in order for the CCP to succeed in attracting women to the Communist Revolution, which promised women's thorough emancipation down the road, the Party had to address women's particular and immediate needs and interests. In practice the two dimensions of women-work presented an inherent source of tension that required tremendous wisdom for CCP feminists to juggle skillfully, as male leaders at all levels tended to treat institutionalized women-work as an auxiliary instrument to fulfill various tasks of the Party. After all, the wars against Japanese invaders and the Nationalist Party provided them with an excuse not to prioritize women's gender-specific interests, but instead to demand women's contribution to the Revolution.

Socialist State Feminist Transformative Practices

China in 1949 was an agrarian society with about 90 percent of its total population of 540 million residing in rural areas, 90 percent of women being illiterate, and an economy devastated by decades of war. Economic recovery with women's participation and increasing women's literacy were high on the CCP's agenda for socialist modernity.[7] The victory of the CCP in 1949 enabled feminists in the Party to wield socialist state power to materialize their feminist dreams. Only 530,000 of the CCP's 1949 membership of 4.49 million were women, but many of these CCP women rose to official positions in administrations ranging from the central government to urban street offices and rural townships, depending on their Party seniority and level of education. Although we do not claim that each CCP woman was a

7. Zhongguo Renquan Yanjiuhui 中国人权研究会 (The Association of Human Rights in China), ed., *Zhongguo Renquan Nianjian* 中国人权年鉴 (The Annals of Human Rights in China) (Beijing: Tuanjie chubanshe, 2007), 580.

conscious feminist, the numbers and power of Chinese socialist state feminists in the early People's Republic of China (PRC) were arguably unprecedented in feminist histories of the world. This was a consequence of a feminist-informed Communist Revolution in the world's most populous nation that attracted female constituents with equality between men and women as an integral goal of the revolution. Upon the founding of the PRC, many CCP feminists, in their official capacity, vigorously initiated and promoted transformative programs to cash the Party's promissory note of women's thorough liberation in a socialist country. This belies the general assumption in much of the scholarship in English that these women were passive followers of a male-dominated party.

The first National Women's Congress, organized by senior CCP feminists Deng Yingchao 邓颖超 and Cai Chang 蔡畅 in March 1949,[8] resolved to set up a national women's organization, the All-China Democratic Women's Federation (ACDWF was changed to All-China Women's Federation in 1957, hence ACWF), an umbrella organization that horizontally united all pro-CCP women's organizations, and an official institution that vertically reached down to the rural villages and urban neighborhoods nationwide. This vast organizational reach enabled socialist state feminists to effectively carry out many transformative actions nationwide. The very first law adopted by the socialist state, the 1950 Marriage Law, drafted by a feminist committee led by Deng Yingchao, was a centerpiece in the socialist feminist mission of transforming Chinese feudalist culture. The law enforced the dismantling of traditional marriage practices such as arranged marriage and

8. Cai Chang joined the CCP in 1923, and Deng Yingchao joined it in 1925. Their Party seniority allowed them to enjoy tremendous respect, especially since they did not pursue high political position with their Party seniority. Cai in 1923 married Li Fuchun 李富春, who became vice premier of the PRC, and Deng in 1925 married Zhou Enlai 周恩来, who became the premier of the PRC. The informal power Cai and Deng enjoyed in the Party was beyond the reach of their successors in the ACWF.

underage marriage, and granted women freedom to divorce and to remarry, establishing new gender norms of equality between men and women with state power.

Women's literacy, equal employment and equal pay, political participation, reproductive health, and new public facilities to reduce working women's burden of childcare and housework were also areas of remarkable feminist achievement in the early PRC. Their efforts to involve and engage rural and urban lower-class women, particularly in all the transformative programs aiming to eliminate class and gender hierarchies, expanded urban elite–based concepts and practices of women's rights from the first half of the twentieth century. That said, the socialist state paradoxically widened the gap between the rural and urban by setting up a two-tier household registration system that offered urban residents more privileges and material goods in order to speed up industrialization.

Socialist feminists' comprehensive vision of Chinese women's liberation crucially hinged on transformation of subjectivities. Senior feminists were acutely aware that without undoing a patriarchal culture that saturated the psyche of the people and of CCP members, efforts to achieve women's equality in all spheres of life would encounter severe obstacles and resistance. Cultural production was thus also an important realm in socialist feminist transformation, a heritage from the May Fourth New Culture Movement, when progressive intellectuals (a cohort that included many men) produced a massive amount of literature and drama to condemn the feudalist patriarchal tradition embodied in Confucianism. The Chinese term *feudalism* in socialist novels, operas, and film (a state-owned industry led by female and male feminist leaders) decidedly represented the Other of the socialist new China. It became a gender-inflected key word encompassing everything we today call sexism, masculinism, patriarchy, male chauvinism, or misogyny. Even illiterate women in rural areas could deploy the term effortlessly to accuse men of chauvinism.[9] "Equality between

9. See the documentary film *Small Happiness*, by Carma Hinton, 1984.

men and women" and "women's liberation," popularized via state-owned media, especially the ACWF's magazine *Women of China* and socialist films accessible even to rural communities, became household slogans intimately connecting gender equality with the authority of the new socialist state. A socialist feminist gender discourse rapidly rose to mainstream discourse in the early PRC.

Chinese socialist state feminists in the early PRC were an integral part of the international women's movement of the socialist camp that was represented by the Women's International Democratic Federation (WIDF). On December 10, 1949, only two months after the founding of the PRC, the All-Asian Women's Congress, attended by 197 representatives from twenty-three countries, was organized by the ACDWF in its new role as a member of the WIDF.[10] Hosting an international conference on women when only about ten socialist countries had established diplomatic relationships with the PRC indicated the CCP leadership's full support for this initiative, as well as the state feminists' high capacity for global networking. The event certainly expressed state feminists' conscious efforts to merge the women's movement in the PRC with socialist women's movements globally. With the Chair of the ACDWF, Cai Chang, serving as the Deputy Chair of the WIDF, Chinese socialist state feminists also played a leading role in the international women's movement until the 1960s, when the CCP split with the Communist Party of the Soviet Union.

The CCP feminists' firm identification with the Party both empowered and constrained them because of the contradictory political environment. Ideologically, the Party's platform endorsed a feminist pursuit of gender equality and "equality between men and women," which was written into the Constitution of the People's Republic of China. Institutionally, however, male Communists assumed leading

10. For a study of WIDF, see Francisca de Haan, "Continuing Cold War Paradigms in Western Historiography of Transnational Women's Organisations: The Case of the Women's International Democratic Federation (WIDF)," *Women's History Review* 19, no. 4 (2010): 547–73.

administrative positions. Many male officials did not eschew male chauvinism during the Communist Revolution even though they vowed to strive for an egalitarian society. *Women of China* in the early 1950s exposed many sexist behaviors of male officials, including blocking women from entering gainful employment.[11] Feminists in the Women's Federation system found their proposals for women's benefits often pushed aside by male officials. Even the institutionalization of a women's mass organization did not resolve the problem of gender hierarchy in the Party. The ACWF,[12] after all, was organized as a Party-led mass organization that was responsible for advocacy, rather than as an executive branch of the government, although everyone in the Women's Federation system was also on the government payroll.

Because each level of the Women's Federation subordinates to the Party committee of the same administrative level, Women's Federation women officials often encountered Party officials who showed little interest in equality between men and women or women-work. Party chair Mao Zedong 毛泽东 was apparently well aware of this situation. On November 12, 1952, in a meeting the ACWF leaders had requested, he instructed them on dealing with different levels of Party committees with these colorful words: *yi song* 一送 (first, submit proposals to the Party committee); *er cui* 二催 (second, push the Party committee to respond); *san maniang* 三骂娘 (if the first two methods did not work, third, just curse and swear).[13] Apparently, though it was

---

11. See chapter 3 in Wang Zheng, *Finding Women in the State: A Socialist Feminist Revolution in the People's Republic of China, 1949–1964* (Berkeley: Univ. of California Press, 2016).

12. The acronym ACWF has two meanings: one, the national women's organization that has six administrative levels paralleling the state administrative structure; two, the national headquarters of the mass organization, based in Beijing. In the following, ACWF is used strictly to refer to the national headquarters, while Women's Federation means the whole system of the national women's organization.

13. Luo Qiong 罗琼 and Duan Yongquiang 段永强, *Luo Qiong Fangtanlu* 罗琼 访谈录 (Interviews with Luo Qiong) (Beijing: Zhongguo funü chubanshe, 2000), 126. Mao's original phrase *san maniang* was changed by women officials into *san*

never an intentional policy, neglecting women's interests was a common practice within the Party that continued into the socialist period; and significantly, the chair's support stopped at the verbal advice without offering any structural rearrangement of power relations, a measure that had not been envisioned, let alone proposed by the ACWF leaders to the supreme Party leader.

Encouraged by Mao's advice, quite a few Women's Federation officials who actually followed his instruction were unfortunately labeled as rightists for their candid criticism of their Party leaders in the Anti-Rightist Campaign in 1957. The subordination of the gender-based mass organization to the male-dominated Party led to subsequent institutional marginalization of the Women's Federation in the state structure of the PRC, which in turn conditioned the routine experiences of feminists in the CCP that women-work was of lesser value, except for those moments when some item on the Party's central agenda required that women be mobilized.

Historically, the CCP used the label of "narrow bourgeois feminism" as a political stick to beat down those outspoken feminists who insisted on the priority of women's interests or raised a critical voice against male chauvinism in the CCP. In this historical context, state feminists in the Women's Federation system routinely operated in a politics of concealment in their endeavors to promote feminist agendas. Since singularly and openly raising a demand on behalf of women would have a slim chance of eliciting the support of male authorities, Women's Federation officials learned to insert feminist items into the Party's agenda in order to gain legitimacy and resources for actions with a clear gender dimension. One example was when the Shanghai Women's Federation organized a large-scale women's rally against American imperialism in 1951 at the request of the municipal Party committee. Using support from the municipal and district

---

piping (三批评 third, criticize) in their public talks, perhaps because of the apparent gender offensiveness and class connotation of the original. Cursing and swearing in profane language were sometimes adopted by lower-class women as a powerful weapon in their resistance, but were forbidden for women of "respectable" families.

governments on this legitimate Party central task, Women's Federation officials swiftly expanded the Women's Federation's institutional development in Shanghai neighborhoods by setting up grassroots women's organizations.[14] Articulating their strong support of the Party's central tasks, state feminists often embedded a hidden script that intended to advance women's diverse interests. In other words, camouflaging a feminist agenda with dominant Party language was a major principle in the politics of concealment. The concealing and self-effacing maneuver appealed to the authority of the Party and glossed over their own struggles behind the scenes.

Receding into the shadows, socialist state feminists were unknown to either the public in China or scholars outside China. Women's dramatic advancements in education, employment, and political participation in the socialist period were noticed by many observers outside China, but without any knowledge of state feminists' endeavors, these observers generally attributed all the accomplishments to a patriarchal party-state that supposedly showed sporadic benevolence to women. A dominant conceptualization of a monolithic socialist state in the field of China studies has disabled scholarly imaginations about possible feminist visions and contentions inside the socialist state.

Socialist state feminists' efforts to eliminate both gender and class hierarchies and transform a patriarchal culture were halted in 1964, when a Maoist class struggle against revisionism and capitalism rapidly ascended to become a dominant agenda of the CCP. The ACWF stopped functioning in the heat of the Cultural Revolution, when all government branches were paralyzed. Though the effects of state feminists' social and cultural transformations in the first fifteen years of the PRC persisted, and institutional mechanisms they developed for gender equality in education and employment continued, their feminist agenda of further transforming gender relations was suppressed by the Maoist class struggle. While working-class young women had

14. See chapter 1 in Wang, *Finding Women*.

more opportunities to be promoted to leadership positions in the Cultural Revolution because of Mao's wife Jiang Qing's 江青 prominent position in the power center, a New Culture agenda highlighting antipatriarchy in cultural production was condemned by Jiang Qing and other radicals as an expression of revisionism. Suppressing a conscious agenda of feminist cultural transformation by state feminists in and outside the ACWF, Maoist radicals did serious harm to the feminist revolutionary cause. When the ACWF revived its function in 1978, the political landscape had already changed so drastically that the surviving first cohort of state feminists found their previous accomplishments for gender equality under severe attack.

A major erasure of socialist state feminists has arisen in the production of historical knowledge of socialism since the late 1970s, when the CCP began to depart from the socialist course after Mao's death in 1976. In Chinese intellectuals' concerted critique of the CCP's crimes under Mao's dictatorship, descriptions of the socialist period were mainly limited to condemnations of its ills, and Mao became synonymous with socialism. The antisocialist discourse was both grossly reductive and openly masculinist. In postsocialist intellectuals' efforts to dismantle both the CCP's authoritarian rule and socialist egalitarian values and practices, socialist state feminist gender ideology and practices that promoted equality between men and women were characterized as the Maoist state's imposition of gender sameness, a crime of the CCP that distorted women's natural femininity and masculinized them.

In an article published in the prestigious Chinese academic journal *Sociological Studies*, Zheng Yefu 郑也夫 argued that contemporary China was falling far behind developed countries in terms of the level of a knowledge economy, as well as the levels of social and material wealth. At the same time, he pointed out the Chinese women's liberation surpassed all countries in the world in terms of women's equal employment and equal pay. Deploring what he viewed as a cause-and-effect situation, Zheng offered a critique that condensed key elements in the backlash against socialist women's liberation:

The immediate consequence of a government-enforced women's liberation outpacing socioeconomic development is dysfunctional family relations. . . . We have failed to explore a new gender division of labor in family life **because, through supporting the weak and suppressing the strong, a strong administrative power has interfered and destroyed the normal division of labor between the strong and the weak in family**. It has even made the weak mistakenly think they are not weak, and made the strong lose confidence in themselves. **Ultimately, it has deprived Chinese society of "real men."** . . . **A women's liberation promoted by politics has also made China lose its women.**[15]

Restoration of gender differentiation was promoted by the urban elite's conflicting proposals: embracing a Western capitalist modernity symbolized by sexualized and commodified women in advertisements, or reviving a Confucian tradition by retrieving so-called Oriental female traditional virtues, which women could express by being self-sacrificing, virtuous mothers and good wives. Rearranging gender practices by promoting a discourse of femininity has been a prominent theme in elite proposals to undo socialist modernity since the early 1980s. The preferred Chinese rendition of *feminism* as *nüxing zhuyi* (女性主义 "feminine-ism") since the early 1990s partly reflects the hegemonic power of this discourse of femininity.

The CCP's turn to privatization and marketization was accompanied by a dismantling of socialist institutional mechanisms that safeguarded gender and class equalities for those working in the public sector, such as equal education, equal employment, equal pay, and state-funded health care and childcare. The state's departure from a socialist egalitarian distribution system was also crucially legitimized by the propagation of a neoliberal ideology that harped on social Darwinism, a discursive maneuver that many male intellectuals eagerly

15. Zheng Yefu 郑也夫, "Nannü Pingdeng de Shehuixue Sikao" 男女平等的社会学思考 (Sociological Reflections on Gender Equity). *Shehuixue yanjiu*, no. 2 (1994): 110 (bold in the original).

adopted. The slogan "Getting rich is glorious" was promoted by the Party's media, and the poor were blamed for being incapable. The much-abused concept of a Maoist class became a convenient excuse for the CCP to abandon class as an analytical category in its embrace of global capitalism.

The profound social, economic, and ideological ruptures that were concealed by one major continuity—the continuous authoritarian political system that sustained the CCP's rule—coincided with the retirement of the first generation of state feminists. Having barely returned to their posts after the ACWF's ten-year hiatus during the Cultural Revolution, the top feminist leaders used the limited time before their retirement to promote compilations of source materials and histories of the Chinese women's movement in diverse locations nationwide, manifesting their will to pass down the heritage of a socialist feminist history. They also started to organize national conferences on research on women, in an attempt to address the myriad problems women confronted in the era of marketization by insisting on a Marxist theory of women's liberation. This theory's fundamental thesis is that women's liberation is based on their participation in social production.

Propagating this Marxist theory of women's liberation was the Women's Federation's feminists' important discursive struggle to resist tremendous masculinist pressures in and outside the government to push women back to the kitchen as a solution to increasing unemployment in marketization. These initiatives recruited and relied on scholars who were showing interest in women's issues, and quickly stimulated a high tide of research on women nationwide beginning in the early 1980s. Discrimination in women's employment and education in a market economy and protection of women's legal rights in marriage and at work were among the hot topics for scholars who aimed to affect public policies with their research. In this period Chinese scholars heavily relied on the Women's Federation's funding and organizational network as well as institutional legitimacy to get involved in research on women. However, feminist scholars from the West tend to ignore the crucial role state feminists played in this research boom, instead focusing on leading women scholars' activities in their effort to identify an autonomous feminist movement vis-à-vis the supposedly Party-controlled women's movement. Literary scholar Li Xiaojiang has been credited as a pioneer of research on women in the 1980s, while much of the work state feminists in the ACWF have done since the late 1970s to initiate and support research on women has gone unnoticed.

In their old age and declining health, many members of the first generation of state feminists vigorously engaged in writing and publishing memoirs and autobiographies. These moves expressed their conscious resistance to the discursive erasure of Chinese socialist feminist struggles. However, when the CCP, now led by Deng Xiaoping 邓小平, had already made decisive moves to merge with global capitalism, which was characterized in the media as a new vision of Chinese modernity, socialist state feminists' claims of their accomplishments in socialist revolution could have little purchase, sounding outdated. Few cared about what these feminists remembered of a time that was condemned as a dark age dominated by Mao's dictatorship in the rising hegemonic discourse of antisocialism. Thus this cohort of socialist state feminists, as well as their endeavors, failed to enter the constructed public memory, or historical knowledge, of a socialist past in the age of capitalist globalization.

The Fourth World Conference on Women and Feminist NGOs

The state accelerated privatization and marketization in the 1980s while opening China to transnational corporations. Urban women workers bore the brunt of this "economic reform," as they became the first to be fired and last to be hired. The labor laws of the socialist period still existed, which required enterprises to pay for reproductive costs, including paid maternity leave and day care. Seeking to maximize profits in a changed economic system, even state-owned sectors began to lay off women disproportionately, as well as close down publicly funded day cares and canteens in the name of optimizing management and improving efficiency. The one-child policy initiated in 1979 placed rural women in a deep predicament, as the simultaneous decollectivization in rural areas installed a household responsibility system, which increased patrilineal peasant families' demands for male labor and male heirs. Female infanticide and forced abortion spread rapidly, resulting in a seriously skewed sex ratio at birth: 117.8 boys born for every 100 girls in 2011.

In the context of a severe backlash against socialist women's liberation in male-dominated public discourse and the state's dismantling of socialist egalitarian institutional mechanisms in a state-controlled market economy, the beneficiaries of socialist gender equality policies rose to form a significant feminist force. A cohort of urban, educated women who were positioned in academic institutions in the 1980s began to participate in research on women in collaboration with the same cohort in the Women's Federations in large cities with the intention to influence public policies. When the Chinese government decided to host the Fourth World Conference on Women (FWCW) in the aftermath of the state suppression of the 1989 Tiananmen Square demonstrations, this cohort of feminists swiftly seized the opportunity to push the political boundaries that curtailed spontaneously organized activities after 1989. Many of these women founded feminist NGOs with resources from international donors, as well as legitimacy granted by the NGO Forum, which was held in tandem with the FWCW and attended by about forty thousand feminists from all over the world.

The ACWF's presence in NGO activities preparing for the FWCW was challenged by global feminist communities due to its ambiguous status as a mass organization on the government's payroll, subordinate to the CCP. A new term, *GONGO*—government organized non-governmental organization—legitimized its participation in the NGO Forum, an ironic moment that made NGO a desirable status even in the eyes of a worried Chinese government. In any case, the monopoly of the ACWF in leading a Chinese women's liberation movement was deconstructed by the rise of feminist NGOs, though the two kinds of organizations worked more in collaboration than in competition in the decade following the FWCW. Two articles published in 2010 presented detailed examinations of the rise of Chinese feminist NGOs in the context of China's hosting of the FWCW.[16] This section highlights a few key features in this cohort of feminist activism from the hindsight of a changed political milieu in 2015.

First, the introduction of a key feminist concept, gender, proved to be enabling and empowering. Gender as a feminist concept was introduced to China by Chinese feminists in diaspora in the process of preparing the FWCW to critically engage with both postsocialist discourse of femininity naturalizing gender hierarchy and a limited Marxist theory of women's liberation unable to explain gendered power relations in all modes of productivity. For this cohort of feminists, who were deeply shaped by the socialist gender discourse of equality between men and women, feminist gender theory provided a powerful critical lens through which to see weaknesses in a state-endorsed and instrumental gender discourse. Li Huiying 李慧英, a leading feminist scholar and activist of the Central Party School, articulated the significance of feminist gender theory for her in these words:

> I think it was a very sad situation in women's pursuit of rights since China's liberation, because women's pursuit of rights has been turned into a means to the end. But now in the concept of gender, the highlighted "rights" are about human autonomy and agency. People should know what rights they have and then should struggle for those rights.[17]

16. Naihua Zhang and Ping-Chun Hsiung, "The Chinese Women's Movement in the Context of Globalization," in *Women's Movements in the Global Era: The Power of Local Feminisms*, ed. Amrita Basu (Boulder: Westview, 2010), 157–92; Wang Zheng and Ying Zhang, "Global Concepts, Local Practices: Chinese Feminism since the Fourth UN Conference on Women," *Feminist Studies* 36, no. 1 (2010): 40–70.

17. Li's interview transcript and video can be accessed on the China site of the University of Michigan's Global Feminisms Project, an online archive of interviews of feminist activists from around the world: https://sites.lsa.umich.edu/global feminisms/interviews/china/china-interviews/. Li Huiying, ed., *Shehui Xingbie yu Gonggong Zhengce* 社会性别与公共政策 (Gender and Public Policy)(Beijing: Dangdai

The attraction of gender, rendered in Chinese as *shehui xingbie* (社会性别, "social sex"), in Li's emphasis, lies in an empowering notion that women should and can control their own destiny without subjecting themselves to the demands of a patriarchal state. The concept of rights is deployed here to demand citizens' rights against an authoritarian state. For this cohort of urban-educated women, liberation had been defined for them by the socialist state. In the 1990s gender theory that emphasized women's agency and explicated gendered power relations and structures illuminated the limitations and constraints of that liberation. It brought about a sort of consciousness-raising for these urban feminists, who began to see the potential of exercising citizen's rights to demand gender equality beyond statist definitions. The expression of citizens' agency, which had been amply demonstrated since the 1980s and brutally suppressed in 1989, now found a vehicle in a timely and legitimate notion of NGOs backed by the FWCW.

Second, the decade after the FWCW witnessed Chinese feminists' innovations in widely circulating the Platform for Action, the Beijing Declaration, and the Convention on the Elimination of Discrimination against Women (CEDAW, which the Chinese government signed in 1980) to hold the government accountable, and in translating global feminist concepts to local practices. They initiated programs to address a wide range of issues, such as domestic violence, gender and development, feminist curricular transformation in higher education, legal aid for women, rural women's political participation, sex ratio imbalances, vocational training for rural women and unemployed urban women, and cultural productions that challenged sexist sexual norms, such as the staging of a Chinese version of *The Vagina Monologues*. Among all kinds of feminist activities, a creative form of gender training was widely adopted.

Utilizing the UN agenda of mainstreaming gender as the basis for legitimate feminist actions, Chinese feminists promoted gender

zhongguo chubanshe, 2002), was the first publication on public policy in China adopting gender as an analytical framework.

training as an important mechanism of social and cultural transformation. Various feminist NGOs conducted gender-training workshops as an integral part of their feminist projects, on themes such as
combating domestic violence, gender and development, and women's
psychological counseling hotlines, to enhance all the participants'
gender sensitivity. The workshops were also offered to various levels of government officials whose responsibilities related to women's
interests. In the context of a rising neoliberal discourse in China since
the 1980s, and when the state collaborated with the intellectual elite
to make a Marxist concept of class a taboo subject in the process of
China's turning into a global sweatshop, promulgating the concept of
gender equality as a mandate from the UN was also a feminist strategy
to uphold social justice as a legitimate goal to pursue, and to hold the
state accountable for its verbal commitment to equality between men
and women.

The third feature most saliently demonstrates the specificity of
Chinese feminism: the collaborative relationship between the Wom-
en's Federations at different levels and feminist NGOs in diverse locations. Instead of drawing a distinct divide between the two kinds
of organizations, feminists from both the Women's Federation and
NGOs often participated in the same projects initiated by NGOs.
And in some cases, feminists in the Women's Federation even organized NGOs when they felt constrained and limited by the official
women's organization.[18] Feminist NGO organizers and feminists
in the Women's Federation were mostly in the same cohort, shaped
by the same socialist ideology and practices of women's liberation.
Moreover, feminists who organized NGOs were, in most cases, respectable academics in universities and academies of social sciences,
all run by the government. Members of the two groups thus were
from not only the same cohort but also the same urban elite class

18. See the University of Michigan's Global Feminisms Project, interviews of
Gao Xiaoxian 高小贤 and Wang Cuiyu 王翠玉.

and enjoyed social prestige and resources due to their positions in the state system.

Fundamentally the collaborative relationship was conditioned on the ACWF's switch from their target constituency, women of lower classes—the masses—in the socialist period to an orientation toward urban professionals in the context of class realignment and social reconfiguration mandated by the state as it merged with global capitalism. Urban professionals' expertise was eagerly sought after in the rising discourse of a scientific modernity in postsocialist China. NGO feminists' scholarly titles allowed them to present themselves as experts to state officials, including the Women's Federation system. NGO feminist organizers who were consciously maintaining an independent position in terms of initiating and managing feminist projects nevertheless needed the vast institutional reach of the Women's Federations at six administrative levels, as well as the official status the Women's Federation offered to effectively promote feminist issues and influence policy making.

The unique collaboration allowed effective feminist intervention in state processes, or to use a less sensitive term, "implementation of gender mainstreaming," in the context of increasing state monitoring of NGO activism. Many issues identified and advocated by feminist NGOs have been incorporated by different levels and regions of the government, and have even entered legislation. Chinese feminists had no leverage to stem the state's merge with global capitalism, which has resulted in officials' massive profiteering from their power to dispose of public assets and regulate the labor of the lower classes, and thus has increased gender gaps as well as class polarization. However, feminists have forged ahead with diverse programs, ranging from legislating against domestic violence and promoting rural women's participation in village management, to transformation of patrilocal marriage systems and land distribution policies to raise rural women's status in villages and change patriarchal cultural norms of son preference. The ACWF also promoted the Reproductive Security Fund at the municipal government level to mitigate the severe impacts on urban women workers of eliminating socialist benefits for women's reproductive work that had previously been guaranteed by state-owned enterprises. The momentous success of this collaboration between feminists in and outside the official system is China's first anti–domestic violence law, passed on December 27, 2015, after two decades of persistent feminist struggles following the FWCW.

Feminist actions and accomplishments have been quite impressive, but they were mostly known only within Chinese feminist circles. The goal of affecting policy making and intervening in government agenda setting in the context of the Chinese political system requires the strategy that socialist state feminists had long adopted: maneuvering behind the scenes and using personal networks and institutional resources. Friends, colleagues, relatives, and classmates positioned in powerful posts can all be accessed for a particular project in a society whose operation heavily relies on the lubricant of personal ties. In this sense, this cohort of feminist leaders of either NGOs or Women's Federations also has acted as lobbyists who absolutely have no intention to publicize their crucial maneuvers. Keeping a low profile is in the best interest of the cause they fight for.

The legitimate concern about the effectiveness of their operations via state power could also become a source of self-censorship, however. This cohort's conscious subversive feminist actions have made them very sensitive to the political parameters set by the state, which paradoxically place them under the influence of a state constantly monitoring NGOs. The state's punishment of the very few feminists who dared to openly raise a dissenting voice and work on taboo issues forcefully demarcated a forbidden zone: issues related to so-called national security, such as labor organizing, ethnic conflicts, and violation of citizens' rights in any form by any government branch. One prominent case is that of feminist literary scholar Ai Xiaoming 艾晓明 of Zhongshan University, who bravely made documentary films recording struggles of village women and men against corrupt officials, rural victims of HIV-contaminated blood in the so-called plasma economy promoted by provincial governments, the injustice of a court ruling in a date rape case, and so on.[19] Her actions, which crossed the line of an exclusive focus on less risky "women's issues," resulted in the discipline of the state in the form of her forced early retirement and nonrenewal of her passport. The personal price is high if one dares to defy the authoritarian state, which has been increasingly corrupt and coercive in the two decades following the FWCW.

The political context has thus served as a critical factor in feminists' choices of what actions to take and what strategies to adopt; it also limits what may be accomplished. The constraints of the context also largely explain this cohort's preoccupation with the feminist concept of gender. Legitimized by the UN mandate, gender has been carved out as a relatively safe zone for feminists to pursue social justice and equality without an open challenge against multiple systems of oppression in the process of a repressive state capitalism. Gender mainstreaming is a circumscribed feminist agenda in comparison to the vision of this cohort's revolutionary foremothers, who pursued women's thorough liberation via political, economic, cultural, and social structural changes. It nevertheless has quietly created new areas of feminist intervention that their foremothers did not envision or where they were unable to intervene. Last but not least, this cohort's tremendous efforts in gender training, especially their efforts to develop women's and gender studies curricula in higher education and to promote feminist knowledge production, have inserted a critical feminist discourse into contemporary China's media and knowledge production, otherwise dominated by blatant sexism and neoliberalism. Such discursive endeavors have paved the way for the rise of a younger generation of daring feminists who reject the ambiguous term *nüxing zhuyi* (女性主义 feminine-ism) and openly embrace *nüquan zhuyi* (女权主义 women's rights/power-ism), a Chinese rendition of feminism shunned

---

19. See the University of Michigan's Global Feminisms Project, interview with Ai Xiaoming; and her documentaries *Taishi Village*, *Stories of the Plain*, and *The Heavenly Garden*.

by mainstream society for its emphasis on women's demand for both rights and power.

New Style of Feminist Actions of Young Feminists

In the second decade following the FWCW, the dynamics in the field of Chinese feminist struggles changed again due to drastic shifts in China's social and economic transformations, as well as its political environment. The feminist pioneers who formed NGOs with the opportunity of the FWCW inspired other groups to follow suit in establishing issue-oriented NGOs nationwide. The rapid growth of various NGOs with massive financial support from diverse international donors alarmed the CCP, which was insecure about its rule and was confronting increasing class and ethnic conflicts domestically and the impact of color revolutions globally. A decade after the NGO Forum hosted in China, the CCP started to tighten up its monitoring and regulation of Chinese NGOs and to restrict their international funding sources, as well as to subvert and co-opt Chinese NGOs.

At the same time, a younger generation of feminists emerged on the stage of social activism, disregarding the tightening political control. Many of the students of the first cohort of feminist NGO leaders, now situated in various urban professions, including universities, the media, and Women's Federations, carried on feminist struggles in new forms and styles. This cohort of feminists in their late thirties to early forties was joined by an even younger group of feminists who were recent college graduates in their twenties. One commonality across the age groups is that they had grown up in postsocialist China, when socialist institutional mechanisms such as equal employment and guaranteed equal pay, along with a position in public enterprises, were largely dismantled in the process of privatization and marketization. In tandem with institutional changes, the socialist gender discourse of equality between men and women was by the 1990s already overshadowed by a discourse of gender differentiation that celebrated a "natural femininity" attained by "modern" consumption of feminine products and by resumption of the traditional role of a virtuous mother and good wife, and a hegemonic masculinity embodied in "successful" men who possess power, wealth, and women. The strong attraction of these young, educated women to feminism is not accidental in a particularly limiting and blatantly sexist political culture.

A demographic factor in combination with China's drastic economic development has made way for the rise of these young feminists. The one-child policy since 1979 resulted in an unprecedented number of single daughters (the lucky ones who were not aborted) who enjoyed all the resources their families from both parents' sides could afford for their education and personal development. The coming of age of these "little princesses" coincided with China's huge expansion of college education, which tapped the educational market on the basis of an expanding middle class.[20] As a result, the proportion of female college students rapidly rose from about 37 percent before 1999 to 51.03 percent in 2012, and the proportion of female Master's degree holders rose to 51.46 percent in 2012.[21]

This college sex ratio, which indicates an opposite trend to the skewed sex ratio in the population, demonstrates female students' superb academic performance, since each applicant has to pass national college entrance examinations to be accepted by various universities according to their test scores. The gender of applicants whose test scores rank among the top regardless of discipline and location has also shown a continuous change, with the male top testers declining

20. College enrollment in China jumped from 2.28 million in 1978 to 29.07 million in 2008. *Xin Zhongguo Liushinian Jiaoyu Chengjiu Zhan* 新中国六十年教育成就展 (An Exhibit of the Accomplishments of Education in the Sixty-Years of the New China), China Education Statistics, www.stats.edu.cn/tjdt/60/新中国60年教育成就展.htm.

21. Zhang Lin 张琳 and Cai Yunqi 蔡蕴琦, "Guanzhu Daxuesheng Xingbiebi: Dushu Nüsheng Youxiu Gongzuo Nan Lingdao Duo" 关注大学生性别比: 读书女生优秀工作男领导多 (Pay Attention to the Sex Ratio of College Students: More Excellent Female Students in School but More Male Leaders in Workplace), *Yangzi wanbao*, September 12, 2012.

from 66.2 percent in 1999 to 39.7 percent in 2008.[22] The consistent high performance of female students has led to an outcry in male-dominated media about *yinsheng yangshuai* 阴盛阳衰—a so-called gender imbalance with a flourishing female (*yin* 阴) and declining male (*yang* 阳). Many universities have adopted discriminatory admission policies that set a higher score for female students to be considered, on the grounds that many more enterprises would like to accept male graduates rather than female graduates. Indeed, blatant gender discrimination in employment has been a well-known reality since the economic reform, and even many government branches have jumped on the bandwagon of posting only male-wanted job advertisements.

A large cohort of well-educated young women from diverse social and economic backgrounds with high aspirations for themselves as well as high expectations from their families, contradictorily, has encountered excessive gender discrimination and pervasive masculinist sexual norms that openly treat women as sex objects and secondary citizens. Inspired by feminism, young women nevertheless have few social resources to make their voices heard, let alone to participate in the policy-making process, as the feminists of older cohorts have been able to. As a feminist organizer of this young cohort commented on the feminist strategy of the second cohort working quietly with and within the official system to generate policy changes, "Their experience is very difficult to replicate. At the time of the FWCW they usually already had some managerial positions in the official system, and they had a circle of friends who were in the decision-making or advisory positions. These factors have served as the lubricant between their NGO programs and the government."[23] It is a sober assessment

22. Liu Bohong 刘伯红 and Li Yani 李亚妮, "Zhongguo Gaodeng Jiaoyu zhong de Shehuixingbie Xianshi" 中国高等教育中的社会性别现实 (A Gendered Reality in China's Higher Education), *Yunnan minzu daxue xuebao* 1, no. 28 (January 2011): 55–64.

23. Li Sipan 李思磐, "Zhongguo Ban Nüquan Zhuyi: Qimeng dao Zijue" 中国版女权主义: 启蒙到自觉 (Chinese Version of Feminism: From Enlightenment to Self-Consciousness), Weibo, February 12, 2015, https://weibo.com/p/100160380885 8006020709.

of the relative deprivation of young urban educated women's social, economic, and political power vis-à-vis that of the cohort who grew up in the socialist period.

Where to find new resources for feminist activism? What forms of action are viable for the young feminists who have hardly any ties with those who have power in the official system? It turns out that social and economic marginality does not necessarily disempower the young educated urban feminists who have been brought up in the age of cyberspace and of new conceptual frameworks circulating globally. The young feminists quickly identified a powerful medium for feminist engagement: the Internet. And because they are not embedded in the official system and have no constraining considerations associated with those who have some social status, they are far less restricted in conceptualizing the possibilities of their actions. As a result, we have witnessed many innovative actions initiated by young feminists who have nothing to lose.

Most prominent among those who engaged in online feminist organizing in the second decade following the FWCW were Feminist Voice in Beijing and New Media Women's Network in Guangzhou. Feminist Voice was an offshoot of Women's Media Monitor Network, a feminist NGO in Beijing founded in 1999. Led by Lü Pin 吕频, who quit her job at the ACWF's newspaper to become a freelance writer to enact her vision of autonomous feminism, Feminist Voice formed a loosely connected feminist network via its website and its electronic journal, which circulated via email. It attracted young feminists who had neither prestigious social status nor available social resources, but who nevertheless possessed abundant imagination and creativity. A loose coalition of young feminists all over the country named Young Feminist Activism (YFA), working closely with Feminist Voice, operated vigorously via website, email, Weibo 微博, and WeChat, with provocative topics and self-initiated actions. Because their intention was to call public attention to violations of women's rights in all aspects of Chinese society as a way to engender feminist social and cultural transformation, they deliberately created shocking images in public spaces and then took photos of their actions to circulate online. Their strategy drastically departed from those of the older cohort of feminist NGO leaders, who were good at maneuvering behind the scenes and inconspicuously running gender training workshops indoors. Visuality became a crucial method for these younger feminists to enable visibility of many unseen and untold violations of women's rights.

A group of Shanghai feminists in 2012 innovatively staged a performance action, first in a Shanghai subway station, with signs saying "I can be slutty, yet you can't harass me" to protest sexual harassment on public transportation. It became an instant social media sensation when photos of a couple of feminists in action were uploaded online. Inspired by the success of the pioneering operation, which did not require many resources yet reached a huge audience with a provocative feminist message via the Internet, the YFA members who were affiliated with Feminist Voice began to stage a range of public performance actions that successfully attracted public attention. They occupied men's rooms in public to demand gender equity in the design of public bathrooms; they shaved their heads to protest gender discrimination in college admissions; they adorned themselves in "blood"-stained white wedding gowns in public to protest domestic violence and posted topless photos online collectively, inscribing anti–domestic violence slogans on their bodies; they launched a feminist cross-country walk to circulate feminist messages; and engaged in many more such creatively eye-catching actions. As the introduction to the YFA photo exhibition in New York City in the fall of 2015 states, "These young people are full of inspiration, talent and bravery at the intersectional space of art, body politics and social movement. Feminism has no doubt become the fountain of their wisdom."[24]

The YFA's most influential performance action took place on March 7, 2015, with the "assistance" of the police, who detained five

24. *Above Ground: Forty Moments of Transformation: A Photography Exhibition of Young Feminist Activism in China*, New York City, September 23–27, 2015. The exhibition was organized by YFA to parallel the UN Global Summit of Women.

young activists preparing to post anti–sexual harassment stickers on public transportation in multiple cities as part of their activities to commemorate International Women's Day. The detention of the Chinese Feminist Five at the moment when global feminists launched Beijing+20 to evaluate feminist progress since 1995 galvanized a global mobilization. Feminists in many countries staged protests, and over 2 million people from all over the world signed the online petitions demanding their release. Chinese feminist activism entered the global spotlight.

Domestically, the detention of the Feminist Five epitomizes the tightening political control of social movements by the state, marking a new era in which NGO feminist activism no longer enjoys a special safe zone in comparison to other social movements that have long been under the state surveillance and suppression. The logic of state control is manifested clearly in the bizarre detention of young feminists: any coordinated and organized activities simultaneously happening in multiple locations indicate the existence of or potential for a cross-regional organization, which has to be crushed regardless of its legitimate agenda of protecting women's rights. In the following years YFA-organized activism was seriously curtailed, and their strategy of pursuing visibility with performance actions is unlikely to continue as police effectively close any public spaces for such actions, especially by activists who are already tightly monitored. At the same time, many more young women demonstrate their enhanced interest in feminism by spontaneously joining online discussions of gender issues to promulgate and expand a feminist discourse via the Internet. The term *nüquan zhuyi* (women's rights/power-ism), unambiguously embraced by this cohort of feminists, is gaining increasing purchase among the young generation while the security system and cyber police are rapidly increasing the scope of their surveillance.

The New Media Women's Network in Guangzhou was initiated and led by journalist Li Sipan 李思磐 and sustained by a core group of young professionals and faculty members in universities in Guangzhou, many of whom had been active participants in feminist programs organized by Ai Xiaoming before her forced retirement. The location of Guangzhou was congenial to social activism, as it is adjacent to Hong Kong. Ideas and resources for civil society frequently flowed from Hong Kong to Guangzhou via various channels.[25]

The New Media Women's Network creatively launched colorful public activities such as public lectures and art exhibitions, as well as online feminist activism. One of the most prominent cases initiated by this group was the anti–sexual harassment campaign in higher education in China in 2014. The group succeeded in collecting about 260 signatures from Chinese professors and scholars transnationally on two petitions: one to the Ministry of Education demanding the implementation of anti–sexual harassment mechanisms in Chinese universities, and one to the president of Xiamen University demanding due punishment of a professor's systematic sexual harassment of his female graduate students. All the transnational mobilization was accomplished via email and WeChat, with the active participation of the YFA, as well as older feminists situated in academic institutions. The widely circulated petitions resulted in the temporary removal of the male professor from his teaching post at Xiamen University (a mild punishment that was unsatisfactory to feminists and his victimized students), and the Ministry of Education's regulation to forbid sexual harassment at universities—a regulation that at this writing remains only on paper without enforcement mechanisms).

Another influential action by the New Media Women's Network was the massive online discussion on the meaning of International Women's Day launched by Li Sipan in a blog post a few days before International Women's Day in 2016. By March 8 it had received 101 million visits: thousands of young people joined the public discussion on how to continue a feminist heritage, join global feminist struggles, and resist capitalist consumerist cooptation of a feminist event as a way to commemorate International Women's Day. Feminism, *nüquan*

---

25. The eruption of Hong Kong's Umbrella Movement in 2014—that is, citizens' protests against the CCP's encroachment on Hong Kong's civil rights— reversed the situation. NGOs in Guangzhou have since been tightly monitored to prevent the impact of Hong Kong's civil society from reaching the mainland.

zhuyi, has never received such massive public attention in China. The Feminist Five and many more people from the YFA also actively participated in the celebration and debates online and even recirculated the anti–sexual harassment stickers that had been evidence of their "crimes" a year before. This huge success of cyber action demonstrates the existence of a rapidly expanding social force that is eager to be informed of feminist heritage, as well as to get involved in feminist actions.

As the Guangdong area has been a center of manufacture for global markets, concentrating tens of millions of migrant workers, feminists in Guangzhou have developed contacts with women workers organizations in recent years, turning increasing attention to the intersection of class and gender. The efforts of young, urban, educated feminists to seek coalition with a more marginalized social group, with full knowledge of the politically sensitive nature of their action, indicate their conscious challenge of political boundaries with an expanding feminist vision. In their online communications, these college-educated young feminists, fluent in English, frequently demonstrate their familiarity with current transnational feminist issues, as well as feminist critiques of capitalist globalization. The critical concept of class has been consciously deployed by this cohort in their articles circulated via WeChat, analyzing migrant women workers' marginality and their predicament, conditioned by both gender and class power relations in today's China. The concept also featured prominently in the online discussion on International Women's Day.

Finally, the most prominent feature distinguishing this young cohort from the previous two cohorts of Chinese feminists examined in this piece is their open defiance of heterosexual normativity. Unlike older feminists who generally avoid open discussion of sexuality (with the exception of Ai Xiaoming, who pioneered the Chinese version of *The Vagina Monologues*, which challenged the taboo of Chinese women's open discussion and display of sexuality), the young cohort displays their diverse sexuality with ease and deeply analyzes the oppressive nature of compulsory heterosexuality. Some young feminists are also active members of gay and lesbian organizations. The determined break from the grip of dominant heterosexual normativity is often inseparable from the empowerment of these courageous young women's and men's exposure to feminism, and embracing a feminist activist identity seems logical to many of them. They are not afraid of being singled out as a minority, sexually or politically, in a largely conformist society. Any individual challenge against homophobia or discrimination based on sexuality receives strong support from this young cohort of feminists.

Though this section presents Feminist Voice and the New Media Women's Network as two cases of autonomous feminist NGOs operated by post-FWCW feminists, the feminist activities of the young generation, whether collectively organized or individually spontaneous, whether covert or overt, are certainly not centered around these two organizations, but rather dispersed on and off the Internet in many sites that defy state surveillance. The emergence of a decentered Chinese #MeToo movement in 2018 may best illustrate how feminist energy has been continuously manifested in ways unexpected by the national security system.

Anti–Sexual Harassment: A Feminist Rallying Point

China's merge with global capitalism has witnessed the rise of a hegemonic and toxic masculinity embodied in "successful men" who flaunt their wealth, power, fame, and possession of young women. Powerful men preying on young female subordinates in all walks of life has become such a prevalent practice that a neologism has long been in public circulation: *the hidden rule* (*qian guize* 潜规则)—that is, young female subordinates, whether in the workplace or educational institutions, are expected to provide sexual service to their male superiors. Understandably many powerless young women have complied unwillingly, and many others have bravely resisted, often bearing painful consequences. In either case the stories would be hidden as a function of the hidden rule.

The earliest media report on a case of brave resistance was the 2009 incident of Deng Yujiao 邓玉娇, a twenty-one-year-old woman working in a public bath center as a pedicurist.[26] In self-defense against attempted rape by a local official client, Deng stabbed him, and this resulted in his death. Deng was arrested but later released after a public uproar on the Internet from people who were enraged about the rampant corruption of government officials. Many men joined the condemnation of the official's sexual assault, and some male lawyers volunteered to provide legal defense to Deng, who, in much of the publicity online, was praised as a heroine who dared to fight against officials to defend her "purity"—that is, her chastity. A few feminists from the Chinese Women's University in Beijing staged a performance action in public to express their support of Deng's resistance and their protest against sexual violence in society.

In 2013 another case of sexual violence enraged the public. A school principal in Haining county, Hainan province, pimped fifth grade girls to local officials who were looking for virgins, and no legal action was taken against them before feminist interventions. Ye Hai-yan, a renowned feminist activist, and Wang Yu, a renowned feminist lawyer, together with four other feminists went to Haining to stage a public protest, demanding legal action against the perpetrators. The photo of Ye Haiyan holding a sign saying, "HEY PRINCIPAL: GET A ROOM WITH ME AND LEAVE THE KIDS ALONE!" went viral online. While school children were too powerless to fight against sexual violence, feminists' heroic struggles in this case gained huge public support, but the effort did not end well. Ye Haiyan was detained and then police harassed her and chased her out of each location where she tried to stay. She had to return to her rural hometown as a result of state persecution because of her feminist action.[27]

---

26. "Deng Yujiao Incident," https://en.wikipedia.org/wiki/Deng_Yujiao_incident.

27. The protest of sexual violence against schoolgirls by Ye and other feminist activists, as well as subsequent police persecution, were recorded and brilliantly represented by film producer Wang Nanfu in her documentary *Hooligan Sparrow* (2016). The feminist lawyer Wang Yu was arrested in the police roundup of over a hundred lawyers nationwide in China on July 9, 2015.

In 2014, when the serial sexual harassment committed by a professor at Xiamen University was exposed via the Internet, the public indignation was mostly expressed by a female audience, and feminists responded strongly with collective actions nationwide and transnationally. By this time the hidden rule had obviously been practiced so widely in the educational system that university administrators did not bother to punish the famous professor, who amassed a huge amount of academic resources, and few men publicly condemned him. Treating young women as their trophies is no longer a corrupt practice confined to the government officials but is now an assumed sexual privilege sought after by many men with some sort of power in all walks of life.

Living with such oppressive masculinist sexual norms, many young women are frustrated, outraged, and eager for action. Wei Tingting, one of the Feminist Five, and her friends conducted a large-scale survey of sexual harassment in higher education in 2016 as a way to raise public awareness of the prevalence of the problem. He Xi, a student at Xi'an Foreign Languages Institute, wrote a letter in 2017 to the president of the school to request that institutional mechanisms be set up to combat sexual harassment. Huang Xueqin, a young journalist, began an online survey of sexual harassment in the media workplace via her WeChat account ATSH in 2017.[28] And in the summer of 2017 leading feminists of two generations gathered in Shanghai for a workshop on how to coordinate feminist efforts for concerted anti–sexual harassment activities.

In the deteriorating political environment, anti–sexual harassment efforts in higher education and the workplace were identified as a relatively low-risk issue for feminist action, though the feminist workshop

---

28. For feminist anti–sexual harassment activities, see 女权学论 Nüquan Xue-Lun, "Zhongguo Mitu Yundong Tuishou Huang Xueqin Zao Juliu" 中国米兔运动推手黄雪琴遭拘留 (Huang Xueqin, Leader in the Chinese #MeToo Movement, Was Detained). www.chinesefeminism.org, November 11, 2019.

was organized confidentially to avoid police attention.[29] Back in May 2017 Song Xiuyan, the Party secretary of the ACWF, in her talk to Women's Federation officials, claimed that "feminism" (女权主义) was promoted by "Western hostile forces," openly invoking a Maoist class-struggle scheme that cancelled the legitimacy of feminism in official discourse.[30] The blatant reversal of the ACWF's congenial relationship with NGO feminists since the FWCW signifies the further encroachment on the official system by national security's new definition of feminism as a social movement instigated by hostile foreign forces to subvert the Chinese state. Feminists at the workshop were fully aware of the drastically changed political climate for feminist activism.

Still, an massive outburst of feminist mobilization against sexual harassment emerged at the beginning of 2018. Luo Xixi, who works in the United States but was once a graduate student at Beijing University of Aeronautics and Astronautics, reached out to Huang Xueqin after observing her online activities against sexual harassment in the media. Inspired by the ongoing #MeToo movement in the United States, Luo decided to expose her former professor Chen Xiaowu, who had sexually harassed her years before and has been continually harassing his current graduate students. Luo had written to the administrator of the university but to no avail. Now Huang, a seasoned journalist, worked with Luo to launch a powerful public exposé via the Internet, openly charging Chen Xiaowu, using Luo Xixi's real name and related evidence, on the New Year of 2018. The first-person exposé became an instant hit on the Internet, and feminists from diverse locations and organizations immediately recognized its significance.

29. The organizers of and participants in this workshop are not revealed here for the sake of their safety.

30. Song Xiuyan 宋秀岩, "Ba Jiang Zhengzhi Guanchuan yu Fulian Gaige he Gongzuo Quan Guocheng" 把讲政治贯穿于妇联改革和工作全过程 (Raising Political Awareness in the Entire Process of the Reform and Work of the Women's Federation System), People.cn, May 19, 2017, http://fj.people.com.cn/n2/2017/0519/c181466-30211002.html, accessed June 26, 2020.

In the following days organized petitions and spontaneous support surged both on social media and in the official media as many young women journalists decided to join the fight. Feminists from the summer workshop of 2017 coordinated to circulate online a petition template to university administrators. To protect current students from retaliation, alumni were contacted to sign petitions to nearly a hundred universities, demanding that mechanisms be set up to combat sexual harassment. Inspired by Luo's example, one young woman after another came out to expose professors and supervisors at diverse workplaces, ranging from universities and the state-run CCTV to NGOs, breaking the cultural taboo of shame that had long been internalized by survivors of sexual violence and sexual harassment. Young women began to adopt a Chinese phonetic transliteration of #MeToo (米兔) to name the ongoing anti–sexual harassment movement in China.

Understandably such large-scale agitation could not escape attention and action from the national security system. Orders to ban reporting on #MeToo in the official media took effect quickly, while cyber police began franticly deleting such content from social media, including WeChat. In the tidal wave of state censorship, Feminist Voice became collateral damage, with its Weibo account shut down permanently. Those in charge of monitoring social movements could not comprehend the decentered and dispersed nature of the surge of feminist activities. They had to punish some organization for its imagined leading role behind the scenes. When various feminist online accounts continued to circulate #MeToo-related information, cyber police moved on to closing down many more Weibo and WeChat accounts and intimidating prominent activists by "treating them to tea," a euphemism referring to police interrogations of activists without due legal procedure. As state suppression intensified, feminists explored diverse means to maintain the momentum of the #MeToo movement. Some sent letters to government officials and legislators; others provided legal support or psychological counseling to survivors of sexual harassment.

While the police accelerated their surveillance, various local governments and various branches of the central government began to respond to the wave of the #MeToo movement. Hangzhou's municipal government was the first to require universities to set up policies dealing with sexual harassment in August 2018. The Ministry of Education followed the trend in November, issuing regulations that included rules against sexual harassment. A proposal to revise the Civil Code in November 2018 included rules against sexual harassment that eventually became the 1010 clause in the Civil Code, which was passed by the People's Congress on May 28, 2020.[31] Besides defining various acts of sexual harassment as illegal, the clause specifies the legal responsibilities of any institution in which sexual harassment occurs. These responsive changes in policy and law indicate feminist operations within the official system, though how to implement the new regulations and law on the ground remains a huge challenge for feminists in and outside the official system.

Conclusion

In 2013, at a meeting with the ACWF leading body, president Xi Jinping instructed: "Special attention should be paid to women's unique role in propagating Chinese family virtues and setting up a good family tradition. This relates to harmony in the family and in society and to the healthy development of children. Women should consciously shoulder the responsibilities of taking care of the old and young, as well as educating children."[32] Emphasizing traditional familial roles

31. On the legal significance of the clause for anti–sexual harassment in the Civil Code, see Wen Juping 温举平, "Minfadian Jiedu: Qiye Ruhe Yingdui Xing-saorao Dailai de Falü Fengxian" 民法典解读: 企业如何应对性骚扰带来的法律风险 (Interpreting the Civil Code: How Can Enterprises Deal with the Legal Risk Caused by Sexual Harassment Cases), Deheng lüshi shiwusuo, May 29, 2020, www.dhl.com .cn/CN/tansuocontent/0008/018697/7.aspx?MID=0902.

32. Xi Jinping 习近平, "Jianchi Nannü Pingdeng Jiben Guoce, Fahui Woguo Funü Weida Zuoyong" 坚持男女平等基本国策, 发挥我国妇女伟大作用 (Upholding the

for women articulates both a masculinist imperative to restore China's presocialist gender order and an increasing social crisis since the state has shed its responsibilities for the care of children, the old, and the sick. The privatization of reproductive labor and the recent population policy that switches from one child to two children added new fuel to the fundamentalist neo-Confucian agitation for reviving patriarchal order, making gender contentions ever more ferocious.

Chinese feminist activists are confronting grave challenges as the male-dominated authoritarian state is turning openly conservative in its gender policy and further tightening its political control of any social activism. With the ominous state narrative claiming that feminist activism is instigated by hostile foreign forces, autonomous feminist NGOs are not only demonized but also delegitimized, a huge regression from the FWCW, when Chinese feminists of the second cohort gained political legitimacy for organizing. Curtailment of domestic NGOs has taken place simultaneously with drastic measures of restricting international donors' support of Chinese NGOs. Thus the resource-poor young feminists confront not only political perils but also financial predicaments for organized activities. Most seriously, the police have also accelerated their control of cyberspace with rapidly advanced high-tech. State censorship is a daily experience for Chinese netizens, when the cyber police constantly delete texts circulating online or via WeChat, or shut down websites. The very space and means of young feminist activism are under the omnipresent surveillance of the police.

Paradoxically, the phrase *equality between men and women*, a legacy of the first cohort of state feminism, remains on the ACWF agenda as well as in state discourse. Not only did Xi Jinping pledge the Chinese government's commitment to equality between men and women at the September 2015 Global Summit of Women, in ACWF leader Song Xiuyan's 2017 talk that condemned feminism, she simultaneously

---

Fundamental State Policy of Gender Equity, Exerting Women's Great Role in Our Country), Xinhua net, October 31, 2013.

claimed to uphold the "fundamental state policy of equality between men and women." Logical consistency has never been a concern of the CCP, but taming social groups that are not immediately under its control has become a top priority in its agenda of "protecting stability" (*weiwen* 维稳), especially in the era of Xi Jinping. The discursive fissures and contradictions can continue to be strategically used by feminists in and outside the official system; that is to say, spaces for feminist actions are not entirely sealed, though the format and content of feminist actions are closely monitored. The effects of operating in a virtual panopticon are serious perils for the development of Chinese feminism.

As we enter the third decade of the twenty-first century, substantial changes in the social setting and political environment have profoundly affected Chinese feminist practices. The ACWF has long lost its first cohort of revolutionary feminist leaders; the second cohort of feminist officials fostered in the socialist period with a commitment to women's liberation is mostly retired; and the women's organization has become part of the state bureaucracy, with officials who generally have less commitment to gender equality than interest in career advancement. While conscious feminists still operate in the official system here and there, institutional constraints often seriously limit their capacity for feminist initiatives.

With neither state power nor ties to those with official power, and with the tightening up of cyber space, the disadvantaged young cohort of feminists nonetheless has access to a crucial power: a critical mass of young women who are increasingly frustrated with gender discrimination and sexual exploitation. As is demonstrated by the sudden surge of the #MeToo movement in 2018, which resulted in both severe suppression by the police and positive changes in government policies and law, feminist organizing around young women's interests is not only feasible but necessary, though such activism has to try to avoid the radar of the police. Diverse and geographically dispersed young feminist groups are continuously operating, mostly within the confines of today's political parameters. If we believe that the current political climate would not remain stable forever, then we have reason to predict that it is only a matter of time before the next burst of concerted feminist interventions pushes political and cultural boundaries. The depth and scope of the next feminist surge by young women, however, will depend on conscious reflections and evaluations of the effects of state censorship and surveillance on individual feminists so as to enable them to explore new areas for feminist breakthrough. Such efforts are beginning to emerge in an otherwise gloomy time.[33]

33. A group of feminists situated in diverse geographic locations hosted an online workshop titled "(Self-)Censorship, Social Activism, and Chinese Feminist Scholarship" on July 10, 2020, exploring constraints on the development of Chinese feminism.

6

Why Don't Mainland Chinese Liberals Support Feminism?

Li Jun (aka Li Sipan)
Translated by Ping Zhu and Tera Mills

In November 2012 a commentary appeared in the *Southern Metropolis Daily* (*Nanfang dushi bao* 南方都市报) in response to a proposal by EU Justice Commissioner Viviane Reding to impose gender quotas on listed companies. The first three-quarters of this commentary recounts divergences in legislation, the views of both sides, and the history of the policy. The author reveals his opinion only at the end of the article: "As for myself, I seem to prefer a passive legal view. In my opinion, individual freedom is the most important of all rights. New morals and values are only effective and worth pursuing when they are chosen by a society."[1] Although proposals and voting are themselves

I would like to thank the many teachers and friends who provided valuable editorial advice, specifically Wang Zheng, Shen Rui, Song Shaopeng, Zhang Nian, Chow Po Chung, Dong Yige, Chien Yeong-Shyang, and Li Lin, the editor of *Sixiang* 思想 (Reflection), where this article was originally published in Chinese in 2013.

1. Chen Jibing 陈季冰, "Oumeng Guiding Gongsi Nüxing Dongshi Bili Xingdetong ma?" 欧盟规定公司女性董事比例行得通吗? (Is the EU's Regulation of the Proportion of Female Directors Feasible?), *Nanfang dushi bao*, November 10, 2012, reposted online as "Duibuqi! Women Buxuyao Zhengfu Zhipai de Nüdongshi" 对不起! 我们不需要政府指派的女董事 (Sorry, but We Don't Need Government-Appointed Female Directors).

part of the process of social choice, here the author seems to imply that gender equality cannot be a spontaneous choice of a society.

This commentary was published online with the title "Sorry, but We Don't Need Government-Appointed Female Directors" (here the idea of legislated regulations is replaced with government appointments). The article even asserts that "legislation dealing with this problem [promoting gender equality] can endlessly segment, eventually stripping away most of people's freedom."[2]

I use this example to show the relationship between Chinese liberalism and feminism because this framework of using freedom to oppose equality, of equating equal rights with the expansion of governmental power, is not a singular case. Since the 1990s more and more liberal intellectuals have used "freedom" to oppose equality and antidiscrimination and have refused to promote the public welfare when they participate in public discussions, both in print media and on online platforms.

In all fairness, the author of the above commentary is a male media writer who has maintained a relatively civil demeanor in addressing the subject of gender. There are more concerning examples. In 2005 a prominent city newspaper began to publish an editorial section featuring social commentaries. After it became the most favored platform of liberal intellectuals, it published two commentaries related to gender. The first commentary states that it is not gender discrimination for Peking University to require higher entry scores for women to enter the minority language programs than for men. There are many statements that would worry someone sensitive to issues of gender equality, such as, "If there were only women in foreign affairs, would they be representing a country of women or the country of China?," and "Girls only have high scores because they are good at rote memorization." The other commentary seems to mock the new addition of the anti–sexual harassment law in China's Women's Rights Protection Act as

2. Chen Jibing, "Duibuqi!"

"nonsense."[3] In the summer of 2012, *Southern Metropolis Daily* published Qiu Feng's article about the "Shanghai Metro Line 2 Incident,"[4] titled "Customs Take Priority Over Rights" (*Lisu youxian yu quanli* 礼俗优先于权力), which supports the metro company's request that women "act respectably" in order to avoid sexual harassment.

It is probably unfair to liberal scholars when we use the media's fast-food culture to criticize contemporary Chinese liberalism. However, the surfacing of liberal thought in China in the 1990s was closely related to the reform of Chinese media led by the market. The bias of mainland Chinese liberals is more conspicuous and influential in mass media. I am often confused as to why mainland Chinese liberals believe that human rights should take priority over women's rights, so that feminism is not necessary. Why are they relatively scornful of the values of economic and social equality, believing that freedom and equality are conflicting and cannot coexist (in other words, believing that equality harms freedom, and is "a road leading to enslavement")? Why are mainland Chinese liberals unable to understand the problem of gender inequality, and why do they always stand on the opposing side of this notion?

When Chinese intellectuals adopted Western liberalism, they also accepted the tension that existed between Western liberalism and feminism without question. Chinese male intellectual elites have been benefactors of the dramatic historical changes of China's postsocialist period, but they are not sensitive to their own social position and barely reflect on their gendered privilege. Under the special political

3. See Yan Lieshan 鄢烈山, "Wei Beida Zhaosheng Bianhu: Zhe Bushi Xingbie Qishi" 为北大招生辩护: 这不是性别歧视 (In Defense of Peking University's Student Enrollment: This Is Not Gender Discrimination), *Nanfang dushi bao*, September 1, 2005; Da Shi 大诗, "Wulitou de 'Xingsaorao' Lifa" 无厘头的"性骚扰"立法 (Nonsensical 'Sexual Harassment' Legislation), *Nanfang dushi bao*, September 3, 2005.

4. The Shanghai Metro Line 2 company's official Weibo account posted images of female passengers wearing revealing clothing, and advised that female passengers "act respectably" to avoid sexual harassment.

economic environment, mainland Chinese liberals cling to the pre-set class identification and elitist way of thinking, purposely avoiding issues of social and economic equality, to the point of viewing them as part of the failed socialist experiment or as a proposition of the Left. As a result, the problem of equality, especially in social class and gender, is deliberately shunned by liberals. However, the development of Chinese feminism had its own problems—for example, uncritical cooperation with the state, the depoliticization tendency of feminism and other social movements, and the lack of theoretical discussions with and critiques of other social ideas all led to the alienation of liberalism and feminism.

"Human Rights" and "Women's Rights"

"Human rights are enough, why do we also need to advocate women's rights?"

"Without human rights, how can you have women's rights? You should only strive for women's rights after human rights have been obtained."

"Chinese feminism has already gone overboard."

These are the opinions often expressed by China's liberal scholars in public discussions. These questions suggest two biases. First, Chinese liberals' understanding of human rights is biased. They see human rights as an abstraction that exists only in principle, a homogenous political right often with the prerequisite of democracy; they do not regard human rights as the safeguard of the functioning and capability[5] of individuals to overcome social oppression and discrimination, which means that because every individual exists in different natural conditions and social structures, human rights should provide

---

5. The idea of a "capability approach" is collaboratively put forward by Amartya Sen and Martha Nussbaum and has been put into practice in international development work and human rights activism. See Martha C. Nussbaum, "Human Rights and Human Capabilities," *Harvard Human Rights Journal* 20 (2007): 21.

diverse contents based on the different needs of different individuals and situations. Second, and perhaps even worse, is that in many people's minds the image of a human is still based on the assumption of the propertied male in classical liberalism, while a woman is viewed as a personal and special subject who does not belong in the public sphere (just as Catharine MacKinnon observed: "'a woman' is not yet the name of a way of being human"[6]), who is lacking in importance at the present stage, or who at most is a topic for the second phase of democratization.

The tension between feminism and liberalism is not unique to China. Feminist political philosophers have already raised abundant criticism on topics ranging from methodologies to basic theoretical concepts, such as why the concepts of liberalism, which should be used to defend gender equality, are so often used to oppose feminism.

Despite the complex internal debates, the principal concepts of liberalism are rational and self-interested individuals; autonomous individuals; individualism; guarantees of individual freedom; and the rights to privacy, equality, and social justice. Many of the demands of feminism are inseparable from two fundamental values of liberalism: individual autonomy and equality. The basic institutional design of liberalism has also played a major role in promoting gender equality throughout history (such as basic human rights, the right to political participation, and equal job opportunities). In this sense, liberalism and feminism are not in opposition. Indeed, many feminist scholars believe that the basic values of liberalism are essential to feminism— that is, liberalism and feminism share some basic principles, especially the view that individuals must be liberated from the hierarchy they are born into to become equal and free.[7]

6. Catharine MacKinnon, *Are Women Human?* (Cambridge, MA: Harvard Univ. Press, 2007), 43.

7. Carole Pateman, "Feminist Critiques of the Public/Private Dichotomy," in Pateman, *The Disorder of Women: Democracy, Feminism, and Political Theory* (Cambridge, UK: Polity, 1989), 118.

However, many feminists point out the numerous insufficiencies that exist in liberalism; they constantly debate with liberal thinkers and thus have helped perfect and deepen liberal ideology. First, liberalism divides social life into two distinct spheres, public and private. The public sphere includes politics and the market, and the private sphere includes personal relationships and family. The public sphere is dominated by men, while the private sphere is where individuals assume social and gender identities. Women are oppressed by the patriarchy in the private sphere, and the gendered division of labor in the home directly influences women's capability to invest in societal work. At this time liberalism has no intention of challenging the inequalities in the private sphere, which is its way of making peace with the gender hierarchy. Thus the oppression and subjugation of women is excluded from the consideration of the political sphere. This kind of split has led to the exclusion of gender justice and the domestic sphere, and thus is the target of the feminist movement. The cries of "gender politics" and "the personal is political" that appeared in the second-wave feminist movement represent feminists' attack on liberalism's logic of the binary public/private division.

In addition, classical liberalism's assumption of a rational, self-interested individual denies the social structure that humans' actions are bound to. As Lisa Schwartzman proposes, the abstractification of liberalism masks the inequalities in power and wealth created by a certain social structure; liberal individualism views the individual as an independent and autonomous decision-maker, rather than a member in a group of oppressors and the oppressed.[8] Susan Moller Okin indicates that this abstract hypothesis has no explanatory power for the people living in gender segregation. The role expectations and process of socialization of the androcentric gender system means that women are less likely to stand up for their rightful share; instead, they

---

8. Lisa H. Schwartzman, *Challenging Liberalism: Feminism as Political Critique* (University Park: Pennsylvania State Univ. Press, 2006), 15.

prioritize the needs of their family members to the point that they are willing to change the course of their entire lives for their family.[9]

Andrea Dworkin and Catharine MacKinnon point out that rather than achieving equality for oppressed and vulnerable groups, the concept of rights tends to protect the current power structure. "Those who have power over others tend to call their power 'rights.'"[10] A typical excuse given by those with vested interests is that social and policy change will erode important rights.

Although the above are all discussions by non-Chinese scholars, they essentially describe the alienation between liberalism and feminism in China. The split of the public and private spheres explains very well why many topics related to feminism, such as domestic violence and marital rape, rarely receive attention from liberal intellectuals. Similarly, gender inequality is treated as a reasonable difference, and liberal intellectuals use differences and pluralism as excuses to defend unequal opportunity. In addition, on the Internet, it is mainly male scholars who start discussions opposing family planning policy, but their opposition focuses on state violence as they emphasize family rights, and they demand reproductive rights to be returned to the family (rather than to women). They do not discuss how women, under the pressure of the patriarchal family system, have been forced to give birth multiple times until they bear a male child. They have also directly imported anti-abortion rhetoric from the United States, trying to interfere with women's reproductive rights in the name of a fetus's human rights. The liberal analysis is too embedded in the power relations that still exist between "free individuals" with equal political rights. As a result, issues of workplace sexual harassment and sexual assault are not discussed as a problem of rights, because liberals

9. Susan Moller Okin, "Justice and Gender: An Unfinished Debate," *Fordham Law Review* 72, no. 5 (2004): 1564.

10. Andrea Dworkin and Catharine MacKinnon, *Pornography and Civil Rights: A New Day for Women's Equality* (Minneapolis, Minn.: Organizing against Pornography, 1988), 17.

view anything but violent coercion as free will, so the women affected are understood to have brought those disastrous consequences on themselves as a result of their own problems.

Male Intellectuals: Unintrospective Gender Beneficiaries

Martha Nussbaum states that the lack of justice in the nontransparent spheres of the home and the workplace, and the use of "private sphere" and "autonomous management of business" as excuses to suppress women's rights are not problems with liberalism itself. Rather, the problem is that some liberal thinkers have not thoroughly carried out liberal ideas. They are not individualistic enough in these areas, as they consider the consolidation or harmony of some collectives or institutions as more important than certain individuals' rights. Perhaps they are concerned about the autonomy and freedom of men and are hoping to set aside more space for men in these areas.[11]

As a result, male intellectuals as a whole barely reflect on the elite gender privileges men have, which may be the main reason for liberalism's alienation from and reaction against the topic of feminism. However, I must emphasize that in mainland China, enmity towards feminism and the lack of interest in understanding the true history of Chinese women's liberation is a shared characteristic of the ideological trends of China's New Left, liberalism, and conservatism.

If we look at market reform's impact on gender in China, especially after the 1990s, we can see a kind of revival of patriarchal capitalism. During the development of the market economy, the state withdrew from most of the social welfare field, citing the reason that a society run by *danwei* 单位, the work unit in state-owned enterprises, has low efficiency.

This proved to have detrimental effects on women. For example, the reform of state-owned enterprises produced many unemployed

11. Martha C. Nussbaum, *Sex and Social Justice* (New York: Oxford Univ. Press, 1999), 65.

women, and 70 percent of the assembly workers with few rights and safeguards in the coastal industrial zone are young unmarried women. Through this process labor once again became gendered. On the other hand, the rising consumerist discourse spearheaded by the market has become a powerful vehicle of gendered discourse and a mighty disciplining force demanding that women perform their traditional role in the home and maintain a feminine body.[12]

The market has bestowed individual rights and private life with legitimacy again. Under the framework of state feminism, the woman question belonged to the public sphere, and women's liberation was considered part of class liberation; but the woman question has been thrown back to the private sphere since the market reforms. Urban women are laid off, rural women have lost land, fewer women participate in politics, gender discrimination has increased, labor rights are undermined, sexual harassment in the workplace has become common, and sexual assault by acquaintances and domestic violence are barely criminalized. But these problems are not only personal dilemmas for women, they are also structural issues that require the government to resolve.

However, these political problems are invisible to most male intellectuals concerned about public issues. They tend to believe that Chinese feminism is overdoing it—ahead of its time or domineering males. Although a part of Chinese intelligentsia was politically suppressed, due to the marketization of education, health care, and other welfare systems in the 1990s, intellectuals have benefited more from the economic reform than have workers and peasants. In a society in which gender discrimination is still severe and women are relatively deprived, male intellectuals have become the beneficiaries of the regendered labor and private spheres.

Of course, the regendering of labor and the private sphere did not emerge spontaneously. While they criticize China's existing

12. The post–World War 2 United States had a similar phenomenon; see Betty Friedan, *The Feminine Mystique* (New York: W. W. Norton, 1963).

institutions, the only thing male intellectuals have never criticized is the gender institution that benefits themselves. In fact, they feel they are not having enough male benefits due to women's liberation in the socialist period, which they view as part of the failed socialist experiment that should be completely discarded. In 1994 China's most important scholarly journal in the field of sociology, *Journal of Sociology Study* (*Shehuixue yanjiu* 社会学研究), published sociologist Zheng Yefu's article "Sociological Reflections on Gender Equality" (*Nannü Pingdeng de Shehuixue Sikao* 男女平等的社会学思考), wherein he states that Chinese women's liberation was a result of state interference: "A kind of immense administrative power, through assisting the weak by suppressing the strong, interfered with and destroyed the normal division of labor between the weak and the strong in the home, to the extent of causing the weak to mistakenly believe they are not weak, and the strong to lose the self-confidence they should have."[13] Zheng believes that gender equality is a practice that sacrifices efficiency for fairness. Men and women getting equal pay for equal work "is an absurd equalitarian principle," he writes. "Politically pushed women's liberation . . . made China lose real men . . . and also made China lose its own women," leading to a "chaotic" China.[14]

Zheng also asserts that "equality is a right, not a result" and that society should "neither impose a ceiling nor fix a floor" for women— that is, "not impose any artificial suppression on women, but "not impose any artificial support either" for their success.[15] Zheng obviously opposes using institutional safeguards to ensure equality, and this is the consensus among Chinese liberals, as Liu Junning points out: "Liberalism is both fully sympathetic with and fully vigilant

---

13. Zheng Yefu 郑也夫, "Nannü Pingdeng de Shehuixue Sikao" 男女平等的社会学思考 (Sociological Reflections on Gender Equity), *Shehuixue yanjiu*, no. 2 (1994): 110.

14. Zheng, "Nannü Pingdeng de Shehuixue sikao," 110–11.

15. Zheng, "Nannü Pingdeng de Shehuixue sikao," 113.

against the ideal of equality. It [liberalism] believes in equality of rights, not equality of outcomes"[16]

Meanwhile, in the discussions set off by Zheng's essay in the *Journal of Sociology Study*, another sociologist, Sun Liping, proposed that the most cost-efficient method for solving China's contemporary unemployment problem was to have more professional women go home.[17] In the mid-1990s, "efficiency and equality" was the buzzword of discussions on economic reform. Sacrificing equality for women to achieve "social efficiency" under economic reform is a typical proposition by male intellectuals.

This type of liberal discourse is a rebound from and overturn of the practices of minimizing class and gender differences during the socialist period. The socialist institution certainly lacked the efficiency of capital, but the new social institution sacrifices the professional space and social position that women have already obtained (which, to women, is not only equality but also freedom) in order to regain efficiency. It means that liberalism has become a weapon of public opinion for some people to increase their own benefits, and is used to expand the gender hierarchy in the era of the market economy.

Compared with those in 1994, today's male intellectuals have barely done more to stop the expanding gender hierarchy. In the era of print media that ended around 2014, almost nothing on women's rights or gender equality appeared in the published articles by renowned liberal intellectuals; rather, there was much misunderstanding about women's liberation and gender rights. We can get a general idea of male intellectuals' attitude toward the gender issue from some of the words and phrases they used. For example, Gan Yang claims that

16. Liu Junning 刘军宁, "Pingdeng de Lixiang, Jingying de Xianshi" 平等的理想, 精英的现实 (Ideals of Equality, Reality of Elitism), blog.bnn.co, http://blog.boxun.com/hero/liujn/51_1.shtml.

17. Sun Liping, "Chongjian Xingbie Juese Guanxi" 重建性别角色关系 (Rebuilding the Gender Roles), *Shehuixue yanjiu*, no. 6 (1994).

gender, race, homosexuality, and queer theory are all trivialities; Qiu Feng asserts that transgender issues are an agenda set by Westerners.[18]

The liberal columnist Xu Zhiyuan wrote about women's liberation in an essay: "In the second half of this century . . . rigid feminists have desperately squeezed all the perfume from women's bodies, making them brave but dry, mistaking masculine behavior and tendencies as strength."[19] When he was a mentor at a youth workshop, he clearly expressed that he did not appreciate the so-called victim mentality (*shouhaizhe xintai* 受害者心态) in feminism's criticism of patriarchal culture. This obviously originates from an aversion to the history of Chinese women's movements. That period in history helped a massive number of women gain equal occupational and educational opportunities, and those women became the social power in many fields to challenge the male elitist monopoly,[20] and so that history has become one of the sources of anxiety for male elites.

I have only encountered two male liberal intellectuals who wrote about gender exclusively. One is Mo Luo, who recently converted to

18. Song Shaopeng 宋少鹏, "Wenhua Minzu Zhuyi de Ruxue Fuxing dui Zhongguo Nüxingzhuyi de Tiaozhan" 文化民族主义的儒学复兴对中国女性主义的挑战 (The Challenge of the Confucian Revival in Cultural Nationalism to Chinese Feminism), manuscript shared by the author.

19. Xu Zhiyuan 许知远, *Naxie Youshang de Nianqingren* 那些忧伤的年轻人 (Those Sad Young People) (Haikou: Hainan chubanshe, 2001), 1.

20. While the proportion of physics majors who are female rose from 9 percent in 1978 to 21 percent in 1999 in the United States, the proportion of physics majors who are female in China dropped. A researcher from the Institute of Physics CAS, Wu Lingan 吴令安, discovered that in the 1950s the average proportion of women in Peking University's physics department was 12.7 percent; in the 1960s it was 20.2 percent; and in the late 1970s it reached 39.5 percent. However, after the 1980s this proportion began to decline, falling from 15.9 percent to today's 9 percent. The proportion of Nanjing University students of physics who are women also fell from 37 percent in the late 1970s to today's 8 precent. See Yang Jianxiang 杨健翔, "Wulixue Weihe Buzai Xiyin Nüxing" 物理学为何不再吸引女性? (Why Does Physics No Longer Attract Women?) Chinese Academy of Sciences, February 5, 2002, www.cas.cn/ky /kyjz/200202/t20020205_1025719.shtml.

a state-nationalist. He published an article *Southern Weekly* in 2007 accusing Chinese women's liberation for harming women's "motherhood"; his article is permeated with resentment toward women's movements, as he asserts that "perhaps modern women's movements are an important reason for this retrogression [of motherhood]."[21] This is not a singular case. Qiu Feng wrote a newspaper article recommending maternity leave; however, he stressed that "the key to doing this is to break with the modern superstition: the first role of females is not as laborers, but as women and mothers."[22] These male intellectuals all hold an essentialist understanding of women's social roles. Rather than protecting motherhood, they are insensitive to the discrimination Chinese women face, and they completely overlook the equal rights and opportunities that women should share with men.

"Liberalism with Chinese Characteristics"

Chinese liberalism has accepted at face value the shortcomings of liberalism. However, feminism and liberalism are compatible in some ways; liberal political practices have helped expand the autonomy of women and members of other underprivileged groups. As Okin observes, liberalism's rejection of the hierarchy and emphasis on individual freedom and equality is essential to feminism.[23] In addition, Okin emphasizes the conceptual tools that John Rawls's theory of justice sets up for feminism's criticism of liberalism, such as "original position," a fair and impartial point of view for our reasoning about justice.[24] In short, liberalism has evolved to absorbing feminist criti-

---

21. Mo Luo 摩罗, "Funü Jiefang Buneng yi Shanghai Muxing Wei Daijia" 妇女解放不能以伤害母性为代价 (Women's Liberation Cannot Be Achieved at the Cost of Undermining Motherhood), *Nanfang zhoumo*, January 10, 2007.

22. Qiu Feng 秋风, "Zhongguo Yingdang Sheli Yuyingjia" 中国应当设立育婴假 (China Should Legalize Family Leave), *Nanfang doushi bao*, November 29, 2011. http://news.ifeng.com/opinion/society/detail_2011_11/29/10972250_0.shtml.

23. Okin, "Justice and Gender," 1546.

24. Okin, "Justice and Gender," 1541.

cisms and adopting feminism's values and methodologies as a way of its self-revision toward pluralism. Rawls's "Justice as Fairness" is precisely this kind of revisionist effort.[25]

Andrea Dworkin's and John Rawls's liberal theories both share some similarities with feminism, which at least serves as a basis for dialogue. However, because of their emphasis on substantive equality, they have been excluded from the field of mainstream Chinese liberalism in mass media. There are divisions among Chinese liberals. For example, Qin Hui attempted to reconcile the left and right to reach a common understanding; however, liberal ideas spread through marketized media and the Internet are still focused on libertarianism.

Political and economic liberalism both value principles such as individual freedom, a free market, and constitutionality, which is why political liberalism was freely propagated in the 1990s. The notion of socialism with Chinese characteristics emphasizes both leftist and rightest mistakes, but mainly leftist mistakes. Because of this, liberals had a fair amount of freedom of expression when they reflected on utopia, the Cultural Revolution, and the French Revolution in the media. The dissemination of a liberalism with Chinese characteristics takes the reflection on the Cultural Revolution, egalitarianism, and totalitarianism as its basis, and it inevitably inherited the Western emphasis on individual freedom and anti-authoritarianism; at the same time, it views equality and social welfare as products of the unsuccessful Communist experiment that should be avoided.

For example, Ren Jiantao believes that we cannot adopt new liberalism simply because it emphasizes social justice and takes into consideration both freedom and equality, or can more readily respond to Chinese politics, or is closer to the moral ideals of intellectuals.[26]

25. John Rawls, "Justice as Fairness," *The Philosophical Review* 67, no. 2 (1958): 164–94.

26. Ren Jiantao 任剑涛, "Zai Gudian Ziyou Zhuyi yu Xin Ziyou Zhuyi Zhijian: Dangdai Zhongguo Ziyou Zhuyi de Lilun Dingwei Wenti" 在古典自由主义与新自由主义之间：当代中国自由主义的理论定位问题 (Between Classical Liberalism and

From the "historical/logical sequence" of the West, in which freedom precedes justice, he infers that Chinese people also must first have systemic safeguards of freedoms—a free constitutional democracy—before they can continue to think about justice.

This can also explain why liberals claim we will only have women's rights after we have human rights (in this respect, these liberals and patriarchal Communists, who claimed that there must first be class liberation before we can have women's liberation, are the same). Liu Junning's American-style conservative position is even more well-known. He has bluntly stated that Chow Po Chung is not a true liberal because Chow has endorsed Rawls's justice theory and criticized the market, thereby producing obstructions for freedom. I have heard that some liberal media people believe that Rawls is not a liberal but a socialist (among some of China's liberals, socialism has seemingly become a stigmatized label, or an option to absolutely be excluded from the sociopolitical blueprint).

In the debates between the liberals and the New Left in the late 1990s, the characteristics of liberalism had been made more conspicuous by its opponents, to the point that we now have liberalism with Chinese characteristics. The Chinese liberals believe that there exists a pure and, in the distribution of resources, omnipotent free market, and they are full of suspicion and are vigilant toward the plea of social justice, worrying that it will bring about the restoration of

---

Neoliberalism: The Issue of Contemporary Chinese Liberalism's Theoretical Positioning), *Aisixiang*, June 15, 2005, www.aisixiang.com/data/7137.html?page=1. Ren Jiantao uses the phrase *new liberalism* to refer to the egalitarian liberalism or leftist liberalism that Rawls, Dworkin, and others discussed. New liberalism is easily confused with neoliberalism. A new liberalism that emphasized equality already existed some time ago, as it points to the political trend of thought started by T. H. Green and others in the second half of the nineteenth century and the early twentieth century. It emphasized social rights and social issues, attacked many of the problems produced by capitalism that is free from interference, and established the theoretical basis for twentieth-century welfare states. Today's left camp likes to criticize neoliberalism, but ignores new liberalism. Perhaps it is because they have overlooked liberalism's historical development.

communism and the totalitarian government. They ignore the fact that in a market economy with Chinese characteristics the market created by the authoritarian state lacks autonomy and sufficient social restraint, and the fact that social justice not only is meaningful for each individual, but also is the foundation for the smooth democratization of the country.

In addition, mainland Chinese liberals are highly elitist. Both Liu Junning and Ren Jiantao recently emphasized the contributions made by political and economic elitists.[27] Chinese intellectuals are disappointed that entrepreneurs as a whole are eager to be joined with power. However, perhaps due to the trauma of being persecuted after joining the revolution during the socialist period, they uphold their class identification with the rising bourgeoisie, which, they believe, will inevitably become the key force of social change, though comparative politics has shown that this is not the universal historical pattern.

Since liberal scholars place the hope for social change on cooperation between elites, they rigidly approach the current problems from the perspective of political freedom, while overlooking the multiple causes for the conundrums of class, gender, race, and cultural identification faced by those groups that are not the male elite, and ignoring the comprehensive means and pluralistic societal forces needed to solve these conundrums.

The blueprint for social reforms led and dominated by elites, liberal democracy that does not take justice into account, and limited government that eschews the welfare problem all exclude relatively disadvantaged groups. They are obviously not ideal for those who adhere to a feminist agenda. Women's submissive status in the gender hierarchy predetermines that they have different starting points compared to males of the same class, and thus women are unable to obtain equal opportunities from a "pure and free market." Women undertake

27. Rong Jian 荣剑, "Zhongguo Ziyou Zhuyi 'Disanbo'—Sixiang Juhui zhi Si" 中国自由主义"第三波"—思想聚会之四 (Chinese Liberalism's "Third Wave"—Symposium No. 4), *Gongfapinglun*, November 2012. www.gongfa.com/html/gongfaxinwen/201211/15-2069.html.

an overwhelming majority of caring work and unpaid reproductive work, and thus have a more urgent need for social welfare. In addition, now feminists believe that patriarchal oppression is implemented and rationalized through various oppressive forces, such as the intersecting oppressions of political power, social class, race, and gender. The lack of examination of hierarchy and conservatism regarding class benefits implies that this kind of plan for change is not committed to everyone's emancipation, but rather leaves room for privileges. Both in social movements and in theoretical research, feminism emphasizes individual consciousness, agency, and empowerment; that is to say, it emphasizes the broad political participation of every citizen. In this sense, exclusionary elite democracy itself implies nondemocracy.

The efforts of liberal scholars in mass communication have enlightened the public. Those active in the civic sphere have a common understanding with liberals: they hope for an accountable government, a public space not under government control but rather where social forces are brought into play, and the rule of law. However, the theoretical strands behind human rights activism are pluralistic and sometimes surpass the scope of mainland liberals' discussions. Two examples are the Marxist theories behind workers, peasants, and feminist movements, and the opposition to global capitalism in areas of fair trade, community economic cooperation, and environmental protection movements. These movements all emphasize citizen participation instead of elite governance. Perhaps contemporary Chinese liberals should focus on citizen action and search for a social revolutionary force that exists in citizen action, and form a localized political theory from their practices.

"Feminism with Chinese Characteristics"

The fresh start of Chinese grassroots feminism is directly related to the Fourth World Conference on Women and the NGO Forum in Beijing in 1995. The authorities tolerated some grassroots feminist organizations joining the NGO Forum, and thus this meeting also became the origin of contemporary Chinese NGOs. The high profile of the World Conference on Women and the related opportunities for exchange promoted the spread of transnational feminist ideas in China. International foundations, mainly the Ford Foundation, have funded the creation of gender studies programs in Chinese universities, and both the All-China Women's Federation (ACWF) system and the nascent women's NGOs received international funding and were influenced by transnational feminist theories.

The Fourth World Conference on Women was a turning point for Chinese authorities' attitude toward the international human rights framework and NGOs. Chinese authorities discovered that the NGO Forum did not lead to the international community's censure of China's human rights record, but rather provided a platform for China to oppose Western hegemony. As a result, the development of feminism and NGOs in China represents a strategic reconciliation between the Chinese government and the international community.[28] Chinese NGOs have mainly been using the international legal framework to gradually expand their freedom of activity since 1995. They mainly used the UN review mechanism for the Convention on the Elimination of Discrimination against Women (CEDAW), which China signed in 1980, and collaboration with the official ACWF system to further women's rights in various areas.

CEDAW requires substantive equality and that the state take up responsibility for eliminating discrimination. The nation's responsibility to eliminate discrimination, and the programs of action based on equality and human rights were mainly proposed by contemporary foreign liberal and feminist scholars. In other words, the main ideological resource of contemporary feminism comes from contemporary liberalism, and yet this fact is neither accepted nor valued by

28. See Wang Zheng, "A Historical Turning Point for the Women's Movement in China," *Signs: Journal of Women in Culture and Society* 22, no. 1 (1996): 192–99. This article describes the swing of the Chinese government's attitude toward NGOs around the time of the World Conference on Women. The anti–US imperialism tendencies of the World Conference on Women NGO Forum eased the Chinese government's concerns about nongovernmental organizations.

mainland Chinese liberals. This paradox deserves our attention, and it also hints at the disparity between Chinese and non-Chinese liberal thought. Unfortunately, even the liberal political platform, Charter 08, does not contain an explicit provision on state responsibility for antidiscrimination.

Despite its liberal core, Chinese feminism is also pluralistic in its practices: there are advocacy and lobbying for policy and legislation, various economic empowerment and community engagement projects for grassroots women, innovations and reforms in media and culture, and an independently developed transgender movement. This ecology of pluralistic coexistence leads to different schools of feminism—socialist feminism, Third World feminism, and lesbian feminism,[29] among others—and their synchronicity in China. That is to say, feminist movements and ideas that emerged outside of China in different historical periods and different regions were translated and localized in China by coexisting feminist movements with different focuses. Yet the discourse of mainland liberals has little overlap with the composite human rights (which include political, economic, and cultural rights) that feminists hope to achieve.

The CCP is the first party in Chinese history to issue a party resolution on women's liberation, and gender equality has been one of the CCP's foundations for legitimacy. Moreover, the Chinese government

29. Socialist feminism is a school of feminist theory that emerged in the 1960s and 1970s, combining Marxist tradition, radical feminist perspectives, and psychoanalytic feminist theories, while rejecting their shortcomings. Its concerns include the gender division of labor and domestic work, the abolition of capitalist wages, and the restructuring of sexual and reproductive and child-rearing relationships. Third World feminism, which emerged in the 1970s, criticizes the feminism created by the dual hegemony of patriarchy and First World feminism. Third World feminism's core idea is that gender oppression is integrated with other forms of oppression, such as those related to class, race, ethnicity, and national differences. Lesbian feminism formed in the late 1970s and early 1980s. It criticizes mainstream feminism's blindness to the hegemony of heterosexuality, and sees this hegemony as an important support of patriarchy. Lesbian feminism tends to separate from both the mainstream feminist movement and the gay movement.

has made promises to the international community to promote human rights and eliminate discrimination (though how effective it has been at keeping those promises is another matter). This is an important reason those Chinese feminists who were active during and after the Fourth World Conference on Women have prioritized cooperating with the government over accountability.[30] These feminist tactics still assume that under the current political structure those in office are more motivated to protect gender equality than those out of office. On the one hand, high-level nationwide gender policies and advocacy projects must be embedded into national policy and official ideology, mainly through the involvement of the ACWF, as there are very few feminists outside of the institution dominated by the ACWF and the government. On the other hand, since grassroots communities are currently under the control of the government, feminists outside the system still rely on the institutional framework of the ACWF to carry out various grassroots projects, including women's economic empowerment, rural communities' political participation, and legal rights safeguards.

Therefore, veteran feminists try their best to not politicize Chinese women's movements. Chinese feminist intellectuals have to seek the greatest degree of improvement within the system; under the premise of sorting out and criticizing the existing institutional resources, they must search for safe ways to collaborate with the government. The main means for promoting women's rights within the system is to raise the awareness of the cadres. Feminists within the system have no way of proposing systematic plans divergent from the interests of the system, so the Chinese feminist movements do not have any systematic theoretical or institutional discourse. Consequently, political or philosophical dialogues with other sociopolitical ideas are incredibly rare in China. Of course, this type of "embedded activism" that both

---

30. In contrast, the young feminist activists who arose in 2012 have demanded government accountability on behalf of the general public.

negotiates with and has tensions with the government is common among contemporary Chinese social movements.[31]

Because of the complexity of Chinese feminism and its relationship with the government, the excessive involvement of the government in advocacy for gender equality policy and legislation, and a lack of mass mobilization, Chinese public, including the liberal community, does not understand Chinese feminism.

Chinese feminists are currently facing a dilemma. Their first choice is to cooperate with the government, which would in turn ensure safeguards according to the international legal framework. However, Chinese feminism does not have an effective channel for government accountability, and furthermore it is prohibited from mobilizing grass-roots forces, and is required to only serve as an aid when the Chinese government needs to respond to the international community. Thus various feminist movements do not move beyond being projects and cannot facilitate the mainstreaming of gender in the ACWF-govern-mental system. The second choice is to demand political reforms in order to realize the feminist agenda, relying on the opportunities provided by political freedom and the legal framework. However, this is currently not an option available for Chinese women. Currently in China policy advocates hope to gain mutual trust with the government, feminist scholars with socialist leanings and Third World international activists have deep misgivings about Western hegemony, and grassroots NGOs simply hope to survive in the gaps. The language of Chinese mainstream liberalism is most forgetful of those who experience intersectional disadvantage based on class, gender, and ethnicity.

Institutional problems are difficult to avoid. It is challenging for a government and women's federation lacking in social response to be changed by grassroots feminism. Even the ACWF still lacks the awareness to make women the agent rather than an object to be helped;

31. See Peter Ho and Richards Edmonds, *China's Embedded Activism: Opportunities and Constraints of a Social Movement* (New York: Routledge, 2008).

their work ethic and methods ironically strengthen patriarchal ideas. The lack of legal and basic political freedom has also hindered Chinese feminism. For example, when the Olympics were held in Beijing in 2008, Ma Xiaoduo's migrant women's community services on the outskirts of Beijing were forced to suspend work. When Ai Xiaoming entered the hamlet of Taishi Village 太石村 in the suburbs of Guangzhou to observe the political participation of female villagers, she witnessed the villagers' autonomy movement, then was threatened and driven out by violence. When a feminist legal assistance NGO (Beijing University Law School Women's Legal Research and Services Center 北京大学法学院妇女法律研究与服务中心) intervened in the case of illegally detained petitioner Li Ruirui, who was raped by a jail guard, the legal involvement brought on a crisis of the legitimacy for the NGO, which was shut down by Peking University.

The stories of these feminist activists indicate that as soon as the definition of aid is overstepped, they are suspected of "making trouble" (*tianluan* 添乱). When touching on sensitive topics such as the scandal of the HIV cases caused by Chinese health officials' blood-for-cash scheme, brutal enforcement of the birth control policy, grassroots democracy and petitioning, or "contentious politics," feminist demands lose their legitimacy with the government. If the principle of gender equality is to be applied consistently, it is impossible not to consider the issue of democratization in China.

A hundred years ago, Chinese men were in a state of anxiety about having been conquered. As their inferiority complex mingled with the desire to become stronger, they took the West as a model. They violently criticized traditional patriarchal culture, and consequently feminism was received as an advanced component of Western culture and become an integral part of Chinese modernity. Gender equality was endorsed by the majority of politicians and thinkers of the generation from the Xinhai Revolution of 1911 to the May Fourth Movement of 1919. Feminists actively participated in various national discussions, proposing anarchism, liberalism, socialism, and other political ideas.

However, despite the fact that today's liberal feminists have spearheaded the international legal framework and discourse of feminist movements, as well as related discussions and actions guided by policies and law, Chinese feminists have never obtained the support of Chinese liberals. On the contrary, the liberals who hope for political progress and reform exclude gender issues from matters of nation-state building. They ambiguously maintain the status quo and even support the restoration of traditional patriarchy. The continuation of this situation implies that Chinese liberals advocate for the suspension of the equal rights of half the population. What can this kind of liberalism do for China? On the other hand, what kind of political argument should feminists develop to criticize the inadequacies of liberalism with Chinese characteristics?

In this historical context we need more dialogues and debates between feminist movements, social movements, and liberalism. The ideas of rights, equality, and freedom, and the vision of a constitutional government should not be monopolized by liberalism. If Chinese liberals continue to obstinately hold to their patriarchal, heterosexual, and procapitalist class position, then they may lose many powerful allies. More important, they may lose a more rational, pluralistic, and rich imagination of Chinese society.

7

The Formation of Chinese Feminist Linguistic Tactics and Discourse

Adapting The Vagina Monologues *for Chinese Women*

Ke Qianting

Translated by Hui Faye Xiao and Tera Mills

Since the late Qing period the discourse of Chinese feminism has gone through three important developments. From the late Qing to the May Fourth Movement in 1919, along with the publication of Jin Tianhe's 金天翮 *Bell of the Women's World* (*Nüjie zhong* 女界钟), Liang Qichao's 梁启超 "On Women's Education" (*Lun Nüxue* 论女学), He-Yin Zhen's 何殷震 "The Issue of Women's Liberation" (*Nüzi jiefang wenti* 女子解放问题), and *The Ladies' Journal* (*Nüzi zazhi* 女子杂志), intellectuals actively participated in a discussion of the woman question (*funü wenti* 妇女问题). Just as Wang Zheng summarized, "With the publication and wide circulation of *Bell of the Women's World*, the term *Nüquan* (women's rights) entered Chinese social and political discourse."[1] The editors of *The Birth of Chinese Feminism* believe that He-Yin established the language of feminism with Chinese characteristics: "*Nannü* [男女], we propose, is a more comprehensive rubric than 'sex-gender,' whereas *shengji* [生计] is a more enabling

---

1. Wang Zheng, *Women in the Chinese Enlightenment: Oral and Textual Histories* (Berkeley: Univ. of California Press, 1999), 40.

rubric than 'class.'"[2] The woman question received widespread attention and discussion, and women's rights and liberation were seen as the foundation for people's liberation, the national cause of antifeudalism and modernization.

After the Chinese Communist Party (CCP) was founded in 1921, the CCP saw feminism as a Western bourgeois product. Instead, it advocated for the political campaign of women's liberation. These competing feminist discourses and movements continued until after the establishment of People's Republic of China (PRC) in 1949. Soon afterward, Marxist views of women and women's liberation discourse took the lead. The issues of women's participation in the labor force and economic independence were considered important, but issues such as domestic violence and gendered division of household work were overlooked. After the economic reform and opening up launched in 1978, "iron girls," who were symbolic of women's active participation in the labor force, received harsh critique for losing their femininity. "Strong woman" (*nüqiangren* 女强人) also became a negative label for a successful career woman. Mainstream media often advocated for women's return to the domestic realm.

The 1995 World Conference on Women, held in Beijing, brought another conjunction of Chinese and global feminist discourses.[3] The Platform for Action (*Xingdong gangling* 行动纲领), discussed and passed by the conference, gave the Chinese women's movement fresh perspectives, and the conference gave birth to multiple social organizations. Some women's organizations that had been established earlier also got further development. Universities established women's and gender studies research centers, with more than thirty universities

2. Lydia H. Liu, Rebecca E. Karl, and Dorothy Ko, eds. *The Birth of Chinese Feminism: Essential Texts in Transnational Theory* (New York: Columbia Univ. Press, 2013), 10.

3. Wang Fengxian 王凤仙 and Mi Xiaolin 米晓琳, "NGO Huayu yu Minjian Funü Zuzhi de Ziwo Rentong" NGO话语与民间妇女组织的自我认同 (NGO Discourse and the Self-Identification of Grassroots Women's Organizations), *Funü yanjiu luncong*, no. 6 (2007): 41–48.

offering classes, promoting the new discipline, and organizing student activities. At the same time, international funds came in to provide financial support for the cause of Chinese women's development.

However, after the initial prosperity, the post-1995 development of Chinese feminism soon reached a bottleneck, and feminism has not been able to enter mainstream discourse. Gender as conceptual terminology and an analytical category was mainly used in women's studies and in training in women's organizations. It did not enter the mainstream academic world; nor did it evoke in-depth discussion about gender-related concepts in other academic disciplines. Activities organized by women's organizations were restrained by the inadequacy of funds and resources, and their popularity and influence were also limited, particularly among young people.

This chapter identifies and analyzes some breakthrough forces against current strictures. If we agree that the post-1995 decade witnessed the establishment of mushrooming women's organizations and gender studies programs, as well as the development of women's capabilities, then the following period was more focused on finding women's voices, media action, and political advocacy. This essay zooms in on the performance of Eve Ensler's *The Vagina Monologues* in China as a case study, analyzing the linguistic tactics used by the Chinese activists and performers to investigate a new feminist discourse in formation.

Telling Local Stories and Representing Different Groups' Lived Experiences

In 1996 Ensler produced her Obie Award–winning *The Vagina Monologues* (TVM), a significant play discussing female sexuality. Two years later she launched the worldwide V-Day campaign, and in 2012 the One Billion Rising worldwide campaign, both of which were global activist movements aimed at ending violence against women. TVM has been translated into forty-eight languages and performed thousands of times around the world. From a play to two global campaigns, from the United States to two hundred countries, TVM has formed a unique kind of vagina culture and vagina discourse. However, unlike in other countries, where TVM has been reenacted as part of a global movement and as a way of fundraising, women's organizations in China are more concerned with local issues in their adaptations of the play.

The First Staging of TVM in China and Its Wide Influence

In 2003 Ai Xiaoming 艾晓明, a professor of gender studies at Sun Yat-sen University, accepted StopDV.net's invitation to become the director of the Chinese version of TVM (TVM in SYSU), and involved students of the university in its local staging. A team made up of teachers and students started with translating and analyzing the script. All those experiences about vagina that had always been regarded as forbidden, shameful, or indescribable topics now were to be spoken of aloud on stage, and must also be able to resonate with the audience. This was a great challenge to the team. When the team uttered words such as *vagina*, *clitoris*, *sex*, and *rape* during rehearsals, they were met with bystanders' shock, resistance, and even threatening phone calls and verbal attacks. Some crew members were worried that these lines and performances could cause misunderstandings that might negatively affect their graduation, employment, and future life. Ai Xiaoming encouraged students and eliminated various obstacles.

Eventually the play was staged at the small theater of the Guangdong Museum of Art, marking the first Chinese-language performance of TVM in China. It received widespread praise and was listed as one of the top ten cultural events of 2003, selected by the *Southern Metropolis Daily* of Guangdong province (*Nanfang dushibao* 南方都市报), a leading liberal news agency. Not long afterward, Ai collaborated with Hu Jie 胡杰, a documentary director, to produce the documentary *The Vagina Monologues: Story from China* in 2004.

Many organizations have since followed in the performers' footsteps. According to Yuping Zhang, "at least 42 Chinese organizations launched performances related to TVM in Mainland China during these 12 years" from 2003 to 2014.[4] The Sex-Gender Education Forum of Sun Yat-sen University, Zhi-he Society of Fudan University, Bcome,[5] Beaver Club, Feminist Spring Society, and Lesgo are some of the most active groups, based in big cities such as Beijing, Shanghai, Guangzhou, and Suzhou, respectively.[6] Except for the Sex-Gender Education Forum, all other organizations were created specifically for performing TVM.

The monologue as a form has brought both great praise and criticism to Ensler and the actors in TVM. Ensler made the performance simple and easy for amateur actors by adopting the form of monologues, which is one of the fundamental skills in drama performance. For the organizations in China, these methods were flexible and portable for amateur teams. Basing a theater production on monologues also made rehearsal much easier, since the director did not need to coordinate the entire cast for each session. A performer named Sophia said, "It is easy to copy the model after we run the theater, and then we share it with other teams. It is a good way to get people involved."[7] Organizers adopted the form of linking together multiple independent plays, a form established by Ensler, which also made script writing and rehearsal easier.

However, these Chinese women's organizations all came to the realization that they could not rigidly follow Ensler's script. Instead, they borrowed her methods and topics to create a Chinese story.

4. Yuping Zhang, "Global Media Activism Made in China: An Extended Case Study on the Circuit of Cultures Based on *The Vagina Monologues* and *Break the Chain*" (PhD diss., Chinese University of Hong Kong, 2016), 138–39.

5. Bcome is an active feminist organization. In 2016 its members staged *Our Vaginas Ourselves* (*Yindao zhi dao*, 阴道之道) in North America.

6. These groups have no independent websites. A set of twelve essays were published by group members on Douban.com on their experiences of producing and performing TVM. See https://site.douban.com/211878/widget/notes/13727777/. Fan Popo also produced a documentary to record their theatrical practices: *Laizi yindao* 来自阴道 (The VaChina Monologues: A Documentary) (Queer Comrades, 2013), www.queercomrades.com/videos/vagina/.

7. Sophia Cai, interview with author, March 12, 2007.

Adapting the Play for Local Agendas

China's gender organizations and TVM crew members gradually developed a set of working methods based on local needs. They communicated with each other, with some participants working across different TVM groups. The methods they used during mobilizing, interviewing, collective writing, and performance responded to local concerns and issues.

First they organized a storytelling workshop for members to tell their own stories or stories they knew of. The workshop encouraged discussion, communication, and self-reflection, all of which were very important for people's self-recognition of their sexual and gender identities and for the bonding of the group. A member from Feminist Spring Society said, "I spent days and nights with team members, sharing experiences, arguing and laughing. We did things that we never had before and became very close friends."[8] Building a space of mutual trust, members shared stories that had been kept in the dark, which deepened their understanding of each other and also motivated them to push for changes together. Their organizational structure was similar to that of women's awareness groups in the 1970s. This is a significant form of continuous self-reflection, which also inspires a collective commitment among group members to criticize the oppressive system.

The members' identities in each newly organized team were always varied, including lesbians, transgender, bisexual, and disabled people. Some people joined the team in the process of discovering themselves as sexual minorities, and others came due to their interest in any form of fringe theater. This diversity of team members made it impossible to have a single dominant perspective for the play. Everyone carried their own slate of experiences and concerns, so that they had to negotiate with each other to decide which topics should be included in the play.

---

8. "Shi'er" 十二, member of the Feminist Spring Society, interview with author, October 25, 2016.

Their stories were heterogeneous and polyphonic, and it was precisely this kind of diversity that allowed them to be fully aware of individual differences and the importance of individual experiences. Through their creation of the script and its staging, they constantly voiced critical reflections on the heteronormative culture and system.

Second, TVM production groups adopted Ensler's method of interviewing to gather writing materials. In addition, they incorporated discussions of current affairs in the content. Starting with Sun Yat-sen University's version (TVM in SYSU), TMV in China had paid special attention to local women's experiences. A sequence of significant events related to gender had taken place: In 2003 a female teacher named Huang Jing 黄静 died during a date, so the issue of dating violence surfaced. In Guangxi province there was a major infant trafficking case in which female infants were transported inside suitcases on a bus, leading to the infants dying from lack of oxygen. Cases of women's rape and murder as well as the rape of rural "left-behind children" had not received enough attention from the media or legal system. Moreover, urban women faced serious problems of workplace sexual harassment, sexual assault, and forced marriages. At the same time, enacting domestic violence legislation became urgent due to a flood of domestic abuse cases and international prodding of the Chinese government to take action on this. Hence the subject of domestic violence had gained the attention of various TVM groups.

Antiviolence is one of the most important issues of "For Vagina's Sake," directed by Professor Song Sufeng 宋素风 at Sun Yat-sen University. Six out of its ten acts are related to gender violence, such as that in the Song Shanmu 宋山木 case, in which a boss raped some of his employees, and the Li Yan 李彦 case, in which a woman killed her husband after suffering years of domestic abuse. On the basis of her historical research, Sophia wrote a scene about sexual violence during the Japanese invasion of China called "You Owe Me an Apology" which gave voice to the comfort women. It was subsequently performed by the group at Southeast Normal University. "Silence" by Xiaoguo 小果, includes three stories about sex trafficking and domestic violence and is a part of the "Words of Vagina" (*Yindao yuyan* 阴道欲言), organized by Lesgo in 2015.

Critical Gender Perspective in Local Stories

Third, TVM production groups analyzed the materials they gathered and created the script from the perspective of feminism. They deployed feminist theories as an analytical lens to interpret women's experiences and agency, and to identify and criticize a sexist culture and gender hierarchy. In the original material gathered by TVM production groups, the female victims in these incidents met with misfortune mainly because they lacked a certain gendered knowledge. If no analysis was carried out to generate a critical vision, then the stories written by TVM production groups might end up reinforcing the stereotype of women as powerless victims. These stories would be filled with sorrow that failed to show women's strength. Hence feminist analysis was an essential tool to help creators find the appropriate creative perspective and a powerful mode of expression.

Women's experiences are never homogenous but are conditioned by their disparate living environments. The act "I Am Worried about My Daughter" (*Wo danxin wode nü'er* 我担心我的女儿) from *For Vagina's Sake* shed light on the dangers, suppression, and cultural pitfalls that Chinese girls might run into while growing up. The maternal figure in this act was put in a dilemma: "I am worried that her ambition will make the road before her difficult and dangerous. But I am more worried that she will lose her ambition." The mother portrayed here shared many mothers' worries about their daughters getting hurt and their hope that their daughters could break past the limitations of reality and realize her dreams. This act used poetic, expressive language not to essentialize the perilous environment a girl finds herself in, or to discipline young daughters, but to expose and criticize the unfair status quo.

The scripts of TVM created by Chinese women's organizations strove to cleverly reveal the restraints and harm that social reality has brought to women in a way that made the audience feel empathetic and empowered, rather than simply denouncing the patriarchal system and its sexist discrimination. For example, when preparing stories about how hard it is for teenage girls who are mocked when dealing with their menarche, Ai Xiaoming told the performers to "try to make the audiences laugh, make them understand that it's wrong to treat a girl like that when you act out these ridiculous stories."[9] Ai recommended the book *Feminism and Contemporary Art: The Revolutionary Power of Women's Laughter* to the students and encouraged them to release the power of laughter in the theater.

The same dark humor could be found in the act "Intrauterine Device (IUD)" of *For Vagina's Sake*. This act registered women's great fear that was brought about by China's family planning measures—forced implantation of an IUD, mandatory annual checkups to make sure the implanted IUD was not secretly removed, and the requirement for doctor's certification of IUD implantation in the mother upon a child's household registration and school enrollment. In order to avoid having an IUD forcefully implanted after marriage, the female lead came up with the idea of filing for divorce every year in the month when the IUD was supposed to be checked.

> B. Arghhhh! So much trouble! You'd better stay single. Only unmarried girls can be exempt from this IUD thing.
> A. Unmarried girls only?
> B. And divorced women. And widows.
> A. This is doable!
> B. What is doable?
> A. After having a child, when it's time for the annual IUD checkup, I'll go get a divorce. Divorced women don't have to do the checkup. Then I can get remarried after the time for the annual checkup is over.
> B. Getting divorced and remarried every year? What a hassle!

9. Jo Anna Isaak, *Feminism and Contemporary Art: The Revolutionary Power of Women's Laughter* (London: Routledge, 1996).

A. No hassle at all. It's easy to get married and divorced now. Look, it only costs nine yuan [approximately 1.3 USD] to get married or divorced. You just need to spend eighteen yuan to keep the award of family planning without having to implant the IUD. This will not violate any law; nor will it cause any trouble for your employer.

B. Sounds reasonable. But how come I still feel there is something not right?

Through acting out various ridiculous ways the female lead invented to cope with the forced birth control, this act highlighted the absurdity of the state's biopolitical management of women's bodies.

Some programs used analysis and deductions to display the absurdity and contradictions of mainstream gender ideology. The act "Bitch" (*biao* 婊) in *Our Vaginas Ourselves* (*Yindao zhidao* 阴道之道) examined how people used *green tea bitch* (*lüchabiao* 绿茶婊), *gutter oil bitch* (*digouyoubiao* 地沟油婊), *pure water bitch* (*chungjingshuibiao* 纯净水婊), and other forms of *bitch* to label and stigmatize women.[10] This act included analysis and deductions: since every woman could possibly be a masked bitch, why didn't we—women on and off the stage—tear off the mask and just call ourselves bitches? *Bitch* is normally considered an insulting term for women. Therefore, ending this act with women characters' self-identification as bitches stirred up huge controversies. Some scholars believed that feminist progress should not be achieved at the cost of lowering moral standards. This act was created jointly by Bcome and the Gender Action Group of Beijing Foreign Studies University. The latter group was maliciously attacked on the Internet when promoting the play, which proved the enormous impact of the provocative script on social and cultural gender norms.

Ai Ke 艾可 of Bcome (a team organized when they performed *Our Vaginas Ourselves*) commented on the creation of the act on

---

10. These derogatory phrases are used in similar ways to the English terms *basic bitch*, *whore*, and so on. These labels are misogynistic ways of describing women as morally reproachable under their deceitful, innocent disguise.

sexual assault, "Pretty much every sentence in the script responds to the myths about rape that we have examined in the workplace. 'Nonexistent' rape, rape by acquaintances, rape ranked among all the sufferings as 'nothing special.'"[11] In other words, their creative work was committed to exposing the denial of the truth about rape in a masculinist rape culture, the overlooking of rape by acquaintances, the pain brought by rape. In the act "No! I Have to Say It" from *For Vagina's Sake*, director Song Sufeng added a voice-over to the performer's monologue in the rape scene, showing the multiple voices of rapists' intimidation and victims' fear, struggle, and breaking free. These instances of violation were embedded in complex cultural, institutional, and legal conditions. Their meanings also shifted, along with the change of mentality of the people involved. Hence the TVM producers were reluctant to make these incidents linear narratives. Instead, they would rather present the acuity of multiple debates and women's process of maturing.

The women were not victims. They had the ability to cope with oppressive situations. The stories they had collected from interviews were mostly sad and cruel. The teams analyzed these materials and understood that these oppressed women were not mere victims but were strong and tough. The play would focus on how these women worked through their difficulties. *For Vagina's Sake* dealt with a couple of these sad stories. In "Boy or Girl" (*Nanhai haishi nühai* 男孩还是女孩), one woman talked about how she had given birth to eight daughters and finally had a son. Some of them had been delivered at home by the mother alone because she had violated the one-child policy and thus had to escape from her hometown and live in solitude. The actor talked proudly, with a strong accent, about how she had wanted to have a son and finally got one after multiple failed attempts. The difficulty and the risk she faced made audiences feel

11. Ai Ke 艾可, "Yindao zhi Dao, BCome he Wo"《阴道之道》、BCome 和我 ("Our Vaginas Ourselves," BCome, and Me), *Kula shibao*, July 12, 2013.

compassionate. Her dialect and humor made audiences laugh and understand that she had tried her best to cope with the situation.

The script, which was created on the basis of feminist analysis and discourse analysis, added a gendered perspective from which women's experiences and voices could be understood and critically reflected on, allowing women's voices to become the starting point of freedom and liberation, to break new paths and suggest a new subject position.

Collaborative Writing, Polyphonic Voices, and Multiple Dialogues

The storytelling form, dramatic style, and stage management presented by TVM in China had obviously deviated from Ensler's original work. Although these performing groups in China continued to use the name *Vagina Monologues* or made explicit reference to it, the differences presented in their plays are not less than those in a parodical adaptation.

The form of monologue could conflict with the polyphonic contents of the play. The script and performance of each scene in Ensler's TVM presented the single perspective of the playwright/actor, even though its title emphasized the plural form *monologues*. Feminist scholar Christine Cooper analyzed the narrative and language of TVM to show how Ensler rewrote the stories of the women she had interviewed through her own point of view. As a result, in the original TVM performance, only a white, heterosexual woman's voice was sounded out on stage. Women of other countries, races, classes, and sexual orientations were represented as possessing neither vagina nor self. Instead they were portrayed as lost and absent.[12] As a result, the

---

12. Christine M. Cooper, "Worrying about Vaginas: Feminism and Eve Ensler's *The Vagina Monologues*," *Signs: Journal of Women in Culture and Society* 32, no.3 (2007): 727–58.

only position for audiences to identify with was that of the single actor on stage at a given time.

Some activists also pointed out the difficulties in performing TVM for local communities. Erin Striff, codirector of TVM at the University of Hartford, critiques this singular perspective, "all monologues are delivered directly to the audience, never to any of the women on stage."[13] Sealing Cheng found that TVM is alien for Asian women: "Read in the transnational context, it is ironic to have one and only one legitimate arbiter of women's experiences in a global movement, while local women's creative participation is actively discouraged."[14] To solve the problems, Striff added roles on stage, "For 'I Was There in the Room' I decided to have the mother and the daughter speak at the same time as the grandmother, to blend with certain words as she spoke them."[15] Cheng created a localized version of TVM: *Stories of Our Little Sisters* (*Xiaoximen de gushi* 小西们的故事). Chinese feminist organizations encountered a similar dilemma and adopted some more flexible methods. In their case, Ensler's original approach, with one center and one perspective and her "vagina-self"[16] framework, were incompatible with the widely varied stories from different communities in China.

While the form of monologue did not work for some stories, double monologue—two actors telling the same story from different perspectives—could provide an appropriate format. Sophia Cai made such a change in her script. She wrote a piece on the issue of *tongqi*

13. Erin Striff, "Staging Communities of Women: Eve Ensler's *The Vagina Monologues* and V-Day Benefit Performances," University of Hartford, March 2, 2004.

14. Sealing Cheng, "Questioning Global Vaginahood: Reflections from Adapting *The Vagina Monologues* in Hong Kong," *Feminist Review*, no. 92 (2009): 23.

15. Striff, "Staging Communities," 9.

16. Christine Cooper critiques TVM'S "vagina-self" myth, in which Ensler uses metonym rather than metaphor to express the idea that "one's vagina is necessarily one's female self." Cooper, "Worrying."

(gay men's wives), in which an elderly woman recounts her sorrow over a depressing marriage with a gay man for more than thirty years. Sophia was not satisfied with this script since she thought the monologue was too sad and could not inspire further thinking or action. She decided that a monologue of the gay husband should be added, since he is also oppressed by socially recognized heterosexual norms. The form of double monologue opens up space for different perspectives and creates a more complicated and nuanced story. Another act, "Rape," a piece from *Our Vaginas Ourselves* (*yindao zhi dao* 阴道之道), written and performed by Bcome, uses triple monologue to achieve a better effect. "Rape" has three roles on stage: the rapist, the victim, and a justice representative. This form shows vividly how the woman speaks and reacts to her rapist, and how the rapist misunderstands her and tries to justify his own criminal behavior. Meanwhile the justice representative alternates between a critical and objective tone, which demonstrates the complicated nature of the institution's role in dealing with violence against women.

The playwrights and directors in China tended to use forms of performance that were familiar to local audiences. Cross talk (*xiangsheng* 相声) and comedy skits (*xiaopin* 小品) were traditional Chinese art forms, featuring comedic dialogues delivered in an exaggerated, playful, and humorous manner. Both local performance art forms were adopted by feminist theater for the power of their humor and irony. For instance, Ai Xiaoming adapted "Moaning" into a comedy skit. This performance featured three women from difference provinces of China who spoke different dialects. While the characters initially felt shameful about discussing orgasm with their female friends, they gradually encouraged each other and ended up moaning together. Ai's version of the "Moaning" skit was set in a specific context that allowed the audience to understand that the student actors were playing stage roles, not themselves. In such a theatric adaptation, it was important to keep the actor at a distance from the role, as there was a risk that the audiences might misinterpret the performance as autobiographical, which would put enormous pressure on the student performer.

The act "Intrauterine Device (IUD)" of *For Vagina's Sake* adopted the traditional stage form of cross talk to allow the bride to speak out all her worries about marriage, her fear of the forced placement of the IUD, and her seemingly bizarre ways of coping with it. This indigenous form of performance highlights the female protagonist's strong feelings of shock and powerlessness and helps to enhance the humorous effect.

The act "Bitch" 婊 in *Our Vaginas Ourselves* took the form of three-person cross talk. The three performers alternated between discussing social phenomena and making critical or ironic comments.

> A. Only if you refuse to act like an obedient good woman—
> B. (*cutting in; speaking simultaneously with A*)Even acting like a "good woman" is not enough. (*Covering her mouth to whisper to the audience with an exaggerated facial expression*) That would earn you the name of pure water bitch.
> A. People would generate all kinds of names to call you, to insult you. So, why don't we just act like bitches?! Milk tea bitch, green tea bitch, gutter oil bitch, pure water bitch, slutty bitch, silly bitch—
> C. —There is always a type fitting you.
> B. Starting from tomorrow, be a bitch. Masturbating, moaning, no bras.
> A. Starting from tomorrow, be a bitch. Acting innocent, acting cute, no sex.
> C. Starting from tomorrow, care about ob/gyn and condoms. Starting from tomorrow, care about orgasm and vagina.
> . . .
> A/B/C. I'd rather be a bitch throughout my life!

This excerpt shows how the three women characters in this act echoed each other with their sarcastic comments. They delivered a long list of misogynistic terms to expose the totalistic social control over and prevailing biases against women. This form deliberately imitated women's everyday speech. Its trivial and gossipy content mocked people's various ways of judging women, which brought the issue of sexist discrimination to audiences' attention. On the stage, performers hung those derogatory labels on their bodies to stress the absurd nature of these names. Women had no choice but to use the patriarchal system of significations, which tended to dismiss or shame women, to express themselves.

The act "An Orgasm Class" (*ziwei ketang* 自慰课堂) in *Our Vaginas Ourselves* mixed together the local stage forms of comedy skit and cross talk to create scenarios of women discussing orgasm while displaying various kinds of orgasmic experiences. With the use of images and role play, the woman teacher responded to students' views, which ranged from conservative to open to mistaken, making the orgasm class more dramatic and entertaining. These script writers and performers were more daring than TVM in SYSU in articulating their views in public. This group invited those who dared to talk about their vaginas, were happy to talk about sex, and were willing to join the movement against domestic violence and sexual insult. The stage roles directly expressed their joys and sufferings to stimulate reflection and a search for individual identification. Their stories were not told from the perspective of a spokesperson—a detached bystander who appears to be an urban-based, heterosexual career woman, or the implied scriptwriter like Ensler's TVM suggests. In other words, the script had multiple characters, viewpoints, and centers; the audience's path to identification was neither fixed nor singular.

The content, form, and style of these scripts were shaped by the method of collaborative writing. Usually the main members of the TVM production team jointly decided which topics their script should focus on. For example, Bcome used the method of voting to choose several important topics out of the many suggested by their members. The team of *For Vagina's Sake* discussed many rampant gender-specific issues in contemporary China and then decided to include the issues of reproduction, birth control, domestic violence, women's growing up, sexual harassment, and sexual pleasure, as well as those concerning the social groups of rural women, transgender people, lesbians, and young girls in their script. In general a script would be divided into eight to ten acts, with the first draft of each act mainly written by one member. However, its material and concepts came from the group's collaborative work. The production group usually made a gendered analysis of the first draft to help novice writers create more profound and powerful plays. Of course, these pieces were far from being professional or perfect, and not every performance could achieve artistic perfection. Their representations of the lives of different groups of women were more of a methodological exploration than the creation of an artistic model.

The process of collaborative creation meant that the acts in these scripts were not signed by any one author. Instead, the copyright was held by the whole production group. None of the groups planned on publishing their scripts; however, they chose to share them. Any other group could apply to get the script and then stage it on their own. This practice had something to do with the fact that they had copied Ensler's TVM concept. Yuping Zhang argues for the pirating or copying of TVM in China as it "is common sense in postsocialist China that culture products should be shared, so that it's acceptable to adopt or use the available script."[17] China's women's organizations did not participate in the V-Day and One Billion Rising worldwide campaigns started by Ensler. Rather, they rewrote the stories and made flexible performances. "The rewritten texts do not exploit TVM but rather apply added meanings to it and make a wider and richer map of the work. . . . Interestingly, Ensler supports the practices of these Chinese groups."[18] Seen from this perspective, China's TVM not only presented a stage dialogue within the theatrical space and a dialogue between performers and audiences, it also conducted a dialogue with the original author of TVM.

17. Zhang, "Global Media Activism," 63.
18. Qianting Ke, "How Can a Radical Sexual Play Work in a 'Conservative' Community?: The Adaptation and Recreation of *The Vagina Monologues* in China," in *Gender Dynamics, Feminist Activism, and Social Transformation in China*, ed. Guoguang Wu, Yuan Feng, and Helen Lansdowne (London: Routledge, 2019), 129.

From Individual Identification to Public Advocacy

During a symposium on Independent Gender Education Theater, Ai Xiaoming made reflective remarks on the limits of the decade-long adaptations of TVM in China: "We act as independent, liberated women on the stage, but we seldom tell our friends about the acting and the theme of the play. . . . TVM in China has a sense of utopian carnival. . . . There are a lot of events that have happened in China that are more cruel, complicated, and controversial than the stories of TVM."[19] Ai pointed out the problem: the theater was disconnected from the outside world. The members could get support within the team, and they were brave enough to tackle a sensitive topic. However, "it's much more challenging for us to work for woman's rights than speaking out on stage."[20] Ai made a prediction for a wider public space for the women's movement, which came true in a short time.

A couple of members from TVM theater went out of university and performed or advocated on the streets, in subways, and in factories and rural areas. They had gained power and skills from the process of organizing the production and performance of TVM, and they wanted to realize the feminist visions they had acquired along the road.

Inspired by the idea that they needed to reach more audiences and should connect their performance with reality, some TVM groups moved their stages to public spaces. Some members of Bcome performed a scene "My Mini Skirt" on the subway train to advocate the legitimacy of laws against domestic violence in China during the 16 Days movement in December 2012. After the performance they

---

19. Feng Yuan 冯媛, ed., "Yindao Dasheng Shuo—Zuowei Xingbie Jiaoyu de Duli Huaju zhi Lu Yantaohui Huiyi Jilu" 阴道大声说—作为性别教育的独立话剧之路研讨会会议记录 (Vagina Speaks Out Loud: Meeting Minutes of the Symposium on Independent Gender Education Theater), Beijing LGBT Center, December 2, 2013, archives of GenderWatch.

20. Feng Yuan, ed., "Yindao Dasheng Shuo."

talked to the audiences, who showed interest in the play and asked them about the topic of vagina. The interaction on the train was a test about how people talked about vagina publicly. Meanwhile, they made videos and uploaded them online so the discussion on the vagina taboo could continue. This team also performed "Who Killed Lesbians" (*shui shasile nü tongxinglian zhe* 谁杀死了女同性恋者) on one of the pedestrian bridges of Beijing. They advocated for lesbians' rights during the International Day against Homophobia in May 2013. By extending the stage from theater to public space and then to the Internet, they got many more opportunities to do public education and policy advocacy.

The volunteers from the Shanghai Zhi-he Society, the Beaver Club, and the Shanghai Nüai 女爱 lesbian NGO group performed on the trains with designed costumes and signboards printed with the lines "It's a Dress, Not a Yes" (*yao qingliang, bu yao selang* 要清凉, 不要色狼) and "Want to Flaunt, Not a Taunt" (*wo keyi sao, ni bu keyi rao* 我可以骚, 你不可以扰) to respond to the announcement at the subway station warning women, "Don't dress skimpily if you want to avoid sexual assault."

Xiaoyan 小燕, one of the members, said, "a couple of the participants in TVM have become activists, and they have done a great job. It is significant for me to join these teams."[21] This activity had been organized tactfully. First, the slogans they came up with were catchy, with a rhyming pattern, and thus easy to remember. Second, they joined the debate and gave the positive answer that women had the right to wear whatever they wanted to wear, which did not mean they were being flirtatious. Third, the costume they designed for this performance had a pointed iron bra which was cool and attractive, so the images were very popular. The language, performance, and images worked together and attracted massive attention.

---

21. Xiaoyan 小燕, "*Yindao Dubai* Zuowei Duoyuan de Pingtai—Zhihe she, Haili she yu *Yin DAO Duoyun*" 《阴道独白》作为多元的平台—知和社、海狸社与《阴DAO多云》 (*The Vagina Monologues* as a Platform for Various Communities: Zhi-he Society, Beaver Club and *Yin DAO Duoyun*), *Kula shibao*, December 6, 2013.

7.1. Anti–sexual harassment action at a subway station. Courtesy of Chen Xiangqi.

The TVM theater in China demonstrated how feminist words could do things. They used words creatively to narrate women's experiences and performed the acts on stage. They could also extend the message to social spaces and advocate women's rights. They did things when they showed up on stage, in the street, or in other public spaces; they did things when they uttered critical words and envisioned a new culture.

Using their bodies as media, they acted out the identities of bald women, female white-collar workers, pregnant women, victims of domestic violence, lesbians, and people with disabilities, appealing to the right to use public space to call for job equality and to advocate for the elimination of discrimination and for legislation against domestic violence. Their catchy, easy-to-chant slogans effectively spread through the media: "Beauty should not cause pain" (*Meili bu shoushang* 美丽不受伤); "There should be two women's toilets for every one of men's, or else women won't be able to hold it in line" (*Cesuo bili er bi yi, fouze nüsheng dengbuji* 厕所比例二比一, 否则女生等不及); "I don't want to become the next Li Yan" (*Wo bu xiang chengwei xia yige Li Yan* 我不想成为下一个李彦); "Proud to give lesbian blood" (*Nü tongxinglian jiaoao xianxue* 女同性恋骄傲献血); "Get a room with me, not with elementary students!" (*Kaifang zhao wo, fang guo xiao xuesheng* 开房找我, 放过小学生); and "My uterus my choice" (*Wo de zigong wo zuo zhu* 我的子宫我作主). Other activities, such as "Walk for feminism" (*Nüquan tubu* 女权徒步), "Feminists boycotting the Spring Festival Gala" (*Nüquan zhan chunwan* 女权战春晚), and "nudity against domestic violence (*luoti fan jiabao* 裸体反家暴), brought together two things that at first glance seemed to have nothing to do with each other. These names and slogans not only made linguistic innovations, but also promoted changes in people's ideas and behavioral patterns.

Plays, street performance art, and media advocacy all used language to do work. The embodied language not only spread ideas, but also shaped the speakers' own identities, constructing new speaking subjects. These speaking subjects dared to voice their own desires and were keen on making social changes. The liberated subjects directly expressed their opinions: they wanted orgasm, not sexual harassment; they did not want beauty standards and life plans set by others. They spoke out for minorities. The words spoken by these new subjects were aimed at analyzing and critiquing the patriarchal society and culture, rather than speaking of difficult problems and then waiting for them to be solved by some therapist or for some advisor to show them the right direction. The subject position they had acquired determined the stance and perspective from which words are spoken; meanwhile, their words and actions also shaped their subjectivity.

The breaking forth of a feminist language needed to seek new motivation, strategies, and momentum. The TVM production groups and other performance art all demonstrated their strength in this breaking forth. First, their works provided new perspectives for analyzing social problems and generated new knowledge. Second, their scripts and slogans could stimulate further public discussions, calling for the formation of a new subject and spurring on the next step of action.

Third, their language had the effect of bringing people together by developing new mechanisms of information dissemination, and thus could evoke responses in various fields. Fourth, their activities had the effect of empowerment, which could provide possible platforms, skills, and motivations to the widest range of people, who could join them and become new speakers and disseminators of the feminist message. Therefore, the knowledge and action growing out of everyday social issues had the potential to form a new discourse to replace the current mainstream gender discourse.

Conclusion

TVM in China serves as an excellent illustration of how contemporary Chinese feminists came up with new approaches and strategies in a heavily censored sociopolitical environment. Many women's organizations around the world joined the two worldwide movements initiated by Ensler. However, Chinese feminist groups could not do it within the purview of Ensler's guidelines. First of all, most Chinese women's organizations are not allowed to fundraise in public or sell tickets for their shows. Therefore, they cannot take part in the global fundraising effort against domestic violence. Second, they cannot organize activities freely during the period between Valentine's Day and the International Women's Day because it is right after the traditional Chinese Spring Festival. More important, this time period also overlaps with the annual meetings of the National People's Congress and the Chinese People's Political Consultative Conference, when sociopolitical surveillance and censorship are ramped up. Third, the narrative and motif of the script prescribed by Ensler for the annual performance fail to align with the ongoing urgent gender-specific issues in contemporary Chinese society. Under such sociopolitical conditions, young Chinese feminists paid close attention to local women's concerns, issues, and needs, and organized activities in a creative and flexible manner to expand a feminist public space.

Focused on the case study of TVM in China, this chapter examines these feminist linguistic tactics. Feminist organizations adapted and rewrote Ensler's script because they yearned for a language of their own to express their needs and desires and to communicate with the public, particularly women. They have gained freedom and power in experimental workshops and group discussions. Shaking off the constraints of the old system of signification, they have engaged in passionate and bold critique of a sexist culture. On the one hand, they have carried on the feminist legacy of women's liberation. On the other hand, they also refused to accept the hegemonic authority and "guidance" of male intellectuals in order to find their own voices on the basis of independent thinking and to make a coalition with other socially disadvantaged groups to develop a more inclusive agenda.

These women's organizations did things with language. They searched for a genuine, powerful, and effective language to write and represent women's stories. They created scripts, made allies with socially marginalized groups, cultivated leadership, and engaged in street performance and media advocacy. They staged their scripts on a wide range of platforms and occasions and organized a series of face-to-face discussions between performers and audiences. They also moved the stage to public squares and subways to speak to a wider audience for the sake of policy advocacy. Most important, new subjects were generated through all these practices. A younger generation with a new gendered awareness also had a stronger sense of civic responsibility. They actively experimented with more creative forms of self-expression to expand the feminist influence with performance art, short videos, and new and old media.

This new feminist movement, mainly launched by a younger generation, has drawn on theoretical and cultural resources of global feminism to develop its own language, platform, public space, and social force in order to challenge and break through the restraining status quo.

Part Three

Chinese Feminisms in Women's Literature, Art, and Film

8

"Am I a Feminist?"

An Interview with Wang Anyi

Liu Jindong
Translated by Ping Zhu

LIU JINDONG. Professor Li Xiaojiang organized a women's studies conference in Zhengzhou in 1991, and you were the only woman writer at the conference. She said you showed some interest in women's literature and women's oral history. She wanted to know why you went to the conference.

WANG ANYI. I did not have to go, but I went because I heard about the conference and some of my friends were going. Besides, I had not been to Zhengzhou.

LIU. So you were not interested in women's studies?

WANG. Li Xiaojiang thought I was interested.

LIU. Have you read Li Xiaojiang's books?

WANG. I have read and own many of her books.

LIU. What do you think about them?

WANG. I appreciate that Li Xiaojiang always speaks from the standpoint of Chinese women—this is very good. The feminist ideas I knew were imported from the West, and as a result, many people

This is an abridged version of Liu Jindong's interview with Wang Anyi, conducted in 2001. The original interview was published in *Zhongshan*, no. 5 (2001): 114–28.

205

with those feminist ideas would involuntarily examine China from the Western perspective.

LIU. Very abstract.

WANG. Those feminist ideas are not only abstract, but also come from a different position. Li Xiaojiang impressed me for always using a Chinese perspective to examine Chinese problems. I have to admit that there are issues in her approach. For example, she cites many fictional works in her books, but fiction is not objective reality. One should not treat fiction as materials—one can only treat fiction writing as reality. Despite this, I still appreciate her position. I thought I would hear many Western theories at the Zhengzhou conference, but I was surprised to see so many participants who engaged in women's work at the grassroots level. They were in plain outfits. I still remember a peasant woman giving a presentation on how backyard production can facilitate women's independence. At that time, I felt Li Xiaojiang was a humanitarian person.

LIU. Now let's turn to your fiction. I think some of your stories, such as *I Love Bill* (*Wo ai Bi'er* 我爱比尔), *A Century on a Hill* (*Gangshang de Shiji* 岗上的世纪), and the Three Love (*Sanlian* 三恋) trilogy can be read as feminist works. The Three Love trilogy, in particular, is a valuable text about women's psychology. What was your original intention in writing those stories?

WANG. My finished works don't belong to me anymore; they are open to anyone's criticism. Li Xiaojiang would be disappointed at my original intention because I have actually rarely conceived my stories from women's point of view. I do not want to solve the women's problem in my works; instead I think the world is shared by men and women together. This balanced ecology cannot be maintained without either side. However, I do have one belief that can be related to feminism: I have created so many female characters because I think women are more aesthetic (*juyou shenmeixingzhi* 具有审美性质) than men, probably because men have been more socialized.

LIU. Many male writers like writing about women too. What does love or sexuality mean to the female characters in your works?

WANG. I think they are associated with women's emotional needs— women both possess and need a great amount of emotions.

LIU. Love and sex have a great transformative power in your stories. For example, in *Love in a Small Town* (*Xiaocheng zhilian* 小城 之恋), the female protagonist was pregnant but she didn't tell other people who the father of her twins was. She raised the kids on her own and felt content, rejecting help from the man. You wrote that the man was surpassed when the woman gave birth to new lives.

WANG. I did not think too much. I had to end their affair so they could walk out from their calamity, the calamity of sex. Sex can only become a healthy relationship when it is supported by emotion and reason. If people lose control of themselves and incessantly ask for pleasure, anesthesia, and stimulation, they would fall into a vicious circle and become irrational. Back to the story: How could they end it? I thought maybe the fruit of sex—pregnancy and childbirth—would bring peace to the woman. This is the natural privilege of women.

LIU. I believe you are right. We can prove this with our own experiences.

WANG. Educated and rational people would have a spiritual demand in love and sex, but the man and woman in *Love in a Small Town* did not. I can only envision something physical as their deus ex machina. The man was actually miserable. He could not escape the tragedy like the woman; he could only struggle in this abyss. There was a huge difference between the man and the woman in the story: the man's identification with the kids was rational, as he could not develop an intuitive relationship with the kids; for the woman, the identification was direct and intuitive.

LIU. Therefore it is possible to read your story from the feminist perspective.

WANG. To be honest, I didn't think of feminism, I simply saw reality.

LIU. But this is how we read your story.

WANG. This is a rather pedantic way of reading, which adds a grave label to my story. I simply needed to find a way out for my protagonists.

LIU. Sometimes sex brings destruction to women. For example, in *I Love Bill*, Ah San loves Bill; once Bill leaves, she falls into degradation.

WANG. I always maintain a distance from the ideology—that is, from the society—but *I Love Bill* is an exception. This is actually a symbolic story, which has little to do with love and sex. I was writing about the Third World situation. Bill is a symbol of the West to Ah San. The biggest contradiction in the story is that Ah San must use her Chinese characteristics to attract Bill, but she also wishes she was not Chinese but rather a Caucasian girl. Therefore, she is simultaneously stressing and effacing her Chinese characteristics.

LIU. This is all because she loves Bill. Bill says he cannot love a girl from a Communist country.

WANG. People are obsessed with the concept of love. Ah San is a girl with a modern dream. She thinks she has connected with Bill, whereas in fact she can never be together with Bill. She meets a French man named Martin later, and she loves Martin too. Martin is different from Bill: Bill is a symbol of modernity, but Martin is not. Like Ah San, Martin has deep cultural roots. But Ah San cannot be together with Martin either: when Ah San forsakes her own culture to approach Martin, Martin does not accept a rootless Ah San; when Ah San keeps her own roots, there is always a distance between Martin and her. I meant to show how a Chinese girl's body and mind are self-destroyed when she approaches the West. *I Love Bill* has nothing to do with love, sex, or feminism, it is a story about a developing country.

LIU. I think *I Love Bill* can be read as a women's story. It is pretty realistic. When Ah San escaped from prison, she found a virgin egg. The warmth of the egg reminded her of her pure virginity.

WANG. It depends on how you read it. The detail you mentioned is related to a previous plot. Ah San was a virgin when she first met Bill. She worried that Bill would be reluctant to have sex with her because she was inexperienced. To be more attractive, she had to show Bill that she was open to sex like all Americans. When they made love for the first time, she covered her virgin blood with a blanket lest Bill see it. She thought it was a shame to have sex for the first time at such a mature age. In the end, she found a virgin egg covered in blood. This is a symbolic story: when we leave our isolation, we lose many things. What has been invaded is not only our resources, but also our economic life and structure of feeling.

LIU. Li Xiaojiang wanted you to talk about how you represent the female consciousness in your stories. You said you are not interested in female consciousness or feminism, but you allow readers to perceive the female consciousness in your stories. Many of your stories, such as *The Song of Everlasting Sorrow* (*Changhen ge* 长恨歌), *Fu Ping* (富萍), *Meitou* (妹头), *Anecdotes of the Cultural Revolution* (*Wenge yishi* 文革轶事), and *Lapse of Time* (*Liushi* 流逝), feature female protagonists from different social classes. Did you have an overall plan for producing those stories?

WANG. There was no overall plan, I simply wrote one story after another. I have no problem with critics putting my stories into different categories, but that was not my plan.

LIU. In your essay "Shanghai Women" (*Shanghai nüxing* 上海女性), you claim that women are representations of Shanghai. Do you write about women in order to write about Shanghai? Or are you interested in women themselves?

WANG. I like writing about women because they are aesthetic. I seldom write about men. I think women are more like a kind of animals, as they have less nurtured qualities. In addition, Shanghai women are full of life. Women are especially suitable for living in the city, where there are crowds and commodities.

LIU. All of the women in those aforementioned stories are trying to make a living. Some of them make a living through work, some of them through love.

WANG. Through love? Not actually. Meitou depends on herself; so
    does Fu Ping.

LIU. Fu Ping would not have come to Shanghai without her engage-
    ment to Granny's grandson.

WANG. Yes, that was a condition for her.

LIU. And she wouldn't be able to settle in Shanghai without the
    crippled man and his mother.

WANG. Although Fu Ping came to Shanghai and settled down
    there through these relationships, she depends on her own labor
    to make a living. She saw many laboring and striving women
    in Shanghai, who became her models. Shanghai women look
    delicate, but they are tough inside. In contrast, northern women
    may look tough, but they are not as malleable as the Shanghai
    women. Just think of Wang Qiyao in *The Song of Everlasting Sor-
    row* as an example: How many other women would have survived
    in her position? Wang Qiyao knew how to compromise, she
    would marry someone just to live the rest of her life.

LIU. Many people, including myself, compare your works with those
    of Eileen Chang. Eileen Chang wrote about the limits of human-
    ity: her characters know that desires are dangerous, but they can-
    not help pursuing their desires, to the extent of self-destruction.
    Many of your stories have characters like this too, they push
    themselves to hopeless situations pursuing their desires.

WANG. There are some similarities between our writings, but not
    too much. People think we are alike because both Chang and I
    wrote about Shanghai, and we are both realistic writers. What
    I appreciate most about Eileen Chang is her secularism. Desire
    (*yuwang* 欲望) is the theorized vocabulary used by intellectuals;
    its vernacular expression is that people want to live better lives.
    Shanghai citizens want to improve their lives bit by bit, it is a
    positive attitude that can take them really far.

LIU. So they don't think about the remote big ideals?

WANG. Urban residents are near-sighted, they don't think about the
    day after tomorrow, they only think about today. They may not
    have aspirations or desires, but they have concrete plans that they

follow one step after another. That's how they laid the foundation for the city.

LIU. Just like the shack dwellers in *Fu Ping*?

WANG. And Granny too. There are many other characters who came to Shanghai down and out, but they managed to settle down and make a living in the city.

LIU. *Fu Ping* is a grassroots story. Its characters, such as the housekeepers and trash collectors, are subalterns. Those people are hardworking and kindhearted. For example, Fu Ping's aunt runs a trash collecting boat in the shanty area. In people's imagination, she must be brusque and petulant. But in the story she is very kind and considerate, and even sensitive. The poor and coarse life didn't undermine her fine human nature. She feels guilty that they didn't take care of Fu Ping years ago. She also has good judgment, so she picked an educated man to be her husband. Her state of mind seems incompatible with her living conditions.

WANG. Maybe this is my biased, subjective view. I set the story before the Cultural Revolution because I wanted to demarcate a utopia in time and space.

LIU. Right, back then people were different.

WANG. Back then there was an order in the society: the old order was not completely discontinued, and the new order was already in. Some intellectuals don't like this statement, because intellectuals were persecuted back then. However, the lives of ordinary folks had improved. I think back then people led a pure and plain life by supporting themselves with their own labor. This healthy lifestyle nurtured honest morality, which in turn enriched their souls. These people were self-sufficient. I meant to express my resistance to contemporary life in this story. I don't like how we live today. There is too much dissipation in terms of time, material, life, emotions, and soul.

LIU. I think you created a new female figure in *Meitou*: unlike all your previous protagonists, Meitou is a real urban petty bourgeois (*xiaoshimin* 小市民).

WANG. Yes, she is a real urban petty bourgeois.

LIU. She is restless, which I think is an important feature of Shanghai residents.

WANG. Not really, Shanghainese residents are absolutely conservative. For example, Meitou will decorate her collar and waistline, but she won't wear a flamboyant outfit, because she is conservative.

LIU. She knows how to make herself and others look attractive. She can make small changes, but these small improvements are not revolutionary.

WANG. You are right, urban petty bourgeois are by no means revolutionary, but they seize every opportunity to live better. In the story, the male intellectual Xiaobai is Meitou's foil. Xiaobai lives in his mind, whereas Meitou lives in reality. Meitou is more powerful than Xiaobai. She looks down on Xiaobai because she thinks his writings are empty and useless. By contrast, Meitou is an interesting figure, who possesses more energy, life, and motivation than Xiaobai. Xiaobai had some vitality when he was with Meitou; however, he lost all his vitality when he moved into the apartment in the new developed area; he became a pale man of culture (*cangbai de wenhuaren* 苍白的文化人).

LIU. So Meitou is leading a better life and Xiaobai is increasingly pale, is this your feminist proposition?

WANG. To a certain degree. It could be my feminist proposition, or my critical view of intellectuals—I think many intellectuals lack vitality.

LIU. Why didn't you create a female intellectual then?

WANG. It wouldn't be realistic. I don't like bizarre stories, such as a female intellectual marrying a male worker. My stories must be reasonable.

LIU. Let's talk about the weak-man problem. I feel the male characters in women writers' works are often pale, mediocre, weak, or ugly.

WANG. Knowledge is feeble, life is robust. Who should embody knowledge and who should embody life in the stories? I think it is better that women embody life, because men do not have women's aesthetic aura (*meigan* 美感) in life. I've barely seen a man full of power and vitality in real life.

LIU. Therefore, in your story *Love on a Barren Mountain* (*Huangshan zhilian* 荒山之恋), the male protagonist is weak and passive compared to the female protagonist? Would women be disappointed at men or heterosexual love in this way?

WANG. Not really. Women have more emotional needs and capacity than men; they would appear more powerful in a romantic relationship. Men have less emotional capacity and needs, so they are more likely to make compromises in a relationship.

LIU. Because men have careers as their foundation, so love is not so important to them.

WANG. It seems that men are not emotional beings. I think women are emotional beings, and it is for this reason that they appear lovely in my eyes.

LIU. I have another question about your novella *Brothers* (*Dixiong men* 弟兄们). In this story the three girls were very close to each other at school, but they grew apart after graduation and marriage. Zhang Jie wrote about the friendship between three women too in her novella *The Ark* (*Fangzhou* 方舟), but her story is very different: in your *Brothers*, the coalition between the three women dissolved under the siege of motherhood and wifehood; in *The Ark*, however, the three female characters continued to live together and support each other in a male-centered society.

WANG. I'm different from Zhang Jie, as I do not have so much resentment toward men.

LIU. You do not project yourself onto your characters, and you rarely hold a feminist stance. Zhang Jie's works have a conspicuous feminist stance and subjective narrative.

WANG. I think Zhang Jie is the only feminist in China.

LIU. So you don't write for women or write with the awareness of the woman question?

WANG. This is a complex question. My head turns muddy as soon as we talk about the woman question. The feminist ideas we learned from the West do not fit squarely with the reality of Chinese women. The reality of Chinese women is more brutal than that of the West; Chinese women's social status was very low due to the backward economy.

LIU. You mentioned this in your earlier conversation with Li Ang.[1] It seems that your concern for women was especially realistic: you wished that women could return to the family and keep a distance from social life, because they were too tired carrying the double burden. But later on you negated yourself, because you felt women would grow more weary pleasing their husbands at home.

WANG. Hence it is hard to find a suitable position for women in society. Speaking of feminism, I do have one relatively unknown story that I wrote consciously for women, it is *Sisters* (*Zimei men* 姊妹们).

LIU. I read it. It is about the lives of the female rusticated youth before they got married. You wrote about the female rusticated youth in other stories too.

WANG. I used the same characters' names in other stories. But this is a story written with a feminist stance and consciousness. The village in the story is very orthodox, regulated, and rigid, but the women are vivacious and beautiful. It is as if I created a Grand View Garden.[2]

LIU. When I read it I didn't perceive a conspicuous feminist voice or stance.

WANG. We tend to view feminist literature as women's conscious revolt against men or women's sober criticism of men. Although in *Sisters* I only wrote about some naive girls, I wrote the story consciously.

---

1. Li Ang and Wang Anyi, "Funü Wenti yu Funü Wenxue" 妇女问题与妇女文学 (The Woman Question and Women's Literature), *Shanghai wenxue*, no. 3 (1989): 76–80.

2. Grand View Garden (*Daguan yuan* 大观园) is a fictional garden in Cao Xueqin's classic novel *Dream of the Red Chamber* (*Honglou meng* 红楼梦); it was once home for many beautiful girls.

LIU. Precisely because these girls are naive, the story is not viewed as a feminist story. Your perspective is objective: you are viewing them, but you are not one of them.

WANG. My stance is very biased. I love them. I think feminist scholars like you always want the female protagonist to speak out.

LIU. Not necessarily. But in *Sisters*, the girls are in a natural state, they are not conscious of their own being, nor can they marry freely. They are not feminists in the common sense.

WANG. What you need is a form of conscious feminism.

LIU. Not exactly. But you can see that the women in *Sisters* do not struggle like those female characters in Zhang Jie's stories.

WANG. I created a beautiful ladies' kingdom. Against the lackluster background, the girls appear so bright and beautiful. They represent my view of women. Do women have to speak out in feminist works?

LIU. At least they have to struggle against their fate. But the women in *Sisters* appear submissive; they don't challenge their fate.

WANG. I'm a writer, not a feminist activist, so I don't directly use my works for that purpose. To me, fiction is art, and it is the object's aesthetic value that determines what I write about.

9

Wang Anyi's New Shanghai

Gender and Labor in Fu Ping

Ping Zhu

The reception of Wang Anyi's literary works has been permeated with a symptomatic desire to construct a continuous and homogenous history of Chinese modernity by connecting Republic of China (ROC)–period petty bourgeois subjectivity with the postsocialist rediscovery of humanity and femininity and by connecting ROC Shanghai modernity with the postsocialist revival of the city's commercial power. This continuous and homogenous history is what Walter Benjamin calls "homogeneous empty time,"[1] which is specifically associated with the capitalist mode of production. One of the effects of such a symptomatic desire to endorse "homogeneous empty time" is the scholars' deliberate omissions of the "socialist stories" in Wang's works. Like my coeditor Hui Faye Xiao points out in a recent essay, few have recognized that "Wang Anyi has paid idiosyncratic attention to the politics and poetics of everyday life and labor aesthetics that underscores the historical legacy of Shanghai's socialist past."[2]

1. Benjamin Walter, "Theses on the Philosophy of History," in *Walter Benjamin, Illuminations*, trans. Harry Zohn (New York: Schocken, 1969), 261.

2. Hui Faye Xiao, "Female Neo-Realism: Masterworks of Zhang Jie, Wang Anyi, and Chi Li," in *Routledge Handbook of Modern Chinese Literature*, ed. Mingdong Gu (New York: Routledge, 2018), 559.

One constant theme in Wang Anyi's stories is the positive influence labor exerts on women. In her first novella, *Lapse of Time* (*Liushi* 流逝, 1982), a rich bourgeois family became impoverished during the Cultural Revolution, yet the daughter-in-law gained self-esteem after she joined the labor force. Many of her novels produced in the twenty-first century, such as *Meitou* (妹头, 2000), *Fu Ping* (富萍, 2000), *Growing Red Water Chestnut Above and Lotus Below* (*Shang zhong hongling xia zhong ou* 上种红菱下种藕, 2001), and *Scent of Heaven* (*Tianxiang* 天香, 2011), feature independent women laborers. However, to this date, a search for "Wang Anyi" and "labor (*daodong* 劳动)" in English and Chinese scholarship yields virtually no result. Instead, Wang's critics overwhelmingly focus on her portrayal of individual psychology, her representations of love and sexuality, and the petit bourgeois lifestyle of Shanghainese residents she depicts. As if eager to prove her emphasis on the significance of labor without distracting people with the spectacle of gender (which she has been lauded for), Wang's 2018 novel, *Artificer's Record* (*Kaogongji* 考工记), narrates how an old-Shanghai dandy gradually transforms into a laborer in socialist China; her most recent novel, *One Chef Knife, A Thousand Words* (*Yibadao, Qiangezi* 一把刀, 千个字) follows the life of a Huaiyang cuisine chef from Shanghai to New York City. Those are no longer women's stories but still laborers' stories.

When I met Wang Anyi in 2017 at the University of Oklahoma, I asked her why she created so many laborers in her stories. She said, "Characters are only possible when their livelihood is explained."[3] This canonical Marxist view explains why she adopts a materialist conception of history and grants labor a preeminent place in her stories. Another important reason that explains Wang's predilection for labor is her deep aversion to the contemporary consumer culture that turns women into objects of desire, which leads to her nostalgia for the effective feminist practices in socialist China, when men and women worked as equal laborers.[4]

3. Ping Zhu, "Seven Short Conversations with Wang Anyi, Dai Jinhua, and Wang Ban," *Chinese Literature Today* 6, no. 2 (2017): 20.

4. Zhu, "Seven Short Conversations," 20–21.

For a long period of time Wang Anyi did not know how to articulate the problem of gender equality. In a 1988 interview with Wang Zheng, for example, Wang Anyi talked about Chinese women's "extra burden" after they gained equality through the socialist revolution and admitted that the problem of women's liberation was "difficult and complex."[5] Wang Anyi's hesitation to endorse the contemporary version of gender equality reflects her sober thinking about the conceptualization and social valorization of gendered labor, which is not a simple gender problem but demands a critique of the economic system.

In China the liberation of women through labor was an invention of the Communist Party. As Dong Limin puts it, "allowing 'women' to enter 'labor' indicates the exploration of a new ideal and an approach to reposition the relationship between women and the world that is different from 'women's liberation' in developed capitalist countries."[6] However, the socialist regime also rendered women's domestic work invisible and insignificant, creating a hierarchy of (masculine) productive work over (feminine) unproductive work. A plethora of films and plays produced during the socialist period, such as *Magnolia Flower in Blossom* (*Malan huakai* 马兰花开, 1956), *Flying Side by Side* (*Biyi qifei* 比翼齐飞, 1959), *Happy Laughter* (*Xiaozhu yankai* 笑逐颜开, 1959), *The Housewife of a Big Family* (*Dajiating zhufu* 大家庭主妇, 1960), and *Li Shuangshuang* (李双双, 1962), aimed to devalue women's traditional domestic work and recruit women for the social productive work under the catchphrase of gender equality. As a result, Chinese women's workforce participation rate has been one of the highest in the world.[7] However, after Chinese women were

5. Wang Zheng, "Interviews with Wang Anyi, Zhu Lin, Dai Qing," *Modern Chinese Literature* 4, nos. 1/2 (1988): 109.

6. Dong Limin 董丽敏, "'Laodong': Funü Jiefang ji qi Xiandu; Yi Zhao Shuli Xiaoshuo wei Ge'an de Kaocha" 劳动: 妇女解放及其限度; 以赵树理小说为个案的考察 ("Labor": Women's Liberation and Its Limits; A Case Study of Zhao Shuli's Fiction), *Zhongguo xiandai wenxue yanjiu congkan* no. 3 (2010), 27.

7. See data collected by The World Bank: https://data.worldbank.org/indicator/sl.tlf.cact.fe.zs.

reindoctrinated into the cult of domesticity in the postsocialist period, they have had to face the double burden (*shuangchong fudan* 双重负担) of work and family and are easily burnt out.[8] To make things worse, a competitive free market has continued to ignore gender differences by devaluing domestic work and leaving legions of women without proper support.

According to Marx, productive labor is the labor that produces surplus value for the capitalist and thus expands the capital. Unproductive labor, in contrast, is labor that is consumed not in order to produce surplus value, but simply in order to satisfy a concrete need.[9] Unproductive labor, therefore, bears a close tie to life itself and does not expand capital. However, Western feminists have pointed out that the concept of productive labor itself was a product of capitalism: "Goods that could be bought and sold, quantities that could be expressed in dollar terms, became the new arbiters of value. Indeed, the growing enthusiasm for social statistics, reflected in new census-taking efforts, deflected attention from activities that could not easily be reduced to a money metric."[10] The capitalist restructuring of economic activities is characterized by its ambiguous conceptualization of the home as a gendered space: "the moral elevation of the home was accompanied by the economic devaluation of the work performed there."[11] For good mothers and wives, women's domestic work was stripped of the exchange value despite its important use value. As Kathleen Canning points out, the dominant social identity and rhetoric of class in the modern period "was cast in terms of a certain idealized relationship to production, a rigid demarcation between

8. Li Xiaojiang 李小江, *Xinggou* 性沟 (Sex Gap) (Beijing: Sanlian shudian, 1989), 92–93.

9. Peter Meiksins, "Productive and Unproductive Labor and Marx's Theory of Class," *Review of Radical Political Economics* 13, no. 3 (1981): 34.

10. Nancy Folbre, "The Unproductive Housewife: Her Evolution in Nineteenth-Century Economic Thought," *Signs: Journal of Women in Culture and Society* 16, no. 3 (1991): 465.

11. Folbre, "Unproductive Housewife," 465.

work and 'nonwork,' production and reproduction, that by definition excluded most of female workers."[12] The unproductive work that is normally performed by women in the domestic sphere thus became invisible as a result of its subordination to the accumulative logic of the capitalist market.

In order to challenge this capitalist configuration of the distinction between productive and unproductive labor that has affected women in both First and Third World countries, Western feminists have drawn inspirations from Michael Hardt's notion of affective labor. According to Hardt, affective labor "is immaterial, even if it is corporeal and affective, in the sense that its products are intangible: a feeling of ease, well-being, satisfaction, excitement, passion—even a sense of connectedness or community."[13] Affective labor "is better understood by beginning from what feminist analyses of 'women's work' have called 'labor in the bodily mode'";[14] however, it is "not only directly productive of capital but at the very pinnacle of the hierarchy of laboring forms."[15] Although affective labor is associated with the pervasive mode of capitalist production, Hardt believes that "the production of affects, subjectivities, and forms of life present an enormous potential for autonomous circuits of valorization, and perhaps for liberation."[16]

The notion of affective labor invites a radical conceptualization of the so-called women's work and opens up new directions for imagining women's liberation. As Li Xiaojiang points out, even though contemporary China is saturated with the ideology of "gender equality," there has not been a feminist revolution in the domains of the family and everyday life.[17] If women's work can be viewed as productive

12. Kathleen Canning, *Languages of Labor and Gender: Female Factory Work in Germany, 1850–1914* (Ithaca, NY: Cornell Univ. Press, 1996), 5.

13. Michael Hardt, "Affective Labor," *Boundary 2* 26, no. 2 (1999): 96.

14. Hardt, "Affective Labor," 96.

15. Hardt, "Affective Labor," 90.

16. Hardt, "Affective Labor," 100.

17. See Li Xiaojiang "Equality and Gender Equality with Chinese Characteristics," in this volume.

of the central constituents of the economic system—networks, communities, and subjectivities—then "economic production has merged with the communicative action of human relations."[18] It is therefore possible to imagine empowered women laborers who engage in "unproductive labor," including kin work and care work. It is also possible to revalorize different types of women's work by recognizing their central roles in developing and sustaining an individual, a community, and a society.

Many of Wang Anyi's new works written after 1995 can be read as a vindication of women's work, which can be illuminated with Hardt's notion of affective labor. Wang Xiaoming has astutely pointed out that Wang Anyi's writing entered a new phase after *Song of Everlasting Sorrow* (*Changhenge* 长恨歌, 1995): it is as if she has deliberately drawn a distance from the 1930s Shanghai and wants to create a different Shanghai story.[19] The protagonist, Wang Qiyao, spent the most peaceful segment of her life during the first seventeen years of the socialist period, working as common laborer—a nurse. Despite the fact this second Shanghai story is often eclipsed by the more alluring story of the glamorous old Shanghai, it is indicative of the author's effort in recreating Shanghai, a time-honored symbol of bourgeois modernity and consumerism, as a city of laborers, thereby rescuing the unique experience of the Chinese working class from the siege of commodity fetishism revived by China's entry into global capitalism. Furthermore, as my reading of Wang Anyi's novel *Fu Ping* 富萍 will show in the following sections, Wang's representation of gendered labor in her stories beseeches us to reevaluate the historical significance of "women's work," which is rendered subordinate in both socialist and capitalist master narratives. Such a reevaluation can lead to radical possibilities for feminist imaginations.

18. Hardt, "Affective Labor," 96.

19. Wang Xiaoming 王晓明, "Cong 'Huaihailu' dao 'Meijiaqiao': Cong Wang Anyi Xiaoshuo de Zhuanbian Tanqi" 从"淮海路"到"梅家桥": 从王安忆小说的转变谈起 (From Huaihailu to Meijiaqiao: On the Transformations of Wang Anyi's Fiction), *Wenxue pinglun*, no. 3 (2002): 5.

Gender, Labor, and the Market

The most exemplary story of Wang Anyi's new Shanghai is *Fu Ping*, which was originally published in the literary journal *Harvest* (*Shouhuo* 收获) in 2000. The story is set in Shanghai in the mid-1960s, right before the Cultural Revolution. Shanghai in the 1960s was an anachronistic space. Wang said in a 2001 interview: "Back then there was an order in the society: the old order was not completely discontinued, and the new order was already in."[20] Shanghai in the mid-1960s is represented as an inclusive place where contradictory ideas and social structures harmoniously coexisted. There was the residue of colonial Shanghai with all its glamorous and exquisite lifestyle; there was the traditional kinship network among migrant workers in Shanghai, especially those migrant groups living in the suburbs; and there was the notion of equality and independence brought by the socialist revolution. The rich and complex lifeworld gives the story a unique setting.

The eighteen-year-old orphan girl Fu Ping was brought to Shanghai from the Yangzhou countryside to temporarily stay with Granny, her future grandmother-in-law. In Shanghai Fu Ping has experienced three different migrant workers' communities: the housekeepers' community on Huaihailu 淮海路 in downtown Shanghai, whose members came to Shanghai before the socialist period and experienced the city's capitalist past; the migrants running trash boats in the poor Zhabei 闸北 district in north Shanghai, with whom Fu Ping temporarily stays, thanks to the kinship relationship; and the shack dwellers in Meijiaqiao 梅家桥 in Zhabei, where she finally settles in by marrying into a poor family consisting of a crippled son and a kind mother.

All three communities are subaltern groups in Shanghai whose members are busy making a living in the big city. However, there is a distinct hierarchy among the three communities: the Huaihailu housekeepers are the most respected due to their connection to the

---

20. Liu Jindong, "'Am I a Feminist?': An Interview with Wang Anyi," in this volume, 211.

old bourgeois Shanghai and their still somewhat exquisite lifestyles; the trash-boat families in Zhabei have stable income and a solid kinship network (as they all came from Yangzhou), and the second generation has already started to blend into Shanghai; and the Meijiaqiao shack dwellers are struggling to make ends meet by doing all kinds of lowly jobs, but they have maintained their dignity by earning their own livelihood.

Fu Ping's trajectory of finding her own place in Shanghai consists of two movements: first she moves from the center of Shanghai to its periphery; second, she moves from the more established subaltern group to the less established subaltern group. Here centrifugal geographical movement is conflated with downward social class movement, unfolding a Shanghai that is very different from the Crystal Palace[21] of colonial modernity, and introducing a different body of Shanghai residents—the laborers. Despite their different social status and dwelling places in Shanghai, the three groups of laborers live a "satisfied and peaceful" life.[22]

In *Fu Ping*, labor is not represented through abstract socioeconomic relations; nor is *laborer* a byword of the proletariat.[23] Instead of reducing history to homogenous and empty time, in *Fu Ping*, Wang Anyi uses labor as a lens through which she can productively create her characters and their world. Labor is how she imagines "the concrete development and cause"[24] of her characters, and the complex social relationships they exist in. Positing labor as the determining

21. Wang Anyi, *Fu Ping* (Changsha: Hunan wenyi chubanshe, 2000), 34. The English version, *Fu Ping: A Novel*, was translated by Howard Goldblatt and published by Columbia University Press in 2019.

22. Wang, *Fu Ping*, 43.

23. Cai Xiang points out that the leftists during the socialist period equated *laborer* with the proletariat, which created a much more rigid definition of the former. See Cai Xiang 蔡翔, *Geming-Xushu: Zhongguo Shehui Zhuyi Wenxue-Wenhua Xiangxiang (1949–1966)* 革命·叙述: 中国社会主义文学-文化想象 (1949–1966) (Revolution and Its Narrative: China's Socialist Literary and Cultural Imaginations [1949–1966]) (Beijing: Beijing daxue chubanshe, 2010).

24. Zhu, "Seven Short Conversations," 20.

factor in people's social activities is nothing new for Marxists. The gist of Marxist historical materialism claims that human society is fundamentally determined at any given time by material conditions—in other words, the relationships that condition people's means of livelihood. The three migrant communities in *Fu Ping* are formed out of those material conditions that allow them to fulfill basic needs, such as food, clothing, and housing for themselves and their families. Through these collective material activities, the people also create history. In *Economic and Philosophical Manuscripts of 1844*, Marx asserts that it is in labor that "all the natural, spiritual, and social variety of individual activity is manifested and is variously rewarded."[25] In the same vein, Wang Anyi has no intention to reduce history to its economic basis and people to *homo economicus*; on the contrary, she likes to use labor as a lens through which she can productively create her characters and their world.

In *The Wealth of Nations*, Adam Smith portrays the market as an "invisible hand"[26] orchestrating all activities and movements of individuals and collectives within its reach. In *Fu Ping*, however, it is labor that functions as the invisible hand, turning the market into an auxiliary existence. If the market always works in the interest of capital, and, in Marx and Engels's words, inevitably reveals the "icy water of egotistical calculation,"[27] labor that orchestrates activities and movements is always embodied and has a human face.

Granny is one of the Huaihailu housekeepers, who takes pride in living in the "real Shanghai."[28] Granny is widowed and has no son, but in Shanghai she is able to save enough money for her old age by doing housekeeping. As an experienced housekeeper, Granny can

---

25. Karl Marx, *Economic and Philosophic Manuscripts of 1844*, trans. and ed. Martin Milligan (Mineola, NY: Dover, 2007), 22.

26. Adam Smith, *The Wealth of Nations*, part 2 (Princeton, NJ: Princeton Univ. Press, 1902), 160.

27. Karl Marx and Friedrich Engels, *Manifesto of the Communist Party*, edited and annotated by Frederick Engels (Chicago: Charles H. Kerr & Company, 1906), 16.

28. Wang, *Fu Ping*, 157.

freely select her employer (*dongjia* 东家) in the local job market. She finally settles with a couple who fought in the Chinese Communist Party's liberation army, with whom she feels free, comfortable, and respected. Granny's best friend, Lü Fengxian, is a shrewd Suzhounese woman who came to Shanghai as a maidservant during the ROC period and chose to stay in Shanghai when her master left for Hong Kong in 1948. She is a registered resident in Shanghai, has her own dwelling, and has grown used to living alone without a man. She makes a living by cooking meals for several families, and she feels "satisfied and peaceful," because she is "earning her livelihood through her own labor, and there is no guilt in her heart."[29] Both Granny and Lü Fengxian depend, to a certain degree, on the local job market to make a living, but it is the network and community of the housekeepers that gives them the strongest support. Most of the Huaihailu housekeepers are described as being "shrewd" (*jingming*), but their shrewdness is the result of a practical and utilitarian survival philosophy instead of mere egotistical calculation. The Huaihailu housekeepers treasure and protect their community with utmost care because the community is not only an invaluable product of their labor activities, but also a shared space that guards them from the troubles and pains of the patriarchal family.

It is the affective dimension of labor that plays a central role in the housekeepers' lives. Complex human interaction takes place through these women's laboring activities, producing connectedness, sociality, and community. Their microchoices have not only changed their own lives, but also affected the choices of other women in their community. The housekeepers are thus not solitary agents in a free market, but friends, acquaintances, and co-workers in a connected laborers' community. The ability to labor is linked with the ability to be integrated into human groups.

Fu Ping is quick to discover the auspices of labor soon after she arrives in Shanghai. She came to Shanghai with a marriage contract

29. Wang, *Fu Ping*, 43.

with Granny's foster grandson Li Tianhua. As an orphan girl, Fu Ping had little bargaining power in the marriage market, but she knew that her future husband Li Tianhua's big family would be her lifelong burden after marriage. In Shanghai, Fu Ping starts to see that the life she wants to live is a life in which she can "make money through her own labor."[30] Labor has also made her realize that she is a useful person and can make a living anywhere.[31] This realization of both the economic and affective dimensions of labor finally helps Fu Ping break the marriage agreement and find her own home in Shanghai, with a poor family in Meijiaqiao doing manual labor to make ends meet.

Fu Ping is shrewd enough to know that unpaid domestic work is an unjust burden for women; but ultimately, it is not paid work but the laborers' communities that help Fu Ping settle down in Shanghai. Kinship relationship is her stepping-stone to join the migrant Yangzhounese community in Zhabei, but it is her ability to work that gains her a place in her uncle's family. It is also through the bonding power of labor that she finds her future home in Meijiaqiao. Therefore, Fu Ping's movements and settling down in Shanghai can be explained with the notion of affective labor: it is through the social relationships she develops in her laboring activities that she becomes integrated into the three migrant communities in Shanghai, one after another. The network of human interaction thus operates as an alternative realm to the market in the story, even though the two realms are connected and sometimes overlap. The network of human interaction is constructed through labor and follows a complex, affective logic in its operation; it is thus a more supportive and freer domain compared with the market.

Scholars in Chinese women's and gender studies have heatedly debated the role of the market in women's liberation. In talking about Li Xiaojiang's advocacy of gender differences and female consciousness, which is discussed in the introduction of this volume, Tani

---

30. Wang, *Fu Ping*, 48.
31. Wang, *Fu Ping*, 194.

Barlow writes that Li "drew on a feminist critique of reason to rework 1980s Marxist humanism, . . . and to relocate the feminist subject in a postpolitical market economy . . . by enlisting women in self-betterment schemes, including lessons in good consumer practices."[32] Barlow perceives a complicit relationship between Li's feminist theories on women and the emerging market economy and consumer society in the post–Cultural Revolution China. For her, Li's feminism "predicated the completion of women as a subject in feminism exclusively in the context of consumer society."[33] Wang Zheng also laments "the radical transformation of state feminists from socialist revolutionaries to market apostles" since the 1980s,[34] and repudiates the masculinist postsocialist discourse that turned woman into an "individualistic, privatized, and sexualized bourgeois consumer who is also commoditized simultaneously."[35] While both Wang Zheng and Li Xiaojiang went through and approve the socialist gender revolution, they differ drastically on women's relationship to the market. For Wang Zheng, since the 1980s, gender differentiation has intensified social (gender, class, and urban versus rural) stratifications, and has facilitated China's merge with global capitalism dominated by hegemonic masculinity.[36]

By contrast, Li Xiaojiang does not share Barlow's and Wang Zheng's negative views of the market and consumption. In her eyes, the market appears to be a depoliticized, open, and fair system that caters to each individual's needs and desires, and such a market can offer concrete benefits and more choices to Chinese women.[37] In a

32. Tani Barlow, *The Question of Women in Chinese Feminism* (Durham, NC: Duke Univ. Press, 2004), 253.

33. Barlow, *Question of Women*, 285.

34. Wang Zheng 王政, *Finding Women in the State: A Socialist Feminist Revolution in the People's Republic of China, 1949–1964* (Berkeley: Univ. of California Press, 2016), 252.

35. Wang Zheng, *Finding Women*, 253.

36. Wang Zheng, *Finding Women*, 241.

37. Li Xiaojiang, *Nüxing/Xingbie de Xueshu Wenti* 女性/性别的学术问题 (Scholarly Discussions on Women/Gender) (Jinan: Shandong renmin chubanshe, 2005), 102.

recent interview, Li says that consumption (*xiaofei* 消费) is a neutral concept that has been turned negative by leftist intellectuals. She argues that consumption is the common reality in a market economy, and individuals should use their moral agency to reject abnormal consumption such as prostitution.[38] It is apparent that Li's benign view of consumption mainly stems from canonical Marxist works, which focus only on production and not consumption. When Marx does discuss consumption, he discusses it in relation to material production. However, later Marxist critics, such as Thorstein Veblen (1857–1929) and Jean Baudrillard (1929–2007), viewed consumption, rather than production, as the driving force of capitalism, thereby turning it into a target of criticism.

Wang Anyi adopts a more dialectical attitude toward the market and commodity culture, neither embracing it enthusiastically nor rejecting it entirely. Setting *Fu Ping* in the mid-1960s represents her effort to explore the historical legitimation of the market when it was not a dominant force in human lives. The mid-1960s is reimagined as a period in which communal networks of support, shared values, trust, and security still exist, and commodities are purchased for their "genuine life-enhancing use value."[39] The migrant laborers in *Fu Ping* live a simple life: they rely on the resources available in the city, including the market, to make a living, and they spend money for good food and clothing, for basic entertainment and social life; yet conspicuous consumption is absent from these people's lives. In Fu Ping's eyes, "the fashionable men and women are pleasant to watch, but they appear unreal, as if they just came out from the movies or theater; the gorgeous garments in the shop windows are not real either—you can look

38. Li Xiaojiang, "Nüren Shenti bei Xiaofei dui Nongye Shehui Daode Shi Dianfuxing de Tiaozhan" 女人身体被消费对农业社会道德是颠覆性的挑战 (The Consumption of Women's Bodies Is a Subversive Challenge to the Morality of an Agricultural Society), Cul.sohu.com, May 30, 2016, http://cul.sohu.com/s2016/lixiaojiang/.

39. Ban Wang, "Love at Last Sight: Nostalgia, Commodity, and Temporality in Wang Anyi's *Song of Unending Sorrow*," *positions: east asia cultures critiques* 10, no. 3 (2002): 687.

at them, but if you put them on, you'd become a freak."[40] Set in the mid-1960s, *Fu Ping* represents the author's effort to reclaim the socialist legacy for an increasingly unsettling contemporary world dominated by the capitalist logic. It reminds us that "market and money are not inventions of capitalism; they existed long before it developed. . . . It is only with the development of capitalism that production of commodities for exchange on the market comes to predominate."[41]

Gendering and Aestheticizing Labor

In *Fu Ping*, the migrant laborers are mainly doing service work, such as housekeeping, cooking, trash picking, and repairing things. These types of labor do not directly result in an increase of the material wealth of a society; instead, they are the general production of life, or subsistence production, often performed by women and the subaltern groups in a society. Michael Hardt has viewed this kind of "unproductive labor" as a form of affective labor that is "strongly configured as gendered labor."[42] Because affective labor involves the production and reproduction of human relations, it is no longer the same as the compulsory wage-earning labor that is felt as oppressive and alienating. Hardt believes that affective labor is an elevated form of labor: "production has become communicative, affective, de-instrumentalized, and 'elevated' to the level of human relations."[43] He discusses affective labor only as a form of labor dominated by and internal to capital, but his notion of affective labor can be used to theorize some often-neglected aspects of gendered labor.

Marx asserts in *Grundrisse*, "Not only do the objective conditions changes in the act of reproduction, . . . but the producers change, too, in that they bring out new qualities in themselves, develop themselves

40. Wang, *Fu Ping*, 33.
41. Sean Sayers, "Individual and Society in Marx and Hegel," *Science & Society* 71, no. 1 (2007): 88.
42. Hardt, "Affective Labor," 98.
43. Hardt, "Affective Labor," 96.

in production, transform themselves, develop new power and ideas, new modes of intercourse, new needs and new language.[44] While productive labor and unproductive labor differ in the extent to which they contribute to material growth, when it comes to the transformation of subjectivities and human interaction, unproductive labor is by no means less productive.

In fact, *Fu Ping* shows numerous examples that "communicative, affective, de-instrumentalized" labor has nurtured people's agency, independence, and confidence. Even the lowest Meijiaqiao dwellers work with dignity: "They earn their clothes and food through their honest work; every penny is exchanged with their sweat. There is a steady, healthy, self-respecting, and self-sufficient vigor beneath the disordered and petty livelihoods."[45] Living off their own labor for years has nurtured the laborers' sense of pride and dignity, and the savings they have accumulated through labor have given them security and peace of mind. One interesting detail is that like Wang Qiyao in *Song of Everlasting Sorrow*, who has a case of gold, Granny keeps a case of jewelries and other valuables. However, Wang Qiyao's case is a fetishized symbol of her self-commodification, and it finally costs her life when the pernicious commodity culture returns after the Cultural Revolution. Granny's case, in contrast, is a symbol of her ability to support herself through labor, and the source of her dignity, safety, and independence.

In *Fu Ping*, Wang Anyi deliberately represents gendered labor as a form of highly aestheticized labor. Labor aesthetics can be traced back to Marx, who, in *Economic and Philosophic Manuscripts of 1844*, discussed the subjective aspect of unalienated labor, which is the activation and development of human sensibility:

Only through the objectively unfolded richness of man's essential being is the richness of subjective *human* sensibility (a musical

44. Karl Marx, *Grundrisse: Foundations of the Critique of Political Economy*, translated by Martin Nicolaus (London: Penguin, 1973), 494.

45. Wang, *Fu Ping*, 232.

ear, an eye for beauty of form—in short, *senses* capable of human gratification, senses affirming themselves as essential powers of *man*) either cultivated or brought into being. For not only the five senses but also the so-called mental senses, the practical senses (will, love, etc.), in a word, *human* sense, the human nature of the senses, comes to be by virtue of *its* object, by virtue of *humanized* nature.[46]

Labor as such produces sensations and aesthetic aura both in and out of the laboring subject; at the same time, it also connects the laboring subject with nature and other humans.

Service work that most of the migrant workers do in *Fu Ping* is the traditionally gendered caring labor that is "entirely immersed in the corporeal, the somatic."[47] It is a mode of labor in which "the sensuous external world" still exists as "a *means of life* in the immediate sense, means for the physical subsistence of the worker."[48] In this sense gendered labor is akin to human senses in the first place, and naturally carries an aesthetic aura.

When Fu Ping first learns from Lü Fengxian how to wash diapers, she also learns how to enjoy the art of labor, as Lü Fengxian shows her: "First, apply a thin layer of soap on the diapers, then pour some half-boiled water on them, so the soap will foam up; rinse twice with clear water and you won't smell soap anymore. It is efficient on both soap and water."[49] In this sequence of actions, human needs and the material world (soap and water) are harmonized and aestheticized, so the laborer can rejoice in the laboring process. Lü Fengxian also teaches Fu Ping to do her best in work so "whatever you get will be well earned."[50] Fu Ping's first lesson on labor has made her both happy and respectful of Lü Fengxian.

---

46. Marx, *Economic and Philosophic Manuscripts*, 108.
47. Hardt, "Affective Labor," 96.
48. Marx, *Economic and Philosophic Manuscripts*, 71.
49. Wang, *Fu Ping*, 47.
50. Wang, *Fu Ping*, 48.

The moment Qi Shifu falls in love with Granny is also depicted as a moment when the beauty of labor blends with the beauty of a woman:

> To the left of the back door there is a north-facing kitchen. A woman is chopping food on the table, with her back to the door. The knife falls rapidly and evenly on the chopping board, letting out a crisp sound. The woman hears his footsteps and turns sideways to take a look, so he can see the carrot pieces neatly lined up on the board. The woman snatches a slice of carrot and puts it in her mouth as she turns back. The pair of golden earrings on her earlobes dances with the movement of her body. The colors of the bright orange carrots, the golden earrings contrasted with the woman's black hair, her pale-yellow face with a slightly chubby chin, and her indigo garment brilliantly enter his eyes.[51]

In Qi Shifu's eyes, the woman with adept skills and smooth movements has gradually merged into an aesthetic scene produced by her labor: Granny is not only producing the aesthetic aura through her labor but is a part of the aesthetic aura at the very moment. Granny's labor, cooking, is represented not as dull and oppressive domestic work, but as an enchanted and aestheticized human activity, a materially and spiritually fulfilling practice, a demonstration of the subject's concrete and autonomous being in the sensuous world.

This aestheticized state is produced by labor that is practiced both *in* the "the concrete, the particular, the bodily" mode and *for* the concrete, the particular, the bodily mode.[52] Reading Marx's *Capital*, Ban Wang points out: "In laboring to produce goods to satisfy the individual's needs and wants, the producer engages in real labor and produces concrete use values. But under the all-encompassing relations of commodity exchange, labor becomes abstract because its sole

---

51. Wang, *Fu Ping*, 82.

52. Dorothy E. Smith, *The Everyday World as Problematic: A Feminist Sociology* (Toronto: Univ. of Toronto Press, 1987), 81.

purpose is to produce commodities for exchange."[53] Wang goes on to analyze how abstract labor affects the producer's subjectivity and relations with the others: "Bodily experience and sensuous particulars are reflected in the producer's work"; by excluding them, abstract labor also excludes the specific qualities of "unalienated" labor, and takes away the latter's aesthetic aura.[54] The bonding of women and labor in *Fu Ping*, in contrast, restores the concrete, the sensuous, and the particular in the laboring process, and revives the aesthetic aura that has been effaced by the mathematical model of capitalist production.

Socialist China had glorified labor and emphasized its aesthetic quality to an unprecedented degree. However, despite some female cadres' claim that domestic work was part of socialist work, the aesthetic aura mostly fell upon those who engaged in productive labor that increased material wealth.[55] This masculine model of labor produced and promoted a one-sided image of women, as iron girls (*tie guniang* 铁姑娘). The gender policy that encouraged women to leave the kitchen to join the productive force was predicated on the assumption that domestic housework is less important when compared with productive labor.[56] It thus devalued the unproductive labor that most

53. Ban Wang, *Illuminations from the Past* (Stanford: Stanford Univ. Press, 2004), 215.

54. Wang, *Illuminations*, 215.

55. In the late 1950s female cadres in the All-China Democratic Women's Federation, such as Cai Chang 蔡畅 and Zhang Yun 章蕴, both emphasized the importance of women's domestic labor. Cai says: "In a socialist society, all kinds of labor that serve socialism is socialist labor; therefore, domestic work is part of socialist labor" (See Cai Chang, *Zhonghua Quanguo Minzhu Funü Lianhehui Zhuyi Caichang de Jianghua* 中华全国民主妇女联合会主席蔡畅的讲话 [Cai Chang's Talks at the All-China Democratic Women's Federation], Beijing: Gongren chubanshe, 1957, 43).

56. Compared with the invisible domestic labor in the private sphere in capitalist society, domestic labor once gained some political recognition in socialist China. See Song Shaopeng 宋少鹏, "Cong Zhangxian dao Xiaoshi: Jiti Zhuyi Shiqi de Jiating Laodong (1949–1964)" 从彰显到消失: 集体主义时期的家庭劳动 (1949–1964) (From Visibility to Disappearance: Domestic Labor in the Age of Collectivism [1949–1964]), *Jiangsu shehui kexue*, no. 1 (2012).

women still had to commit to, thereby reinforcing the existing hierarchy of gendered work. Wang Anyi's focus on unproductive labor
reverses this masculine model of labor during the socialist period, and
thus adds a missing piece to the established political representations of
Chinese laborers. In fact, Wang's sensuous depictions of women's labor
in *Fu Ping* suggests that the kind of labor that contributes to the general production of life or subsistence production is naturally endowed
with more aesthetic aura, as it exemplifies with utmost directness and
spontaneity the unification of production and consumption, need and
intention, as well as the bodily and the spiritual.

A New Shanghai

Toward the end of the story, Fu Ping's uncle is showing Fu Ping
around the Zhabei district, and they come across a pond. The uncle
explains to Fu Ping that the aquatic plants floating on the surface of
water are duckweeds (*fuping* 浮萍), whose name is a homophone of
Fu Ping 富萍. If Fu Ping's life is like that of duckweeds, the migrant
communities who make a living near the Suzhou River in Zhabei and
the Huaihailu migrant housekeepers who came to Shanghai via the
Huangpu River are like rootless duckweeds too. Duckweeds need
water to survive; water is mobile and flexible, accommodating and
nurturing at the same time. In traditional Chinese philosophy, water
is associated with the feminine (*yin*). Apparently Wang Anyi purposely
made Fu Ping the name of the female protagonist to convey her feminist ideas about migrant and subaltern people, especially migrant and
subaltern women: they thrive in a society that is flexible and supportive like water. In *Visceral Cosmopolitanism*, Mica Nava argues that
"women were more likely to identify with the migrants"[57] and "on the
whole more sympathetic to outsiders than were men."[58] As a recurring

---

57. Mica Nava, *Visceral Cosmopolitanism: Gender, Culture, and the Normalisation of Difference* (Oxford: Berge, 2007), 99.

58. Nava, *Visceral Cosmopolitanism*, 107.

image in the novella, water is a metaphor of this gendered identification, empathy, and support.

It is for this reason that the novel culminates in the chapter titled "Great Flood" (*dashui* 大水), in which the torrential summer rain has infiltrated everything and turned streets into rivers. However, in Shanghai "everything is still the same, and there is even an extra tint of liveliness."[59] Shanghai looks more beautiful and alive in the rain: "The buildings in this city have taken a darker color. The red bricks, the yellow gravel on the walls, the black tiles, and the ashen rooftops all appear darker. It is not a depressing kind of darkness, but saturated color with a fine texture, which appears vivid and flowing in the falling rain."[60] The city also appears softer in this rainy season: "The humid air softens up the hardness of the steel pier, adding a graceful touch to it."[61] Even the sirens of the trains sound "soft, flexible, and less sharp."[62] The lanes and corners of Shanghai are bustling with liveliness despite the various inconveniences brought by the rain and floods: all businesses are open as usual. During the day children wade through the water on the streets for fun; at night the light rain becomes a soothing lullaby.

What Wang Anyi presents in this chapter is a panoramic picture of the sensuous lifeworld in mid-1960s Shanghai—in Zhang Xudong's words, "the real sociopolitical dynamism of a seemingly ossified everyday world as the city plummets into the vortex of the Cultural Revolution."[63] This Shanghai is flexible, mobile, accommodating, and supporting like water. The dynamic scene of Shanghai can be traced to the inclusive and diverse *haipai* culture formed in the early twentieth century. People from different places and backgrounds came to

59. Wang, *Fu Ping*, 249.
60. Wang, *Fu Ping*, 251.
61. Wang, *Fu Ping*, 249.
62. Wang, *Fu Ping*, 252.
63. Xudong Zhang, "Shanghai Nostalgia: Postrevolutionary Allegories in Wang Anyi's Literary Production in the 1990s," *positions: east asia cultures critiques* 8, no. 2 (2000): 356.

Shanghai and were able to settle down there. Fu Ping's centrifugal and downward movements in Shanghai resemble the movement of water too. It is also in Shanghai that she realizes that "all things are subject to change, so there are no set rules."[64] At the end of the novel, when Fu Ping is found pregnant, she is sitting on a boat in the flood water, as if she is thriving thanks to the nurture and support of water, a symbol of the conjugation of gender and labor in Shanghai.

In his book *Liquid Modernity*, Zygmunt Bauman writes that ever since the capitalist period, the economic order has come to dominate the totality of human life because whatever else might have happened in that life has been rendered irrelevant and ineffective as far as the relentless and continuous reproduction of that order is concerned.[65] The economic order was a more "solid" order because "it was immune to the challenge from non-economic action,"[66] and this solid order has dominated not only capitalism but also communism.[67] Seen in this light, it can be said that many leftist mistakes made during the socialist period in China resulted from preoccupation with the economic order, which would lead to a totalitarian society of compulsory and enforced homogeneity. By contrast, what Wang Anyi does in *Fu Ping* is to reverse the domination of the economic order by making what was once rendered irrelevant and ineffective in Chinese history relevant and effective again. Her representations of the myriad and concrete relationships developed through labor, and of the ethical and aesthetic dimension of labor, add a feminist thrust that softens up the otherwise hard narrative of history.

Dai Jinhua has criticized white middle-class feminism for either neglecting or concealing the problems of subaltern working women

---

64. Wang, *Fu Ping*, 30.

65. Zygmunt Bauman, *Liquid Modernity* (Malden, MA: Polity, 2000), 4.

66. Bauman, *Liquid Modernity*, 4.

67. Communism, Bauman writes, "wished only to clean up . . . that malignant market-generated chaos which stood in the way of the ultimate and total defeat of accidents and contingency and made rational planning less than all-embracing" (*Liquid Modernity*, 57).

in the city and of peasant women in the countryside.[68] Therefore community in *Fu Ping* is particularly important as it allows subaltern women and marginalized individuals to coexist while having the space and the freedom to choose their own ways of living. This resembles the ideal socialist community that Song Shaopeng envisions, where differences between different groups, including gender, are accommodated, and where women can participate in the communal life comprehensively and equally.[69] This form of "community-based socialist feminism" can help women "resist the destructive erosion of society by both nationalism and the market economy."[70]

But even this feminine Shanghai is not free of masculine symbols. For example, Wang Anyi depicts Fu Ping's traumatic encounter with the Great World (*dashijie* 大世界), an indoor amusement arcade and entertainment complex that was built in 1917 when Shanghai was a treaty port. As a landmark of Shanghai, the Great World is the epitome of the highly developed commodity culture of the city, the center of the "crystal palace"—a metaphor for the glory of Shanghai's colonial modernity. In cultural representations since the 1990s, landmarks such as the Great World are often associated with "a coercive ideological discourse whose free-market dogmatism and empathy with a bourgeois universal history underscore the pleasure of the cultural fashion of nostalgia."[71]

In the novel the Great World is a tall and dazzling building, but it is nothing more than a mere background of Shanghai in Fu Ping's

68. Dai Jinhua 戴锦华, "Liangnan Zhijian Huo Tuwei Keneng?" 两难之间或突围可能? (A Dilemma or a Breakout?), in *Funü, Minzu yu Nüxing Zhuyi* 妇女、民族与女性主义 (Women, Nation, and Feminism), ed. Chen Shunxin and Dai Jinhua (Beijing: Zhongyang bianyi chubanshe, 2002), 35.

69. Song Shaopeng, "Ziben Zhuyi, Shehui Zhuyi he Funü: Weishenme Zhongguo Xuyao Chongjian Makesi Zhuyi Nüquan Zhuyi Pipan" 资本主义、社会主义和妇女:为什么中国需要重建马克思主义女权主义批判 (Capitalism, Socialism, and Women: Why China Needs to Rebuild a Marxist Feminist Critique), *Kaifang shidai*, no. 12 (2012), 109–10.

70. Song, "Ziben Zhuyi," 99.

71. Zhang, "Shanghai Nostalgia," 354.

eyes; she even finds it "gaudy, uncouth, and somewhat vulgar."[72] Fu Ping's only tour of the Great World turns out to be a traumatic experience. First, she is forced to look at warped reflections of herself in the distorting mirrors (*hahajing* 哈哈镜), then she gets lost after going to the bathroom alone. As she fights her way through the crowd, she gets scolded for stepping on someone's shoe. Finally, she feels someone in the crowd groping her breasts. At this point,

> Fu Ping has lost all confidence. Trembling, she keeps walking down until she reaches the lobby and exits from the front gate. Cars are rushing on the street. Their headlights and the streetlamps have conjoined into a luminous river. Fu Ping walks in this luminous river, the neon lights flashing above her head, and the grating horns beside her ears.[73]

The Great World appears to be chaotic, bizarre, exhausting, and even dangerous for Fu Ping because it is not a space for laborers, but a spectacle for consumers. The varied interpersonal relationships in labor in the outside world are replaced by the one-dimensional relationship between consumers and commodities in the Great World. Fu Ping feels powerless here because her agency as a laborer is useless; she can only blindly follow the crowd to consume commodities she feels indifferent to. She is also easily disoriented in this space because the crowds in the Great World have no organization or pattern, because as consumers they are not connected with each other in any way. The Great World is not a community.

In the 2001 interview "Am I a Feminist?" (*Woshi nüxingzhuyizhe ma?* 我是女性主义者吗?), collected in this volume, Wang Anyi confesses that the reason for writing *Fu Ping* is her dissatisfaction with the current consumer culture: "I think back then people led a pure and plain life by supporting themselves with their own labor. This healthy lifestyle nurtured honest morality, which in turn enriched

72. Wang, *Fu Ping*, 139.
73. Wang, *Fu Ping*, 181.

their souls. These people were self-sufficient. I meant to express my resistance to contemporary life in this story. I don't like how we live today. There is too much dissipation in terms of time, material, life, emotions, and soul."[74]

Fu Ping's escape from the Great World is thus symbolic: it is an escape from consumer society and global capitalism. Bauman warns us about the next phase after the early phase of "solid" modernity, which he calls "light modernity." In the age of global capitalism, he observes, "It is the patterns of dependency and interaction whose turn to be liquefied has now come,"[75] and this is a disastrous trend. In *Fu Ping*, family, class, hometown, profession, and neighborhood are some of the bonds that lay foundations for individual choices, and they, in Bauman's words, "interlock individual choices in collective projects and actions."[76] Removing these relations is tantamount to removing life substance for subaltern people. It would turn the world into the "luminous river" Fu Ping walks in after she exits the Great World: it is a river without water, a river that constantly harasses and threatens her without giving her any form of support. The absence of labor and community has made the Great World and its surroundings a chaotic, bizarre, exhausting, and dangerous space, an emblem of masculinist desires.

Wang Anyi is trying to chart a different Shanghai with a different feminine substance. Shanghai has been viewed as a feminine city in the modern period under the Western gaze, when sexualized women gained more visibility under the auspices of consumer culture.[77] However, consumer culture not only marginalizes subaltern groups but also produces them. One symptom of consumer culture is the view

74. Liu Jindong, "Am I a Feminist?," in this volume, 211.

75. Bauman, *Liquid Modernity*, 8.

76. Bauman, *Liquid Modernity*, 5.

77. See Shu-mei Shih, *The Lure of the Modern: Writing Modernism in Semi-Colonial China, 1917–1937* (Berkeley: Univ. of California Press, 2001), 318–22; and Ping Zhu, *Gender and Subjectivities in Early Twentieth-Century Chinese Literature and Culture* (New York: Palgrave, 2015), 99–128.

that links manual labor with social and economic weakness. Wang Zheng has pointed out that in the postsocialist period, there is "an intertwined regime of gender and class that places women doing manual labor outside the home at the bottom of the social hierarchy."[78] Dai Jinhua also points out in a recent interview that women who are incapable of consumption simply "do not exist" in today's mainstream culture.[79] A Shanghai immersed in consumer culture, therefore, is by no means women-friendly.

Wang Anyi's representation of mid-1960s Shanghai, by contrast, valorized women's labor and the lifeworld produced by their labor. This laborers' culture has decisively questioned and dissolved the artificial bond between women and consumption. Escaping the Great World thus represents the author's effort to unlink Shanghai with consumer culture and reclaim it as a different feminine city: a noncapitalist, nonmasculinist space for working people, especially working women.

Coda: Is Wang Anyi a Feminist?

In the interview "Am I a Feminist?," Wang Anyi explicitly voiced her dissatisfaction with the indiscriminate application of Western middle-class feminism in the Chinese context. As the interviewer Liu Jindong[80] tried to interpret Wang's works through a feminist lens, she was frequently rebutted by Wang, who firmly denied she was a feminist (*nüxing zhuyi zhe* 女性主义者) and bluntly questioned the validity of Western middle-class feminism in the context of China, a developing country. Despite Liu's repetitive hints, Wang only emphasized

---

78. Wang, *Finding Women in the State*, 104.

79. Dai Jinhua, "Xiaoxianrou, Danmei, Xingbie Kunjing" 小鲜肉·耽美·性别困境 (Little Fresh Meat, Slash Fiction, Gender Dilemma). *Jiliu*, September 18, 2018, http://jiliuwang.net/archives/76694.

80. Liu Jindong is a colleague of Li Xiaojiang, the founder of China's women's studies at Dalian University. Liu conducted the interview at Li Xiaojiang's request.

that she liked writing about women simply because women are "more aesthetic" than men.

It is probably disappointing to feminist-minded readers that Wang Anyi, who is known for her many stories about women, rejects the label *feminist*. However, the right question to ask probably is not why Wang Anyi is not a feminist, but rather what it means to be a feminist in China. In her preface to the volume *Women, Nation, and Feminism* (*Funü, minzu, yu nüxing zhuyi* 妇女、民族与女性主义), Dai Jinhua writes that the greatest significance of feminism is not gender equality or sex war, but "the search for different worlds and alternative possibilities other than global capitalism" and "through women's, especially Third-World women's thinking of nationalism, to reveal the plurality of historical processes, so as to open a broader space for thoughts, criticisms, and social practices."[81] What Dai proposes is a broader application of the feminist slogan "the personal is political" beyond the terrain of sex and gender; in other words, she calls for a methodological feminism that is able to challenge the patriarchal premises in world order and historical processes. In the post–Cold War period, this kind of feminism includes all alternative, pluralistic, and peripheral practices, imaginations, and thinking that can be used as antidotes for global capitalism. Therefore, one can be viewed a feminist if one engages in the search for different social and historical imaginations of Chinese history and reality, even if one is not directly advocating women's rights or exclusively representing women's oppression.

In *Fu Ping*, there is no sex war, no depiction of women's sexual desires, and no declaration of women's rights. However, the author has drawn from the socialist history of China to create a flexible, supportive, and aesthetic feminine utopia, one that is both an amendment to the sex-blind socialist history and an alternative to the capitalist world. If, as Dai Jinhua suggests, "feminism is utopia,"[82] Wang's imagination of a utopic Shanghai can be viewed as a kind of feminism with

81. Dai, "Liangnan Zhijian Huo Tuwei Keneng?," 29.
82. Dai, "Xiaoxianrou, Danmei, Xingbie Kunjing."

Chinese characteristics because her imagination is rooted in Chinese history and reality. Wang Anyi's focus on subaltern women combines class and gender as lived realities and structuring processes, and her emphasis on the affective dimension of labor allows her to avoid the reductionist pitfall, which reduces culture and politics to mere reflections of economy. This is her way of reconciling feminism and Marxism in order to imagine a different space for women and a different future for the world. This makes *Fu Ping* a significant text in global feminisms, since it presents a feasible alternative, derived from China's history, to the capitalist empire we all live in today.

10

"I Am Fan Yusu"

Baomu *Writing and Grassroots Feminism against the Postsocialist Patriarchy*

Hui Faye Xiao

On April 25, 2017, an eight-thousand-character essay titled "I Am Fan Yusu" (*Wo shi Fan Yusu* 我是范雨素) was first published on Zhengwu Gushi, a WeChat public account featuring nonfictional writings.[1] This article is an autobiographical account of a *baomu* (保姆 "domestic worker") named Fan Yusu who currently lives in Picun, on the outskirts of Beijing. It deals with the author's everyday experiences of performing and violating various gender and class roles (daughter, wife, single mother, primary school teacher, migrant worker, and *baomu*) at different stages of her forty-four years of life. Fan's self-writing is not the first time migrant women workers have written their own life stories. For example, in 1998–99, *Rural Women Knowing All* (*Nongjia nü baishitong*), a monthly publication directed at rural women, organized a writing competition for migrant women.[2] There

---

1. Fan Yusu 范雨素, "Wo Shi Fan Yusu" 我是范雨素 (I Am Fan Yusu), *Zhengwu Gushi*, April 25, 2007, https://news.qq.com/a/20170425/063100.htm?fbclid=Iw AR0ULJ8wDiukyQ5ASRXicLRWAtl-92lUTQxyMHPTkbkz8PJHccIZvT5RauU.

2. Arianne Gaetano, and Tamara Jacka, *On the Move: Women and Rural-to-Urban Migration in Contemporary China* (New York: Columbia Univ. Press, 2004), 279. Thanks to an anonymous reviewer for bringing this writing competition to my attention.

are also *Migrant Women Workers* (*Dagong mei*), a magazine founded in 2003 by the All-China Women's Federation, and *Chinese Women's News* (*Zhongguo funü bao*). However, Fan's piece is arguably the most widely discussed essay, and its influence went beyond rural and migrant women in the age of new media.

Within twenty-four hours, this essay was viewed over one hundred thousand times and was disseminated quickly and widely through social media. This unexpected "Fan Yusu Heat" even spread to state media. *People's Daily*, the mouthpiece of the Chinese Communist Party, published an op-ed, "Thanks to Those Who Still Cherish Literature in Their Hearts" (*Ganxie Naxie Xinhuai Wenxue de Ren* 感谢那些心怀文学的人), in which Fan is called a legendary figure (*qiren* 奇人) in the modern world.[3] *The Beijing News*, affiliated with the Publicity Department of the Beijing Municipal Committee, has reached the conclusion that Fan's unexpected sweeping popularity bears witness to city dwellers' irrepressible yearnings for spiritual freedom that find their personification in this one-of-a-kind norm-bending *baomu*.[4]

How shall we read Fan Yusu's autobiographical account, one of the few self-writings by a *baomu* who is positioned at the margins of the culture dominated by urban middle class in postsocialist China? What gender and class ramifications do we perceive in Fan's self-writing? What literary traditions, cultural memories, and historical legacies have been mobilized and reinvented that make this new tale of *baomu* simultaneously feminist and "Chinese" in an age characterized by economic globalization, as well as a backlash of neoconservative patriarchy in China and beyond?

To address these central issues, this chapter investigates the synchronous and diachronous links of Fan's writings with feminist literary

---

3. Zhang Tie 张铁, "Ganxie Naxie Xinhuai Wenxue de Ren" 感谢那些心怀文学的人 (Thanks to Those Who Still Cherish Literature in Their Hearts), *Renmin ribao*, April 26, 2017, 5.

4. He Xiaoshou 何小手, "'Fan Yusu' Shuapin, Women Shi Bei Ziyou de Linghun Jingyan dao le" 《范雨素》刷屏, 我们是被自由的灵魂惊艳到了 ("Fan Yusu" Flooding the Feed Because We Are Shocked by a Free Soul), *Xinjing bao*, April 25, 2017.

traditions, as well as the local literary practices of her cohorts. The following sections combine a historical study of shifting literary and media representations of *baomu* from the May Fourth generation to the postsocialist period and a close textual analysis of Fan Yusu's writings. Instead of reading Fan as an exceptional and legendary *baomu* writer as mainstream media commentaries have suggested, I argue that Fan serves as a node in a new literary network that is buttressed by collective efforts in the spirit of an emerging grassroots feminism. On the one hand, Fan's self-writing about the figure of *baomu* as both individual identity and collective denominator cannot squarely fit the discursive models of state feminism and market feminism. Rather, grassroots feminism highlights the cultural creativity and historical agency of a multidimensional gendered subject of *baomu* generated at the intersection of multiple forms of inequalities along gender, class, generational, and regional divisions. On the other hand, the formation of such an intersectional subject is made possible only by the construction of a larger literary and social collectivity consisting of a group of emerging grassroots writers, as well as intellectual volunteers working in Picun, an obscure urban village (*cheng zhong cun* 城中村) on the periphery of Beijing.

Writing *Baomu*: Mother Earth, Master Storyteller, and "Low-*Suzhi* (Quality)" Home Wrecker

Baomu, as a representative persona of disadvantaged social groups, has been an important subject of Chinese realist literature since its birth. In the humanist-spirited works composed by left-leaning male writers, *baomu* is often portrayed as the very icon of Chineseness, or a typical traditional Chinese woman who silently puts up with all kinds of sufferings and social injustices like the "dark, kindly Mother Earth."[5]

5. Lu Xun, "Ah Chang and the *Book of Hills and Seas*," in *Dawn Blossoms Plucked at Dusk*, trans. Yang Hsien-yi and Gladys Yang (Beijing: Foreign Languages Press, 1976), 25.

Ai Qing thus depicts his *baomu* Dayanhe in his canonical poem "Da-yanhe—My Wet-Nurse":

> Smiling, she washed our clothes,
> Smiling, she carried the vegetables, and rinsed them in the icy
>   pond by the village,
> . . .
> Dayanhe, in order to survive,
> After the milk in her had run dry,
> She put those arms, arms that had cradled me, to work.[6]

Underlining the plight of *baomu* and their families in every corner of the Chinese society, leftist writers seek to bring together all these *baomu* representatives into a humanitarian imagined community. Because these aging figures are often memorized and mourned in the retrospective narratives of adult male writers, they often appear to be the voiceless object of male observation and nostalgia, as well as the target of male enlightenment and salvation.

In comparison to these nostalgic tales featuring a silently or smilingly suffering *baomu*, Lin Haiyin's writings display a more distinct and self-reflective gender consciousness. The chapter "Donkey Rolls" in her widely read semi-autobiographical work *Memories of Peking: South Side Stories* (*Cheng nan jiu shi* 城南旧事, 1960) does not take God's perspective to recall the life trajectory of Song Ma (Mother Song), a *baomu* working in a middle-class family residing in south Beijing during the Republican period. Rather, the narrative unfolds through Song Ma's own oral account and daily interaction with those around her. Sitting in the courtyard, surrounded by a group of her employer's children, Song Ma assumes the role of a master storyteller who occupies center stage with her possession of the enunciative power of language. Through the mediation of Song Ma's colloquial feminine

6. Ai Qing, "Dayanhe—My Wet-Nurse," in *Selected Poems of Ai Qing*, trans. and ed. Eugene Chen Ouyang (Bloomington: Indiana Univ. Press, 1982), 27–28.

language, which, of course, is remediated through Lin's writing pen, readers get to hear the *baomu*'s her-story about how and why she left behind her own children with her husband in the village in order to make a living in Beijing.

Following chronological order, "Donkey Rolls" is the last installment in Lin's semi-autobiographical memoir that marks the end of the character Yingzi's childhood. If we connect the dots between this last episode of childhood memories and previous chapters, a networked narrative is formed. In place of an isolated text, a constellation of similar accounts weave together an outpouring of gendered dilemmas and everyday struggles experienced simultaneously by a series of domesticated women: a mad woman who loses her illegitimate daughter; a runaway concubine who was sold to cover her sick brother's mounting medical bills; as well as Yingzi's mother, a middle-class homemaker who takes care of seven children while her husband visits courtesan houses. In this vein, Lin's literary writing about a *baomu* can be read as an attempt to open up an intersubjective gendered space crossing the boundaries between different homes, generations, and social strata. This literary exploration of an alternative form of sociality has been continued and expanded in Wang Anyi's fictional works, published a few decades later at a different historical juncture.

Among contemporary Chinese writers, Wang Anyi probably is the most prolific when it comes to the subject matter of *baomu*. Raised by a *baomu* from Yangzhou, Wang shares Lin's daily interactions with and deep concerns for this social group. With her fictional accounts "A War between Cuckoos and Magpies" (*Jiu que yi zhan* 鸠 鹊一战, 1986), *Fu Ping* (富萍, 2000), "Nannies" (*Baomu men* 保姆们, 2002) and "Home in the World" (*Xiangguan chuchu* 乡关处处, 2017), Wang has been paying constant attention to the gendered labor of *baomu* and their fluid identity between family and outsider, as well as between local Shanghainese and provincial migrants. Diligently creating a literary archeology of rich everyday life details of various social segments embedded in the socialist and postsocialist urban space of Shanghai, Wang shows her readers possibilities of forging cross-class and intergenerational ethical and affective ties outside of the closed space of urban middle-class family.[7]

Since China's opening up and economic reform, its economic boom has generated unprecedented social stratification and accelerating spatial mobility. A rising urban middle class resorts to purchasing commodified private homes as well as commodified domestic labor to fulfill a dream of domestic bliss. As a result, China has also witnessed a vast group of rural women leaving their families behind in the countryside to enter urban middle-class homes as domestic workers. Therefore, a new economy of affective labor and domestic care (*zhaoliao jingji* 照料经济) is on the rise in postsocialist Chinese society. In other words, we see a dual trend of gendering and classing everyday labor within the domestic space: the provision of domestic and affective labor for household chores and raising up the next generation has been considered women's job or even the essential core of the feminine identity, and then is further shifted from the female homemaker of the middle-class family to the *baomu*, usually female laborers coming from the outside—of the family, the city, and the middle class).

However, the physical and emotional closeness of the *baomu* to their employers, as depicted in these literary works, starts to be regarded as a problem, even a threat to the maintenance of the proper domestic order. Therefore, *baomu* have been redefined as intimate strangers, or an alien existence awkwardly inserted into the domestic interior. In developmentalist discourse about modernization, *baomu* are often labeled as a "low-quality" (*suzhi di* 素质低) social group who need to constantly improve themselves with proper training and discipline that urban civilization can provide to them so they can fill the role of a "high-quality" (*suzhi gao* 素质高) workers in a middle-class domestic space.[8] Meanwhile, a different sense of uneasiness is generated by the physical presence of an alien body inside the domestic

---

7. For a full-length discussion of Wang Anyi's *baomu* writing, see Ping Zhu's chapter in this volume.

8. YAN Hairong, *New Masters, New Servants: Migration, Development, and Women Workers in China* (Durham, NC: Duke Univ. Press, 2008).

space. In comparison to the affectionate image of aging *baomu* in the republican and socialist eras, the image of little *baomu* (*xiao baomu* 小保姆) starts to dominate a deluge of literary and media representations of *baomu*.

The nature of a *baomu*'s littleness is obviously conceived from her employer's perspective. First, this sense of littleness is an indication of her low social status. Second, it is also closely related to the lowered average age of the *baomu*. The emphasis on a *baomu*'s youthful body not only shows the middle-class employers' concern for her physiological capacity to perform domestic labor, but also implies the sexual appeal of a young woman to her male employer occupying the same domestic space, and thus constitutes a potential threat to the proper affective order supposedly under the firm control of the female employer in the urban middle-class family. This sexualization and stigmatization of *xiao baomu* reinforce middle-class apprehension while totally ignoring domestic workers' sense of insecurity. Due to lack of social support, secure housing, and private space, female migrant workers are vulnerable to sexual harassment and exploitation.[9]

Riding this wave of middle-class anxiety, some celebrity writers have published commentaries to reinforce this sense of insecurity and fear felt by urban families that cannot function properly without the labor of *baomu*. Wu Zhihong, who gained overnight fame as "the most popular psychologist in China" for his bestselling volume *The Nation of Giant Infants* (Ju Ying Guo 巨婴国, 2016), attributed the root cause of rampant social problems to the developmental stagnancy of Chinese people who fail to outgrow the mother-infant symbiosis to become independent individuals.[10] Following the same logic, Wu contends that today's middle-class family needs to shake off the shackles of any forms of symbiotic bonding to develop a heightened consciousness of

9. Can Tang, "Sexual Harassment: The Dual Status of and Discrimination against Female Migrant Workers in Urban Areas," *Social Sciences in China* 19, no. 3 (1998): 64–71.

10. Wu Zhihong 武志红, *Ju Ying Guo* 巨婴国 (The Nation of Giant Infants), Hangzhou: Zhejiang renmin chubanshe, 2016.

boundaries (*jiexian yishi* 界限意识) between employers and employees.[11] In order to maintain the proper boundaries of a respectable and orderly middle-class domestic space, according to Wu, the labor of *baomu* is still essential, but the destructive potential of an "evil *baomu*" should be exterminated through the redrawing of a more rigid and impenetrable border between affective bonding and financial transaction, between family and *baomu*, or between us and them.

Baomu Writing: Mother, Woman Cadre, and Political Sisterhood

Against such a postsocialist patriarchal setting, in which the cultural imagination of an intersubjective commons across class and generation has been replaced by an increasingly strict master-servant class order infected with an eroticized gender hierarchy, Fan Yusu's autobiographic writing can be viewed as a conscious self-ethnography. It chronicles her life and work, providing an alternative *baomu* narrative in a female migrant laborer's own words and giving voice to those silenced and scattered at the peripheries of the patriarchal power structure. In this sense Fan's *baomu* narrative continues the tradition of feminist writings against patriarchal hegemony.

"I Am Fan Yusu," the title of her widely circulated online autobiographical essay, is a loud call to the vast world, like a confident declaration of the author's existence. This titular self-interpellation is a proud speech act of self-assertion, indicating an ambition of constructing an individual subjectivity through self-writing that rehumanizes the masses of nameless and faceless silent laborers. However, this self-writing does not limit itself in the tradition of the individualist "private writings" (*si xiezuo* 私写作) that were trendy in 1990s feminist

11. Wu Zhihong 武志红, "Zonghuo de Baomu, yu Xiaoshi de Bianjie," 纵火的保姆, 与消失的边界 (Nanny Arsonist and Disappearing Boundaries), *Sina* blog, June 26, 2017, http://blog.sina.com.cn/s/blog_547645590102x9oi.html. This article was first published on Wu's WeChat public account and the *Sina* blog on June 26, 2017, then was republished on multiple venues of traditional and new media.

literature. Rather, the very existence of the "I," or Fan's gendered and classed identity, is firmly built on the foundation of the author's everyday interaction and close bonding with other laborers, both male and female. In this chapter I examine two dimensions of the imagined commons in and out of the domestic space: sisterhood in the form of mother-daughter bonding, and the literary commons of Picun.

Born in 1973 to a rural family in Dahuo Village, Hubei province, Fan Yusu first worked as a primary school teacher in the village after graduating from middle school. Later she went to Beijing as a migrant worker, first as a waitress and later as a *yu'ersao* (育儿嫂), or live-in nanny, a different name for *baomu*. Fan's life path is typical of millions of women migrant workers in postsocialist China. In comparison to Song Ma in *Memories of Peking*, Fan is empowered by loving memories of her mother, whose image clearly evokes the socialist legacies of women's liberation, mobilization, and political participation. Actually, the original title of Fan's self-ethnography was "Mother" (*muqin* 母亲). Talking about the most admirable person in the world, Fan Yusu names her mother with no hesitation:

> My mother, Zhang Xianzhi, was born July 20, 1936. At the age of fourteen, she was democratically elected the Director of the Local Committee of the Women's Federation, because she had a way with words and excelled at helping others solve conflicts. She began in 1950 and held the office for 40 years, outlasting political strongmen like Saddam Hussein and Gaddafi.[12]

This portrayal of an ordinary Chinese woman cadre at the grassroots level deviates from the iconic images of silent and oppressed rural woman, such as Xianglin's wife (*Xianglin sao* 祥林嫂) or the old *baomu* Dayanhe (大堰河), under the pen of left-leaning male writers in the republican period. It is also radically different from the

---

12. An excerpt of Philip Bradshaw and Keegan Sparks's translation of "I Am Fan Yusu" has been published in *World Literature Today* (Spring 2021), www.world literaturetoday.org/2021/spring/i-am-fan-yusu-fan-yusu.

mainstream media construction of "low-quality" rural women who flood into the city to take the job of *xiao baomu* in the postsocialist era. On the contrary, although she is illiterate and young, Zhang Xianzhi is respected in the local community for being resourceful and outspoken. Through her mastery of oral language in its everyday use, Zhang is able to successfully solve people's problems and thus intervene in the communal affairs of the village. Therefore she is elected director of the local committee of the Women's Federation to join the grassroots governance of the country.

Zhang's politically charged strong-woman image is reminiscent of a series of rural women cadre characters created during the socialist period, such as Li Shuangshuang (in the film *Li Shuangshuang* 李双双, 1962), Jinhua (in the film *Five Golden Flowers* 五朵金花, 1959), and Du Wanxiang (in Ding Ling's 1978 story "Du Wanxiang" 杜晚香), who are witty, sharp-tongued, and active in managing public affairs in the village. Such an unprecedented cultural imagination testifies to the governmental efforts in liberating and mobilizing rural women who were largely illiterate and of the lower class to contribute to the cause of socialist revolution. The convergence of the gender line and the mass line in the process of state formation in the early years of the People's Republic of China highlights the significance of women's agency in revolutionizing political, economic, and social lives and interrogates the conventional "assumption of the total dominance of a socialist state patriarchy."[13]

However, this socialist feminist construction of women cadres has been disrupted in postsocialist literary and cinematic works. From Wang Shouxin in Liu Binyan's famous work of reportage literature *Between Humans and Monsters* (*Renyao zhijian* 人妖之间, 1979), to Li Guoxiang in Gu Hua's *Hibiscus Town* (*Furong Zhen* 芙蓉镇, 1981), to Duan Lina in Chi Li's bestselling novel *To and Fro* (*Lailai wangwang*

13. Wang Zheng, *Finding Women in the State: A Socialist Feminist Revolution in the People's Republic of China, 1949–1964* (Berkeley: Univ. of California Press, 2016), 2.

来来往往, 1998), the figure of woman cadres has been portrayed as ugly, selfish, cunning, and most importantly sexually undesirable and thus failing to fit the new model of femininity in postsocialist China. Chen Rong's award-winning story "At Middle Age" (*Ren dao zhong-nian* 人到中年, 1980) popularizes the label of "old granny of Marxist Leninism" (*Ma lie zhuyi lao taitai* 马列主义老太太), making it a misogynist shorthand term that compares women cadres to robotic adherents of outdated and dogmatic ideologies.

As a result, in postsocialist Chinese literature and film, women cadres are often condemned as ambitious and conniving women and have been portrayed as the source of a feminine polluting force that unsettles the proper order. What is worth noting here is the linking of unruly feminine sexuality that unleashed chaos with the ten turbulent years of the Cultural Revolution in a highly misogynist narrative of Jiang Qing as an ambitious vixen, a female usurper who manipulated Mao Zedong with her dangerous sexual charms and treacherous political machinations.[14] With this narrative the popular imagination defends the authority of patriarchal morality, regarding Jiang as "*hongyan huoshui*" 红颜祸水, or the femme fatale who leads the great helmsman astray and brings the nation to the verge of collapse. Ann Anagnost argues that "this 'feminization of evil' has now become a pervasive image of the Cultural Revolution period. The irony of this image lies in the fact that the Cultural Revolution, despite its horrors, was the most successful period in the erasure of gender inequality in its assaults on Confucian ideology."[15] Discussing the changes in women's political participation after the end of the Cultural Revolution,

14. Natascha Vittinghoff, "Jiang Qing and Nora: Drama and Politics in the Republican Period," in *Women in China: The Republican Period in Historical Perspective*, eds. Mechthild Leutner and Nicola Spakowski (Münster: LIT, 2005), 208–41.

15. Ann Anagnost, "Transformations of Gender in Modern China," in *Gender and Anthropology: Critical Reviews for Research and Teaching*, ed. Sandra Morgan (Washington DC: American Anthropological Association, 1989), 313–42. For a more elaborate discussion of the feminization-of-evil discourse, see chapter 2 in Hui

Wang Qi also points out that "the proportion of basic-level woman cadres has declined sharply since the early 1980s."[16] Countering such a backlash of conservative patriarchal morality in postsocialist political life and cultural imagination, Fan Yusu's loving depiction of Zhang Xianzhi, a caring mother and a respected village leader at the same time, contests the demonization of women cadres in the mainstream postsocialist cultural imagination.

The centrality of such a woman cadre figure in Fan's self-ethnography is also manifested in the significance of the act of naming that alludes to the lineage of socialist women cadres. In the earlier literary and cinematic works about the changing image of rural women, the textual titles are often directly derived from the female characters' names. For example, in Li Zhun's story "A Short Biography of Li Shuangshuang" (*Li Shuangshuang Xiao Zhuan* 李双双小传, 1960), the first paragraph tells about how the female protagonist had been known as Xiwang's wife or Xiaoju's mom or simply "the one who cooks for me" (*an zuofan de* 俺做饭的) until she participated in managing public affairs during the Great Leap Forward. In other words, the process of getting her own name is indicative of the process of rural woman participating in grassroots government and changing their status in and out of the family.[17] In comparison to earlier literary figures of rural women, such as Xianglin's wife and Dayanhe, who have gotten no names of their own and can be addressed only by their deceased husband's name or even their hometown's name, these women cadres are not only called by their own names, but even provide defining meaning to the literary texts with their names.

Faye Xiao, *Family Revolution: Marital Strife in Contemporary Chinese Literature and Visual Culture* (Seattle: Univ. of Washington Press, 2014).

16. Wang Qi, "State-Society Relations and Women's Political Participation," in *Women of China: Economic and Social Transformation*, ed. Jackie West, Zhao Minghua, Chang Xiangqun, and Cheng Yuan (New York: St. Martin's, 1999), 19.

17. Li Zhun 李准, "Li Shuangshuang Xiao Zhuan" 李双双小传 (A Short Biography of Li Shuangshuang), *Renmin wenxue*, no. 3 (1960): 11.

The political and cultural soil for asserting the historical significance of rural women's names has been eroded in the postsocialist period when moving to the city as migrant workers has become a typical path of mobility for this social group. As Lü Tu, a sociologist who worked on an assembly line for a short time, has observed, migrant workers, both male and female, working in the foreign-invested enterprise are rarely addressed by their names: "The workshop is a nameless world."[18] Deprived of their names, migrant workers are managed not as human beings but as dehumanized tools of production, not unlike the industrial machinery used on the assembly line. Put into a similar situation, domestic workers are also often nameless. Instead, they are referred to as *xiao ayi* ("little nanny") by middle-class city dwellers. The value of their existence in the History of capital is reduced to the commodified value of labor extracted out of these nameless bodies.

Against such a nameless world ruled by the capitalist patriarchy, the politics of naming in Fan Yusu's self-writing is particularly noteworthy. She not only asserts the presence of a *baomu* by putting her own name in the title, but also juxtaposes the name of her mother, a grassroots woman cadre in socialist China, with the well-known names of Saddam and Gaddafi to bring out a sense of black humor that pokes fun at the usual gender hierarchy and political rankings in male-dominated world politics. The importance of gendered agency in naming is well-registered under Fan Yusu's pen. While providing readers with her mother's full name and life story, her self-ethnography renders her father into a shady, nameless character with few stories: "From my earliest memories, the impression I had of my father was like that of the shadow of a big tree: visible but useless. My father never spoke. He was in poor health, and incapable of physical labor. One house, five kids, and everyone relied on mom alone for support."

18. Lü Tu 吕途, *Zhongguo Xin Gongren: Wenhua yu Mingyun* 中国新工人: 文化与命运 (Chinese New Workers: Culture and Prospects) (Beijing: Falü chubanshe, 2015), 36.

In comparison to the strong woman cadre image of Fan's mother, this paternal figure is depicted as silent and weak, like "the shadow of a big tree." Not only does he lose his name in his daughter's narrative, he also has given away the conventional patriarchal power of naming his children in real life. All five children's names were given by Fan's mother. Fan Juren is the youngest one. At the age of twelve, Fan Juren finished reading *Misty Rain* (*Yan yu mengmeng* 烟雨濛濛, 1983), a popular work of romance fiction, and took over the agency of self-naming to change her own name to Fan Yusu. This meticulous account of girls' and women's naming process in a rural family is especially meaningful if we take into account the central significance of naming in Confucian patrilineage. The loss of naming power not only testifies to the weakening of patriarchal power but also highlights the essential role played by the mother in Fan Yusu's growing experience, self-knowledge, and appropriation of conventional gender roles.

Positioned against the patriarchal system, this cross-generational intersubjectivity continues the literary tradition of writing sisterhood in modern China: works from Ding Ling's *Mother* (*Muqin* 母亲, 1932–1933), to Zhang Jie's *The Ark* (*Fangzhou* 方舟, 1981), to Wang Anyi's *Brothers* (*Dixiongmen* 弟兄们, 1989) are centered on exploring a utopian female-female relationship (mother-daughter bonding for Ding and sisterly camaraderie for Zhang and Wang) outside of the heterosexual and patrilineal matrix. Rooted firmly in this literary lineage, Fan Yusu's self-writing further expands and enriches it by bringing the usually neglected grassroots perspective and rural women's political agency into the gendered literary commons.

In place of a voiceless and self-sacrificing Mother Earth, the woman cadre image of Fan's mother evokes the socialist legacy of women's liberation and mass mobilization. In this sense, the intergenerational bonding between Fan Yusu and Zhang Xianzhi can be characterized as political sisterhood. In discussing Ding Ling's work *Mother*, Tani Barlow uses the phrase *political sisterhood* to depict "a reinvented, politically defined, female identity" embedded in a historicized time-space rather than a universal female identity defined on the anatomical basis of "sexual differentiation and sexual categories."[19] The political legacy of the mother-daughter bonding is carried out in a different form, since mass mobilization and rural women's participation in grassroots-level governance have become a diminishing tradition in the postsocialist period. Rather than being elected as women cadres managing public affairs in the local communities, a vast number of rural women leave the village to work as migrant laborers to be managed by the productivity-driven capitalist regime.

In this sense, Fan's trajectory is typical for a postsocialist rural woman whose life path strikes a sharp contrast with that of the maternal woman cadre during the socialist era. However, the intergenerational political sisterhood still binds them together. Like her mother, Fan Yusu is good with words, in written form this time. With her literary text Fan registers her loving memory of the maternal woman cadre, which rekindles the past in the present by retrieving a missing figure in postsocialist political life, popular culture, and even feminist literature. Moreover, Fan herself carries on the socialist woman cadre's legacy of engaging with public affairs and community building with her literary writing, which exposes gender and class-based social inequalities and redefines the meaning and form of home outside of the postsocialist patriarchy. In this sense Fan's literary production should be viewed as a social act of constructing a grassroots lifeworld not recognized by the History of capital, and "a historically situated practice" of retrieving and reenacting the forgotten feminist legacy.[20] Her contribution to subaltern (*diceng*) literature revitalizes the heritage of the socialist revolution and women's liberation, as Xueping Zhong's chapter in this volume similarly suggests.

19. Tani E. Barlow, "Gender and Identity in Ding Ling's *Mother*," *Modern Chinese Literature* 2, no. 2 (1986): 124.

20. Sheldon Pollock, "Introduction," in *Literary Cultures in History: Reconstructions from South Asia*, ed. Sheldon Pollock (Berkeley: Univ. of California Press, 2003), 18.

Unmaking a Patriarchal Home(town), Remaking a Literary Home

At the age of twenty Fan went to Beijing as a migrant worker. In this most expensive megacity of postsocialist China, Fan not only experiences class-based bias on a daily basis, but also has to deal with gender-specific life situations. After a brief marriage with an abusive husband, Fan became a single mother with two young daughters. She works as a live-in nanny to look after other people's young children while leaving her own daughters in a rented room in Picun. Her family feels like rootless duckweeds floating in Beijing. What sustains Fan's everyday life is the cross-generational affection and bonding flowing between three generations of women who cannot fit in any patriarchal family.

This sense of migrant women as homeless has been further enhanced by the awkward positionality of *baomu* as isolated workers in a closed domestic space. In comparison with other manual laborers, *baomu* have a gender- and class-specific identity that is unique and hard to define. Their voluminous reproductive, caring, and affective labor as surrogate mothers blurs the fine line between work and familial bonding. This leads to the ambivalent positionality of *baomu* in middle-class families: on the one hand, *baomu* live and interact with their employers in the same domestic space, but on the other hand, their existence is still regarded as alien to that of their employers. The *baomu*'s physical existence reveals the effaced traces of the labor of bourgeois domesticity and exposes the hierarchical positionality of women of different social rankings.

Unlike industrial workers and peasants living and working in the same village, a *baomu* has to live in a home(town) that is not her own. Meanwhile, this job not only involves long hours of work, but also tends to be centered on household chores and reproductive care, which is often seen as an extension of women's natural instincts and therefore categorized as unproductive labor even in classical Marxism. As a result, the everyday living and working environment of the *baomu* is even more isolating than that of other groups of workers, leaving little potential for the formation of organized action or a collective class consciousness. To make things even worse, the provision of legal protection of workers' rights and professional training for cultivating new skills demanded by other possible new jobs is far from adequate. No wonder the life trajectory of many *baomu* is nonstop movement from one home to another: the father's, the employer's, the husband's, but never their own.

A similar sense of homelessness is also manifest in Fan's description of her bourgeois employer, who is a full-time "house-concubine," or "second mistress" (*ernai* 二奶) of a local tycoon who was on Rupert Hoogewerf's "China Rich List." Despite the opulent comfort of her living conditions, the mistress's life appears to be as lonely and isolated as Fan's:

> My female employer was 25 years younger than my male employer. Sometimes I would get up in the middle of the night to comfort the baby and would see her sitting on the sofa with her delicate make-up, waiting for her husband to come home. Her figure was more graceful than a model's, and her face was prettier than that of film star Fan Bingbing. But she was still like an imperial concubine from a palace drama, painstakingly flattering her husband as if she would not be fed if she did not honor him. . . .
>
> Every time, I would absent-mindedly ask myself if I was living in the Tang dynasty, in the Qing dynasty, or if this was the new socialist China. But I had no supernatural powers to time-travel![21]

Fan's acerbic narrative, on the one hand, shows the irony of a young woman's voluntary self-negation in "the new socialist China," or indeed a postsocialist China. Several decades after women's liberation, the convergence of global consumerism and a resurgent conservative gender ideology has brought back the institution of concubinage. On the other hand, her narrative also highlights the common gender

---

21. Fan Yusu, "I Am Fan Yusu," trans. Philip Bradshaw and Keegan Sparks, *World Literature Today* (Spring 2021), www.worldliteraturetoday.org/2021/spring/i-am-fan-yusu-fan-yusu.

dilemma of a second mistress and a laboring nanny, both of whom serve the wealthy patriarch with either a well-groomed sexualized body or diligent caring labor to raise up male offspring. Locked into a closed domestic space, both domesticated women have no home of their own. In other words, the patriarchal family provides "an illusion of community based on isolation and the freezing of difference" along gender and class lines in an increasingly stratifying and fragmenting postsocialist society.[22]

Living in such an alienating working environment as a homeless *baomu*, Fan feels so disconnected from others that she even diagnoses herself as suffering from "civilization phobia" (*wenming kongju zheng* 文明恐惧症). Therefore, she seeks to forge affective and ethical ties outside of the closed domestic space through reading literature, creative writing, and sharing her writings with fellow migrant workers in Picun, which is located between the Fifth and Sixth Ring Road of Northeastern Beijing. With its narrow streets and dilapidated buildings, this type of shantytown is often located on the borderline of the urban and the rural areas of big cities, and is thus called an urban village. Zheng Xiaoqiong, a migrant worker–poet pinpoints *urban village* as the best metaphor for the liminal positionality of migrant workers: "Just as these places are neither completely rural nor completely urban, these workers are neither salaried workers nor farmers. They work in the city but are not accepted by it."[23]

Although the revving engine noise of airplanes taking off is unbearable due to Picun's geographic proximity to the Capital International Airport, its cheap rental housing prices and low living costs still draw tens of thousands of migrant workers. Wang Dezhi and Sun Heng are two migrant workers living in Picun. With assistance of several co-workers, they rented two courtyards in Picun and founded the

22. Chandra Talpade Mohanty, *Feminism without Borders: Decolonizing Theory, Practicing Solidarity* (Durham, NC: Duke Univ. Press, 2003), 117.

23. Qin Xiaoyu, "Introduction: Remembering the Anonymous," in *Iron Moon: An Anthology of Chinese Migrant Worker Poetry*, ed. Qin Xiaoyu, trans. Eleanor Goodman (Buffalo, NY: White Pine Press, 2016), 22.

Workers Home (*Gongyou zhi jia* 工友之家). In this communal space, several supporting units were also established: Tongxin Huhui Store to lower migrant workers' living costs; Tongxin Experimental School to provide education for migrant workers' children; Tongxin Center of Career Development, which was later developed into the Workers University, to equip young workers with better education and up-to-date professional training; and the Migrant Workers Museum.[24] The small urban village, "home to more than ten thousand rural migrants and a thousand or so local residents, is now the center of rural migrant community cultural activism and is a hotbed for the politicization and radicalization of rural migrant workers."[25]

The Picun Literature Group (*Picun wenxue xiaozu* 皮村文学小组) is one of the communal units that aim to facilitate workers' everyday lives and forge a sense of community among them. The Literature Group of the Workers Home was organized by Fu Qiuyun, a woman migrant laborer who graduated from the Workers University. When she worked in the library of the Workers Home, Fu noticed that many migrant workers were eager to write their own stories. Therefore, she took the initiative to establish the Literature Group for these workers in the fall of 2014. She also facilitated the publication of *Picun Literature* (*Picun Wenxue* 皮村文学), a grassroots literary journal publishing migrant workers' creating writings, and helped type and print workers' handwritten manuscripts.[26] In putting together and managing the daily operations of the Literature Group, Fu is pursuing a mission that could be seen as analogous to that of an educated cadre who

---

24. Zhang Lijiao 张黎姣, "Beijing Wuhuan wai de Gongyou zhi Jia" 北京五环外的工友之家 (A Workers' Home outside of Beijing's Fifth Ring), *Zhongguo qingnian bao*, August 6, 2013, 9.

25. Wanning Sun, *Subaltern China: Rural Migrants, Media, and Cultural Practices* (Lanham, MD: Rowman & Littlefield, 2014), 133–34.

26. Picun wenxue xiaozu 皮村文学小组, "Picun Wenxue Xiaozu: Liuxia Zhezuo Shuyu Women Ziji de Bowuguan" 皮村文学小组: 留下这座属于我们自己的博物馆 (The Picun Literature Group: Preserve Our Own Museum), *Picun gongyou*, July 19, 2017, http://mp.weixin.qq.com/s/4yuelhe06nBd2ubGTa3yeA.

10.1. Entrance of the Workers Home. Photo by Hui Faye Xiao.

was assigned the job of cultivating working-class writers and building a cultural home for workers from different walks of life during the socialist period. Different from the socialist women cadres embedded securely within the state bureaucracy, Fu is positioned within the grassroots community that receives NGO assistance and voluntary help from workers, activists, and intellectuals in and out of Picun.

To find a literary counselor for the group, Fu posted an announcement, which drew Zhang Huiyu's attention. Zhang had studied with feminist critic Dai Jinhua and had earned his PhD in Marxism and Cultural Studies at Peking University. He volunteered to join the group. Since the first class was offered on September 21, 2014, every Sunday evening, in a classroom set inside the Museum of Migrant Workers' Culture and Art, Zhang has guided the participants in the Literature Group to discuss current affairs and to read and discuss canonical writers such as Lu Xun, Xiao Hong, Tolstoy, and Balzac side by side with

10.2. Migrant Workers Museum. Photo by Hui Faye Xiao.

migrant workers' creative writings. According to Zhang, cultivating a sociohistorical consciousness is as important as learning rhetorical skills for self-expression.[27] In addition to Zhang, Liang Hong, Huang Deng, Liu Chen, Li Yunlei, Shi Chengbin and other writers and scholars have also given lectures there.[28] Thus the Literature Group has become a significant united front where intellectuals and workers can mingle, interact, and form the kind of border-crossing literary alliance that had been annulled in the postsocialist era.[29]

27. Picun wenxue xiaozu, "Picun Wenxue Xiaozu."

28. Bukebang 布客帮, "Picun Wenxue Gushi: Naxie zai Liushuixian shang Xie Shi de 'Xin Gongren'" 皮村文学故事: 那些在流水线上写诗的"新工人" (Stories of Literature in the Pi Village: "New Workers" Write Poems at the Assembly Line), *Beijing wanbao*, May 20, 2017.

29. Thanks to Ling Zhang for bringing this to my attention.

10.3. A Picun Literature Group meeting with Zhang Huiyu (top right). Courtesy of Fu Qiuyun.

Fan Yusu was one of the first participants in the group and attended nearly every class before she moved out of Picun to work as a live-in nanny. Explaining the irrepressible urge to engage in creative writing, Fan Yusu said, "I need to do something beyond basic everyday needs to satisfy my spiritual pursuit."[30] Fan's remark resonates with the Marxist ideal of aesthetic practice that is less constrained by utilitarian purposes. In this light, Aili Mu's comments on contemporary commonfolk (*pingmin* 平民) writers could be well applied to Fan's literary pursuit: "Living through writing beyond instrumental reason, they come close to aesthetic freedom that Karl Marx envisioned: work during the day, appreciate literature in the evening, and create their

30. Ji Wei 计巍, "Wo Shi Kao Kuli Chifan de, Bu Kao Xie Wenzhang Mousheng" 我是靠苦力吃饭的, 不靠写文章谋生 (I Make a Living with Manual Labor, Not with Creative Writings), *Zhongguo qingnian bao*, April 26, 2017.

own on weekends."[31] This investment in "nonproductive" literary labor in her off hours is Fan's effort of resisting the totalistic taming and disciplining of laborers made possible through organizing, managing, and optimizing "productive labor" in the capitalist economy. Rejecting such productivity-driven regimentation of her time and bodily capacity, Fan redefines her existence through aesthetic enactment that liberates her from the constraints of the hierarchical class and the gender-based division of labor.

In comparison with audiovisual media such as DV cameras, writing (journal, memoir, and other forms of personal narrative) is an easier means of self-ethnography for domestic workers.[32] It is more affordable and less intrusive in a closely monitored middle-class domestic space. Fan's reflective self-writing on subaltern experiences builds up affective and spiritual linkages among domestic workers who are scattered and locked in the depth of each gated space of middle-class interiority. Moreover, Fan's active involvement in Picun literary activities does not identify her as an isolated worker-turned-writer whose overnight fame is only a result of middle-class curiosity about and constant hunting for the exotic and the sensational. Rather, Fan's literary trajectory starts with her love for books since childhood and develops in her daily interaction with fellow worker-writers living in the closely knit local community of the Picun Literature Group.

Unembedded from her patriarchal home(town), the homeless *baomu* finds a new home not in the urban middle-class space but in the fast-growing Literature Group, which is compared to Yan'an by Wang Chunyu, Fan's groupmate who is a migrant worker from Hebei province. Wang wrote, "Just like revolutionaries at wartime who trekked thousands of miles to get to Yan'an, I rush to Picun as

---

31. Aili Mu, "The Rise of the Short-Short Genre," in *China and New Left Visions: Political and Cultural Interventions*, ed. Ban Wang and Jie Lu (Lanham, MD: Lexington, 2012), 164.

32. Sun, *Subaltern China*, 146.

if marching on a pilgrimage journey, as if traveling back home."[33] In the Literature Group these migrant workers, male and female, share their love for reading and writing. Having found their right to speak and to express themselves with words, these outsiders in the city feel connected and respected. Writing is no longer a privilege reserved exclusively for intellectuals or professional writers. Workers can also pick up a pen to articulate their thoughts and tell their own stories. Their writings are not isolated texts competing for the recognition of mainstream literary history. Rather, they speak to each other to weave together an intertextual network of literary self-ethnographies.

Fan Yusu, in her autobiographical essay, quotes another piece of creative writing, "The Dogs in Picun" (*Picun ji gou* 皮村记狗), by Guo Fulai, a construction worker from Hebei province. Having joined the Literature Group in 2015, Guo remarks: "In my forty years of life, I have never been to such a place where everyone is close and connected as a big family, and where everyone can utter their voices."[34] His daughter Guo Jun wrote about her pain regarding quitting school to make money: "I wish I could sit in a classroom and study like my younger brother. But that is impossible. Why? I don't know. Is it because of gender inequity? Or sexist discrimination? . . . but we women workers also want to speak up! We want to cry out the word from the bottom of our hearts: equality!"[35]

Similar to what Fan conveys in her self-ethnography, in addition to the exploitation of female labor in the factory workshop, Guo Jun bears the violence of gender hierarchy within her own family. Given the limited financial resources of the working-class family, she is forced to drop out of school and become a worker to support her younger

33. Bukebang, "Picun Wenxue Gushi."

34. Wu Jingya 武靖雅, "Picun Wenxue Xiaozu: Dang Chenmo de Daduoshu Naqi Bi" 皮村文学小组: 当沉默的大多数拿起笔 (The Picun Literature Group: When the Silent Majority Picks up a Pen), *Sohu.com*, July 7, 2017, www.sohu.com/a/155302421_747149.

35. Wu, "Picun Wenxue Xiaozu."

brother's education. Joining the Literature Group provides her with a rare opportunity to communicate her gender dilemmas and to gain moral support outside of the patriarchal home. With literary writings, the twenty-one-year-old Guo Jun is able to voice a woman worker's questions, sentiments, and protests to interrogate multiple inequalities and oppressions along the divisions of gender, class, age, and urban/rural differences in postsocialist China.

Despite the massive number of female migrant workers in postsocialist China, very few of them have turned to creative writing to utter their voices. According to Qin Xiaoyu, who edited several anthologies of poems composed by migrant workers, "This lack of parity is only one indication that women are still treated as inferior in the countryside, where the patriarchal system still dictates. Girls are taught to be timid and are forced into silence, even after they have left home."[36] Under such hostile circumstances, the female workers' organization of and participation in the Picun Literature Group are particularly significant. These female worker-writers, such as Fan and Guo, are especially sensitive about their intersectional identity, defined by double inequalities of economic exploitation and sexist discrimination not only in the countryside but also in the urban heart of the capitalist regime.

The women workers' highly reflective self-ethnographic writings seek to unmake the patrilineal home(town) in the countryside, as well as the bourgeois patriarchal home built on private ownership and an unequal gendered and classed division of labor. Meanwhile, with their creative writings and everyday interactions, these grassroots workers seek to remake a cultural home based on class and gender solidarity rather than blood ties or heterosexual marriage. Blurring boundaries between public and private, individual and collective, and male and female, the remaking of a cultural home reconfigures a liminal time-space (the urban village exiled outside of high modernity, and

36. Qin, "Introduction," 27.

off hours outside of the productivity-driven capitalist regime) into a utopian moment of grassroots creativity and community building that revitalizes and reconnects the feminist tradition and the socialist legacy of workers' literary writings.

Conclusion

Postsocialist China has witnessed a transformation of middle-class domestic space. On the one hand, the sweeping privatization of home ownership provides a spatial form to China's socioeconomic differences and the middle-class dream of a "private paradise," a historical process dubbed "spatialization of class."[37] On the other hand, with the dismantling of the state welfare system, this middle-class dream cannot be fulfilled without a vast investment of time, energy, and affective labor, often designated as the wife's or the *baomu*'s duty in the reconfigured family structure and gender politics. The simultaneous historical processes of privatizing and gendering domestic space bear testimony to a revival of a patriarchal gender ethics that redraws the boundaries between male and female, exterior and interior, and public and private.

Positioned against such a postsocialist patriarchy, Fan's writings not only lend a voice to an otherwise silent group of *baomu*, but also bear great potential for building up organic connections through literary practices among atomized *baomu* scattered in each and every enclosure of the urban bourgeois family. Fan and her working-class cohorts based in and out of Picun bring together a reading community in which people come together to share their lived experiences and everyday writings to rebuild a cultural home. In this light, their literary practices and activities redefine the meaning of home outside of traditional patrilineality and capitalist private ownership: it has

---

37. Li Zhang, *In Search of Paradise: Middle-Class Living in a Chinese Metropolis* (Ithaca: Cornell Univ. Press, 2010).

offered them a shelter to cultivate interpersonal bonding and sentiments, while simultaneously serving as a public space in which each "family" member can discuss individual writings and common social issues on a more equal footing, as well as explore fluid identities and subjectivities based on their everyday interactions.

The grassroots-level literary efforts and intersubjective communication have transformed the obscure urban village into a place of collective creativity and resistance against the spatialized hierarchy in the capitalist regime. Through exploring a reconnection of individual experience with feminist traditions and historical legacies, Fan and her cohorts manage to reinvent a cultural and political vocabulary to articulate their critical reflections on the social injustice encountered by migrant workers in general and the gender-specific problems faced by female laborers. Their writings continue the tradition of Chinese women's literature while expanding it with their grassroots perspectives and bringing back the class dimension to postsocialist feminist thoughts and practices.

Acknowledgments

I am thankful for the support of the American Philosophical Society Franklin Research Grant, University of Kansas International Affairs, and the University of Kansas Center for East Asian Studies to fund my international research trip in summer 2019. I cannot thank enough Fu Qiuyun, Zhang Huiyu, Fan Yusu, and other participants in the Picun Literature Group for their generous help during my field work and when I was writing this chapter. Thanks to Geraldine Fiss, Noah Smith, and Ping Zhu for inviting me to present different versions of this paper at various conference and symposium venues. I received invaluable comments and suggestions from fellow panelists and audiences at all those occasions. I am also grateful for the following colleagues and friends who have read this paper in its different forms at different points of time and shared with me their most insightful feedback: Tani E. Barlow, Maghiel van Crevel, Michel Hockx, Wu

Qin, Ren Qiran, Ling Zhang, Xueping Zhong and Ping Zhu. Last but not least, my heartfelt thanks go to Philip Bradshaw and Keegan Sparks, two of my former students at KU, who completed translating Fan Yusu's autobiographical essay and gave me permission to use it for teaching and research purposes.

11

Over 1.5 Tons
Subversive Destruction and Counter-Monumentality to the Phallic Archetype

Shuqin Cui

Works of art by women, centered on female experience and explored from the perspective of gender politics, have claimed a significant place in Chinese contemporary art. Women's art has contributed not only to art history but also to discussions and debates over feminisms in terms of theory and practice. In response to the call for feminism with Chinese characteristics in a plural form, this chapter takes the reader-viewer to the art scenes where notions of feminism inform artistic practice to demonstrate a special metamorphosis with Chinese characteristics. Women's art and its feminist potential have been seen as a transnational and plural endeavor for a long time. In the 1990s the call for global feminism from the West and the response by Chinese women artists forged a transnational exchange. Western introduction of feminist concepts, translated into Chinese, prompted a response to theory by Chinese artists in their practices and experimental endeavors.

The transnational flow of Western concepts into China evoked an artistic reaction that challenged and extended the notion of feminism in plural and multiple modes. Global feminism, for instance, addressed the "'common difference' between women from various cultures, nations, religions, ethnicities, and sexualities" to create "a

11.1. Jiang Jie, *Over 1.5 Tons* (2014). Epoxy resin, textile, iron, 1000cm × 4000cm × 4800cm.

larger dissonant narrative" about feminism.[1] Unlike Western assumptions, where feminist rhetoric took sexual difference as its core thesis and gender politics as a political strategy, women and art in contemporary China did not appear oppositional to either sociopolitical conditions or the conventions of mainstream art. In other words, Chinese women artists were interested not so much in political subversion or gender confrontation as in the negotiation of positional difference *within* rather than *against* the system of gender or sexual relations.

In addition, the notion of feminism in the era of the transnational flow of theories and discussions remains conceptual and rhetorical,

1. Maura Reilly and Linda Nochlin, eds. *Global Feminisms: New Directions in Contemporary Art* (New York: Brooklyn Museum and Merrell Publishers, 2007), 31.

sourced in English and translated into Chinese via the mode of "translingual practice."[2] Translingual practice in the domain of woman and art demonstrates how theoretical terminology encounters linguistic limitations as well as connotative ambiguity when translation flows across different languages. Notions of women's art and feminist art translated respectively as *"nüxing yishu"* (女性艺术) and *"nüxing zhuyi yishu"* (女性主义艺术) in Chinese suggest different meanings, for instance. Few Chinese woman artists would welcome the label of feminist artist or categorize their work as feminist art even if the feminist dimensions of their practices were clearly evident. The problem remains an issue of catachresis as social-gender conditions and sufficient referents have to be considered through the translation of theoretical assumptions from English into Chinese and vice versa. In other words, the flow of feminism between two different linguistic domains prompts discursive inspiration on the one hand and obstacles to perception on the other.[3]

The denial of a feminist identity and the rejection of feminist readings of artworks while engaging with feminist practices remain a compelling aspect of feminism with Chinese characteristics in the art world. The phenomenon represents a lingering paradox asking for serious consideration of feminism in plural forms and under China's gender-political conditions. Against a postsocialist landscape, where Western concepts of feminism remain a translated vocabulary and China's dynamic economy complicates gender politics, the question of how to read women's works of art from the perspective of gender is perplexing.

A case study of Jiang Jie's 姜杰 recent massive sculpture installation *Over 1.5 Tons* (*Dayu yidunban* 大于一吨半) invites as well as

---

2. This terminology is traced from Lydia Liu, *Translingual Practice: Literature, National Culture, and Translated Modernity—China, 1900–1937* (Palo Alto, CA: Stanford Univ. Press, 1995), which examines the transformations between word and meaning under translations.

3. For detailed reference, see Shuqin Cui, *Gendered Bodies: Toward a Women's Art in Contemporary China* (Honolulu: Univ. of Hawai'i Press, 2015).

intimidates the desire for a feminist reading. A phallic-shaped dying monster wrapped with colored lace and snagged by iron hooks, the work presents a metaphor of despair. Through her selection of subject and material, and in the context of Chinese visual culture, the female sculptor creates a feminist art practice that is both alluring and repulsive. In this chapter, I argue that in the hands of the female sculptor the phallic imagery no longer signifies desire or symbolizes power, but rather points to an impotent, vulnerable, and fragmented body, the phallus in its death throes. Its survival and constancy depend on a special sculptural form and material support, created as well as manipulated by the female artist. Moreover, role reversals between subject and object, signifier and signified, and castrated and castrator have generated sculptural as well as discursive subversion in Chinese contemporary art. I will show how psychoanalytical and visual subversion can produce counter-monumental destruction, removing the mighty symbol of the phallic archetype from its monumental position and rendering it a hopeless part-object. Finally, in a comparative discussion of *Over 1.5 Tons* with other recent public installations and hanging sculptures, I will consider how contemporary Chinese art is viewed through transnational as well as gendered perspectives.

Materiality from a Psychoanalytical Perspective

Over 1.5 Tons simultaneously invites and subverts the concept of psychoanalysis, as the phallus archetype serves as the primary subject and form of the sculpture. We understand that psychoanalytical discourse, Freudian or Lacanian, comes to terms via infantile psychological development as the conceptual origin. Notions of an Oedipus complex and castration anxiety result from relationships of boys and girls with their parents. Realization of the phallus as a signifier of desire or lack and of symbolic power predominates one's formation of identity and sexual difference. The phallus, as Anika Lemaire states, "takes on the symbolic meaning of absence of lack [. . .] because of its form, because of its erectile power, because of its function of penetration. It is that which denies the lack, that which fills the empty space."[4] But consider what happens when the power of the phallic archetype wanes—the loss of the phallus and the death of fathers, in other words. Jiang Jie's *Over 1.5 Tons* captures the most embarrassing and hopeless moment of the phallus, no longer the upright totemic symbol demanding worship but rather a deflated and spent form.

As an impotent form, and in its vulnerable condition, the phallic-shaped sculptural work extends the Lacanian notion of symbolic power to a postsymbolic crisis. This shift reflects a psychoanalytical reversal, where the symbolic phallus is troubled by various anxieties, fearful of losing its power, and suffering a lack of driving energy at its late stage of life. In other words, the crisis reflects an anxiety resulting less from the lack of the phallus than from the loss of its function, and thus the symbolic force. As a result, the symbolic phallus "comes to stand in the place of everything the subject loses."[5] In its impotence it inverts the function it once stood for when associated with what Lacan terms the "symbolic father." The immediate question is what happens as the phallus is falling from its throne of power and becoming impotent in its penetrating function.

Reversal between Subject and Object

The artist, via sculptural form and material innovation, projects all those anxieties and fears onto the dying phallus, thereby reversing the psychoanalytical dichotomies between subject and object. The artistic subversion begins with a subject-object reversal in terms of art-object. With the phallus purposely selected as her sculptural subject but reconstructed intentionally as a subordinate object, the artist proposes the

4. Anika Lemaire, *Jacques Lacan*, trans. David Macey (Boston: Routledge & Kegan Paul, 1970), 59.

5. Dino Felluga, "Modules on Lacan: On Psychosexual Development," in *Introductory Guide to Critical Theory*, Purdue University, www.purdue.edu/guideto theory/psychoanalysis/lacandevelop.html.

notion of phallus-as-part-object. "What really characterizes the phallus and reappears in all its figurative embodiments," as Jean Laplanche and Jean-Bertrand Pontalis explain in *The Language of Psychoanalysis*, "is its status as a detachable and transformable object."[6] Removed from the body and exaggerated in size, the transformed part-object comes to us not as a symbolic signifier of power, embodying either monumental or totemic authority, but as a (re)castrated and vulnerable phallus in its late stage of life. After being rendered into a body-piece, the isolated phallus makes us realize that the law of the father is far more vulnerable than we had imagined. Falling and paranoid, it desperately needs protection and salvation. Or in Leo Steinberg's comments, "Fragmentation and discontinuity of the parts is implacable and literal, not symbolic."[7]

The part-object is often associated with part-sculpture, specifically phallic sculpture in Jiang Jie's case. The dialectical interrelations between part-object and part-sculpture pose the possibility of transforming bodily fragments into sculptural reproduction. *Over 1.5 Tons* offers a special case in point but does not stand alone. In fact, it may be argued that "there is a dominant trend toward the representation of a body-in-pieces, of what is, in Kleinian theory, termed the part object, that runs, like an insistent thread, a sustained subtext, through much of American artistic production . . . art objects as part objects."[8] For Jiang Jie, sculptural reproduction does not entail mechanical repetition but rather critical recreation, pursuing multiple and excessive potentials. In addition, the dialectic also brings about intersections between psychic and social implications. In doing so, phallus as part-object and part-sculpture appears "not only as a theoretical

6. Jean Laplanche and Jean-Bertrand Pontalis, *The Language of Psychoanalysis*, trans. Donald Nicholson-Smith (London: Hogarth, 1973), 313.

7. Leo Steinberg, "Jasper Johns: The First Seven Years of His Art," *Other Criteria* (London: Oxford Univ. Press, 1972), 37.

8. Annette Michelson, "Where Is Your Rupture?: Mass Culture and the Gesamtkunstwerk," *October* 56, (1991): 48.

proposition, but as a logic of artistic practice and political resistance."[9] The tendency toward resistance by artists marks a divergence from phallocentric discourse and a subversion of master narratives.

Material Tensions between Softness and Resilience

In order to subvert master narratives, the artist first invests the sculptural trope of the phallic totem with a material subversion. The selection and application of hybrid materials are a primary source and agent of sculptural construction. The formed materiality, in its distinct quality and function, generates a process of gendering the sculpture and destructing the phallic symbol. Jiang uses fiberglass, dyed lace, and iron hooks to negotiate or transgress the boundaries of masculinity and femininity, construction and destruction, the corporeal and the psychological. More specifically, the gendered materials feminize the phallic hierarchy with colored lace and constrain it with iron hooks.

The foundation or primary form of the sculpture is made of scrap metals. Metal materials—iron, steel, or bronze—are traditionally associated with stability and durability, and with strength, hence masculinity. From antiquity to modernity and from West to East, for instance, metallic materials have been used to commemorate figures of authority, often in the form of prominent statues. Jiang Jie's *Over 1.5 Tons*, however, subverts social and visual conventions by wrapping and sealing the noble material and masculine form with dyed lace fabrics. The supersession of metal by fabric, with the latter encasing the former, is a radical reversal. The soft confines the hard; the feminine dominates the masculine.

The sculpture posits a material tension between softness and resilience. In considering how to color the sculpture, the artist turned to fabric and lace for wrapping and coloring materials. The phallic object,

9. Mignon Nixon, "Part-Object Part Sculpture," *October* 119, (2007): 99.

11.2. *Over 1.5 Tons*, maquette.

structured by iron and fiberglass, is swathed in layers of soft fabric, creating a material encounter where softness and toughness clash and embrace. The tangible feel of the textiles, which resembles a woman's bodily texture and temperature, generates a sensation of sexual intercourse through material blending. In this symbolic sexual encounter, the powerful and masculine is subordinate to the feminine when sheathed by the fleshy and drippy laces. As a result, the phallic symbol, once unbendable and strong, yields to its feminine counterpart. In so doing, the phallic part-object, wrapped first by the feminine, sexual fabric, then constrained by the sculptural materiality, bows to the artist's designation and discursive reversal.

The strategy that the artist plays with is the notion of fabricability: the fabric's ability to shape and frame its object. The sculptor of *Over 1.5 Tons* has used textiles precisely to challenge and refute an iron-steel counterpart. A commenter about Rozsika Parker's pioneering book *The Subversive Stitch* suggests that cloth can be viewed "as

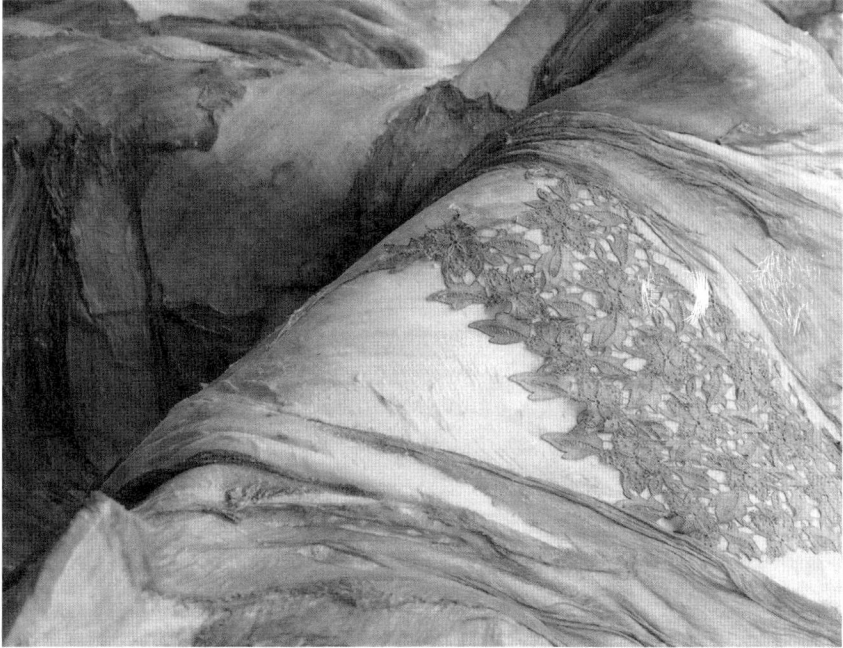

11.3. *Over 1.5 Tons*, detail.

a strategy for subversion and political engagement."[10] The artist uses material less to insert femininity than to assert a subjective position, with woman as the creator who is able to (re)shape the phallic symbol and rewrite the conventional discourse of gender politics. In other words, the feminine could challenge as well as subvert the masculine via its flexible and contradicting materiality. In addition, the intercourse of metal and lace suggests intermateriality on the one hand and transmateriality on the other. That is, when objects cross material boundaries, they may simultaneously disturb discursive realms.

10. "The Subversive Stitch Revisited: The Politics of Cloth," Goldsmiths website forum, organized by Pennina Barnett and Jennifer Harris, June 2014, www.gold.ac.uk/subversivestitchrevisited/. See also Rozsika Parker, *The Subversive Stich: Embroidery and the Making of the Feminine* (London: Women's Press, 1986).

Push and Pull by Iron Hooks

The reversal from phallus-as-signifier to phallus-as-object radically alters gender dynamics and sculptural rhetoric: subject is transformed into object, signifier into signified, and castrator into castrated. In addition to the material tension between softness and resilience, the push and pull of gravity is also an important aspect of *Over 1.5 Tons*, where the falling phallic part-object relies on iron hooks to remain aloft. The contrast between the object's vulnerable condition and the forceful intrusion of the iron hooks raises the question of postcastration anxiety. The artwork suggests that the castration complex does not end in its imaginary and symbolic stages but rather continues towards a post- or (re)castration crisis.

The Lacanian concept of the castration complex has it emerging first from an imaginary fantasy, where the child attempts to be mother's desiring object, the phallus as signifier of desire. In the symbolic stage, the child realizes the father's prohibitory power, his possession of the phallus, and experiences the threat of castration; the child is forced to abandon his attempt to become and must submit to the name of the father. Castration anxiety does not end in its imaginary and symbolic stages, however. As Lacan points out in his second contribution to the *Cahiers pour l'Analyse*, "castration anxiety is related to the possibility of a fundamental 'impossibility,' of no longer being able to desire. The child thus experiences a 'being-towards-castration' that is prior to 'being-towards-death.'"[11]

The notion of the castration complex needs to be extended beyond the child stage and into a senior phase, however. The aged phallus experiences (re)castration anxiety after competing in the world of the father and realizing its lack or loss of function. The phallus is the dominant totem of the arena of competitive struggle, which men

11. "Castration," Concept and Form: The *Cahiers pour l'Analyse* and Contemporary French Thought website, http://cahiers.kingston.ac.uk/concepts/castration .html.

are pushed to enter. As Jeanne Willette observes, "Men are energized by the threat of castration and live uneasily within a phallocentric message that intimidates men and forces them to enter into rivalry with those who seem to possess more Phallus/power."[12] The threat of defeat and extinction are omnipresent. "Lack and Loss," Willette explains, "are the very reasons of Desire."[13] Moreover, as Christian Muller points out, the "re-emergence and intensification of the anxiety which lies at the root of numerous pathological phenomena can be attributed to the impinging necessity of coming to grips with death and loss."[14] Woman, by contrast, is defined from her infantile stage by the lack of a penis, thus the phallus.

Jiang Jie's *Over 1.5 Tons* nonetheless reverses the Oedipus complex to position the female artist-self as the castrating subject and the phallus as the castrated. In other words, the artist transgresses the boundaries of gender hierarchy, turning herself into a phallic woman and rendering the phallic object into lack or loss. The phallic woman in general possesses traditionally masculine characteristics. Taking this position, the artist uses iron hooks to penetrate the impotent phallic part and insert feminist sculptural implications. We see from the installation that the falling phallic part-object is first helplessly hooked by the chain of iron hooks and then lifted up via steel wires. The application of the selected materials strings up the falling phallic object and thereby ridicules its waning power. As the artist explains, she explores the potential force that is able to "lift up, expand, and erect" the incapable phallus. "The dragging and pulling gravity between the hooks and wires mean to save the dying symbol from its degradation."[15] By

---

12. Jeanne S. M. Willette, "Jacques Lacan and Women," *Art History Unstuffed*, July 19, 2013, https://arthistoryunstuffed.com/jacques-lacan-and-women/.

13. Willette, "Jacques Lacan and Women."

14. Christian Muller, "The Influence of Age on Schizophrenia," in *Process of Aging: Social and Psychological Perspectives*, ed. Richard H. Williams, Clark Tibbits, and Wilma Donohue (London: Aldine Transaction, 2009), 504.

15. See *Huakan*'s special interview with Jiang Jie 姜杰, "Cuiruo, Wuneng, Wugu Shi Shengming de Yizhong: Jiang Jie Zhuanfang" 脆弱、无能、无辜是生命的一种: 姜杰

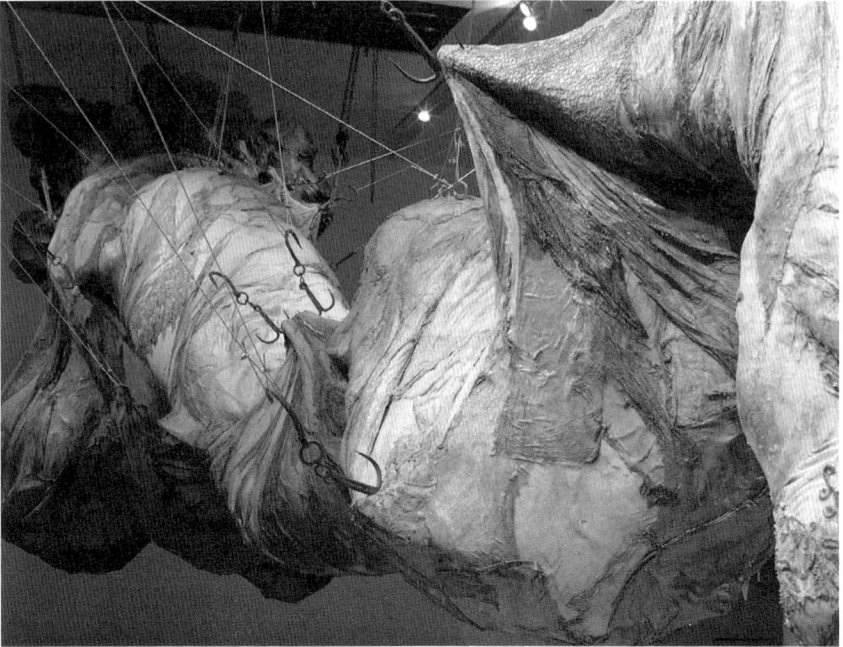

11.4. *Over 1.5 Tons*, detail.

lifting the frail or paralyzed phallus, the hooks and wires impose a
sharp visual contrast: firmness in contrast to softness, uplifting to
sinking, dominance to subordination. The contrast further reflects
the law of gravity, where the powerful and the vulnerable pull and
push each other through mass transgressions.

As an inserted force the hooks and wires attempt to awaken or
re-erect the dysfunctional phallus from its castration and impotence.
The chosen materials would typically represent masculine force and
phallic authority, but in the hands of the female sculptor, the material
enacts a subversive force to generate feminist power and sculptural
destruction. And the sculptor does so in the name and language of

专访 (Weak, Incapable, and Vulnerable Is a Mode of Life: An Interview with Jiang
Jie)," *Huakan*, no. 2 (2015): 27.

the father. The significance of the materiality seen from gender and psychoanalytical perspectives is that the dialectical interdependence between the restraining devices and the dropping object rearranges gender dynamics so that the female subject claims the dominant position over the phallic object. The reversal of gendered positions then redefines notions of castration anxiety. The female artist as subject/creator returns as a phallic woman, and man reexperiences the threat of castration in his late and declining stage. The conceptual and visual reversal through materiality subverts not only conventional psychoanalytical discourse but also sculptural rhetoric. As the artist claims, "*Over 1.5 Tons* is my most confident, unrestricted, and radical work."[16]

The proximate reference from which we might comprehend Jiang Jie's *Over 1.5 Tons* may be found in the work of the American artist Louise Bourgeois, especially her *Fillette*. This sculpture is probably the best known image by Bourgeois, a phallic piece either hung from a butcher's hook in the Tate Modern or tucked under her arm in a photograph by Robert Mapplethorpe. As to what Bourgeois thought she was doing with *Fillette*, a gallery label has this to say:

> The title of this phallic sculpture means "little girl," an ironic disjunction of word and object. Bourgeois has talked about this work in relation to her experiences as a wife, and a mother to three boys, which led her to see masculinity as far more vulnerable than she had imagined. "From a sexual point of view, I consider the masculine attributes to be extremely delicate," she explained. "They're objects that the woman, myself, must protect." The photographer Robert Mapplethorpe famously portrayed Bourgeois with a version of this work tucked playfully under her arm.[17]

The two female artists may share the perception of the phallus as powerful as well as vulnerable and in need of protection. Bourgeois's

16. *Huakan*, "Cuiruo," 28.

17. Tate exhibition gallery label, October 2016, www.tate.org.uk/art/artworks /bourgeois-fillette-sweeter-version-l02885.

sculptural phallus reflects the artist's unspoken emotions about her family and her psychological world. Yet *Fillette* showcases not only personal expression but also a response to the awakening of female consciousness and the emergence of the feminist movement in the late 1960s in the United States. Jiang Jie's *Over 1.5 Tons* intends to explore the potential archetypal meanings of the phallus, which could be psychological and sociopolitical, or sexual and theological. The artist explains that "the phallus symbol preoccupies a significant position in multifaceted disciplines. The worship and totem of the phallus, for instance, is evidenced in pillars, high-rises, and monuments."[18] The evidence of sculptural subversion and destruction leads to the conception of a counter-monumental discourse.

Beyond sculptural subversion and psychoanalytical rearticulation through materiality, *Over 1.5 Tons* involves counter-monumentality. "Counter-monuments," as James E. Young defines them, "are those which reject and renegotiate the traditional forms and reasons for public memorial art."[19] The counter-monument (re)defines the commemorative—the conventions and collective memories associated with the monument. "Possibly the most notable and most common feature of anti-monumentality is its opposition to conventional monumental form and the employment of alternative, contrasting design techniques, materials and duration."[20] Historically, monumental constructions in the Chinese art and architectural tradition have shaped the collective memories and political consciousness of social groups. Monuments have often been built in the form of phallic symbols—intentionally or unintentionally—to project the seat of power. Such affirmative and permanent monuments monopolize China's geopolitical landscapes: for instance, stone steles and the Great Wall from

18. *Huakan*, "Cuiruo," 29.

19. James E. Young, "The Counter-Monument: Memory against Itself in Germany Today." *Critical Inquiry* 18, no. 2 (1992): 272.

20. Quentin Stevens, Karen A. Franck, and Ruth Fazakerley, "Counter-Monuments: The Anti-Monumental and the Dialogic," *The Journal of Architecture* 17, no. 6 (2012): 956.

traditional times; Mao's mausoleum and the Monument to the People's Heroes in socialist China; hegemonic high-rises and invasive landscapes in contemporary China.

Public Sculpture, Public Space, and Anti-Monumentality

A counter-monumental encounter occurs in the relation between public art and public space, especially in the intertwined relations of sculpture and cityscape. Jiang Jie's *Over 1.5 Tons* defines itself in opposition to traditional monumental principles, forms, and rhetoric. The artist reconsiders how the sculpture relates to the surrounding space, explaining in an interview that "the work could be installed either indoors or outdoors. Or could be placed in a hospital, church, or school. Problems would occur wherever the sculpture is located, however."[21] *Over 1.5 Tons* was invited to participate in the Shanghai Pujiang OCT Ten-Year Public Art Project (*Shanghai pujiang huaqiaocheng shiian gonggong yishu jihua* 上海浦江华侨城十年公共艺术计划). The OCT is a newly developed urban district designed by Italian firm Gregotti Associati International.[22] The new urban center features classical Western city architecture and ancient Chinese tradition, and it opens a public space for the potential of public art. The OCT Public Art Project has curated art shows since 2007 and has drawn well-known artists such as Sui Jianguo 隋建国, Wang Guangyi 王广义, Gu

21. Zhang Wenzhi 张文志 and Jiang Jie 姜杰, "Diaosu Chuangzuo Zhong de Chonggao yu Gonggongxing" 雕塑创作中的崇高与公共性 (Sculptural Sublime and Public Spheres), news.artron.net, November 28, 2014, https://news.artron.net/2014 1128/n682274_4.html.

22. For detailed information see the New City of Pujiang page at http://us.archello.com/en/project/new-city-pujiang. See also Peng Fei 彭菲, "Mianhuai yu Chonggou: 'Pujiang Huaqiaocheng Shinian Gonggong Yishu Jihua' Jinru Dishinian" 缅怀与重构:"浦江华侨城十年公共艺术计划"进入第十年 (Retrospection and Reconstruction: OCT Public Art Project Enters Its Tenth Year," news.artron.net, December 18, 2016, https://news.artron.net/20161218/n894759.html.

Wenda 谷文达, and Lin Tianmiao 林天苗. Jiang Jie's *Over 1.5 Tons* was
created especially for its Ten-Year Public Art Project in 2014.

Public works of art are "not displayed in museums and galleries,
but performed or materialized in streets, squares, and other public
spaces."[23] The art speaks to its location, as the public sculpture cor-
responds with the surrounding environment. But how an artwork
relates to its setting may turn out to be problematic rather than harmonious. Because of the "inappropriate phallic form" of Jiang Jie's
sculpture, the location for the installation was changed from the open
space of China-Italy Square to OCT's exhibition hall. To sequester
the work indoors detaches the sculpture from an open and widely
available environment, thereby defeating the purpose of public art for
public space. The walled exhibition hall and the confined sculpture
could only be accessed by special visitors, scholars, and art critics, not
the general public.

Although the indoor setting physically separates the sculpture
from open surroundings, the site does generate discursive connections. The sculpture, with its ambiguous subject and monstrous
form, does not blend into its surroundings but clashes against the
contemporary urban center in spatial and discursive dimensions.
Over 1.5 Tons is a fallen giant on life support, a graphic reflection of
the grave consequences of China's socioeconomic madness, where
hypercharged urbanization and economic expansion have grievously
violated the environment and distorted traditional values. The newly
developed OCT city expansion, for instance, presents precisely what
Over 1.5 Tons intends to visualize. In this urban district one sees
industrial factories, rural remnants, housing blocks, university campuses, and transnational corporations such as Microsoft and Coca-
Cola.[24] The massive size of *Over 1.5 Tons* thus visualizes the sheer

23. Ash Amin, "Collective Culture and Urban Public Space," *City* 12, no. 12
(2008): 5–24

24. See Huang Ping's 黄平 discussion comments in Ouyang Jianghe, ed., *Jiang
Jie: Dayu Yidunban* 姜杰: 大于一吨半 (Jiang Jie: Over 1.5 Tons), exhibition catalogue,
Shanghai Pujiang, October 2015, 92.

scale of China's urbanization on the one hand and the collapse of massive overbuilding on the other. One may say that the sculptor is less interested in the question of how to immerse her work in the spatial setting as a monument than in its possibilities for counterdiscourse and counter-monumentality.

Against Shanghai's affluent urban setting, the monstrous installation announces its anti-monumental intentions. Anti-monumental approaches, however, "remain ambiguous and resist any unified interpretation; their meanings are often dependent on visitors' historical knowledge or supplementary information."[25] When the work was unveiled to the public, viewer perceptions of the sculpture lingered on the question of what it is or what it is not. A totemic monster or phallic alternative generates both thematic and visual ambiguity; it is an enigma. Nonetheless, the artist and viewers can project multifaceted meanings, whether sociohistorical or psychoanalytical, totemic or monumental. As Natalia Krzyżanowska states in her study of *Stolpersteine*, counter-monumental installations "carry multiple meanings and have multiple functions which allow for diverse patterns of interaction with past/present."[26] No matter the perspective taken to read the sculpture, the viewer's inevitable puzzlement leads to the recognition that the artist is out to subvert a hegemonic archetype.

The counter-monumental mode of *Over 1.5 Tons* takes aim at official monuments such as the Monument to the People's Heroes (*Renmin yingxiong jinian bei* 人民英雄纪念碑) in Tiananmen Square. There are stark differences in material forms and discursive purposes. With its granite obelisk and marble stele, the national monument is designed to commemorate those who sacrificed their lives for China's revolutionary cause; it is an architectural medium for the inscription of state-sanctioned rhetoric. Its historical and political implications are clear, as Hung Wu observes about the square and its monuments:

25. Stevens, Franck, and Fazakerley, "Counter-Monuments," 961.

26. Natalia Krzyżanowska, "The Discourse of Counter-Monuments: Semiotics of Material Commemoration in Contemporary Urban Spaces," *Social Semiotics* 26, no. 5 (2016): 465.

"The square has been and will continue to be a prime visual means of political rhetoric in modern China to address the public and actually to constitute the public itself."[27] Yet the historical and national monument can be read differently. The French art historian Simon Leys views the national monument as an assault on the sublime architectural harmony of old Beijing, castigating it as "the Maoist rape of the ancient capital" or "an insignificant granitic phallus receiving all its enormous significance from the blasphemous stupidity of its location."[28] If we take the national monument and its monumentality as a phallic symbol of the Chinese Communist Party, signifying its revolutionary past and authoritarian present as well as future, Jiang Jie's *Over 1.5 Tons* radically and mercilessly subverts its historical and political monumentality.

In contrast to all the obelisks and phallic monuments, traditional or contemporary, *Over 1.5 Tons* repositions the phallic signifier from vertical to horizontal and changes the material from granite to fabric. As the art critic Ouyang Jianghe comments: "the eternally erect, metaphysical and incarnate phallic symbol has now, without a moment's notice, been rendered horizontal, just like a distortion intuition."[29] The phallic object, suspended from the ceiling by the iron hooks and cables, is a purposeful display of horizontality. Without support from the floor, the large object looks forlorn and vulnerable. The horizontal position subverts the convention, whereas sculpture oriented on a vertical axis represents social, political, and historical force. The uprightness of the sculptural tradition throughout sociopolitical history stands for social power and masculine form: totemic symbols in ancient times, political statues in a revolutionary past, or high-rises in the modern era. By making the shaft horizontal, the sculptor not

27. Hung Wu, "Tiananmen Square: A Political History of Monuments," *Representations*, no. 35 (1991): 85.

28. Simon Leys, *Chinese Shadows* (New York: Viking, 1977), 53–54.

29. Ouyang Jianghe 欧阳江河, ed., *Jiang Jie: Dayu Yidunban* 姜杰: 大于一吨半 (Jiang Jie: Over 1.5 Tons), exhibition catalogue: Shanghai Pujiang, October 2015, 100.

only shifts the orientation of the axis but also transforms its embedded meanings. In his study of Alberto Giacometti and Jacob Epstein's sculptural works, David Getsy claims that "For sculpture, uprightness was a primary sign of subjectivity and mental activity while horizontality was, by inference, a sign of weakness or vulnerability."[30] Indeed, the axis shift from vertical to horizontal turns *Over 1.5 Tons* from an upright, erect phallus into an impotent and vulnerable dependent. Detached from public space and reliant on supporting devices, *Over 1.5 Tons* rejects not only a freestanding position but also a longstanding tradition in monumentality.

The change in axis also affects the viewer, as conventional political and collective perceptions yield to alternative and individual viewpoints. The sculpture's suspended horizontal layout allows the viewer to circle around the hanging object and observe it from one side to the other. The ambulating viewer gains access to details from all directions. And the moving relation of spectator to sculpture generates "kinetic possibilities," where "we might choose to move through the sculpture or we imagine for the sculpture."[31] The kinetic possibilities available in close interactions between the sculpture and its viewers can lead to alternative perceptions and discursive resistance, especially from the perspective of gender. The symbolic phallic part-object rejects a masculine reception; in fact, in its sorry state it embarrasses male vision, negating the male power of possession or pleasure in desire. The exposed and defenseless creature is left to an alternative salvation, hoisted aloft by a female sculptor concerned about female spectatorship. Manipulated by both female authorship and female spectatorship, the phallic part-object is stripped of its monumentality.

30. David J. Getsy, "Fallen Women: The Gender of Horizontality and the Abandonment of the Pedestal by Giacometti and Epstein," in *Display and Displacement: Sculpture and the Pedestal from Renaissance to Post-Modern*, ed. Alexandra Gerstein (London: Courtauld Institute of Art Research Forum and Paul Holberton Publishing, 2007), 122.

31. Susanne Langer, *Feeling and Form: A Theory of Art* (New York: Charles Scribner's Sons, 1953), 90.

Over 1.5 Tons in the Realm of Chinese Contemporary Art

Sculptures and installations that engage in counter-monumentality contribute significantly to the experiment of Chinese contemporary art. These works stand in opposition to traditional or official monumental discourses. Gu Wenda's 谷文达 *Forest of Stone Stele: Retranslation and Rewriting of Tang Poetry* (1993–2005) (*Beilin: Tangshi houzhu* 碑林: 唐诗后著), for instance, transforms original historical records from monumental steles into unreadable texts carved on stones. The juxtaposition between past and present or historical and contemporary comes to terms through rewriting via calligraphy and ink rubbing on the one hand and translations between Chinese and English on the other. The mode of textual rewriting and linguistic translation radically deconstructs the original, traditional monumentality that the stone steles embodied.[32] In a similar vein, Xu Bing 徐冰, in his *Ghosts Pounding the Wall* (*Gui da qiang* 鬼打墙, 1990–1991), uses ink rubbing to duplicate piece by piece the worn body of the Great Wall. The contrast between the Wall as national monument and the Wall in its ink-rubbed paper copies reflects the artist's intention to rewrite or reinterpret history as a deconstructive parody.

While Gu Wenda and Xu Bing choose traditional and hegemonic monuments as targets for counter-monumental destruction, Wang Qingsong's 王庆松 sculpture installation *Past, Present, and Future* (*Guoqu, xianzai he jianglai* 过去, 现在和将来) aims at socialist monumental giants that commemorate the so-called people's heroes and evoke the collective memory of revolutionary history. The artist begins his counter-monumental subversion by miniaturizing the monumental and inserting himself into the frame as a bystander. An individual observer can confront the monuments of collective commemoration

32. For online information on publication and the process of making the work, see Asia Art Archive, "Translating Visuality—Gu Wenda: Forest of Stone Steles, Retranslation and Rewriting of Tang Poetry," Asia Art Archive, https://aaa.org.hk /en/collection/search/library/translating-visuality-gu-wenda-forest-of-stone-steles -retranslation-rewriting-of-tang-poetry-59236.

and create a connection between past and present, as well as between history and memory. Also counter to the monument of people's heroes was the Goddess of Democracy, a statue erected by students from the Central Academy of Fine Arts during the student movement in 1989 and installed at the center of the solemn site of Tiananmen Square, facing Mao's portrait on the Gate of Heavenly Peace. The Goddess of Democracy survived for only a few days before military tanks crushed it. The monumental implication of the statue marked Chinese political history and commemorated those in the democracy movement who lost their lives.

Considering Jiang Jie's sculpture in the context of other counter-monumental works of art, one can say that *Over 1.5 Tons* seizes the most fundamental essence of monumental origin, the phallic symbol, as her counter-monumental endeavor. Once worshiped and idolized, the phallus often signifies either a specific monumental implication or a collective commemoration—traditional or modern, sociopolitical or material. But in the hands of the woman sculptor, the castrated phallus loses all magnificence and appears limp, enervated. In other words, *Over 1.5 Tons* declares a war against the world ruled by the power of the phallus. In addition, beyond the significance of its counter-monumental statement, *Over 1.5 Tons* extends sculptural rhetoric to installation art, especially as large-scale, hanging work.

Examples of suspended sculptures can be found among works by prominent Chinese artists such as Xu Bing. His massive sculpture installation, *Phoenix* (*Fenghuang* 凤凰), for instance, features two magnificent birds (*fenghuang*) made of industrial debris from China's construction sites. The large-scale, paired work— one hundred feet long and weighing twelve tons—has attracted attention in public exhibitions around the world. Its cultural implications and material innovations have opened *Phoenix* to multifaceted readings. Along with the dragon, *fenghuang* have been sociocultural monuments, commemorated and worshiped in China for their symbolic implications. The dragon signifies power and strength; the phoenix is auspicious for harmony. The counter-monumental intention becomes possible when the totemic birds and construction remnants meet. The contrast reflects the artist's concern that behind the affluence and lavishness of the birds—an emblem of China's rising economy and wealth—lies the hard labor of construction workers and devastation of the environment.

The massive public artwork by this prominent artist has traveled across the globe. Different sites have favored different meanings, influencing the spectacle of the bird sculpture. After two exhibitions in China—outside the Today Art Museum in Beijing and at the World Expo in Shanghai in 2010—*Phoenix* made its overseas debut at the Massachusetts Museum of Contemporary Art Mass (MoCA) from December 22, 2012, to October 27, 2013. Mass MoCA was originally housed in the old Sprague Electric factory building in North Adams. When Beijing factory number 718 began to make capacitors in 1955, it put Sprague Electric out of business. The Beijing factory later became part of Beijing's art district 798.[33] The arrival of Xu Bing's *Phoenix*, hung from the roof of what had been one of Sprague's old factory buildings, invested the site with both historical and translocal meanings. The exhibition site and the spectacle of the sculpture reflect a historical past in Massachusetts and a contemporary local art scene in China. Once defined by industrial production, the Massachusetts factory site returns through the sight of a sculpture constructed from industrial waste. The very notion of manufacturing, and the materials used, unite the old factory and the current installation, both juxtaposing and dislocating past and present, Massachusetts and China.

After Mass MoCA, *Phoenix* traveled to the Smithsonian's Arthur M. Sackler Gallery in Washington, DC, with the exhibition title "Nine Deaths and Two Births: Xu Bing's Phoenix Project" (April 27 to September 1, 2013). The exhibit explored the inspirations and challenges behind the artist's new work. Thus the curatorial approach was

---

33. For exhibition information, see the museum webpage, https://massmoca .org/event/xu-bing-phoenix/. Information on the connection between the Sprague Electric factory in North Adams and the 798 art district in contemporary China can be found in Ellen Pearlman, "A Tale of Two Phoenixes," *Hyperallergic*, July 3, 2013, https://hyperallergic.com/74458/a-tale-of-two-phoenixes/.

to "document the project's development through preparatory draw-
ings, technical diagrams, scale models and a new film made especially
for this presentation."[34] The Smithsonian's curators and scholars provided the sculpture on show with written and visual records that, when
institutionalized and exhibited to the public, served as official recognition and visual evidence that legitimized the documents of *Phoenix* as
an integral part of the Freer and Sackler galleries' permanent collection. The chief curator stated that Xu Bing's sculpture "offers a unique
opportunity to draw on the Galleries' historical collections to enhance
our understanding of the work of a major contemporary artist."[35]
The museum exhibition and its curatorial documentation claimed Xu
Bing's work for an institutional system and discursive rhetoric that are
internationally orthodox.

Phoenix kept traveling, moving on to St. John the Divine in New
York City. So the Phoenix arose from construction ashes in China
to float in the divine space of a New York cathedral. A special public space received the unusual installation art to create a meaningful
spectacle as the largest cathedral in the world embraced the massive
phoenixes from China. The host of the exhibition explained that "in
western mythology the phoenix is associated with the sun and symbolizes rebirth and resurrection."[36] The artist saw the cathedral as
"monumental and very lofty, and the phoenixes now have a sacred
quality."[37] The cathedral space and the sculpture installation created
hybrid monumentalities: Western mythology and Chinese rituals,
Christian divinity and modern technology, cathedral architecture and

34. Smithsonian, "New Exhibition Documents the Rise of Xu Bing's Monumental 'Phoenixes,'" Smithsonian news release, April 9, 2013, www.si.edu/newsdesk
/releases/new-exhibition-documents-rise-xu-bing-s-monumental-phoenixes.

35. Smithsonian, "New Exhibition."

36. Liz Leafloor, "Symbolism of the Mythical Phoenix Bird: Renewal, Rebirth
and Destruction," Ancient Origins, www.ancient-origins.net/myths-legends/ancient
-symbolism-magical-phoenix-002020.

37. Carol Vogel, "Phoenixes Rise in China and Float in New York," *New York
Times*, February 14, 2014.

installation art. Thus we may say that *Phoenix* took flight from China and landed in New York, both mechanically and discursively.

In comparison to Xu Bing's *Phoenix*, Jiang Jie's *Over 1.5 Tons* did not draw much public attention, especially outside China. In its radical counter-monumentality, *Over 1.5 Tons* could make art institutions and public spaces uncomfortable. Imagine what might happen if the phallic monster, impotent and vulnerable, were hung inside the Sackler or in the nave of the cathedral St. John the Divine, as the sculptural installation work ridicules the very essence of sociocultural norms—official, institutional, and spiritual. In contrast, *Phoenix* is less a counter-monumental work than a newly created monument, rising from the ashes of construction debris and reborn in the artist's conceptual, sculptural articulations. The regenerated monumentality invites interpretations that vary with the public space of the installation. Few would question the labor that went into the making of the art or the capital needed for a world tour, even as we gaze at the documented social reality behind the magnificent birds: China's voracious urbanization. Junjie Jiang sees in rampant urban growth "two sides of Chinese society: the harsh realities of cheap labor and environmental pollution as well as the miraculous economic prosperity and the Chinese dream."[38] In a critical view one should realize that the construction of urban skyscrapers and the creation of the monumental birds, although utterly different projects, consume labor in a similar way.

Jiang Jie's *Over 1.5 Tons* (2014) also calls for a comparison with Chen Zhen's 陈箴 *Precipitous Parturition* (*Zaochan* 早产, 1999), which was selected for a special exhibition at the Guggenheim's exhibition *Art and China after 1989: Theater of the World.* The large sculptural and installation work, using multiple materials, was suspended and displayed from the ceiling of the museum's central rotunda. Although

---

38. Junjie Jiang, "The Doubleness of Sight/Site: Xu Bing's Phoenix as an Intended Public Art Project," *Yishu: Journal of Contemporary Chinese Art* 17, no. 2 (2018): 37.

thematically and materially distinct, these works by Chen and Jiang Jie share similarities in size and appearance, and one can imagine a dialectical conversation between them. Viewed as a "writhing dragon"[39] by the curators and a "most spectacular work"[40] by the media, Chen's sculpture consists of bicycle parts, black rubber inner tubes woven together, and plastic toy cars; it is a comment on China's shift from a bicycle kingdom to car-crazed culture.

Like Jiang Jie's *Over 1.5 Tons*, *Precipitous Parturition* takes the form of a phallus or dragon, a large body suspended from the ceiling. The artist expresses his concern about the socioeconomic and material transitions roiling China. The dragon body has become a womb, but instead of producing the countless bicycles that once defined city life, it now experiences a precipitous parturition, birthing ever more automobiles. The phallic dragon embodies a masculine socioeconomic force that works through the female body. In other words, female reproduction serves masculine production, and this is a signal, or prophesy, of the economic and environmental catastrophe looming over China's socioeconomic landscape. Created in their own cultural moments, Jiang Jie's *Over 1.5 Tons* and Chen's *Precipitous Parturition* advance different themes and visual purposes. From the perspective of gender, however, one may say that for Chen the phallic part-object is a powerful prophesy of economic-environmental catastrophe, but for Jiang Jie it is a public execution of the hegemonic power driving that catastrophe.

Although both works are imposing and provocative, they received contrasting public receptions that reflected the exhibition space and political milieu. Installed in the central rotunda of the Guggenheim museum and enthusiastically praised by the *New York Times*, Chen's

39. Guggenheim, "Chen Zhen's Precipitous Parturition," Guggenheim website, October 26, 2017, www.guggenheim.org/audio/track/chen-zhens-precipitous-parturition.

40. Holland Cotter, "From Innovation to Provocation: China's Artists on a Global Path," *New York Times*, October 6, 2017.

Precipitous Parturition drew global attention and accrued monumental implications.[41] The global status of Chen's installation arose in part from the American media's portrayal of the 1990s as China's entrance into the global economy and the international art scene. Completed in 1999, *Precipitous Parturition* corresponded well to the curatorial vocabulary and rhetoric of art criticism in the West. The work marks the passing of the era of "pedal-driven proletarian culture" and the arrival of "head-spinning urban speed, pollution, and technological encasement."[42] It also exemplifies how, beginning in the 1990s, Chinese contemporary art has attracted worldwide attention for its counter-official positions and avant-garde experiments. For this reason, the artworks selected for the Guggenheim exhibition were monumental in the sense of historical and discursive significance.

Although the show was titled "Art and China after 1989: Theater of the World" and the American media presented it as characteristic of Chinese art since 1989, viewers did not acquiesce; they protested and insisted that the museum withdraw three pieces of work. Cooperation between contemporary Chinese artists and museums and markets in the West has been bumpy because of the changing sociopolitical and economic landscape. During an interview the chief curator, Alexandra Munroe, asked, "Are contemporary Chinese artists, whose recent history has been one of cultural lockdown, still negotiating the principles of modernism along with 21st-century concepts? Is there a certain freedom that comes with not being mired in Western traditions and the attendant market?"[43] On the other side of the globe, where Jiang Jie's *Over 1.5 Tons* was on show at the Sishang Art Museum in 2015, the curator asked a similar question: "Do Chinese artists have to follow the history of Western aesthetics

41. Cotter, "From Innovation to Provocation."

42. Cotter, "From Innovation to Provocation."

43. Alexandra Munroe, "Eyes Wide Open: How Chinese Contemporary Art Went Global," *Christie's*, December 18, 2017, www.christies.com/features/Art-and -China-after-1989-Theater-of-the-World-8579-1.aspx.

in their artistic practice? How to be free from Western art discourses that have influenced the Chinese contemporary art world and seek self-independence?"[44]

In response to these questions, *Over 1.5 Tons* presents a promising example, demonstrating how innovative and experimental the artwork could be on its own terms. The sculpture installation cannot be tagged by either Chinese or Western terminologies; few, for instance, would categorize the work in terms of established discourses of Chinese contemporary art: realism, avant-garde, iconographic abstraction, or political pop. The significance of *Over 1.5 Tons* lies in its challenge to the discursive conceptions and rhetoric of art criticism in both Chinese and English. If Chen's installation, together with 150 other artworks selected for exhibition by the Guggenheim, exemplifies Chinese contemporary art since 1989, Jiang Jie's sculpture challenges the status quo with its simultaneous invitation and rejection of conventional readings. The embedded ambiguity, as well as the alluring potential in terms of subject concerns, multilayered materials, method of installation, and exhibition space, extend contemporary Chinese art beyond the worldviews of either 1989 discourse or the rhetoric of modernism. In other words, *Over 1.5 Tons* stands on its own and refuses to be viewed simply as another work of Chinese contemporary art, whose artists are often described as political resisters to ideological imperatives, avant-garde experimentalists, participants in modernist exploration, or favored latecomers to the global art market. *Over 1.5 Tons* seems to embody everything simultaneously, whether the perspective is historical or political, experimental or alternative, sexual or psychoanalytical, modern or postmodern. The sculptural work marks a monumental turning point for the artist herself as well as for contemporary Chinese art.

---

44. Yu Ya, "Dialogue with Images: Methodology of Visual Image (De)construction," news.artron.net, April 28, 2015, https://news.artron.net/20150428/n735411.html.

Conclusion

Jiang Jie's *Over 1.5 Tons* is a special and unusual work unprecedented in the recording of contemporary Chinese art. Radical and innovative, the sculpture installation fundamentally challenges the phallus-ruled world through visual subversion and discursive contestation. In the hands of the female sculptor, the phallic archetype appears to no longer embody the law of the father; instead, it appears as an impotent, falling creature. The reversal from powerful subject to vulnerable object prompts a reconsideration of the psychoanalytical notions of castration anxiety and identity formation. The application of hybrid materials, especially iron hooks and lace fabric, suggests a shift in gender relations, where female authorship exercises the power of manipulation in both narrative articulation and sculptural construction. Subversive and drastic, *Over 1.5 Tons* provides viewers with a counter-monument that stands firmly and strategically in opposition to the many grandiose monuments that populate China's landscape. In comparison with other critical hanging sculptures that take the phallic archetype as thematic subject and visual form, *Over 1.5 Tons* stands out as an acutely subversive and destructive work; it knocks the phallic symbol off its pedestal.

Although it has left a significant mark on the history of Chinese contemporary art, Jiang Jie's sculpture installation faces a challenge in maintaining its visibility. Public art needs public space for display; it needs public perception to influence discourse. In an art world still under the sway of politically correct thinking and mainstream visual aesthetics, who will invite a giant phallic-shaped monster to hang from the ceiling, or value the aesthetics of the work? Spectacular when on display and strikingly innovative, this counter-monument has an uncertain future. Following a couple of exhibitions in China, where is it now? The examples of its counter-monumentality and sculpture as a subversive gesture remain open for discussion.

12

Screen Feminisms with Hong Kong Characteristics

Gina Marchetti

Hong Kong's feminist discourses reflect the territory's unique history and current geopolitical position as a Special Administrative Region (SAR) of the People's Republic of China since the end of British colonial rule in 1997. As Ya-Chen Chen points out in *The Many Dimensions of Chinese Feminism*: "Since 1842, the history of feminism in Hong Kong has been different from the Mainland, whether that of the late Qing Dynasty, Republican China, or the PRC."[1] The colonial period of agitation against foot-binding, forced marriage, and the "mui tsai" 妹仔 system of female domestic slavery parallels the advent of the motion picture in Hong Kong. After World War 2, colonial Hong Kong gradually dominated East and Southeast Asian screens and emerged as a global force in the latter half of the twentieth century before the 1997 Handover.

Women played key roles as producers, distributors, directors, screenwriters, and performers throughout the history of Hong Kong cinema. Esther Eng 伍锦霞, for example, made her mark during the

---

Although Hong Kong uses traditional Chinese characters, this essay uses simplified Chinese characters common in mainland China and Singapore in order to conform to the style of the rest of the book.

1. Ya-chen Chen, *The Many Dimensions of Chinese Feminism* (New York: Palgrave, 2011), 4.

Sino-Japanese/World War II era with films such as *National Hero-*
ine (民族女英雄, 1937),[2] and with *The Arch* (董夫人, 1969), Tang Shu-
Shuen 唐书璇[3] set the stage for Hong Kong's New Wave arthouse
successes a decade later. Women filmmakers within the orbit of the
New Wave broke new ground with films focusing on female protagonists and their struggles within a male-defined and dominated society.
Ann Hui's 许鞍华 *The Secret* (疯劫, 1979), Mabel Cheung's 张婉婷 *An*
Autumn's Tale (秋天的童话, 1987),[4] and Clara Law's 罗卓瑶 *The Rein-*
carnation of the Golden Lotus (潘金莲之前世今生, 1989),[5] to mention a
few films, provide critiques of the sexual status-quo. Angie Chen's 陈安
琪 *My Name Ain't Suzie* (花街时代, 1985), in particular, directly tackles
Hollywood's Orientalist fantasies of exotic Chinese women involved
in the city's sex trade, exemplified by *The World of Suzie Wong* (1960).

In Mayfair Yang's groundbreaking anthology *Spaces of Their Own:*
Women's Public Sphere in Transnational China, several of the con-
tributors, including Dai Jinhua, Shih Shu-Mei, and Elaine Yee Lin
Ho, consider cinema to be a vital part of the feminist public sphere in
transnational China.[6] In fact, many feminist scholars critique screen
depictions of women across the Chinese-speaking world, including
Rey Chow, Shih Shu-Mei, Olivia Khoo, Cui Shuqin, Chris Berry,
Esther Yau, Stephanie Hemelryk Donald, Jenny Lau, Helen Leung,
S. Louisa Wei, Yau Ching, E. Ann Kaplan, Berenice Reynaud, Hsiu-
Chuang Deppman, Zhang Zhen, Audrey Yue, Meaghan Morris, Stac-
ilee Ford, Wendy Gan, Sylvia Martin, and the late Esther Cheung, to

2. See S. Louisa Wei's documentary *Golden Gate Girls* (2013).

3. For more on Tang, see Ching Yau, *Filming Margins: Tang Shu Shuen, a For-*
gotten Hong Kong Woman Director (Hong Kong: Hong Kong Univ. Press, 2004).

4. Stacilee Ford, *Mabel Cheung Yuen-Ting's An Autumn's Tale* (Hong Kong:
Hong Kong Univ. Press, 2008).

5. Steve Fore, "Tales of Recombinant Femininity: *The Reincarnation of Golden*
Lotus, the *Chin P'ing Mei*, and the Politics of Melodrama in Hong Kong," *Journal*
of Film and Video 45, no. 4 (1993): 57–70.

6. See Mayfair Mei-hui Yang, *Spaces of Their Own: Women's Public Sphere in*
Transnational China (Minneapolis: Univ. of Minnesota Press, 1998).

name only a few of the most prolific. The subtitle of Lingzhen Wang's anthology, *Chinese Women's Cinema: Transnational Contexts*, notes the crucial role cross-border networks play in the careers of women filmmakers, and Hong Kong women have particularly robust global connections.[7]

Marie-Paule Ha, for example, zeroes in on the similarities between constructions of gender in Hong Kong and those throughout the Chinese diaspora, which demand a transnational and multicultural feminist critique:

> As postcolonial Chinese, we find ourselves in the same intermediate position as the Chinese overseas. Like them, we also have to engage in multicultural social practices, including those of gender, which are informed not only by different bodily schemas but also by different social gender orders, such as the neo-Confucian one and the Euro-American one.[8]

In *Transnational Feminism and Women's Movements in Post-1997 Hong Kong: Solidarity beyond the State*, Adelyn Lim calls specifically on Hong Kong women to build "transnational feminist solidarity through their conceptualization of feminism as a collective action frame rather than a collective identity."[9]

As Hong Kong female filmmakers travel farther and more frequently beyond the territory's borders as well as in the Sinosphere, the ways in which they circulate feminism with or without Chinese characteristics merits serious study. Many of these filmmakers deal with issues that resonate within and beyond the HKSAR, including

7. Lingzhen Wang, *Chinese Women's Cinema: Transnational Contexts* (New York: Columbia Univ. Press, 2011).

8. Marie-Paule Ha, "Double Trouble: Doing Gender in Hong Kong," *Signs: Journal of Women in Culture and Society* 34, no. 2 (2009): 443.

9. Adelyn Lim, *Transnational Feminism and Women's Movements in Post-1997 Hong Kong: Solidarity beyond the State*. (Hong Kong: Hong Kong Univ. Press, 2015), 18.

the impact of the growth of China's economy on the world, cross-border migration, families divided within the Chinese diaspora, sex work, sexual harassment and violence, romance and marriage, gender discrimination in the workplace, LGBTQ issues, and women's basic political rights, such as suffrage and representation in government. These issues testify to the diversity of Hong Kong women filmmakers' political interests.

However, the range of feminisms depicted by women on Hong Kong screens has not been given adequate attention. Speaking specifically of the dearth of scholarship on female auteurs, feminist filmmaker and scholar Yau Ching laments: "Unlike certain examples of woman writers in China who have been identified by Western critics as 'feminist,' like Qiu Jin and Ding Ling, Hong Kong female and feminist authorship has largely gone unnoticed."[10]

Some Hong Kong women filmmakers have been reluctant to identify themselves as auteurs or feminists. Hong Kong's most celebrated and prolific filmmaker, Ann Hui, for example, has avoided associating herself with either label throughout most of her career.[11] Over time Hui has modified her view and, like her character Macy (Sandra Ng 吳君如) in *All About Love* (得閒炒飯, 2010), wants to put the *is* back in *feminism*. Defining what *is* feminism in the HKSAR poses certain challenges, however. Ya-Chen Chen sees the diversity of Hong Kong's feminists as a particular strength, but Hong Kong feminisms also reflect deep political fissures in the territory that find their expression on screen. The prolabor, collective, feminist championing of sex workers' rights in *Whispers and Moans* (性工作者十日談, scripted by Yeeshan Yang 楊漪珊, 2007)[12] seems worlds apart, for

10. Yau, *Filming Margins*, 9.

11. Pang Li, "Ann Hui: A Director Who Captures Ordinary Women's Lives," China.org.cn, April 15, 2010, www.china.org.cn/arts/2010-04/15/content_1982 0089.htm.

12. See Gina Marchetti, "The Gendered Politics of Sex Work in Hong Kong Cinema: Herman Yau and Elsa Chan (Yeeshan)'s *Whispers and Moans* and *True Women for Sale*," *Alphaville: Journal of Film and Screen Media* 10 (2015): 1–19.

12.1. Sandra Ng as Macy in *All About Love* (Ann Hui, 2010).

example, from the aspirational, individualistic, neoliberal feminism of *Wonder Women* (女人本色, directed by Barbara Wong 黄真真, 2007),[13] made the same year on the tenth anniversary of the 1997 Handover.

In the years leading up to the Handover, controversy surrounding inheritance rights for women in villages in the New Territories,[14] the creation of an Equal Opportunities Commission, and Hong Kong's participation in the UN Convention on the Elimination of Discrimination against Women (CEDAW) spurred many women into action. Several groups, including the Hong Kong Federation of Women,[15]

13. See Marchetti, "Lean In or Bend Over? Postfeminism, Neoliberalism, and Hong Kong's *Wonder Women*," in *Emergent Feminisms: Complicating a Postfeminist Media Culture*, ed. Jessalynn Keller and Maureen E. Ryan (New York: Routledge, 2018), 193–210.

14. Eliza Chong-lai Chan, "Negotiating Daughterhood: A Case Study of the Female Inheritance Movement in the New Territories, Hong Kong" (master's thesis, Chinese University of Hong Kong, 1995), http://repository.lib.cuhk.edu.hk/tc/item/cuhk-320613.

15. The Hong Kong Federation of Women's website is at www.hkfw.org/eng/.

advocated for greater participation of women in the political sphere, and female leaders, such as Elsie Tu 杜葉錫恩, Christine Loh 陸恭蕙, Anna Wu 胡紅玉, and Emily Lau 劉慧卿 emerged. The HKSAR government established a Women's Commission, appointed by the chief executive, in 2001,[16] and the nongovernmental organizations HER Fund[17] and the Women's Foundation,[18] both established in 2004, continue to raise money to support women's initiatives in the territory. Female politicians have a limited, but visible presence. Hong Kong's chief executive Carrie Lam 林鄭月娥 provides a notable example.[19]

Feminists claim both sides of the political divide between pro-Beijing and antiestablishment forces. However, for women opposed to Beijing's tight control over Hong Kong's domestic governance, the prodemocracy/antiestablishment camp has a distinctly feminist quality, since the Beijing-backed All-China Women's Federation has come under attack for various policies, including the regulation of female sexuality through the one-child policy and the promotion of the notion of "left-over women."[20]

In fact, perhaps more than any other issue, Hong Kong's status vis-à-vis mainland China creates a border between feminists in the city. As Lisa Fischler notes, this split became acutely visible during the 1995 World Conference on Women in Beijing, in which two Hong Kong coalitions participated, reflecting the schism between

16. The Women's Commission's website is at https://www.women.gov.hk/en/index.html.

17. The HER Fund's website is at www.herfund.org.hk/.

18. The Women's Foundation website is at https://twfhk.org/.

19. For more on women in Hong Kong in the 1980s and 1990s, see Eliza Wing-Yee Lee, ed., *Gender and Change in Hong Kong: Globalization, Postcolonialism, and Chinese Patriarchy* (Hong Kong: Hong Kong Univ. Press, 2004). For a look at four women who have headed political parties in Hong Kong, see Lauren Ho, "Four Women Blaze Trail in Hong Kong Politics," *South China Morning Post*, February 7, 2013.

20. See Leta Hong Fincher, *Leftover Women: The Resurgence of Gender Inequality in China* (London: Zed, 2014).

pro–People's Republic of China (PRC) and prodemocracy forces that was exacerbated by the June 4, 1989, crackdown on demonstrations in Tiananmen Square.[21] In fact, virtually all films made by women in the years following the 1997 Handover include some mention of Hong Kong–PRC tensions, often embodied by mainland Chinese characters and dramatized through cross-border romances, marriages, and various other sexual liaisons.

Whispers and Moans and *Wonder Women*, for example, both include tense cross-border sexual encounters, and Barbara Wong's documentary, *Women's Private Parts* (女人那话儿, 2000),[22] details Hong Kong–PRC erotic connections, as does Crystal Kwok's 郭锦恩 *The Mistress* (迷失森林, 1999).[23] Yau Ching's 游静 *Ho Yuk: Let's Love Hong Kong* (好郁, 2002) and Mak Yan-Yan's 麦婉欣 *Butterfly* (蝴蝶, 2004) depict cross-border lesbian relationships.[24] Hong Kong women filmmakers' proximity to and distance from their sisters across the border renders key divisions among the city's feminists visible as issues involving competition for housing, jobs, and access to education and social services, as well as sexual partners, strain the one country, two systems policy.

21. Lisa Fischler, "Women's Activism during Hong Kong's Political Transition," in *Gender and Change in Hong Kong: Globalization, Postcolonialism, and Chinese Patriarchy*, ed. Eliza Wing-Yee Lee (Hong Kong: Hong Kong Univ. Press, 2004), 49–77.

22. Gina Marchetti, "Handover Bodies in a Feminist Frame: Two Hong Kong Women Filmmakers' Perspectives on Sex after 1997," *Screen Bodies* 2, no. 2 (December 2017), 1–24.

23. Patricia Brett Erens, "*The Mistress* and Female Sexuality," in *Hong Kong Screenscapes: From the New Wave to the Digital Frontier*, ed. Esther M. K. Cheung, Gina Marchetti, and See-Kam Tan (Hong Kong: Hong Kong Univ. Press, 2010), 239–252; Stacilee Ford, *Troubling American Women: Narratives of Gender and Nation in Hong Kong* (Hong Kong: Hong Kong Univ. Press, 2011), 167–72.

24. Gina Marchetti, "Handover Women: Hong Kong Women Filmmakers and the Intergenerational Melodrama of Infidelity," *Feminist Media Studies* 16, no. 4 (June 2016), 590–609.

Women's Activism On-Screen

Examining the depiction of female political activists by Hong Kong women filmmakers provides one way of charting splits within the territory's feminisms. Ann Hui, for example, has made several films that include female activists involved with political or social movements designed to improve the lives of Hong Kong women. *Ordinary Heroes* (千言万语, 1999) features a female activist, herself a rape victim, who takes up the cause of the "boat women" constantly threatened with deportation because of their floating domiciles. Made ten years after the 1989 Tiananmen protests and two years after the Handover, the film serves as a commentary on the promise and perils of political involvement for ordinary women in the territory. Although the film's female protagonist does not take up any political causes, Clara Law's *Farewell China* (爱在别乡的季节, 1990) notes the global reach of demonstrations in support of the Tiananmen Square protests with a shot of a New York City Goddess of Democracy near the end of the film.[25] Mak Yan-Yan's *Butterfly* also places its story of thwarted lesbian romance against the background of Hong Kong's demonstrations in support of the 1989 Tiananmen protests.

Tammy Cheung 张虹, a participant-observer of the Hong Kong political scene, takes a very different approach to women in the public arena in her documentary practice. Several of her documentaries, including *July* (七月, 2004) and *Election* (选举, 2008), reflect back on her own intervention as a filmmaker in the political development of Hong Kong, as well as providing portraits of key women involved in activist causes and runs for elective offices.[26]

25. Gina Marchetti, "The Gender of GenerAsian X in Clara Law's Migration Trilogy," in *Ladies and Gentlemen, Boys and Girls: Gender in Film at the End of the Twentieth Century*, ed. Murray Pomerance (Albany: State Univ. of New York Press, 2001), 71–87.

26. Gina Marchetti, "Hong Kong as Feminist Method: Gender, Sexuality, and Democracy in Two Documentaries by Tammy Cheung," in *Hong Kong Culture and*

It is difficult to imagine a film less like Cheung's *July* and *Election* than *Whispers and Moans*. However, this exploitation exposé of prostitution in the HKSAR stands as a rare Hong Kong fiction film that features a feminist activist in a major role. The activist Elsie Yan Ng 吳日言 frames the various stories told by and about the sex workers in the narrative. As a loose stand-in for scriptwriter Elsa Chan/Yang Yeeshan, Elsie intervenes to "raise the consciousness" of Hong Kong's prostitutes as women as well as workers. Nodding to the actual efforts of the sex worker advocacy group Zi Teng 紫藤, "purple vine,"[27] *Whispers and Moans* acknowledges the existence of feminism as part of the political fabric of Hong Kong. In a very different vein, Joanna Bowers's nonfiction film *The Helper* (守护者, 2017) also highlights the role NGOs play in agitating for the rights of female foreign domestic workers in Hong Kong. Male filmmaker Gabriel Ordaz's *Erwiana: Justice for All* (2016) takes a darker view by focusing on the egregious case of the abuse of Indonesian migrant worker Erwiana Sulistyaningsih, and the collective action that propelled her quest for legal redress.

Going beyond local Hong Kong activists, Clara Law's *Letters to Ali* (给阿里的信, 2004) follows the journey of Australian human rights activist Trish Kerbi as she travels to the internment camp where a young Afghan political refugee, Ali, awaits the determination of his request for asylum. The multilayered film is not only about Trish and Ali, but also about Trish's road trip with her family and Law—uncovering their own stories of displacement, exile, and loss. The kinship Law clearly feels for Trish becomes part of a cosmopolitan exchange that includes Hong Kong, Europe, Australia, and the Middle East.[28]

Society in the New Millennium: Hong Kong as Method, ed. Yiu-Wai Chu (Singapore: Springer, 2017), 59–76.

27. See the About page of the Zi Teng website: www.ziteng.org.hk/aboutus /aboutus_e.html

28. Gina Marchetti, "Clara Law, Asia, and World Cinema," in *The Palgrave Handbook of Asian Cinema*, ed. Aaron Han Joon Magnan-Park, Gina Marchetti, and Tan See-Kam (London: Palgrave, 2018), 689–707.

Ann Hui returns to the theme of women activists in *Night and Fog* (天水围的夜与雾, 2009) and *All About Love* (2010).[29] However, in these two films the women take the lead in explicitly feminist street demonstrations against gender-based discrimination in housing and employment. Both films expressly link gender bias in the wider society to sexual violence. While the tone of the former is tragic, and that of the latter comic, both films show women agitating for a range of reforms central to a Hong Kong feminist agenda, from the right of abode to mandatory maternity leave, and her female characters occupy an expressly political space within the territory's cinematic landscape. The fact that the HKSAR's screen women can take their issues to the streets models the potential—however utopian—for a democratic public sphere available to those who have been marginalized by a heterosexual, male-dominated society. Taken together, along with features by male directors such as Evans Chan 陈耀成,[30] these films depict women taking political action collectively for specifically feminist causes and, for Hong Kong filmmakers, women's role in governance becomes key to their efficacy in advancing women's rights in the territory.

Digital Democracy and Umbrella Feminism

Hong Kong's 2014 Umbrella Movement, calling for a more open procedure for vetting candidates for its first scheduled exercise in universal suffrage in the election of its chief executive in 2017 (which did not happen), does not have an explicitly feminist agenda.[31] However,

29. Gina Marchetti, "Feminism, Postfeminism, and Hong Kong Women Filmmakers," in *A Companion to Hong Kong Cinema*, ed. Esther M. K. Cheung, Gina Marchetti, and Esther C. M. Yau (Hoboken, NJ: Wiley-Blackwell, 2015), 237–64.

30. Gina Marchetti, *From Tian'anmen to Times Square: Transnational China and the Chinese Diaspora on Global Screens, 1989–1997* (Philadelphia: Temple Univ. Press, 2006).

31. For more on the broader history of the current demonstrations, see Arif Dirlik, "The Mouse that Roared: The Democratic Movement in Hong Kong," *b2o*,

women have been active in all aspects of the movement. Many Hong Kong feminists see suffrage as fundamental to addressing other concerns, including immigration, employment, education, LGBTQ rights, religious liberties, and access to services such as women's health clinics, childcare, and domestic violence shelters. Eliza W. Y. Lee 李咏怡 articulates this in her "Prospects for the Development of a Critical Feminist Discourse" written before the Umbrella Movement:

> In the next few years, there will be a constitutional review to determine the method of selection of the chief executive and the members of the legislature (the legislative council) in 2007 and thereafter. The review will provide opportunities for social activists to mobilize popular demand for democratization. Strategically, the women activists should seize the chance by aligning with other socially disadvantaged groups to launch a civil rights movement on the one hand and participate in the emerging democratic space movement on the other. Hopefully, all these will open up more discursive space for women activists to articulate a feminist discourse on democratic citizenship as an essential ingredient for the construction of a just polity."[32]

Suffrage has long been a defining issue of feminism, particularly in its so-called first wave of militant suffragists imprisoned for agitating for the vote. Images of Hong Kong women on city streets demanding a voice in the interpretation of election rules conjures up this history and serves as an important corrective to an account of women's

---

October 6, 2014, https://www.boundary2.org/2014/10/the-mouse-that-roared -the-democratic-movement-in-hong-kong-2/, and Jeffrey Wasserstrom, "No Tiananmen Redux: Picking the Right Analogy for the Protests in Hong Kong," *Foreign Affairs*, October 5, 2014.

32. Eliza W. Y. Lee, "Prospects for the Development of a Critical Feminist Discourse," in *Gender and Change in Hong Kong: Globalization, Postcolonialism, and Chinese Patriarchy*, ed. Eliza W. Y. Lee (Hong Kong: Hong Kong Univ. Press, 2004), 205.

suffrage that neglects its importance to women outside of Europe and the United States.[33]

From the outset, women filmmakers have made stunning use of cell phones, lightweight cameras and sound recording devices, first-person engagement, observational as well as interview formats, available and nondiegetic sound, and sophisticated montage techniques to provide a compelling vision of the Umbrella Movement. Most of these films fall into the category of agitprop. Although mainstream media missed much of the gendered nature of the events, these women highlight female involvement and, arguably, the implicitly feminist nature of much of the movement, even if the term *feminism* rarely becomes part of the filmed discourse.

Some of the videos speak to the gendered nature of the Umbrella Movement more eloquently than others. Female activist-journalist Glacier Kwong's 鄺頌晴 YouTube talking head reports for the NGO Keyboard Frontline stand out. The focus on her body and voice as an authoritative witness to the Occupy protests speaks to the important role women play in pleading Hong Kong's case to the world. Kwong condemns the use of tear gas against peaceful protesters and includes her own footage of police action, as well as images of counterdemonstrators and visual evidence of sexual assaults on female protesters. She speaks directly to the camera in English to an implied global audience and says "universal suffrage may be so common in your country, which is a democratic state, but it is not common in Hong Kong at all." Given her choice to highlight the particular problems faced by women in the movement in their attempts to participate in peaceful protests, suffrage again becomes a feminist issue when women's right to assemble is not adequately protected by the police.[34] Mabel Au 區美寶 of Amnesty International also condemned police inaction in several other instances involving men grabbing women's breasts

33. Louise Edwards, *Gender, Politics, and Democracy: Women's Suffrage in China* (Stanford: Stanford Univ. Press, 2008).

34. Keyboard Frontline Facebook page, at www.facebook.com/Keyboard Frontline/.

and groins during the demonstrations.[35] Although the international media lauded the generally peaceful protests, male counterdemonstrators zeroed in on female protesters, and women activists had to face these particular challenges when exercising their rights to free speech and public assembly.

Likely because of the student-led nature of the movement, many of the motion pictures coming out of the protests are the creations of teachers and students who are involved as activists. Shannon Walsh, an assistant professor in the School of Creative Media at the City University of Hong Kong at the time of the protests, created the short *Under the Umbrella* (2014),[36] which documents her female students' involvement as young filmmakers embroiled in the demonstrations. The first voice heard and face seen is that of a young woman saying, "OK, rolling"; this testifies to women's involvement in documenting their own political engagement in the protests. Seeing a female production teacher working together with young women from her program to produce this tribute to women's commitment to political change underscores the implicitly feminist nature of many of these motion pictures. One subtitle reads "Three young women are recording their perspectives in video," over an image of an anonymous woman's arm holding up a camera recording the protests.

Interviewee Vicky Do introduces herself as an MFA student from the "south of Vietnam . . . Ho Chi Minh City, although I don't like that name," implying her opposition to the ruling Communist Party of Vietnam. The choice of Vicky Do as one of the interviewees speaks to several elements of Hong Kong's political culture that are neglected by mainstream media. In addition to the general neglect of the political needs of women, Vicky Do's statements reveal that many residents

35. Amnesty International, "Hong Kong: Women and Girls Attacked as Police Fail to Protect Peaceful Protesters," Amnesty International online news, October 3, 2014, www.amnesty.org/en/for-media/press-releases/hong-kong-women-and-girls-attacked-police-fail-protect-peaceful-protesters-.

36. AJ+, "Under the Umbrella of Hong Kong's Protest," AJ+ YouTube channel, 8:16, November 25, 2014, https://www.youtube.com/watch?v=_nULwJ6yJNc.

of Hong Kong are not ethnic Chinese, that the territory has hosted political refugees from other parts of Asia over the years (including, ironically, Ho Chi Minh himself), and that its long-standing problems with the integration and resettlement of Vietnamese refugees continue to haunt the former colony because of its Cold War past. However, Do is not a political refugee, but an exchange student who has also spent time in the United States, benefiting from the relaxation of tensions between the former enemies. Because of continuing political constraints in Vietnam, Do is attracted to the Umbrella Movement as a model of greater political inclusiveness for her own country. She is particularly impressed by the creativity and artistic expression at the heart of the protests, which many observers have linked to a climate of freedom guaranteed by law. For her, the role of the filmmaker should involve documenting the people's political aspirations for social change.

Another woman, Wang Jing Jing, comes from Shanghai. She talks about focusing on mainland exchange students at the protest sites. She feels nervous because she does not support the protesters, and she records the sentiments of her fellow mainland students who find the Umbrella Movement "useless." Thus political divisions between some mainland and local women find expression in the documentary. The third female student profiled is Ansah Malik, born in Hong Kong as part of the fourth generation of a South Asian family that settled in the territory. A social work student, she has gotten involved in distributing free food to the protesters. As an ethnic minority, she sees herself as a potential target for retaliation by those opposed to political change. However, Ansah Malik's experiences in the Umbrella Movement prove to be quite positive, and, using words such as "surprised" and "amazed," she testifies to the fact that for the first time she has received recognition from her Chinese peers that she, too, is a citizen of the HKSAR.

Produced by a newcomer to Hong Kong and featuring three women outsiders (two born outside the territory, in Vietnam and the PRC, and one Hong Kong–born ethnic minority woman), this documentary underscores the range of political sentiments and the wide variety of challenges faced by women in the HKSAR. Even Wang Jing Jing, who sees the demonstrations as pointless, understands that the territory's body politic exhibits a diversity unknown in even a major mainland city such as Shanghai. Making the film presupposes an expectation for freedom of speech seldom experienced in mainland China. She laments that even though her documentary takes a negative view of the demonstrations, it likely could not be shown in Shanghai.

Vicky Do, in particular, was shocked by the use of tear gas on the student demonstrators. She is taken with the way the lights at night in the urban center can blend her shadow as a filmmaker with the shadow of the city itself, and poetic images of Do filming in the evening concretizes her voice-over commentary on the way in which her aesthetic sensibility blends with her political engagement in the street protests. Even though she is an outsider, she feels her shadow belongs in the city where she resides. In Vietnam she tries to escape from the "big shadow of China," but she can express her sentiments openly in Hong Kong. Do calls the actions of the students "utopian," and the film ends with a shot of a woman leading a group of protesters acknowledging the power of youth as a vanguard for social change.

None of the women mentions feminism as a motivating force, although all three—with widely varied political, social, and ethnic backgrounds—see the importance of their presence at the demonstrations, and the choice of Shannon Walsh to focus on aspiring female filmmakers reflects on the importance of women educating women to play an active part in the creation of media representations visualizing women's participation in civil society.

Professional journalist and filmmaker Daria Marchenko picks up on Vicky Do's idea of shadows in her poetic short film *Drops* (2014),[37] which begins with an anonymous female voice saying, "I love Hong Kong," over the shadow of a human figure on a wall. Over images of the protesters, another female voice says, "No, I am not afraid." A

---

37. Daria Marchenko, "Hong Kong's Occupy Central fight for democracy," Vimeo video, 1:20, 2015, https://vimeo.com/114971342.

rainstorm breaks out at the protest site, but a drawing of the iconic yellow umbrella ends the short on a note of hope for weathering the political storm ahead. Linking female voices to love and courage makes a statement about the determination of Hong Kong women to be heard as a committed presence within the political sphere.

Vicky Do's own short, *Stranger from Paradise* (2014),[38] provides a very personal political perspective on the Umbrella Movement by linking Hong Kong's situation to the Communist movement in Vietnam. Do begins by condemning her mother for being a member of the Communist Party of Vietnam. As shadows move across a wall at the Occupy site devoted to posters and written messages of support from people from around the world, she continues off-screen, "Actually we hardly talked in recent years, especially about sensitive topics such as democracy." As a disembodied voice, she goes on to question the gap between the rich and the poor in the city and why some choose to work so hard to make others wealthy.

The off-screen commentary parallels the images on-screen of the filmmaker's shadow on the pavement and against the urban walls of Central, at the heart of Hong Kong's downtown financial district. Do continues by expressing the frustration of helping others fight for democracy rather than being able to engage in similar political actions at home in Vietnam. She reflects on the rise of China in Asia and the fact that Western powers really do not care about the balance of power in the East as long as they can continue to exploit its cheap labor and natural resources. In fact, Do remains suspicious of the utopian aspirations of Hong Kong's protesters, since the Communist movement was born out of similar yearnings for a more just and equitable society. However, she also has a strong connection to the city that she expresses by comparing the glass façade of Hong Kong's skyscrapers to crystal—hard but fragile. The short ends with dedications to Hong Kong, Saigon, and the filmmaker's mother.

38. Vicky Do, "Stranger from Paradise: Vicky," Vimeo video, 5:38, 2015, https://vimeo.com/118096291.

Do's piece brings out the theme of divided nations and families in the aftermath of the Vietnam War, and the fact that this younger generation of women still lives with the constraints imposed by Cold War ideology, which has retarded democratic development on both sides of the political divide. Here, again the mother-daughter relationship speaks to the way the Communist movement, particularly in Vietnam during the war against the United States, held out promise for women's emancipation that the younger generation feels has not been realized.

Another student-produced documentary, *The Umbrella Movement* 雨伞运动 (2014),[39] created by journalism students at the University of Hong Kong and shown on MSNBC's digital channel, was a team effort that included production editor Joyce Liu 刘晨阳, a female student from the PRC. Although it is difficult to say whether the mixed-gender production crew had any deliberations on the inclusion of women in the piece, the fact that female interviewees provided candid assessments of the protests speaks to the team's sensitivity to gender in the selection and filming of the subject.

A segment called "Hope," directed by one of the women on the production team, Jane Li 李林晋, profiles female student Fish Cheng, who talks about going to the Occupy site after school to finish her homework and teach people how to fold yellow paper umbrellas in support of the movement. When her friends arrive after work, she helps them with a project to construct a large umbrella. With the Post-it Notes of Lennon Wall as a backdrop,[40] she reveals that her mother supports the students' demonstration, while her father does not.

Young women embroiled in these family conflicts often deal with assumptions about the role women should or should not play in public life—assumptions that their brothers manage to avoid. In this case,

---

39. MSNBC, "'And Then Hell Broke Loose,'" MSNBC video, 22:42, December 6, 2014, www.msnbc.com/msnbc/watch/and-then-hell-broke-loose-367963715731.

40. John Lennon and Yoko Ono became symbolic icons of blessing for the student demonstrators, harking back to the couple's commitment as artists and entertainers to the anti-war movement in the 1960s and 1970s.

while her father "does not think democracy is that important for Hong Kong," mother and daughter urgently see the need. While Fish does not articulate a feminist analysis of these family dynamics, the fact that these women see democracy as more critical may reflect on their marginalized status within a patriarchal society. The film also includes an interview with Fish's mother, who speaks Mandarin and indicates that she is not native to Hong Kong. Several shots show mother and daughter holding hands to signify their intimacy. Fish mentions that she still loves her father, but also feels the need to lie to him about her political activities. The documentary balances Fish's story with a vignette on a father and daughter in which the father takes the lead in the family in support of the protesters and the daughter has mixed feelings about the dangers her father faces trying to protect the students from anti-Occupy agitators.

In *The Umbrella Movement* politician Claudia Mo 毛孟静 introduces the situation in Mong Kok, the district that saw the preponderance of violent clashes between protesters and counterdemonstrators during Occupy. The close-up of a yellow ribbon on her necklace indicates her support for the demonstrators, so her political position finds visual expression without the need to introduce her further. Shown in one shot wearing a yellow construction helmet to protect against blows, Mo talks about her role in the protests as helping to bring an element of order into what had become a chaotic situation.

A female videographer, Nora Lam 林子穎, produced another University of Hong Kong student documentary, this one made for Campus TV, titled *Midnight in Mong Kok* 旺角黑夜 (2014).[41] This short documentary features testimony from female as well as male protesters in Mong Kok. One woman, whose face is not shown on-screen, recounts how she used Facebook to help organize the occupation of

41. Nora Lam 林子穎, *Wangjiao Heiye-Jilupian* 旺角黑夜—纪录片 (Midnight in Mong Kok: A Documentary), YouTube video, 15:57, November 9, 2014, www.youtube.com/watch?v=in32UFyghWE&feature=youtu.be.

Mong Kok as a site more convenient for residents from Kowloon and the New Territories, who might find it difficult to commute to Causeway Bay or to Central, Hong Kong's principal business district, on a daily basis. The video does a superb job of conveying the demonstrators' frustrations with police refusal to take action against violent counterdemonstrators. Singing "Happy Birthday to You" became one of the primary ways demonstrators expressed their anger by silencing the opposition with music.

The documentary also highlights the very different roles played by men and women in the movement. While one of the principal male subjects, shown in a close-up, calmly claims the street by lying on the pavement during his interview, the main female informant does not show her face at all. Visually she becomes a series of shots of nervous hand gestures and legs against the pavement. She highlights the importance of the Internet to her ability to participate in the movement, and she does not exhibit the same confident command of the pavement as the men do. Lam went on to make an additional feature on the Umbrella Movement, *Road Not Taken* 未竟之路 (2016).

Liu To's 廖韜 short, *A Tiny Handheld Camera* 手持摄影机的人 (2014), narrates a direct confrontation with the police. The filmmaker herself provides first-person documentation of a chance encounter with the authorities. During a visit to the University of Hong Kong on February 16, 2015, Liu discussed the genesis of the film. Beginning with a simple walk around the protest sites, her footage became a documentary at the point when an officer demanded to know why she was filming in the streets. He expressed his incredulity by saying, "I don't believe you are making a documentary," which made Liu even more determined to use her footage to document the encounter as visible evidence of the fraught relationship between the police and the public in Mong Kok. Likely the male officer's incredulity resulted in part from the size of the equipment used for the documentary and the gender of the filmmaker. Referring to her gender and youth, one male officer told her, "Go back to your father now." To compound her determination to show the demonstrations on-screen, Liu made two other films in Mong Kok, the feature *Like an Abortion, for the Very First Time* 扯旗、我要真普选和 (2018) and the short *Mongkok Story* 徒弟仔 (2018).

In *A Tiny Handheld Camera*, Liu films in Mong Kok at the height of the protests. While she is crossing the street, a male police officer asks her what she is filming and does not seem satisfied with her response that she is simply crossing the street. Pausing on the pedestrian island in the middle of the road, Liu stands up for herself by asking why the officer is being provocative and overreacting to her presence in the crosswalk. Avoiding their faces, she focuses her camera on the officers' hands and their weapons in their belts as symbols of the threat of violence always at the ready in any encounter with the public. One officer says, "You can take videos but you cannot show our heads, because it indicates a lack of respect." Indeed, Liu keeps the shots of the officers out of focus and backlit, so they remain shadowy forms rather than identifiable individuals. Her handheld videography adds to the emotional nature of the encounter by keeping the field of vision in constant flux. One officer uses a light to disrupt her filming by pointing it directly into her lens. The battle between the female filmmaker and the patriarchal state for control over representation of the public sphere becomes blindingly clear at that moment.

An officer continues the awkward exchange by taking out his cell phone and suggesting that they film each other. The camera on the officer's shirt shows the filmmaker as a little image on his chest. He points out that a crowd has gathered to watch the exchange, and indeed, Liu's shot over the officer's shoulder shows spectators in the background. The police accuse her of disturbing the peace, and she asks them why they are surrounding her. When a man comes to congratulate the police on their actions, a female officer accuses Liu of pushing and yells at her to move along. The police finally turn and abruptly move away. Liu wonders why a "safe island" in the middle of the road should be so hazardous, and the video ends with a remark from one of the male bystanders that "our taxes are used to feed bastards who bully good citizens." The end credits of the piece confirm that the film is indeed a documentary by Liu To.

拍吧 我們繼續互拍吧
Let's go on and record each other

12.2. Confrontation with police in Mong Kok, *A Tiny Handheld Camera* (Liu To, 2014).

Female filmmaker Nate Chan's 陈千憓 documentary *Do You Hear the Women Sing?* 伞不走的女声 (2015),[42] focuses exclusively on women in the Occupy Movement. Taking its title from the musical *Les Misérables* and its hit song, "Do You Hear the People Sing?," the film replaces the "angry men" of France with the female protesters of the Umbrella Movement. The interviewees identify as students, teachers, mothers, secretaries, insurance sales staff, and journalists. One woman, Kani, introduces herself specifically as someone who works in a women's organization devoted to eliminating sexual violence and

42. HKCC Gender Justice Ministry, *San Bu Zou de Nüsheng* 伞不走的女声 (Do You Hear the Women Sing), YouTube video, 25:45, November 26, 2014, www.youtube.com/watch?v=ENH43yWYFnI.

promoting gender equality. Another woman, Valerie Ho, identifies as a lesbian. Identifying as a lesbian, in this case, highlights the issue of LGBTQ rights in the territory as subject to legislative action.

According to the credits, the film was sponsored, at least in part, by the Hong Kong Christian Council Gender Justice Group. Although the film includes many secular voices of women active in the Umbrella Movement, it pays particular attention to female activists' Christian religious convictions. This underscores the important role religion plays in the movement's origins in the Occupy Central with Love and Peace campaign, inspired by Christian figures associated with non-violent civil disobedience, such as Martin Luther King Jr. Before the movement became a student-led protest, the original organizers of Occupy Central, Baptist minister Chu Yiu-ming and university professors Benny Tai Yiu-ting and Chan Kin-man, pointed to Christian principles as the foundation for the suffrage movement. The film's subtitle references the Beatitudes, found in the Gospel according to Matthew, quoting Jesus Christ's words, "Blessed are the meek, for they will inherit the earth." Other Bible verses punctuate the interviews and footage of the demonstrations as a way of highlighting the moral and philosophical justification for breaking the law in the name of a higher sense of justice.

Pastoral assistant Tam Ka Ying explains the relationship between retired cardinal Joseph Zen and the longstanding tension between the Roman Catholic Church and the authorities in Beijing. A substantial portion of the antiestablishment movement in Hong Kong is fueled by religious sentiment, since many Christian denominations, as well as Buddhist groups such as the Falun Gong, have been systematically persecuted in the PRC. Some people of faith in Hong Kong are motivated by fear of the loss of religious freedom if they are denied access to democratic representation through a freely elected government. As in many parts of the world, even though women may not be church leaders, they represent a substantial portion of the active congregation and feel a particular need to demonstrate on behalf of their faith.

Given the fact that conservative Christians have often been at odds with the LGBTQ community in the HKSAR, the reasoning behind identifying one of the women featured in the Christian-sponsored documentary as a lesbian not only speaks to the demographics of the movement, but draws a line between an inclusive vision of Christianity and the beliefs of those fundamentalists who are in opposition to the LGBTQ community. In another documentary in which Nate Chan participated, Evans Chan's *Raise the Umbrellas* (2016), popular chanteuse Denise Ho, a vocal supporter of LGBTQ rights who came out publicly as a lesbian in 2012, narrates an encounter between herself and a devout Christian woman. The woman confides in Ho that her church teaches that homosexuality is a sin, but she refuses to believe it after seeing Ho's devotion to the Umbrella Movement and knowing the sacrifices she made to participate. Thus across divides of religion and sexuality, Hong Kong women can find common ground in their commitment to suffrage.

Several of the testimonies delivered by the interview subjects in *Do You Hear the Women Sing?* underscore the ways in which the women protested as groups. Many women mobilized in response to the use of tear gas by police on September 28, 2014. This brought sympathetic parents and older adults out to support the students, whom many considered to be victims of excessive police violence. One student, Charis Hung, shares her story of feeling intimidated as a young woman, small in stature, who does not dare wear a yellow ribbon to show her support of the Umbrella Movement out of fear of harassment. However, she does muster the courage to attend the Occupy protests with her church group. When an older boy told her not to go to the front lines, she said to herself, "I am on the front line because you're not." Her experience reveals the role gender plays in the tactics used by the demonstrators. Women feel frustrated by the perception that they are too weak or frail to participate effectively, while men, often hypocritically, do not step up in times of crisis. Clearly young women such as Charis Hung take active roles in confrontations with police—putting their bodies into service to make their political perspective known.

Feminist activist Kani talks candidly about the tactics used by counterdemonstrators to target female activists. Gangs of men—purportedly triad members hired by the opposition—groped women

12.3. Kani speaks about sexual harassment, *Do You Hear the Women Sing?* (Nate Chan, 2015).

protesters. *Do You Hear the Women Sing?* catches one particularly egregious example on film, in which a man pulls at a woman's shirt during a street confrontation. One interviewee in *Do You Hear the Women Sing?*, identified only as Miss P, a secretary, gives an account of a male counterdemonstrator grabbing her breasts during a heated confrontation. Kani analyzes this systematic sexist intimidation of women by noting the patriarchal belief that the best way to control women's behavior is by threatening to violate their sexual purity.

This segment on sexual harassment is followed by an interview with student leader Yvonne Leung (Lai Kwok) from the University of Hong Kong, who was the only female leader to take part in a televised debate on October 21, 2014, between student representatives and members of the HKSAR government. In the interview Leung comments on gender differences in the Occupy demonstrations:

> Women did help guard the metal barricades and even slept in front of the barricades. The movement has embodied the gender equality in our society. Certain roles are simply better for women while others are better for men. When women try to move something, men would like to take over. They are not looking down on

women, but have got used to their roles. But women and men are actually equal.

Leung's description of gender divisions in the Umbrella Movement highlights the ways in which firmly entrenched attitudes continue to plague women involved in the public sphere. Bringing men and women together to sing one song in harmony speaks to the power of the movement to provide a clear direction to very different people who have often opposing stakes in an open and fair electoral system. *Do You Hear the Women Sing?* makes this feminist point by juxtaposing verbal and visual evidence of the violation of women's rights to the failure of political leaders to recognize women's rights as an integral part of the call for democracy.

The range of motion pictures produced by women during the Occupy demonstrations indicates several progressive tendencies from a feminist perspective. Women who make documentaries self-reflexively comment on their social position as filmmakers in a cultural climate that remains suspicious of women with cameras (as seen, for example, in *A Tiny Handheld Camera*). They also display an awareness of the importance of established women filmmakers empowering a younger generation of female students to take up the camera, giving them confidence to express themselves in a medium traditionally dominated by men (most clearly seen in *Under the Umbrella*).

In collaborative modes such as documentary film production or video journalism, the leading roles women take seem to be correlated with the inclusion of a wider range of female voices as part of the Umbrella Movement—including young women and their mothers (as seen in the *Umbrella Movement*) and women's rights activists (in *Do You Hear the Women Sing?*). All films implicitly link women's rights to democratic rights by demonstrating the fact that women must have access to the political process in order to guarantee adequate representation of their needs. This is most vividly shown in *Do You Hear the Women Sing?* and Glacier Kwong's YouTube dispatches, which voice concern about counterdemonstrators' use of sexual violence targeting women in order to get them off the streets. They link this to police inaction and call out the authorities' tendency to concentrate on containing civil unrest rather than prosecuting men who are sexually assaulting women. Sexism on the part of the police is shown most vividly, of course, in Liu To's *A Tiny Handheld Camera*.

However, throughout these videos produced by women, the term *feminism* receives little attention. Presumably Kani, who works for a women's organization, would identify herself as a feminist, but most of the other women involved in these films fail to link feminism to suffrage explicitly. The films demonstrate sexism exists; however, they do not articulate a feminist solution to this problem. Ho Chi-kwan 何芝君, a founding member of Hong Kong's Association for the Advancement of Feminism, sheds light on this disconnect between feminism and Hong Kong's overall political development in the years leading up to the Umbrella Movement: "We felt that, yes, we were part of that big movement, but we also felt that women's issues were not being attended to. And sometimes we even felt that women's issues were put at a disadvantaged position in favor of the so-called 'big' issues. That's why we insisted we should have our own movement."[43] Women in Hong Kong are now visible across the political spectrum as activists and elected members of the legislature; however, this does not mean that the fight for gender equality has been won. Unfortunately the visible record, as seen in these films made by women during the Umbrella Movement, proves otherwise. Even if not verbalized, the urgent need for a specifically feminist critique seems clear.

#MeToo Hong Kong

As film producer Harvey Weinstein allegations opened up the depth and breadth of sexual harassment in Hollywood in 2017, Weinstein's associates in Hong Kong, most notably Bey Logan,[44] came under

43. Quoted in Lim, *Transnational Feminism*, 37.

44. Niall Fraser, "Harvey Weinstein Scandal Deepens as Producer Accused of Sexual Misconduct at Hong Kong Hotel," *South China Morning Post*, December 15, 2017; Christina Zhao, "Harvey Weinstein's Friend Bey Logan Accused of Sexual

scrutiny as well. This fed the evolving #MeToo moment in Hong Kong and highlighted the transnational connections linking women globally. Hong Kong women became involved with #MeToo, as they had in the Umbrella Movement, through digital technology. As a result, the feminist screen activism associated with both movements bears the marks of new technologies: screens connected via the Internet, facilitated by the accessibility of cell phone videography. Women marginalized by a motion picture industry and mainstream media journalism dominated by men found other means of expression and public platforms for their grievances outside the commercial cultural industries.

#MeToo also highlights important differences between feminist activists on either side of the Chinese border. In mainland China state censors moved to stem the tide of allegations on the Internet, and the Chinese characters for *rice* 米 (mi) and *rabbit* 兔 (tu) began to stand in for the English #MeToo. The global movement combines social media with an established form of second-wave feminist organizing based on the consciousness raising work of groups that facilitate the sharing of personal experiences of sexism and discrimination. This is similar to the Chinese 诉苦 (*suku*) during the socialist period, which refers to the expression of grievances more generally but has been used by women to voice their oppression. As these grievances span the worlds of entertainment, higher education, and beyond, the manner in which business, violence, and sexual politics form transnational links from China through Hong Kong to Hollywood makes Weinstein's story transnational in some unexpected ways.

Not unique to the US film industry, a business model that includes intimidation and sexual harassment pervades both Hong Kong and Hollywood. In Hong Kong, triad gangsters cast a sexist shadow over the quotidian operations of film production. In *Haunted: An*

Assault By Multiple Women in Hong Kong," *Newsweek*, December 13, 2017; Vivienne Chow, "'Crouching Tiger' Actress Accuses Harvey Weinstein Asia Associate of Sexual Misconduct," *Variety*, December 15, 2017.

Ethnography of the Hollywood and Hong Kong Media Industries, anthropologist Sylvia Martin notes this connection between triad influence and misogyny in the local industry:

> Several informants confided that their families disapproved of their on- and off-screen obligations, which included sexualized portrayals on camera and sexualized demands made of them off screen. An actress, at the beginning of her acting career, was expected to entertain dubious producers and their cronies at late-night parties and karaoke bars as a supplement to her paltry income. The prevalence of male gangsterism in the industry has reinforced the patriarchal characteristics of capitalism—characteristics that . . . likely contribute to why there are fewer female directors and few female cinematographers.[45]

As Martin shows, sexual harassment is part of a misogynist production culture that keeps women from professional advancement and contributes to a cycle that also limits how and by whom women are portrayed on-screen.

Given the similarities in the business cultures, it comes as no surprise that Harvey Weinstein would have the same expectations of compliance with his sexual demands in Hong Kong as he did in the United States, and several women associated with the Hong Kong industry have come forward. In transnational coproductions, Orientalist sexual predation targets ethnic Chinese actresses. In *The Hypersexuality of Race: Performing Asian/American Women on Screen and Scene*,[46] Celine Parreñas Shimizu points out the racial dimension of these encounters. Although not speaking specifically of Weinstein, Shimizu notes that Euro-American men assume Asian women's sexual

45. Sylvia J. Martin, *Haunted: An Ethnography of the Hollywood and Hong Kong Media Industries* (Oxford: Oxford Univ. Press, 2016), 145–46.

46. Celine Parreñas Shimizu, *The Hypersexuality of Race: Performing Asian/American Women on Screen and Scene* (Durham, NC: Duke Univ. Press, 2007).

availability. Weinstein worked with acclaimed female stars Joan Chen on the television series *Marco Polo* (2014–16) and Michelle Yeoh on the movie *Crouching Tiger, Hidden Dragon: Sword of Destiny* (2016). Although Chen has not commented, Yeoh stated to the Associated Press: "I knew he was a bully and not always honorable. I wasn't exposed to this side of him, otherwise he would have experienced the full effect of years of martial arts training."[47] Given Yeoh's own difficulties doing stunt work in films such as Ann Hui's *The Stunt Woman* 阿金 (1996), the idea that marital arts training of any kind could protect women from sexual harassment and the disempowerment they may feel on set seems a bit disingenuous. In fact, Yeoh's relationship with the producer was complicated by the fact that Weinstein was also a major contributor to amfAR, an AIDS charity, in which Yeoh serves as an official ambassador.

However, looking at Weinstein's productions in Asia, such as *Marco Polo*, the "need" to see female talent naked becomes clear, since women appear nude on-screen more often than their male counterparts, even in martial arts roles.[48] In "The Visual Language of Oppression,"[49] film educator Nina Menkes links on-screen portrayals of women to male control of the industry and a male-dominated production culture, and #MeToo in Hong Kong connects the various ways women suffer on both sides of the camera with these sexist assumptions.

Arguably, #MeToo Hong Kong would not exist without the cyber-support network it has made available to victims, and the anonymity available to those who prefer not to enter the criminal justice system

47. Angela Chen, "Michelle Yeoh: Weinstein Was a 'Bully,' 'Not Always Honorable,'" Associated Press, October 17, 2017, https://apnews.com/article/c3d1f39 273ad4853bc0ad494cbf04956.

48. For the history of the naked and the nude in Western art, see John Berger, *Ways of Seeing* (New York: Penguin, 1990).

49. Nina Menkes, "The Visual Language of Oppression," *Filmmaker*, October 30, 2017, https://filmmakermagazine.com/103801-the-visual-language-of-oppression -harvey-wasnt-working-in-a-vacuum/#.XGWxZWQzY6U.

with their complaints. The accused have also taken to the Internet to push back against allegations. Bey Logan, for one, went online to offer an apology for his behavior:

> Over the years of my adult life, I have made advances to women.
> Sometimes they were rebuffed and sometimes they were reciprocated. I have had a too-carefree attitude towards physical encounters with women. I have made inappropriate comments lightheartedly or after a few drinks.
> I now see I was wrong and I have made mistakes for which I can't forgive myself, and must live with them. I regret that any action I might have taken could have caused distress to anyone.[50]

However, these apologies fail to do justice to the harm done by a violently sexist culture that belittles the professional contributions of women on a massive scale and denies them access to employment behind the camera.

Sexual misconduct allegations have also been leveled against Brett Ratner,[51] known for his successful collaboration with Jackie Chan in the *Rush Hour* series, as well as many notable celebrities in India, South Korea, and elsewhere in the region. Indeed, Ratner took advantage of the Paris filming location to cast his friend Roman Polanski in a cameo in *Rush Hour 3* due to the fact Polanski cannot travel to the United States because he jumped bail after being convicted of statutory rape in 1978. These transnational webs linking alleged and convicted sexual predators point to the need for a feminist response that takes the intertwined nature of capitalism, misogyny, and media representation into full account.

As a major media hub in Asia, Hong Kong sits on the front line of feminist #MeToo activism in the Chinese-speaking world. However,

---

50. Niall Fraser, "Harvey Weinstein's Hong Kong Associate Bey Logan Accused of Sexual Misconduct," *South China Morning Post*, December 13, 2017.

51. Amy Kaufman and Daniel Miller, "Six Women Accuse Filmmaker Brett Ratner of Sexual Harassment or Misconduct," *Los Angeles Times*, November 1, 2017.

backlash against #MeToo continues, as does women's drive for visibility within the film industry. Everyone involved in screen culture needs to take a long critical look at gender at the intersection[52] of class, race, nation, ethnicity, and other markers of identity to redress the debilitating ways predatory figures such as Weinstein have limited what we can see on global screens.

#ProtestToo and the 2019 Anti-ELAB Movement

In her insightful book on the Hong Kong protests, *The Appearing Demos: Hong Kong during and after the Umbrella Movement*, scholar Laikwan Pang highlights the role played by women in the 2014 and 2019 movements. In her list of people supporting the 2019 protests, for example, she notes, "Housewives came out loud to support their protesting children and threatened to launch their own strikes at home."[53] Women form a vital part of the ongoing protests that continue to define contemporary Hong Kong culture. Screenings of Nora Lam's *Lost in the Fumes* 地厚天高 (2017), focusing on Edward Leung's 梁天琦 battle to stay out of prison for his involvement in confrontational street demonstrations, became part of several 2019 protest rallies involving opposition to the Fugitive Offenders and Mutual Legal Assistance in Criminal Matters Legislation (Amendment) Bill (ELAB), which would allow extradition to mainland China for trials under the PRC's dramatically different legal system. Leung is credited with coining the phrase "liberate Hong Kong; revolution of our times" for his 2016 election campaign, and this slogan became the defining cry of the 2019 protests.

Whereas the preponderance of complaints involving sexual harassment were lodged against counterdemonstrators in the 2014

52. Kimberlé Crenshaw, "Mapping the Margins: Intersectionality, Identity Politics, and Violence against Women of Color," *Stanford Law Review* 43, no. 6 (1991): 1241–99.

53. Laikwan Pang, *The Appearing Demos: Hong Kong during and after the Umbrella Movement* (Ann Arbor: Univ. of Michigan Press, 2020), 5.

Umbrella Movement, accusations against the police dominated feminist calls for action in 2019. Allegations of gender-specific misconduct on the part of the authorities include male officers partially disrobing a woman by mishandling her during an arrest, inappropriate use of strip searches, routine sexist invective, sexual assault, and rape.[54] #ProtestToo emerged as an outgrowth of the Anti-ELAB movement to highlight sexual violence suffered by women protesters. A rally held on August 28, 2019, demanded an investigation into these incidents, and human rights advocates maintain a spotlight on other cases of abuse that followed. On December 20, 2019, Amnesty International filed a report detailing allegations of sexual violence by police involving protesters:

> Allegations of the sexual harassment and assault of protesters have been circulating since Hong Kong's current protest movement began. . . .
>
> The few women who have spoken out about the issue have faced a massive backlash. Some have had their personal details leaked online; others have been targeted with fake sex tapes or received harassing phone calls. Although much of this abuse comes from anonymous trolls, the Hong Kong authorities have created a climate where such abuse thrives by smearing protesters and failing to establish an independent investigation into police misconduct.[55]

The US-based National Women's Studies Association published a statement on December 10, 2019:

54. Gina Marchetti, "Extradition as a 'Women's Issue,'" *Women's Studies Research Centre*, December 6, 2019, https://www.wsrcweb.hku.hk/wp-content/uploads/2019/12/Gina-Marchetti-Extradition-as-a-Womens-Issue.pdf. https://www.wsrcweb.hku.hk/wp-content/uploads/2019/12/Gina-Marchetti-Extradition-as-a-Womens-Issue.pdf

55. Amnesty International. "Sexual Violence against Hong Kong Protesters: What's Going on?" Amnesty International online news, December 20, 2019, https://www.amnesty.org/en/latest/news/2019/12/sexual-violence-against-hong-kong-protesters/.

12.4. Female demonstrators forming a human chain to pass water bottles in order to wash away tear gas and extinguish flaming gas canisters. From *Not One Less* (Kanas Liu, 2019).

As transnational feminists, we are appalled by the unfolding political and humanitarian crisis in Hong Kong. The recent police crackdowns on demonstrations have turned Hong Kong into a de facto police state. We unequivocally condemn Chinese authorities' use of surveillance tactics, policing on university campuses, escalating violence, and violations of human rights and freedom of speech and assembly. We extend our solidarity to the protesters.[56]

Female director Kanas Liu 廖洁雯, a veteran of Umbrella Movement filmmaking, has made several short films on the 2019 protests.

56. National Women's Studies Association, "NWSA Statement on Hong Kong," public statement, December 10, 2019, https://mailchi.mp/nwsa/hong-kong ?fbclid=IwAR14Orvv_byzVx-VhpN2EE3NziQkJ7FK6xA_3cOKhD4P9Gb4GyG2 NrlnISg.

In *Not One Less* 缺一不可 (2019, codirected with Sam Tsang 曾锦山), Liu focuses on clashes with the police during the August 31st demonstrations and the subsequent rally outside the Lai Chi Kok detention facility, in which protesters remained in custody during the mid-Autumn festival, which celebrates family unity. Taking a participant-observer approach to the protests, the short provides only minimal commentary, in the form of titles, and does not include voice-over narration or talking-head interviews.

On the frontlines with the protesters as they confront the police, the filmmaker shows female demonstrators forming a human chain to pass water bottles in order to wash away tear gas and extinguish flaming gas canisters. Along with their male peers, women work to minimize the effect of the gas, as well as take up the megaphone to announce shifts of the demonstrations to other parts of the city. At one point in the film a male protester says he does not want to see his "sisters" get arrested and asks them to retreat before the police over-run their line. Some women can be heard to object. Although the film does not provide context, the fact that women suffered sexual harassment and violence in police custody was generally known at the time. The last segment of the film begins with a close shot of a woman playing "Glory to Hong Kong" on a harmonica at the gates of the Lai Chi Kok facility, underscoring the importance of women to the struggle.

As Hong Kong faces the trials of COVID-19 and the National Security Law dictated by the powers in Beijing in 2020, women such as Kanas Liu, with short documentaries that include *The Time of the Individual* 用自己方式的时代, *Comrades* 手足, and *Trial and Error* (all 2019), continue to bring to the screen voices from the political margins that highlight the importance of sexual and gender diversity within the protest movement. Films such as Sue Williams's *Denise Ho: Becoming the Song* (2020) underscore the transnational foundations of Hong Kong feminism by focusing on the appeal of celebrities, such as the Cantopop chanteuse Denise Ho, who is an icon of lesbian activism, LGBTQ advocacy, and Hong Kong protest culture. As she appears before the US Congress and the United Nations, Ho crosses borders in ways that show the importance of Hong Kong cosmopolitanism to its unique feminist politics. Adelyn Lim eloquently articulates this:

> Hong Kong as a transnational space allows for the possibility of women activists to construct transnational identifications and organizations in response. At the same time, it is also when women activists are reflecting upon more extensive and inclusive representations of feminism to overcome hierarchies of class, gender, ethnicity, and nationality that transnational feminist solidarity poses the greatest challenge. For this reason, women's activism in Hong Kong constitutes a strategic case for the articulation of new conceptions of transnational feminism.[57]

Free from the firewall that constrains cyber-expression across the border, Hong Kong plays a critical role in feminist attempts to transform all aspects of a culture that limits the ways in which women can express themselves on transnational screens. This fact underscores the deep connection between the Umbrella Movement, the Anti-ELAB movement, #ProtestToo, and #MeToo feminism in Hong Kong.

Acknowledgments

Research for this chapter was partially funded by a General Research Fund award, "Gendered Screens, Chinese Dreams: Women Filmmakers and the Rise of China in the Twenty-First Century," Research Grants Council, Hong Kong, 2019–2021 (HKU17612818). Many thanks to Georgina Challen and Louis Lu Yu, who helped to prepare the manuscript.

57. Lim, *Transnational Feminism*, 13–14.

Bibliography

Contributor Biographies

Index

Bibliography

Ackerly, Brooke A., and Bina D'Costa. "Transnational Feminism: Political Strategies and Theoretical Discussions." Working paper, Department of International Relations, Australian National University, January 2005.

Ai Ke 艾可. "Yindao zhi Dao, BCome he Wo" 《阴道之道》、BCome和我 ("Our Vaginas Ourselves," BCome, and Me). *Kula shibao*, July 12, 2013.

Ai Qing. "Dayanhe—My Wet-Nurse." In *Selected Poems by Ai Qing*. Translated and edited by Eugene Chen Ouyang, 26–30. Bloomington: Indiana Univ. Press, 1982.

AJ+. "Under the Umbrella of Hong Kong's Protest." AJ+ YouTube channel, 8:16. November 25, 2014. www.youtube.com/watch?v=_nULwJ6yJNc.

Amin, Ash. "Collective Culture and Urban Public Space." *City* 12, no. 1 (2008): 5–24.

Amnesty International. "Hong Kong: Women and Girls Attacked as Police Fail to Protect Peaceful Protesters." October 3, 2014. Amnesty International online news. www.amnesty.org/en/for-media/press-releases/hong -kong-women-and-girls-attacked-police-fail-protect-peaceful-protesters-.

———. "Sexual Violence against Hong Kong Protesters: What's Going on?" December 20, 2019. Amnesty International online news. https:// www.amnesty.org/en/latest/news/2019/12/sexual-violence-against -hong-kong-protesters/.

Anagnost, Ann. "Transformations of Gender in Modern China." In *Gender and Anthropology: Critical Reviews for Research and Teaching*, edited by Sandra Morgan, 313–42. Washington, DC: American Anthropological Association, 1989.

Asia Art Archive. "Translating Visuality—Gu Wenda: Forest of Stone Steles, Retranslation and Rewriting of Tang Poetry." Asia Art Archive. https://aaa.org.hk/en/collection/search/library/translating-visuality

-gu-wenda-forest-of-stone-steles-retranslation-rewriting-of-tang-poetry
-59236.

Bai Di 柏棣. "Cong Makesi Zhuyi de Jiaodu Kan Zhongguo Nüxing Wenhua Sanshinian" 从马克思主义的角度看中国女性文化三十年 (On Chinese
Women's Culture of the Last Three Decades from a Marxist Perspective). www.wyzxwk.com/Article/lishi/2015/10/352841.html.

———. "Lishi Shiming de Zhongjie? Zai Ziben Zhuyi Weiji Zhong Sikao
Nüxing Zhuyi yu Ziben Zhuyi de Guanxi (xia)" 历史使命的终结? 在资本主
义危机中思考女性主义与资本主义的关系(下) (Is It the End of the Historical
Mission? A Study on the Relationship between Feminism and Capitalism in the Capitalist Crisis [Part Two]). *Shandong nüzi xueyuan xuebao*,
no. 4: (2014) 1–6.

Bao Hong 鲍红. "Weixiao de Zhongguo Nüxingzhuyi" 微笑的中国女性主义
(A Smiling Chinese Feminism). *Chuban cankao*, no. 11 (2004): 14.

Barlow, Tani E. "Asia, Gender, and Scholarship under Processes of Re-
regionalization." *Journal of Gender Studies (Ochanomizu University)* 5
(2002): 1–14.

———. "Asian Women in Reregionalization." *positions: east asia cultures critique* 15, no. 2 (2007): 285–318.

———. "Gender and Identity in Ding Ling's *Mother*." *Modern Chinese Literature* 2, no. 2 (1986): 123–42.

———. "Introduction." In *The Power of Weakness*, edited by Tani E. Barlow,
1–25. New York: Feminist Press, 2007.

———. *The Question of Women in Chinese Feminism*. Durham, NC: Duke
Univ. Press, 2004.

Barnett, Pennina, and Jennifer Harris. "The Subversive Stitch Revisited: The
Politics of Cloth." Goldsmith's website forum, June 2014. www.gold
.ac.uk/subversivestitchrevisited/.

Bauman, Zygmunt. *Liquid Modernity*. Malden, MA: Polity, 2000.

Beahan, Charlotte L. "Feminism and Nationalism in the Chinese Women's
Press." *Modern China* 1, no. 4 (1975): 379–416.

Berger, John. *Ways of Seeing*. New York: Penguin, 1990.

Bowring, John. "Chinese Characteristics." *Fortnightly Review* 1 (1865):
561–71.

Boxer, Marilyn J. "Rethinking the Socialist Construction and International
Career of the Concept 'Bourgeois Feminism.'" *The American Historical
Review* 112, no. 1 (2007): 131–58.

Bukebang 布客帮. "Picun Wenxue Gushi: Naxie zai Liushuixian shang Xie Shi de 'Xin Gongren'" 皮村文学故事: 那些在流水线上写诗的"新工人" (Stories of Literature in the Pi Village: "New Workers" Write Poems at the Assembly Line). *Beijing wanbao*, May 20, 2017.

Cai Chang 蔡畅. *Zhonghua Quanguo Minzhu Funü Lianhehui Zhuyi Caichang de Jianghua* 中华全国民主妇女联合会主席蔡畅的讲话 (Cai Chang's Talks at the All-China Democratic Women's Federation). Beijing: Gongren chubanshe, 1957.

Cai Xiang 蔡翔. *Geming/Xushu: Zhongguo Shehui Zhuyi Wenxue-Wenhua Xiangxiang (1949–1966)* 革命/叙述: 中国社会主义文学-文化想象 (1949–1966) (Revolution and Its Narrative: China's Socialist Literary and Cultural Imaginations [1949–1966]). Beijing: Beijing daxue chubanshe, 2010.

Canning, Kathleen. *Languages of Labor and Gender: Female Factory Work in Germany, 1850–1914*. Ithaca, NY: Cornell Univ. Press, 1996.

Cao Zhenglu 曹征路. "Ni Hong" 霓虹 (Neon Lights). In *Cao Zhenglu Wenji* 曹征路文集 (Collection of Cao Zhenglu's Works), vol. 3, 55–112. Shenzhen: Haitian chubanshe, 2014.

"Castration." Concept and Form: The *Cahiers pour l'Analyse* and Contemporary French Thought website. http://cahiers.kingston.ac.uk/concepts/castration.html.

Chan, Eliza Chong-lai. "Negotiating Daughterhood: A Case Study of the Female Inheritance Movement in the New Territories, Hong Kong." Master's thesis, Chinese University of Hong Kong, 1995. http://repository.lib.cuhk.edu.hk/tc/item/cuhk-320613.

Chen, Angela. "Michelle Yeoh: Weinstein Was a 'Bully,' 'Not Always Honorable.'" Associated Press, October 17, 2017. https://apnews.com/article/c3d1f39273ad4853be0ad494cbf04956.

Chen Fang 陈方. "Xinxing de Xueke, Kaifang de Kecheng" 新兴的学科, 开放的课程 (A New Discipline and an Open Curriculum). *Funü yanjiu luncong*, no. 1 (2003): 61–65.

Chen Jibing 陈季冰. "Oumeng Guiding Gongsi Nüxing Dongshi Bili Xingdetong ma?" 欧盟规定公司女性董事比例行得通吗? (Is the EU's Regulation of the Proportion of Female Directors Feasible?). *Nanfang doushi bao*, November 10, 2012. Reposted online as "Duibuqi! Women Buxuyao Zhengfu Zhipai de Nüdongshi" 对不起! 我们不需要政府指派的女董事 (Sorry, but We Don't Need Government-Appointed Female Directors).

Sina Weibo. http://blog.sina.com.cn/s/blog_593bcdce0101equr.html ?tj=2.

Chen Ran 陈染. *Siren Shenghuo* 私人生活(Private Life). Nanjing: Jiangsu renmin chubanshe, 1996.

Chen Shunxin 陈顺馨. "Nüxing Zhuyi dui Minzu Zhuyi de Jieru" 女性主义对民族主义的介入 (Feminist Intervention of Nationalism). In *Funü, Minzu yu Nüxing Zhuyi* 妇女、民族与女性主义 (Women, Nation, and Feminism), edited by Chen Shunxin 陈顺馨 and Dai Jinhua 戴锦华, 1–26. Beijing: Zhongyang bianyi chubanshe, 2002.

Chen Shunxin 陈顺馨 and Dai Jinhua戴锦华, eds. *Funü, Minzu yu Nüxing Zhuyi* 妇女、民族与女性主义 (Women, Nation, and Feminism). Beijing: Zhongyang bianyi chubanshe, 2002.

Chen, Ya-chen. *The Many Dimensions of Chinese Feminism*. New York: Palgrave, 2011.

Cheng, Sealing. "Questioning Global Vaginahood: Reflections from Adapting *The Vagina Monologues* in Hong Kong." *Feminist Review*, no. 92 (2009): 19–35.

Chizuko, Ueno 上野千鹤子, and Li Xiaojiang 李小江. "'Zhuyi' yu Xingbie" "主义"与性别 ("-isms" and Gender). *Dushu*, no. 8 (2004): 39–49.

Chow, Rey. *Woman and Chinese Modernity: The Politics of Reading between West and East*. Minneapolis: Univ. of Minnesota Press, 1991.

Chow, Vivienne. "'Crouching Tiger' Actress Accuses Harvey Weinstein Asia Associate of Sexual Misconduct." *Variety*, December 15, 2017.

Cong, Xiaoping. *Marriage, Law, and Gender in Revolutionary China, 1940–1960*. Cambridge, UK: Cambridge Univ. Press, 2016.

Conway, Janet M. "Troubling Transnational Feminism(s): Theorising Activist Praxis." *Feminist Theory* 18, no. 2 (2017): 205–27.

Cooper, Christine M. "Worrying about Vaginas: Feminism and Eve Ensler's *The Vagina Monologues*." *Signs: Journal of Women in Culture and Society* 32, no. 3 (2007): 727–58.

Cotter, Holland. "From Innovation to Provocation: China's Artists on a Global Path." *New York Times*, October 6, 2017. https://www.nytimes.com/2017/10/06/arts/design/guggenheim-museum-art-and-china-review.html.

Crenshaw, Kimberlé. "Mapping the Margins: Intersectionality, Identity Politics, and Violence against Women of Color." *Stanford Law Review* 43, no. 6 (1991): 1241–99.

Cui, Shuqin. *Gendered Bodies: Toward a Women's Visual Art in Contemporary China*. Honolulu: Univ. of Hawai'i Press, 2015.

Da Shi 大诗. "Wulitou de 'Xingsaorao' Lifa" 无厘头的"性骚扰"立法 (Nonsensical 'Sexual Harassment' Legislation). *Nanfang dushi bao*, September 3, 2005.

Dai Jinhua 戴锦华. *After the Post–Cold War: The Future of Chinese History*. Durham, NC: Duke Univ. Press, 2018.

———. "Liangnan Zhijian Huo Tuwei Keneng?" 两难之间或突围可能? (A Dilemma or a Breakout?). In *Funü, Minzu yu Nüxing Zhuyi* 妇女、民族与女性主义 (Women, Nation, and Feminism), edited by Chen Shunxin 陈顺馨 and Dai Jinhua 戴锦华, 27–38. Beijing: Zhongyang bianyi chubanshe, 2002.

———. *Shedu zhi Zhou: Xinshiqi Zhongguo Nüxing Xiezuo yu Nüxing Wenhua* 涉渡之舟: 新时期中国女性写作与女性文化 (A Boat Crossing the Ocean: New-Period Chinese Women's Literature and Culture). Beijing: Beijing daxue chubanshe, 2007.

———. "Xiaoxianrou, Danmei, Xingbie Kunjing" 小鲜肉·耽美·性别困境 (Little Fresh Meat, Slash Fiction, Gender Dilemma). *Jiliu*, September 18, 2018. http://jiliuwang.net/archives/76694.

———. *Yinheng* 印痕 (Marks). Shijiazhuang: Hebei jiaoyu chubanshe, 2002.

Davin, Delia. *Woman-Work: Women and the Party in Revolutionary China*. Oxford: Clarendon, 1976.

de Haan, Francisca. "Continuing Cold War Paradigms in Western Historiography of Transnational Women's Organisations: The Case of the Women's International Democratic Federation (WIDF)." *Women's History Review* 19, no. 4 (2010): 547–73.

Dirlik, Arif. "The Mouse that Roared: The Democratic Movement in Hong Kong." *b2o*, October 6, 2014. www.boundary2.org/2014/10/the-mouse-that-roared-the-democratic-movement-in-hong-kong-2/.

Do, Vicky. "Stranger from Paradise: Vicky." Vimeo video, 5:38. 2015. https://vimeo.com/118096291.

Dong Limin 董丽敏. "'Laodong': Funü Jiefang ji qi Xiandu; Yi Zhao Shuli Xiaoshuo wei Ge'an de Kaocha" 劳动: 妇女解放及其限度; 以赵树理小说为个案的考察 ("Labor": Women's Liberation and Its Limits; A Case Study of Zhao Shuli's Fiction). *Zhongguo xiandai wenxue yanjiu congkan*, no. 3 (2010): 16–28.

———. "Nüxing Zhuyi: Bentuhua ji qi Weidu" 女性主义: 本土化及其维度 (Feminism: Indigenization and Its Purview). *Nankai xuebao*, no. 2 (2005): 7–12.

———. "Xingbie Yanjiu: Wenti, Ziyuan he Fangfa; Dui Zhongguo Xingbie Yanjiu Xianzhuang de Fansi" 性别研究: 问题、资源和方法: 对中国性别研究现状的反思 (Gender Studies: Problems, Resources and Methods; Rethinking the Current Situation of China's Gender Studies). *Shehui kexue*, no. 12 (2009): 164–72.

———. "Yan'an Jingyan: Cong 'Funü Zhuyi' dao 'Jiating Tongyi Zhanxian'—Jian Lun 'Geming Zhongguo' Funü Jiefang Lilun de Shengcheng Wenti" 延安经验: 从"妇女主义"到"家庭统一战线"—兼论"革命中国"妇女解放理论的生成问题 (The Yan'an Path: From "Feminism" to the "United Family Front"—The Rise of a Theory of Women's Liberation in "Revolutionary China"). *Funü yanjiu luncong*, no. 6 (2016): 19–27.

Dooling, Amy. *Women's Literary Feminism in Twentieth-Century China*. New York: Palgrave, 2005.

Du Fangqin 杜芳琴. "Lijie, Bijiao yu Fenxiang: Yazhou Funüxue de Jueqi—'Yazhou Funüxue Congshu' Shuping" 理解、比较与分享: 亚洲妇女学的崛起—"亚洲妇女学丛书"书评 (Understanding, Comparing, and Sharing: The Rise of Asian Women's Studies—A Review of the "Book Series on Asian Women's Studies"). *Funü yanjiu luncong*, no. 9 (2005): 76–80.

———. "Quanqiu Shiye zhong de Bentu Funüxue—Zhongguo de Jingyan: Yige Wei Wancheng de Guocheng" 全球视野中的本土妇女学—中国的经验: 一个未完成的过程" (Indigenous Women's Studies in a Global Horizon—the Chinese Experience: A Process that Is Not Yet Completed). *Funü yanjiu*, no. 6 (2001): 33–42.

———. "Zai Gongxing yu Chayi zhong Fazhan Yazhou Funüxue" 在共性与差异中发展亚洲妇女学 (Developing Asian Women's Studies within Commonalities and Differences). *Funü yanjiu luncong*, no. 1 (2002): 28–33.

"Dushu" Zazhi, ed. *Yazhou de Bingli* 亚洲的病例 (Asia's Pathology). Beijing: Sanlian shudian, 2007.

Dworkin, Andrea, and Catharine MacKinnon. *Pornography and Civil Rights: A New Day for Women's Equality*. Minneapolis, Minn.: Organizing against Pornography, 1988.

Edwards, Louise. *Gender, Politics, and Democracy: Women's Suffrage in China*. Stanford: Stanford Univ. Press, 2008.

Erens, Patricia Brett. "*The Mistress* and Female Sexuality." In *Hong Kong Screenscapes: From the New Wave to the Digital Frontier*, edited by Esther M. K. Cheung, Gina Marchetti, and See-Kam Tan, 239–52. Hong Kong: Hong Kong Univ. Press, 2010.

Fan Popo 范坡坡. *Laizi Yindao* 来自阴道 (The VaChina Monologues: A Documentary). Queer Comrades, 2013. www.queercomrades.com/videos /vagina/.

Fan Yusu 范雨素. "I Am Fan Yusu." Translated by Philip Bradshaw and Keegan Sparks. *World Literature Today* (Spring 2021). www.worldliterature today.org/2021/spring/i-am-fan-yusu-fan-yusu.

———. "Wo Shi Fan Yusu" 我是范雨素 (I Am Fan Yusu). Zhengwu Gushi, April 25, 2007. https://news.qq.com/a/20170425/063100.htm?fbclid =IwAR0ULJ8wDiukyQ5ASRXicLRWAtl-92lUTQxyMHPTkbkz 8PJHccIZvT5RauU.

Felluga, Dino. "Modules on Lacan: On Psychosexual Development." In *Introductory Guide to Critical Theory*. Purdue University. www.purdue .edu/guidetotheory/psychoanalysis/lacandevelop.html.

Feng Yuan 冯媛, ed. "Yindao Dasheng Shuo—Zuowei Xingbie Jiaoyu de Duli Huaju zhi Lu Yantaohui Huiyi Jilu" 阴道大声说—作为性别教育的独 立话剧之路研讨会会议记录 (Vagina Speaks Out Loud: Meeting Minutes of the Symposium on Independent Gender Education Theater). Beijing LGBT Center, December 02, 2013. Archives of GenderWatch.

Fincher, Leta Hong. *Betraying Big Brother: The Feminist Awakening in China*. New York: Verso, 2018.

———. *Leftover Women: The Resurgence of Gender Inequality in China*. London: Zed, 2014.

Fischler, Lisa. "Women's Activism during Hong Kong's Political Transition." In *Gender and Change in Hong Kong: Globalization, Postcolonialism, and Chinese Patriarchy*, edited by Eliza Wing-Yee Lee, 49–77. Hong Kong: Hong Kong Univ. Press, 2004.

Folbre, Nancy. "The Unproductive Housewife: Her Evolution in Nineteenth-Century Economic Thought." *Signs: Journal of Women in Culture and Society* 16, no. 3 (1991): 463–84.

Ford, Stacilee. *Mabel Cheung Yuen-Ting's An Autumn's Tale*. Hong Kong: Hong Kong Univ. Press, 2008.

———. *Troubling American Women: Narratives of Gender and Nation in Hong Kong*. Hong Kong: Hong Kong Univ. Press, 2011.

Fore, Steve. "Tales of Recombinant Femininity: *The Reincarnation of Golden Lotus*, the *Chin P'ing Mei*, and the Politics of Melodrama in Hong Kong." *Journal of Film and Video* 45, no. 4 (1993): 57–70.

Fraser, Nancy. "Feminism, Capitalism and the Cunning of History." *New Left Review* 56 (2009): 97–117.

Fraser, Niall. "Harvey Weinstein Scandal Deepens as Producer Accused of Sexual Misconduct at Hong Kong Hotel." *South China Morning Post*, December 15, 2017.

———. "Harvey Weinstein's Hong Kong Associate Bey Logan Accused of Sexual Misconduct." *South China Morning Post*, December 13, 2017.

Friedan, Betty. *The Feminine Mystique*. New York: W. W. Norton, 1963.

Fukuyama, Francis. "The End of History?" *The National Interest*, no. 16 (1989): 1–18.

Gaetano, Arianne, and Tamara Jacka. *On the Move: Women and Rural-to-Urban Migration in Contemporary China*. New York: Columbia Univ. Press, 2004.

Gao Xiaoxian 高小贤. "Zhongguo Minjian Funü Zuzhi de Kongjian he Celüe" 中国民间妇女组织的空间和策略 (The Space and Strategies of Chinese Feminist NGOs). In *Shen Lin "Qi" Jing—Xingbie, Xuewen, Rensheng* 身临"奇"境: 性别、学问、人生 (Being in Wonderland: Gender, Knowledge, and Life), edited by Li Xiaojiang 李小江, 215–36. Nanjing: Jiangsu renmin chubanshe, 2000.

Getsy, David J. "Fallen Women: The Gender of Horizontality and the Abandonment of the Pedestal by Giacometti and Epstein." In *Display and Displacement: Sculpture and the Pedestal from Renaissance to Post-Modern*, edited by Alexandra Gerstein, 114–29. London: Courtauld Institute of Art Research Forum and Paul Holberton Publishing, 2007.

Gilmartin, Christina K. *Engendering the Chinese Revolution: Radical Women, Communist Politics, and Mass Movements in the 1920s*. Berkeley: Univ. of California Press, 1995.

Grewal, Inderpal, and Caren Kaplan. "Introduction: Transnational Feminist Practices and Questions of Postmodernity." In *Scattered Hegemonies: Postmodernity and Transnational Feminist Practices*, edited by Inderpal Grewal and Caren Kaplan, 1–33. Minneapolis: Univ. of Minnesota Press, 1994.

Guggenheim. "Chen Zhen's Precipitous Parturition." Guggenheim website, October 26, 2017. www.guggenheim.org/audio/track/chen-zhens-precipitous-parturition.

Ha, Marie-Paule. "Double Trouble: Doing Gender in Hong Kong." *Signs: Journal of Women in Culture and Society* 34, no. 2 (2009): 423–49.

Hai Nan 海男. *Shengming Shengjing* 生命圣经 (Bible of Reproduction). Beijing: Zuojia chubanshe, 1998.

Han Dongping 韩东屏. "Liangxing Hexie" 两性和谐 (Harmony between the Sexes). *Hunan shehui kexue*, 2 (2006): 22–24.

Hardt, Michael. "Affective Labor." *Boundary 2* 26, no. 2 (1999): 89–100.

Harvey, David. *A Brief History of Neoliberalism*. Oxford, UK: Oxford Univ. Press, 2005.

He Xiaoshou 何小手. "'Fan Yusu' Shuapin, Women Shi Bei Ziyou de Linghun Jingyan dao le." 《范雨素》刷屏, 我们是被自由的灵魂惊艳到了 ("Fan Yusu" Flooding the Feed Because We Are Shocked by a Free Soul). *Xinjing bao*, April 25, 2017.

Hershatter, Gail, Emily Honig, and Lisa Rofel. "Reflections on the Fourth World Conference on Women, Beijing and Huairou, 1995." *Social Justice/Global Options* 23, nos. 1/2 (1996): 368–75.

He-Yin Zhen. "Economic Revolution and Women's Revolution." In *The Birth of Chinese Feminism: Essential Texts in Transnational Theory*, edited by Lydia H. Liu, Rebecca E. Karl, and Dorothy Ko, 92–104. New York: Columbia Univ. Press, 2013.

———. "On the Question of Women's Liberation." In *The Birth of Chinese Feminism: Essential Texts in Transnational Theory*, edited by Lydia H. Liu, Rebecca E. Karl, and Dorothy Ko, 53–71. New York: Columbia Univ. Press, 2013.

HKCC Gender Justice Ministry. *San Bu Zou de Nüsheng* 伞不走的女声 (Do You Hear the Women Sing). YouTube Video, 25:45. November 26, 2014. www.youtube.com/watch?v=ENH43yWYFnI.

Ho, Lauren. "Four Women Blaze Trail in Hong Kong Politics." *South China Morning Post*, February 7, 2013.

Ho, Peter, and Richards Edmonds. *China's Embedded Activism: Opportunities and Constraints of a Social Movement*. New York: Routledge, 2008.

Huakan. "Cuiruo, Wuneng, Wugu Shi Shengming de Yizhong: Jiang Jie Zhuanfang" 脆弱、无能、无辜 是生命的一种: 姜杰专访 (Weak, Incapable, and Vulnerable Is a Mode of Life: An Interview with Jiang Jie), *Huakan*, no. 2 (2015): 27–30.

Huang Lin 荒林. "Zuowei Nüxing Zhuyi Fuhao de Linglei Changjing: Ximeng Bofuwa, Hanna Alunte, Sushan Sangtage de Zhongguo Yuedu" 作为女性主义符号的另类场景：西蒙·波伏娃、汉娜·阿伦特、苏珊·桑塔格的中国阅读 (Another Scene of Feminist Symbols: The Reading of Simone de Beauvoir, Hannah Arendt, and Susan Sontag in China). *Zhongguo tushu pinglun*, no. 5 (2006): 78–84.

Huang Shuqin 黄蜀芹. "Nüxing, zai Dianyingye de Nanren Shijie li" 女性，在电影业的男人世界里 (Women, in the Men's World of the Film Industry). *Dangdai dianying*, no. 5 (1995): 69–71.

Isaak, Jo Anna. *Feminism and Contemporary Art: The Revolutionary Power of Women's Laughter*. London: Routledge, 1996.

Jaschok, Maria, and Shui Jingjun. "'Outsider Within': Speaking to Excursions across Cultures." *Feminist Theory* 1, no. 1 (2000): 33–58.

Ji Wei 计巍. "Wo Shi Kao Kuli Chifan de, Bu Kao Xie Wenzhang Mousheng" 我是靠苦力吃饭的，不靠写文章谋生 (I Make a Living with Manual Labor, Not with Creative Writings). *Zhongguo qingnian bao*, April 26, 2017.

Jiang, Junjie. "The Doubleness of Sight/Site: Xu Bing's Phoenix as an Intended Public Art Project." *Yishu: Journal of Contemporary Chinese Art* 17, no. 2 (2018): 29–45.

Judge, Joan. "Talent, Virtue, and the Nation: Chinese Nationalisms and Female Subjectivities in the Early Twentieth Century." *American Historical Review* 106, no. 2 (2001): 765–803.

Kaufman, Amy, and Daniel Miller. "Six Women Accuse Filmmaker Brett Ratner of Sexual Harassment or Misconduct." *Los Angeles Times*, November 1, 2017.

Ke, Qianting. "How Can a Radical Sexual Play Work in a 'Conservative' Community?: The Adaptation and Recreation of *The Vagina Monologues* in China." In *Gender Dynamics, Feminist Activism, and Social Transformation in China*, edited by Guoguang Wu, Yuan Feng, and Helen Lansdowne, 123–43. London: Routledge, 2019.

Ko, Dorothy, and Wang Zheng. "Introduction: Translating Feminisms in China." *Gender & History* 18, no. 3 (2006): 463–71.

Krzyżanowska, Natalia. "The Discourse of Counter-Monuments: Semiotics of Material Commemoration in Contemporary Urban Spaces." *Social Semiotics* 26, no. 5 (2016): 465–85.

Lam, Nora 林子穎. *Wangjiao Heiye-Jilupian* 旺角黑夜—紀錄片 (Midnight in Mong Kok: A Documentary). YouTube video, 15:57. November 9, 2014. www.youtube.com/watch?v=in32UFyghWE.

Langer, Susanne. *Feeling and Form: A Theory of Art*. New York: Charles Scribner's Sons, 1953.

Laplanche, Jean, and Jean-Bertrand Pontalis. *The Language of Psychoanalysis*. Translated by Donald Nicholson-Smith. London: Hogarth, 1973.

Leafloor, Liz. "Symbolism of the Mythical Phoenix Bird: Renewal, Rebirth and Destruction." *Ancient Origins*, www.ancient-origins.net/myths -legends/ancient-symbolism-magical-phoenix-002020.

Lee, Eliza Wing-Yee, ed. *Gender and Change in Hong Kong: Globalization, Postcolonialism, and Chinese Patriarchy*. Hong Kong: Hong Kong Univ. Press, 2004.

———. "Prospects for the Development of a Critical Feminist Discourse." In *Gender and Change in Hong Kong: Globalization, Postcolonialism, and Chinese Patriarchy*, edited by Eliza W. Y. Lee, 200–207. Hong Kong: Hong Kong Univ. Press, 2004.

Lemaire, Anika. *Jacques Lacan*. Translated by David Macey. Boston: Routledge & Kegan Paul, 1970.

Leys, Simon. *Chinese Shadows*. New York: Viking, 1977.

Li Ang 李昂 and Wang Anyi 王安忆. "Funü Wenti yu Funü Wenxue" 妇女问题与妇女文学 (The Woman Question and Women's Literature). *Shanghai wenxue*, no. 3 (1989): 76–80.

Li Huiying, ed. 李慧英. *Shehui Xingbie yu Gonggong Zhengce* 社会性别与公共政策 (Gender and Public Policy). Beijing: Dangdai zhongguo chubanshe, 2002.

Li, Pang. "Ann Hui: A Director Who Captures Ordinary Women's Lives." China.org.cn, April 15, 2010. www.china.org.cn/arts/2010-04/15 /content_19820089.htm.

Li Sipan 李思磐. "Zhongguo Ban Nüquan Zhuyi: Qimeng dao Zijue" 中国版女权主义: 启蒙到自觉 (Chinese Version of Feminism: From Enlightenment to Self-Consciousness). *Weibo*, February 12, 2015, https://weibo .com/p/1001603808858006020709.

Li Xiaojiang 李小江. "50 Nian, Women Zou dao le Nali?: Zhongguo Funü Jiefang yu Fazhan Licheng Huigu" 50年, 我们走到了哪里?: 中国妇女解放与发展历程回顾 (Fifty Years, Where Have We Reached?: Looking Back onto the Project of Chinese Women's Liberation and Development). *Funü yanjiu*, no. 2 (2000): 58–64.

———. "Daoyan: Cong Gender (Xingbie) Zai Yijie Zhong de Qiyixing Tanqi" 导言: 从Gender(性别)在译介过程中的歧义性谈起 (Introduction: On the Ambiguity of Gender in Translation). In Li Xiaojiang et al., *Wenhua, Jiaoyu yu Xingbie Bentu Jingyan yu Xueke Jianshe* 文化, 教育与性别——本土经验与学科建设 (Culture, Education, and Gender: Local Experiences and the Construction of a Discipline), 1–14. Nanjing: Jiangsu renmin chubanshe, 2002).

———. "From 'Modernization' to 'Globalization': Where are Chinese Women?" Translated by Tani E. Barlow. *Signs: Journal of Women in Culture and Society* 26, no. 4 (2001): 1274–78.

———. "Funü Yanjiu de Yuanqi, Fazhan ji Xianzhuang" 妇女研究的缘起、发展及现状 (The Origin, Developments, and Current Status of Chinese Women's Studies). *Funü yanjiu*, no. 1 (1999): 128–33.

———. *Gaobie Zuotian* 告别昨天 (Bidding Farewell to Yesterday). Zhengzhou: Henan renmin chubanshe, 1995.

———. *Guanyu Nüren de Dawen* 关于女人的答问 (Questions and Answers on Women). Nanjing: Jiangsu renmin chubanshe, 1997.

———. "Nüren Shenti bei Xiaofei dui Nongye Shehui Daode Shi Dianfuxing de Tiaozhan" 女人身体被消费对农业社会道德是颠覆性的挑战 (The Consumption of Women's Bodies Is a Subversive Challenge to the Morality of an Agricultural Society). Cul.sohu.com, May 30, 2016. http://cul.sohu.com/s2016/lixiaojiang/.

———. *Nüxing Shenmei Yishi Tanwei* 女性审美意识探微 (Inquiry into Women's Aesthetic Consciousness). Zhengzhou: Henan renmin chubanshe, 1989.

———. *Nüxing/Xingbie de Xueshu Wenti* 女性/性别的学术问题 (Scholarly Discussions on Women/Gender). Jinan: Shandong renmin chubanshe, 2005.

———. *Nüzi yu Jiazheng* 女子与家政 (Women and Homemaking). Zhengzhou: Henan renmin chubanshe, 1986.

———. "Qianyan: 'Qi' zai Nali?" 前言: "奇"在哪里? (Foreword: In What Way Are We "Strange"?). In *Shen Lin "Qi" Jing: Xingbie, Xuewen, Rensheng* 身临"奇"境: 性别、学问、人生 (Being in Wonderland: Gender, Knowledge, and Life), edited by Li Xiaojiang, 1–6. Nanjing: Jiangsu renmin chubanshe, 2000.

———. "Quanqiuhua Beijing xia Zhongguo Funü Yanjiu yu Guoji Fazhan Xiangmu" 全球化背景下中国妇女研究与国际发展项目 (Chinese Women's

Studies and International Development Projects under Globalization). *Funü yanjiu luncong*, no. 3 (2005): 55–61.

———. *Rang Nüren Shuohua: Qinli Zhenzheng* 让女人自己说话: 亲历战争 (Let Women Speak for Themselves: Experiencing the War First Hand). Beijing: Sanlian shudian, 2003.

———. "With What Discourse Do We Reflect on Chinese Women? Thoughts on Transnational Feminism in China." In *Spaces of Their Own: Women's Public Sphere in Transnational China*, edited by Mayfair Meihui Yang, 261–77. Minneapolis: Univ. of Minnesota Press, 1999.

———. *Xiawa de Tansuo* 夏娃的探索 (Eve's Exploration). Zhengzhou: Henan renmin chubanshe, 1988.

———. *Xinggou* 性沟 (Sex Gap). Beijing: Sanlian shudian, 1989.

Li Xiaojiang 李小江 and Paek Won-dam 白元淡. "Jieji, Xingbie yu Minzu Guojia" 阶级, 性别与民族国家 (Class, Gender, and the Nation State). *Dushu*, no. 10 (2004): 3–14.

Li Xiaojiang and Zhang Xiaodan. "Creating a Space for Women: Women's Studies in China in the 1980s." *Signs: Journal of Women in Culture and Society* 20, no. 1 (1994): 137–51.

Li Xiaojiang et al. *Wenhua, Jiaoyu yu Xingbie: Bentu Jingyan yu Xueke Jianshe* 文化, 教育与性别—本土经验与学科建设 (Culture, Education, and Gender: Local Experiences and the Construction of a Discipline). Nanjing: Jiangsu renmin chubanshe, 2002.

Li Yunlei 李云雷. *Xinshiji Diceng Wenxue yu Zhongguo Gushi* 新世纪底层文学与中国故事 (*Diceng* Literature in the Twenty-First Century and the Stories of China). Guangzhou: Zhongshan daxue chubanshe, 2014.

Li Zhun 李准. "Li Shuangshuang xiao zhuan" 李双双小传 (A Short Biography of Li Shuangshuang). *Renmin wenxue*, no. 3 (1960): 11–27.

Lim, Adelyn. *Transnational Feminism and Women's Movements in Post-1997 Hong Kong: Solidarity beyond the State*. Hong Kong: Hong Kong Univ. Press, 2015.

Lin Bai 林白. "Yigeren de Zhanzheng" 一个人的战争 (One Person's War). *Huacheng*, no. 2 (1994): 4–80.

Lin Chun. "China's Lost World of Internationalism." In *Chinese Vision of World Order: Tianxia, Culture, and World Politics*, edited by Ban Wang, 177–211. Durham, NC: Duke Univ. Press, 2017.

———. "Chinese Socialism and Global Capitalism." In *China and Global Capitalism: Reflections on Marxism, History, and Contemporary Politics*, edited by Lin Chun, 43–61. New York: Palgrave, 2013.

Liu Bohong 刘伯红. "95 Shijie Funü Dahui he Zhongguo Funü Yanjiu" 95 世界妇女大会和中国妇女研究 (The 1995 World Conference on Women and Chinese Women's Studies). *Funü yanjiu*, no. 2 (1999): 46–51.

———. "Zhongguo Funü Fei Zhengfu Zuzhi de Fazhan" 中国妇女非政府组织的发展 (The Development of Chinese Women's NGOs). *Zhejiang xuekan*, no. 4 (2000): 110–11.

Liu Bohong and Li Yani 李亚妮. "Zhongguo Gaodeng Jiaoyu zhong de She-huixingbie Xianshi" 中国高等教育中的社会性别现实 (A Gendered Reality in China's Higher Education). *Yunnan minzu daxue xuebao* 1, no. 28 (January 2011): 55–64.

Liu, Jieyu. *Gender and Work in Urban China: Women Workers of the Unlucky Generation*. New York: Routledge, 2007.

Liu Junning 刘军宁. "Pingdeng de Lixiang, Jingying de Xianshi" 平等的理想, 精英的现实 (Ideals of Equality, Reality of Elitism). Blog.bnn.co. http://blog.boxun.com/hero/liujn/51_1.shtml.

Liu, Lydia H. "Invention and Intervention: The Making of a Female Tradi-tion in Modern Chinese Literature." In *Chinese Femininities/Chinese Masculinities: A Reader*, edited by Susan Brownell and Jeffrey N. Was-serstrom, 149–74. Berkeley: Univ. of California Press, 2002.

———. *Translingual Practice: Literature, National Culture, and Translated Modernity—China, 1900–1937*. Palo Alto, CA: Stanford Univ. Press, 1995.

Liu, Lydia H., Rebecca E. Karl, and Dorothy Ko, eds. *The Birth of Chinese Feminism: Essential Texts in Transnational Theory*. New York: Columbia Univ. Press, 2013.

Liu Xu 刘旭. *Diceng Xushi: Cong Daiyan dao Ziwo Biaoshu* 底层叙事: 从代言到自我表述 (*Diceng* Narratives: From Representation by Others to Self-Representation). Shanghai: Shanghai renmin chubanshe, 2013.

———. *Diceng Xushu: Xiandaixing Huayu de Liexi* 底层叙述: 现代性话语的裂隙 (*Diceng* Narration: Fractures in Modernity Discourse). Shanghai: Shanghai guji chubanshe, 2006.

Lü Pin 吕频. "'Nüquan Wu Jiemei' Si Zhounian, Nüquan Hexin Zuzhizhe de Pinkun, yu Pinkun de Nüquan Yundong" 女权五姐妹"四周年, 女权核心组织者的贫困, 与贫困的女权运动 (The Fourth Anniversary of the "Feminist

Five": The Poverty of Core Feminist Activists and the Impoverished Feminist Movement). *The Initium*, March 8, 2019. https://theinitium .com/article/20190308-opinion-lvpin-feminist-and-metoo/.

Lu Taiguang 鲁太光. "Sikai Shidai de Chenmo: 'Wo Shi Fan Yusu' Beihou de Shehui Qishi" 撕开时代的沉默："我是范雨素"背后的社会启示 (Tearing apart the Silence: Understanding the Social Implications in "I Am Fan Yusu"). *Honggehui*, December 15, 2017. www.szhgh.com/Article /gnzs/worker/2017-12-15/155952.html.

Lü Tu 吕途. *Zhongguo Xin Gongren: Wenhua yu Mingyun* 中国新工人：文化与命运 (Chinese New Workers: Culture and Prospects). Beijing: Falü chubanshe, 2015.

Lu Xun. "Ah Chang and the *Book of Hills and Seas*." In *Dawn Blossoms Plucked at Dusk*. Translated by Yang Hsien-yi and Gladys Yang, 17–25. Beijing: Foreign Languages Press, 1976.

———. "What Happens to Nora after She Walks Out." In *Jotting under Lamplight*, edited by Eileen Cheng and Kirk Denton, 258–59. Cambridge, MA: Harvard Univ. Press, 2017.

Luo Qiong 罗琼 and Duan Yongquiang 段永强. *Luo Qiong Fangtanlu* 罗琼访谈录 (Interviews with Luo Qiong). Beijing: Zhongguo funü chubanshe, 2000.

MacKinnon, Catharine. *Are Women Human?* Cambridge, MA: Harvard Univ. Press, 2007.

Marchenko, Daria. "Hong Kong's Occupy Central Fight for Democracy." Vimeo video, 1:20. 2015. https://vimeo.com/114971342.

Marchetti, Gina. "Clara Law, Asia, and World Cinema." In *The Palgrave Handbook of Asian Cinema*, edited by Aaron Han Joon Magnan-Park, Gina Marchetti, and Tan See-Kam, 689–707. London: Palgrave, 2018.

———. "Extradition as a 'Women's Issue.'" Women's Studies Research Centre, December 6, 2019. www.wsrcweb.hku.hk/wp-content/uploads /2019/12/Gina-Marchetti-Extradition-as-a-Womens-Issue.pdf.

———. "Feminism, Postfeminism, and Hong Kong Women Filmmakers." In *A Companion to Hong Kong Cinema*, edited by Esther M. K. Cheung, Gina Marchetti, and Esther C. M. Yau, 237–64. Hoboken, NJ: Wiley-Blackwell, 2015.

———. *From Tian'anmen to Times Square: Transnational China and the Chinese Diaspora on Global Screens, 1989–1997*. Philadelphia: Temple Univ. Press, 2006.

———. "The Gender of GenerAsian X in Clara Law's Migration Trilogy." In *Ladies and Gentlemen, Boys and Girls: Gender in Film at the End of the Twentieth Century*, edited by Murray Pomerance, 71–87. Albany: State Univ. of New York Press, 2001.

———. "The Gendered Politics of Sex Work in Hong Kong Cinema: Herman Yau and Elsa Chan (Yeeshan)'s *Whispers and Moans* and *True Women for Sale*." *Alphaville: Journal of Film and Screen Media* 10 (2015): 1–19. http://www.alphavillejournal.com/Issue10/PDFs/ArticleMarchetti .pdf.

———. "Handover Women: Hong Kong Women Filmmakers and the Intergenerational Melodrama of Infidelity." *Feminist Media Studies* 16, no. 4 (June 2016): 590–609.

———. "Hong Kong as Feminist Method: Gender, Sexuality, and Democracy in Two Documentaries by Tammy Cheung." In *Hong Kong Culture and Society in the New Millennium: Hong Kong as Method*, edited by Yiu-Wai Chu, 59–76. Singapore: Springer, 2017.

———. "Lean In or Bend Over?: Postfeminism, Neoliberalism, and Hong Kong's *Wonder Women*." In *Emergent Feminisms: Complicating a Postfeminist Media Culture*, edited by Jessalynn Keller and Maureen E. Ryan, 193–210. New York: Routledge, 2018.

Martin, Sylvia J. *Haunted: An Ethnography of the Hollywood and Hong Kong Media Industries*. Oxford: Oxford Univ. Press, 2016.

Marx, Karl. *Economic and Philosophic Manuscripts of 1844*. Translated and edited by Martin Milligan. Mineola, NY: Dover, 2007.

———. *Grundrisse: Foundations of the Critique of Political Economy*. Translated by Martin Nicolaus. London: Penguin, 1973.

Marx, Karl, and Friedrich Engels. *Manifesto of the Communist Party*. Edited and annotated by Frederick Engels. Chicago: Charles H. Kerr & Company, 1906.

Meiksins, Peter. "Productive and Unproductive Labor and Marx's Theory of Class." *Review of Radical Political Economics* 13, no. 3 (1981): 32–42.

Menkes, Nina. "The Visual Language of Oppression." *Filmmaker*, October 30, 2017. https://filmmakermagazine.com/103801-the-visual-language -of-oppression-harvey-wasnt-working-in-a-vacuum/#.XGWxZWQzY6U.

Michelson, Annette. "Where Is Your Rupture?: Mass Culture and the Gesamtkunstwerk." *October* 56, (1991): 42–63.

Min Dongchao 闵冬潮. "Awakening Again: Traveling Feminism in China in the 1980s." *Women's Studies International Forum* 28, no. 4 (2005): 274–88.

———. "*Duihua* (Dialogue) In-Between: A Process of Translating the Term 'Feminism' in China." *Interventions: International Journal of Postcolonial Studies* 9, no. 2 (2007): 174–93.

———. "Gender (Shehui xingbie) zai Zhongguo de Youxing Pianduan" Gender (社会性别) 在中国的游行片段 (Fragments of the Travel of Gender in China). *Funü yanjiu*, no. 1 (2004): 3–19.

———. "Yige Youxing de Gainian: Gender (Shehui xingbie)—Yi Bei'ou, Dong'ou he Nanmei dui gender de Fanyi wei Li" 一个游行的概念: Gender (社会性别)—以北欧, 东欧, 和南美对 gender 的翻译为例 (A Traveling Concept: Gender [*Shehui Xingbie*]—A Case Study of Translating Gender in Northern and Eastern Europe and South America). *Zhejiang xuekan*, no. 1 (2005): 209–14.

Mo Luo 摩罗. "Funü Jiefang Buneng yi Shanghai Muxing wei Daijia" 妇女解放不能以伤害母性为代价 (Women's Liberation Cannot Be Achieved at the Cost of Undermining Motherhood). *Nanfang zhoumo*, January 10, 2007.

Mohanty, Chandra Talpade. *Feminism without Borders: Decolonizing Theory, Practicing Solidarity*. Durham, NC: Duke Univ. Press, 2003.

———. "Transnational Feminist Crossings: On Neoliberalism and Radical Critique." *Signs: Journal of Women in Culture and Society* 38, no. 4 (2013): 967–91.

Moretti, Franco. "Lukács's Theory of the Novel." *New Left Review* 91 (2015): 39–42.

MSNBC. "'And Then Hell Broke Loose.'" MSNBC video, 22:42. December 6, 2014. www.msnbc.com/msnbc/watch/and-then-hell-broke-loose-367963715731.

Mu, Aili. "The Rise of the Short-Short Genre." In *China and New Left Visions: Political and Cultural Interventions*, edited by Ban Wang and Jie Lu, 159–80. Lanham, MD: Lexington, 2012.

Muller, Christian. "The Influence of Age on Schizophrenia." In *Process of Aging: Social and Psychological Perspectives*, edited by Richard H. Williams, Clark Tibbits, and Wilma Donohue, 504–12. London: Aldine Transaction, 2009.

Munroe, Alexandra. "Eyes Wide Open: How Chinese Contemporary Art Went Global." *Christie's*, December 18, 2017. www.christies.com /features/Art-and-China-after-1989-Theater-of-the-World-8579-1 .aspx.

Nan Fan 南帆. "Xingbie, Nüquan Zhuyi yu Jieji Huayu" 性别、女权主义与阶级话语 (Gender, Feminism, and Class Discourse). *Dangdai zuojia pinglun*, no. 3 (2017): 4–16.

National Women's Studies Association. "NWSA Statement on Hong Kong." Public statement, December 10, 2019. https://mailchi.mp/nwsa/hong -kong?fbclid=IwAR14Orvv_byzVx-VhpN2EE3NziQkJ7FK6xA_3cOK hD4P9Gb4GyG2NrlnISg.

Nava, Mica. *Visceral Cosmopolitanism: Gender, Culture, and the Normalisation of Difference*. Oxford: Berge, 2007.

Negra, Diane. *What a Girl Wants?: Fantasizing the Reclamation of Self in Postfeminism*. New York: Routledge, 2008.

Newman, W. Lawrence. *East Asian Societies*. Ann Arbor, MI: Association for Asian Studies, 2014.

Nixon, Mignon. "Part-Object Part Sculpture." *October* 119, (2007): 98–127.

Nüquan Xue Lun 女权学论. "Zhongguo Mitu Yundong Tuishou Huang Xueqin Zao Juliu" 中国米兔运动推手黄雪琴遭拘留 (Huang Xueqin, Leader in the Chinese #MeToo Movement, Was Detained). chinesefeminism .org, November 11, 2019.

Nussbaum, Martha C. "Human Rights and Human Capabilities." *Harvard Human Rights Journal* 20 (2007): 21–24.

———. *Sex and Social Justice*. New York: Oxford Univ. Press, 1999.

Okin, Susan Moller. "Justice and Gender: An Unfinished Debate." *Fordham Law Review* 72, no. 5 (2004): 1537–67.

Ouyang Jianghe 欧阳江河, ed. *Jiang Jie: Dayu Yidunban* 姜杰: 大于一吨半 (Jiang Jie: Over 1.5 Tons). Exhibition catalogue, Shanghai Pujiang, October 2015.

Pan Jintang 潘锦堂. "Wo Kan 'Shehui Xingbie Lilun' ji qi Liuxing" 我看"社会性别理论"及其流行 (My View on 'Gender Theory' and Its Popularity). *Funü yanjiu*, no. 1 (2003): 59–60.

Pang, Laikwan. *The Appearing Demos: Hong Kong during and after the Umbrella Movement*. Ann Arbor: Univ. of Michigan Press, 2020.

Parker, Rozsika. *The Subversive Stich: Embroidery and the Making of the Feminine*. London: Women's Press, 1986.

Pateman, Carole. "Feminist Critiques of the Public/Private Dichotomy." In Carole Pateman, *The Disorder of Women: Democracy, Feminism, and Political Theory*, 118–40. Cambridge, UK: Polity, 1989.

Pearlman, Ellen. "A Tale of Two Phoenixes." *Hyperallergic*, July 3, 2013. https://hyperallergic.com/74458/a-tale-of-two-phoenixes/.

Peng Fei 彭菲. "Mianhuai yu Chonggou: 'Pujiang Huaqiaocheng Shinian Gonggong Yishu Jihua' Jinru Dishinian" 缅怀与重构:"浦江华侨城十年公共艺术计划"进入第十年 (Retrospection and Reconstruction: OCT Public Art Project Enters its Tenth Year). news.artron.net, December 18, 2016. https://news.artron.net/20161218/n894759.html.

Picun wenxue xiaozu 皮村文学小组. "Picun Wenxue Xiaozu: Liuxia Zhezuo Shuyu Women Ziji de Bowuguan" 皮村文学小组: 留下这座属于我们自己的博物馆 (The Picun Literature Group: Preserve Our Own Museum). *Picun gongyou*, July 19, 2017. http://mp.weixin.qq.com/s/4yuelhe06nBd2ubGTa3ycA.

Pollock, Sheldon. "Introduction." In *Literary Cultures in History: Reconstructions from South Asia*, edited by Sheldon Pollock, 1–36. Berkeley: Univ. of California Press, 2003.

Qin Xiaoyu. "Introduction: Remembering the Anonymous." In *Iron Moon: An Anthology of Chinese Migrant Worker Poetry*. Translated by Eleanor Goodman and edited by Qin Xiaoyu, 14–31. Buffalo, NY: White Pine, 2016.

Qiu Feng 秋风. "Zhongguo Yingdang Sheli Yuyingjia" 中国应当设立育婴假 (China Should Legalize Family Leave). *Nanfang doushi bao*, November 29, 2011.

Qu Yajun 屈雅君. "Nüxingzhuyi Wenxue Piping Bentuhua Guocheng zhong Ying Zhuyi de Wenti" 女性主义文学批评本土化过程中应注意的问题 (Issues to Be Noted in the Process of Localizing Feminist Literary Criticism). In Li Xiaojiang et al., *Wenhua, Jiaoyu yu Xingbie: Bentu Jingyan yu Xueke Jianshe* 文化, 教育与性别——本土经验与学科建设 (Culture, Education, and Gender: Local Experiences and the Construction of a Discipline), 154–78. Nanjing: Jiangsu renmin chubanshe, 2002.

Rawls, John. "Justice as Fairness." *The Philosophical Review* 67, no. 2 (1958): 164–94.

Reilly, Maura, and Linda Nochlin, eds. *Global Feminisms: New Directions in Contemporary Art*. New York: Brooklyn Museum and Merrell Publishers, 2007.

Ren Jiantao 任剑涛. "Zai Gudian Ziyou Zhuyi yu Xin Ziyou Zhuyi Zhijian: Dangdai Zhongguo Ziyou Zhuyi de Lilun Dingwei Wenti" 在古典自由主义与新自由主义之间: 当代中国自由主义的理论定位问题 (Between Classical Liberalism and Neoliberalism: The Issue of Contemporary Chinese Liberalism's Theoretical Positioning). *Aisixiang*, June 15, 2005. www .aisixiang.com/data/7137.html?page=1.

Riegl, Aloïs. "The Modern Cult of Monuments: Its Character and Its Origin." Translated by Kurt W. Forster and Diane Ghirardo. *Oppositions*, no. 25 (Fall 1982): 21–51.

Rofel, Lisa. *Other Modernities: Gendered Yearnings in China after Socialism*. Berkeley: Univ. of California Press, 1999.

Rong Jian 荣剑. "Zhongguo Ziyou Zhuyi 'Disanbo'—Sixiang Juhui zhi Si" 中国自由主义"第三波"—思想聚会之四 (Chinese Liberalism's "Third Wave"— Symposium No. 4). *Gongfapinglun*, November 2012. www.gongfa.com /html/gongfaxinwen/201211/15-2069.html.

Rottenberg, Catherine. "Neoliberal Feminism and the Future of Human Capital." *Signs: Journal of Women in Culture and Society* 42, no. 2 (2017): 329–48.

Sangari, Kumkum, and Sudesh Vaid. "Recasting Women: An Introduction." In *Recasting Women: Essays in Colonial History*, edited by Kumkum Sangari and Sudesh Vaid, 1–26. New Brunswick, NJ: Rutgers Univ. Press, 1989.

Sayers, Sean. "Individual and Society in Marx and Hegel." *Science & Society* 71, no. 1 (2007): 84–102.

Schwartzman, Lisa H. *Challenging Liberalism: Feminism as Political Critique*. University Park: Pennsylvania State Univ. Press, 2006.

Seth, Sanjay. "Nationalism, Modernity, and the 'Woman Question' in India and China." *The Journal of Asian Studies* 72, no. 2 (May 2013): 273–97.

Shih, Shu-Mei. *The Lure of the Modern: Writing Modernism in Semi-Colonial China, 1917–1937*. Berkeley: Univ. of California Press, 2001.

———. "Towards an Ethics of Transnational Encounter, or 'When' Does a 'Chinese' Woman Become a 'Feminist'?" *differences: A Journal of Feminist Cultural Studies* 13, no. 2 (2002): 90–126.

Shimizu, Celine Parreñas. *The Hypersexuality of Race: Performing Asian/ American Women on Screen and Scene*. Durham, NC: Duke Univ. Press, 2007.

Smith, Adam. *The Wealth of Nations*. Part 2. Princeton, NJ: Princeton Univ. Press, 1902.

Smith, Arthur Henderson. *Chinese Characteristics*. Shanghai: North China Herald, 1890.

Smith, Dorothy E. *The Everyday World as Problematic: A Feminist Sociology*. Toronto: Univ. of Toronto Press, 1987.

Smithsonian. ""New Exhibition Documents the Rise of Xu Bing's Monumental 'Phoenixes.'" Smithsonian news release, April 9, 2013. www.si.edu/newsdesk/releases/new-exhibition-documents-rise-xu-bing-s-monumental-phoenixes.

Somers, Margaret R. "Narrativity, Narrative Identity, and Social Action: Rethinking English Working-Class Formation." In *The History and Narrative Reader*, edited by Geoffrey Roberts, 354–74. London: Routledge, 2001.

Song Shaopeng 宋少鹏. "Cong Zhangxian dao Xiaoshi: Jiti Zhuyi Shiqi de Jiating Laodong (1949–1964)" 从彰显到消失: 集体主义时期的家庭劳动 (1949–1964)(From Visibility to Disappearance: Domestic Labor in the Age of Collectivism [1949–1964]). *Jiangsu shehui kexue*, no. 1 (2012): 116–25.

———. "Wenhua Minzu Zhuyi de Ruxue Fuxing dui Zhongguo Nüxingzhuyi de Tiaozhan" 文化民族主义的儒学复兴对中国女性主义的挑战 (The Challenge of the Confucian Revival in Cultural Nationalism to Chinese Feminism). Manuscript shared by the author.

———. "Ziben Zhuyi, Shehui Zhuyi he Funü: Weishenme Zhongguo Xuyao Chongjian Makesi Zhuyi Nüquan Zhuyi Pipan" 资本主义、社会主义和妇女:为什么中国需要重建马克思主义女权主义批判 (Capitalism, Socialism, and Women: Why China Needs to Rebuild a Marxist Feminist Critique). *Kaifang shidai*, no. 12 (2012): 98–112.

Song Xiuyan 宋秀岩. "Ba Jiang Zhengzhi Guanchuan yu Fulian Gaige he Gongzuo Quan Guocheng" 把讲政治贯穿于妇联改革和工作全过程 (Raising Political Awareness in the Entire Process of the Reform and Work of the Women's Federation System). People.cn. May 19, 2017. http://fj.people.com.cn/n2/2017/0519/c181466-30211002.html.

Spakowski, Nicola. "'Gender' Trouble: Feminism in China under the Impact of Western Theory and the Spatialization of Identity." *positions: east asia cultures critique* 19, no. 1 (2011): 31–54.

———. "'Ihr hört uns nicht an und verliert dadurch viel': Zum Dialog der chinesischen und der westlichen Frauenforschung und Frauenbewegung" ("You Don't Listen to Us and Thereby Lose a Lot": On the Dialogue between Chinese and Western Women's Studies and Women's Movement). *Newsletter Frauen und China* 2 (1992): 26–29.

———. "Socialist Feminism in Postsocialist China." *positions: east asia cultures critique* 26, no. 4 (2018): 561–92.

———. "The Internationalization of China's Women's Studies." *Berliner China: Hefte/Chinese History and Society* 20, (2001): 79–100.

———. "The Internationalisation of China's Women's Movement—'Global Sisterhood' between Western Domination and Chinese Self-Definition." In *Negotiating Space for Gender Studies: Disciplinary Frameworks and Applications*, edited by Özen Odag and Alexander Pershai, 47–65. Hamburg: Peter Lang, 2005.

———. "Von der Befreiung zur Entwicklung. Modernisierungsbegriff und Emanzipationsstrategie im feministischen Diskurs der VR China" (From Liberation to Development: Theories of Modernization and Emancipation in Chinese Feminism). *Berliner China-Hefte* 10, (1996): 11–47.

———. "'Women Studies with Chinese Characteristics'? On the Origins, Issues, and Theories of Contemporary Feminist Research in China." *Jindai Zhongguo funüshi yanjiu*, no. 2 (1994): 297–322.

Steinberg, Leo. "Jasper Johns: The First Seven Years of His Art." *Other Criteria*. London: Oxford Univ. Press, 1972.

Stevens, Quentin, Karen A. Franck, and Ruth Fazakerley. "Counter-Monuments: The Anti-Monumental and the Dialogic." *The Journal of Architecture* 17, no. 6 (2012): 951–72.

Striff, Erin. "Staging Communities of Women: Eve Ensler's *The Vagina Monologues* and V-Day Benefit Performances." University of Hartford. March 2, 2004.

Sun Liping 孙立平. "Chongjian Xingbie Juese Guanxi" 重建性别角色关系 (Rebuilding the Gender Roles). *Shehuixue yanjiu*, no. 6 (1994): 65–68.

Sun Shaoxian 孙绍先. "'Guizuhua' de Zhongguo 'Nüxing Zhuyi'" "贵族化" 的中国"女性主义" ("Aristocratized" Chinese "Feminism"). *Tianya*, no. 1 (2005): 23–25.

Sun, Wanning. *Subaltern China: Rural Migrants, Media, and Cultural Practices*. Lanham, MD: Rowman & Littlefield, 2014.

Tan Shen 谭深. "Funü Yanjiu de Xin Jinzhan" 妇女研究的新进展 (The New Developments of Women's Studies). *Shehuixue yanjiu*, no. 5 (1995): 66–74.

Tang, Can. "Sexual Harassment: The Dual Status of and Discrimination against Female Migrant Workers in Urban Areas." *Social Sciences in China* 19, no. 3 (1998): 64–71.

Tsing, Anna. "The Global Situation." *Cultural Anthropology* 15, no. 3 (2000): 327–60.

UN Women. "World Conferences on Women." www.unwomen.org/en/how-we-work/intergovernmental-support/world-conferences-on-women (accessed February 15, 2019).

Vittinghoff, Natascha. "Jiang Qing and Nora: Drama and Politics in the Republican Period." In *Women in China: The Republican Period in Historical Perspective*, edited by Mechthild Leutner and Nicola Spakowski, 208–41. Münster: LIT, 2005.

Vogel, Carol. "Phoenixes Rise in China and Float in New York." *New York Times*, February 14, 2014.

Walter, Benjamin. "Theses on the Philosophy of History." In Walter Benjamin, *Illuminations*. Translated by Harry Zohn, 252–64. New York: Schocken, 1969.

Wang Anyi 王安忆. *Fu Ping* 富萍. Changsha: Hunan wenyi chubanshe, 2000.

———. *Fu Ping: A Novel*. Translated by Howard Goldblatt. New York: Columbia Univ. Press, 2019.

———. *The Song of Everlasting Sorrow: A Novel*. Translated by Michael Berry and Susan Chan Egan. New York: Columbia Univ. Press, 2008.

Wang, Ban. *Illuminations from the Past*. Stanford: Stanford Univ. Press, 2004.

———. "Love at Last Sight: Nostalgia, Commodity, and Temporality in Wang Anyi's *Song of Unending Sorrow*." *positions: east asia cultures critiques* 10, no. 3 (2002): 669–94.

Wang Fengxian 王凤仙 and Mi Xiaolin 米晓琳. "NGO Huayu yu Minjian Funü Zuzhi de Ziwo Rentong" NGO 话语与民间妇女组织的自我认同 (NGO Discourse and the Self-Identification of Grassroots Women's Organizations). *Funü yanjiu luncong*, no. 6 (2007): 41–48.

Wang Gan 王干 and Dai Jinhua 戴锦华. "Nüxing Wenxue yu Gerenhua Xiezuo" 女性文学与个人化写作 (Women's Literature and Private Writing). *Dajia*, no. 1 (1996): 193–203.

Wang, Lingzhen. *Chinese Women's Cinema: Transnational Contexts*. New York: Columbia Univ. Press, 2011.

———. "Wang Ping and Women's Cinema in Socialist China: Institutional Practice, Feminist Cultures, and Embedded Authorship." *Signs: Journal of Women in Culture and Society* 40, no. 3 (2015): 590–93.

Wang Qi. "State-Society Relations and Women's Political Participation." In *Women of China: Economic and Social Transformation*, edited by Jackie West, Zhao Minghua, Chang Xiangqun, and Cheng Yuan, 19–44. New York: St. Martin's, 1999.

Wang Xiaoming 王晓明. "Cong 'Huaihailu' dao 'Meijiaqiao': Cong Wang Anyi Xiaoshuo de Zhuanbian Tanqi" 从"淮海路"到"梅家桥": 从王安忆小说的转变谈起 (From Huaihailu to Meijiaqiao: On the Transformations of Wang Anyi's Fiction). *Wenxue pinglun*, no. 3 (2002): 5–20.

Wang, Zheng 王政. "Detention of the Feminist Five in China." *Feminist Studies* 41, no. 2 (2015): 476–82.

———. *Finding Women in the State: A Socialist Feminist Revolution in the People's Republic of China, 1949–1964*. Berkeley: Univ. of California Press, 2016.

———. "A Historical Turning Point for the Women's Movement in China." *Signs: Journal of Women in Culture and Society* 22, no. 1 (1996): 192–99.

———. "Interviews with Wang Anyi, Zhu Lin, Dai Qing." *Modern Chinese Literature* 4, nos. 1/2 (1988): 99–148.

———. "'Nüxing Yishi', 'Shehui Xingbie Yishi' Bianyi" "女性意识"、"社会性别意识"辨异 (Distinguishing between "Women's Consciousness" and "Gender Consciousness"). *Funü yanjiu*, no. 2 (1997): 17–23.

———. "Shehui Xingbie Gainian zai Zhongguo de Yunyong" 社会性别概念在中国的运用 (The Application of the Concept of Gender in China). *Funü yanjiu*, no. 2 (2000): 3.

———. "We Had a Dream that the World Can Be Better than Today." *Revolution* 59 (2006), accessed March 21, 2019, http://revcom.us/a/059/some-of-us-en.html.

———. *Women in the Chinese Enlightenment: Oral and Textual Histories*. Berkeley: Univ. of California Press, 1999.

Wang Zheng and Ying Zhang. "Global Concepts, Local Practices: Chinese Feminism since the Fourth UN Conference on Women." *Feminist Studies* 36, no. 1 (2010): 40–70.

Wasserstrom, Jeffrey. "No Tiananmen Redux Picking the Right Analogy for the Protests in Hong Kong." *Foreign Affairs*, October 5, 2014.

Watkins, Susan. "Which Feminisms?" *New Left Review* 109, nos. 1–2 (2018): 5–76.

Wen Juping 温举平. "Minfadian Jiedu: Qiye Ruhe Yingdui Xingsaorao Dailai de Falü Fengxian" 民法典解读: 企业如何应对性骚扰带来的法律风险 (Interpreting the Civil Code: How Can Enterprises Deal with the Legal Risk Caused by Sexual Harassment Cases). Deheng lüshi shiwusuo. May 29, 2020. www.dhl.com.cn/CN/tansuocontent/0008/018697/7.aspx?MID=0902.

Wesoky, Sharon R. "Bringing the *Jia* Back into *Guojia*: Engendering Chinese Intellectual Politics." *Signs: Journal of Women in Culture and Society* 40, no. 3 (2015): 647–66.

Willette, Jeanne S. M. "Jacques Lacan and Women." *Art History Unstuffed*, July 19, 2013. https://arthistoryunstuffed.com/jacques-lacan-and-women/.

Wu, Hung. "Tiananmen Square: A Political History of Monuments." *Representations*, no. 35 (1991): 84–117.

Wu Jingya 武靖雅. "Picun Wenxue Xiaozu: Dang Chenmo de Daduoshu Naqi Bi" 皮村文学小组: 当沉默的大多数拿起笔 (The Picun Literature Group: When the Silent Majority Picks up a Pen). *Sohu.com*, July 7, 2017. www.sohu.com/a/155302421_747149.

Wu Zhihong 武志红. *Ju Ying Guo* 巨婴国 (The Nation of Giant Infants). Hangzhou: Zhejiang renmin chubanshe, 2016.

———. "Zonghuo de Baomu, yu Xiaoshi de Bianjie" 纵火的保姆, 与消失的边界 (Nanny Arsonist and Disappearing Boundaries). *Sina* blog, June 26, 2017. http://blog.sina.com.cn/s/blog_547645590102x9oi.html.

Xi Jinping 习近平. "Jianchi Nannü Pingdeng Jiben Guoce, Fahui Woguo Funü Weida Zuoyong" 坚持男女平等基本国策, 发挥我国妇女伟大作用 (Upholding the Fundamental State Policy of Gender Equity, Exerting Women's Great Role in Our Country). Xinhua net, October 31, 2013.

Xiao, Hui Faye. *Family Revolution: Marital Strife in Contemporary Chinese Literature and Visual Culture*. Seattle: Univ. of Washington Press, 2014.

———. "Female Neo-Realism: Masterworks of Zhang Jie, Wang Anyi, and Chi Li." In *Routledge Handbook of Modern Chinese Literature*, edited by Mingdong Gu, 553–66. New York: Routledge, 2018.

Xiaoyan 小燕. "*Yindao Dubai* Zuowei Duoyuan de Pingtai—Zhihe she, Haili she yu *Yin DAO Duoyun*" 《阴道独白》作为多元的平台—知和社、海

狸社与《阴DAO多云》(*The Vagina Monologues* as a Platform for Various Communities: Zhi-he Society, Beaver Club and *Yin Dao Duo Yun*). *Kula shibao*, December 06, 2013.

Xin Zhongguo Liushinian Jiaoyu Chengjiu Zhan 新中国六十年教育成就展 (An Exhibit of the Accomplishments of Education in the Sixty-Years of the New China). China Education Statistics. www.stats.edu.cn/tjdt/60/新中国60年教育成就展.htm.

Xing Zheng 邢郑. "Geti Siying Jingji Cheng Xina Jiuye 'Xushuichi'" 个体私营经济成吸纳就业 "蓄水池" (Private Enterprises Have Become the "Reservoir" for Absorbing Labor). People.cn, October 28, 2015. http://finance.people.com.cn/n/2015/1028/c1004-27747492.html.

Xu Ping 许平. "Yi ge Zhongguo Nanren Tushengtuzhang de Nüxing Zhuyi Guandian" 一个中国男人土生土长的女性主义观点 (A Chinese Man's Local Feminist Viewpoint). In *Nüxing? Zhuyi: Wenhua Chongtu yu Shenfen Rentong* 女性? 主义: 文化冲突与身份认同 (Femin?ism: The Clash of Cultures and Identity), edited by Li Xiaojiang, 227–41. Nanjing: Jiangsu renmin chubanshe, 2000.

Xu Xiaobin 徐晓斌. "Shuangyu Xingzuo" 双鱼星座 (Pisces). *Dajia*, no. 2 (1995): 10–44.

Xu Zhiyuan 许知远. *Naxie Youshang de Nianqingren* 那些忧伤的年轻人 (Those Sad Young People). Haikou: Hainan chubanshe, 2001.

Yan, Haiping. *Chinese Women Writers and the Feminist Imagination, 1905–1948*. New York: Routledge, 2006.

YAN Hairong. *New Masters, New Servants: Migration, Development, and Women Workers in China*. Durham, NC: Duke Univ. Press, 2008.

Yan Lieshan 鄢烈山. "Wei Beida Zhaosheng Bianhu: Zhe Bushi Xingbie Qishi" 为北大招生辩护: 这不是性别歧视 (In Defense of Beijing University's Student Enrollment: This Is Not Gender Discrimination). *Nanfang doushi bao*, September 1, 2005.

Yang Jianxiang 杨健翔. "Wulixue Weihe Bu Zai Xiyin Nüxing" 物理学为何不再吸引女性? (Why Does Physics No Longer Attract Women?). Chinese Academy of Sciences, February 5, 2002. www.cas.cn/ky/kyjz/200202/t20020205_1025719.shtml.

Yang, Mayfair Mei-hui. *Spaces of Their Own: Women's Public Sphere in Transnational China*. Minneapolis: Univ. of Minnesota Press, 1998.

Yau, Ching. *Filming Margins: Tang Shu Shuen, a Forgotten Hong Kong Woman Director*. Hong Kong: Hong Kong Univ. Press, 2004.

Young, James E. "The Counter-Monument: Memory against Itself in Germany Today." *Critical Inquiry* 18, no. 2 (1992): 267–96.

Young, Marilyn. *Women in China: Studies in Social Change and Feminism.* Ann Arbor: University of Michigan Center for Chinese Studies, 1973.

Yu Ya. "Dialogue with Images: Methodology of Visual Image (De)construction." news.artron.net, April 28, 2015. https://news.artron.net /20150428/n735411.html.

Zhang, Li. *In Search of Paradise: Middle-Class Living in a Chinese Metropolis.* Ithaca: Cornell Univ. Press, 2010.

Zhang Lijiao 张黎姣. "Beijing Wuhuan wai de Gongyou zhi Jia" 北京五环外的 工友之家 (A Workers' Home outside of Beijing's Fifth Ring). *Zhongguo qingnian bao*, August 6, 2013, 9.

Zhang Liming 章立明. "Quanqiuhua Yujing Zhong de Zhongguo Funüxue Jianshe" 全球化语境中的中国妇女学建设 (On the Construction of Women's Studies in China in the Context of Globalization). *Sixiang zhanxian*, no. 4 (2006): 54–60.

Zhang Lin 张琳 and Cai Yunqi 蔡蕴琦. "Guanzhu Daxuesheng Xingbiebi: Dushu Nüsheng Youxiu Gongzuo Nan Lingdao Duo" 关注大学生性别 比: 读书女生优秀工作男领导多 (Pay Attention to the Sex Ratio of College Students: More Excellent Female Students in School but More Male Leaders in Workplace). *Yangzi wanbao*, September 12, 2012.

Zhang, Naihua, and Ping-Chun Hsiung. "The Chinese Women's Movement in the Context of Globalization." In *Women's Movements in the Global Era: The Power of Local Feminisms*, edited by Amrita Basu, 157–92. Boulder: Westview, 2010.

Zhang Tie 张铁. "Ganxie Naxie Xinhuai Wenxue de Ren" 感谢那些心怀文学 的人 (Thanks to Those Who Still Cherish Literature in Their Hearts). *Renmin ribao*, April 26, 2017. 5.

Zhang Wenzhi 张文志 and Jiang Jie 姜杰. "Diaosu Chuangzuo Zhong de Chonggao yu Gonggongxing" 雕塑创作中的崇高与公共性 (Sculptural Sublime and Public Spheres). news.artron.net, November 28, 2014. https://news.artron.net/20141128/n682274_4.html.

Zhang, Xudong. *Postsocialism and Cultural Politics.* Durham, NC: Duke Univ. Press, 2008.

———. "Shanghai Nostalgia: Postrevolutionary Allegories in Wang Anyi's Literary Production in the 1990s." *positions: east asia cultures critiques* 8, no. 2 (2000): 349–87.

Zhang, Yuping. "Global Media Activism Made in China: An Extended Case Study on the Circuit of Cultures Based on *The Vagina Monologues* and *Break the Chain*." PhD diss., Chinese University of Hong Kong, 2016.

Zhao, Christina. "Harvey Weinstein's Friend Bey Logan Accused of Sexual Assault by Multiple Women in Hong Kong." *Newsweek*, December 13, 2017.

Zhao Xifang 赵稀方. "Zhongguo Nüxing Zhuyi de Kunjing" 中国女性主义的困境 (The Predicament of Chinese Feminism). *Wenyi zhengming*, no. 4 (2001): 74–79.

Zheng Bijun 郑必俊. "Nüxingxue Xueke zai Beijing Daxue de Jianshe Shijian ji Sikao" 女性学学科在北京大学的建设实践及思考 (Practice of and Reflections on Constructing Women's Studies at Peking University). In Li Xiaojiang et al., *Wenhua, Jiaoyu yu Xingbie: Bentu Jingyan yu Xueke Jianshe* 文化, 教育与性别—本土经验与学科建设 (Culture, Education, and Gender: Local Experiences and the Construction of a Discipline), 15–40. Nanjing: Jiangsu renmin chubanshe, 2002.

Zheng Yefu 郑也夫. "Nannü Pingdeng de Shehuixue Sikao" 男女平等的社会学思考 (Sociological Reflections on Gender Equity). *Shehuixue yanjiu*, no. 2 (1994): 108–13.

Zheng Yongfu 郑永福. "Funüshi yu Da Lishi Jiaoxue zhong de Hudong: Yi Lishi Zhuanye Zhongguo Jindaishi wei Li" 妇女史与大历史教学中的互动: 以历史专业中国近代史为例 (Interaction between Women's History and the Teaching of Macro History: The Example of Modern Chinese History for History Majors). In Li Xiaojiang et al., *Wenhua, Jiaoyu yu Xingbie: Bentu Jingyan yu Xueke Jianshe* 文化, 教育与性别—本土经验与学科建设 (Culture, Education, and Gender: Local Experiences and the Construction of a Discipline), 131–53. Nanjing: Jiangsu renmin chubanshe, 2002.

Zheng Yongfu 郑永福 and Lü Meiyi 吕美颐. *Jindai Zhongguo Funü Shenghuo* 近代中国妇女生活 (The Life of Modern Chinese Women). Zhengzhou: Henan renmin chubanshe, 1993.

Zhong Xueping 钟雪萍. "Cuozhi de Jiaolü" 错置的焦虑 (Worries about Wrong Positions). *Dushu*, no. 4 (2003): 47–53.

———. "*Internationale* as Specter: Na'er, 'Subaltern Literature,' and Contemporary China's 'Left Bank.'" In *China and New Left Visions: Political and Cultural Interventions*, edited by Ban Wang and Jie Lu, 101–20. Lanham, MD: Lexington, 2012.

Zhongguo Renquan Yanjiuhui 中国人权研究会 (The Association of Human Rights in China), ed. *Zhongguo Renquan Nianijan* 中国人权年鉴 (The Annals of Human Rights in China). Beijing: Tuanjie chubanshe, 2007.

Zhou Weihui 周卫慧. *Shanghai Baobei* 上海宝贝 (Shanghai Baby). Jilin: Chunfeng wenyi chubanshe, 1999.

Zhu, Ping. *Gender and Subjectivities in Early Twentieth-Century Chinese Literature and Culture*. New York: Palgrave, 2015.

———. "Seven Short Conversations with Wang Anyi, Dai Jinhua, and Wang Ban." *Chinese Literature Today* 6, no. 2 (2017): 14–21.

Zhu Yanfang 朱彦芳. "'Liang Xing Hexie': Zhongguo Nüxing Zhuyi de Zhongji Zhuiqiu: Di Qi Jie Zhongguo Nüxing Wenxue Xueshu Yantaohui Zongshu" "两性和谐": 中国女性主义的终极追求——第七届中国女性文学学术研讨会综述 ("Harmony between the Two Sexes": The Ultimate Goal of Chinese Feminism: Report on the Seventh Academic Conference on Chinese Women's Literature). *Luoyang shifan xueyuan xuebao*, no. 6 (2005): 18–20.

Contributor Biographies

Shuqin Cui is a professor of Asian studies and cinema studies at Bowdoin College. Her research interests extend across interdisciplinary fields such as film studies, cultural studies, and visual art studies, with a focus on gender politics. She is the author of *Women Through the Lens: Gender and Nation in a Century of Chinese Cinema* (2003) and *Gendered Bodies: Toward A Women's Visual Art in Contemporary China* (2015). She is also the editor of a special issue, "(En)Gendering: Chinese Women's Art in the Making," *positions: asia critique* 28, no. 1: 2020.

Dai Jinhua is a professor in the Institute of Comparative Literature and Culture at Peking University. She is a leading feminist critic, cultural critic, and film critic in China. She is the author of more than ten scholarly monographs, including *Breaking out of the Mirror City* (1995), *Invisible Writing: Cultural Studies in China in the 1990s* (1999), *Gendering China* (2005), *Cinema and Desire: Feminist Marxism and Cultural Politics in the Work of Dai Jinhua* (ed. Jing Wang and Tani Barlow, 2002), *Scenery in the Fog: Chinese Cinema Culture, 1978–1988* (2006), and *After the Post–Cold War: The Future of Chinese History* (2018). Her works have been translated into English, French, German, Italian, Spanish, Japanese, and Korean. Her literary, film, and TV commentaries have addressed an expanding audience in China, Taiwan, and Hong Kong over the last several decades.

Ke Qianting is an associate professor of Chinese language and literature at Sun Yat-sen University. She holds a PhD in comparative literature and world literature, and her research interests focus on feminist theory and its applications to literature, film, media and cultural studies. She has published numerous journal articles and the book *Body, Gender, and Trauma: On*

Chinese Contemporary Literature (2009), and has edited three volumes in Chinese on issues of gender studies.

Li Jun (aka Li Sipan) has a PhD in political sociology and is an associate professor at Shantou University. Before entering the academic world, she was already a well-known feminist activist and journalist nationwide. In 2004, she established the feminist organization Women Awakening Network (*Xinmeiti Nüxing*) in Guangzhou, which focuses on gender equality in journalism and communication. Her organization is committed to advocating gender equity in journalism; conducting media criticism; monitoring, investigating, and reporting on gender issues ignored by mainstream media; and training journalists on gender issues. Moreover, as a journalist with the pen name Li Sipan, she has long cooperated with lawyers and organizations to report cases of sexual assault in workplace and education. Her research focuses on generational differences in Chinese feminist activism, media and gender, and digital activism.

Li Xiaojiang is a special researcher at the Institute for Advanced Studies in Humanities and Social Sciences, and honorary director of the Women's Culture Museum at Shaanxi Normal University. Since the 1980s she has contributed pioneering work on women's studies in China and was a visiting scholar at McGill University, Harvard University, Ochanomizu University, and Nara Women's University. She served as the chief editor for *Chinese Women's Oral History in the 20th Century* (2003), and contributed to *Engendering China* (1995–2000) and the Women's Studies Research Series (1987–92). Her recent monographs include *Archaeology in Mind: Spiritual Archives of New China's People* (2014), *Dialogue with Wang Hui: Case Studies of Scholarism in Mainland China, 1990–2011* (2014), *Wolf Totem and the Post-Mao Utopian: A Chinese Perspective on Contemporary Western Scholarship* (ed. Edward Mansfield Gunn, Jr., 2018) and *Women's Utopia* (2016).

Liu Jindong is an associate professor of literature at Dalian University. She received her PhD in literary studies at Capital Normal University. Her main research interests include Chinese women's literature and modern Chinese poetry. She is the author of *Jiefangqu Qianqi Shige Yanjiu, 1936–1942*

(Study of the Chinese Poetry in the Early Period of the Liberated Areas, 1936–1942 [2014]).

Gina Marchetti is a professor in the Department of Comparative Literature at the University of Hong Kong. In 1995 her book *Romance and the "Yellow Peril": Race, Sex and Discursive Strategies in Hollywood Fiction* won the award for best book in the area of cultural studies from the Association for Asian American Studies. Her other books include *From Tian'anmen to Times Square: Transnational China* (2006), *Andrew Lau and Lan Mak's Infernal Affairs: The Trilogy* (2007), *The Chinese Diaspora on Global Screens* (2012), and the coedited volume *Chinese Connections: Critical Perspectives on Film, Identity, and Diaspora* (2009).

Nicola Spakowski is a professor of Sinology at the University of Freiburg in Germany. She previously held positions at the Free University of Berlin and Jacobs University Bremen. Her research is dedicated to twentieth-century and contemporary China, in particular concepts of time, approaches to history and the future, feminism and women's studies, and the history of socialism in China. She is the author and coeditor of several books, including *"Mit Mut an die Front": Die Militärische Beteiligung von Frauen in der Kommunistischen Revolution Chinas, 1925–1949* ("Courageously to the Front": Women's Military Participation in the Chinese Communist Revolution, 1925–1949, 2009) and *Women in China: The Republican Period in Historical Perspective* (2005). She has covered developments in contemporary Chinese feminism in numerous articles, including "Socialist Feminism in Post-Socialist China" (*positions: asia critique*, 2018).

Wang Anyi is an award-winning Chinese writer and a leading figure in contemporary Chinese literature. She is the chair of the Shanghai Writers' Association, vice-chair of the China Writers Association, and a professor in Chinese literature at Fudan University. Wang was the laureate of France's *Ordre des Arts et des Lettres* in 2013, and was the winner of the fifth Newman Prize in Chinese Literature in 2017. Her most representative works include *Lapse of Time* (1993), *Baotown* (1985), *Love on a Barren Mountain* (1986), *Love in a Small Town* (1986), *Brocade Valley* (1987), *Reality and Fiction* (1994), *Utopian Verses* (1991), *The Song of Everlasting Sorrow* (1995),

Fu Ping (2003), *Scent of Heaven* (2011), and *Artificer's Record* (2018). Her works have been widely translated into other languages.

Wang Zheng is a professor of women's studies and history and a research scientist of the Institute for Research on Women and Gender at the University of Michigan. She is the author or editor of *Women in the Chinese Enlightenment: Oral and Textual Histories, From the Soil: The Foundations of Chinese Society, Translating Feminisms in China*, and *Some of Us: Chinese Women Growing Up in the Mao Era*, and *Finding Women in the State: A Socialist Feminist Revolution in the People's Republic of China, 1949–1964* (2017). A long-term academic activist promoting gender studies in China, she is the founder and codirector of the University of Michigan–Fudan Joint Institute for Gender Studies at Fudan University. She has also authored two books and coedited nine volumes on feminism and gender studies in Chinese.

Wu Haiyun received her master's degree in Media and Cultural Analysis from Loughborough University Analysis in 2005 and graduated with a doctoral degree in Cultural Studies from Si-mian Institute for Advanced Studies in Humanities at East China Normal University in 2015. She was a visiting fellow at the Harvard-Yenching Institute from 2013 to 2014 and has worked for *Jiefang Daily*, *Phoenix Weekly*, and *The Paper*. Currently she is a senior editor at the news website Sixth Tone: www.sixthtone.com.

Hui Faye Xiao is a professor of Chinese at the University of Kansas. She is the author of *Family Revolution: Marital Strife in Contemporary Chinese Literature and Visual Culture* (2014) and *Youth Economy, Crisis, and Reinvention in Twenty-First-Century China: Morning Sun in the Tiny Times* (2020). She is currently working on a third monograph tentatively titled *The Hen Cackles in the Morning: Gendered Soundscape and Female Leadership in Modern Chinese Literature and Culture*.

Xueping Zhong is a professor of Chinese literature and culture in the Department of International Literary and Cultural Studies, Tufts University. Her publications include *Mainstream Culture Refocused: Television Drama, Society, and the Production of Meaning in Reform Era China* (2010) and *Masculinity Besieged?: Issues of Modernity and Male Subjectivity in Chinese Literature of the Late Twentieth Century* (2000). She cotranslated and coedited *Revolution and Its Narratives*, by Cai Xiang (2016). Her other coedited volumes include *Debating the Socialist Legacy and Capitalist Globalization in China* (2014), *Cultural and Social Transformations: Theoretical Framework and Chinese Context* (2013), *Culture and Social Transformations in Reform Era China* (2010), *Some of Us: Chinese Women Growing Up in the Mao Era* (2001).

Ping Zhu is an associate professor of Chinese literature at the University of Oklahoma and serves as the acting editor-in-chief of the biennial literary journal *Chinese Literature Today*. She is the author of *Gender and Subjectivities in Early Twentieth-Century Chinese Literature and Culture* (2015) and the coeditor of *Maoist Laughter* (2019), which won *Choice*'s Outstanding Academic Title in 2020. She is currently working on a monograph titled *The Discourse of Labor in Modern China, 1893–1976*.

Index

aesthetics, 33, 215, 264–65, 296, 298, 313; of women, 206, 209, 213, 241. *See also* labor

affective labor, 220–21, 226, 229–31, 248, 258, 268; women's service work in *Fu Ping*, 229, 231. *See also* Hardt, Michael

Ai Qing, 246; "Dayanhe—My Wet-nurse" (poem), 246, 251, 254

Ai Xiaoming, 138, 145, 147, 178, 183, 188, 197; "Moaning," 193

alienated labor. *See* labor

All About Love (film). *See* Hui, Ann

All-China Democratic Women's Fed-eration (ACDWF), 123, 125. *See also* All-China Women's Federation

All-China Women's Federation (ACWF): 118, 126n12, 154–55, 251–52, 304; history of, 9–10, 123–29; relationship to NGO, 17–20, 133, 136–38, 143, 151, 174–77. *See also* All-China Demo-cratic Women's Federation

Ankur (film), 32, 90–91

Anti-ELAB movement, 329–30, 333

Ark, The (novella). *See* Zhang Jie

baomu, 255, 258–60, 265, 268; narrative, 250; representations of,

245–50; self-writing, 243–45. *See also* "I Am Fan Yusu"

Barlow, Tani, 6, 15, 78, 226–27, 256–57

Bauman, Zygmunt, 236, 239

Between Humans and Monsters (reportage). *See* Liu Binyan

body writing (*shenti xiezuo*), 13

Bowers, Joanna, 307; *The Helper* (film), 307

Butterfly (film). *See* Mak Yan-Yan

Cai Chang, 123, 123n8, 125, 233n55

Cai Xiang, 9, 81, 223n23

Cao Zhenglu, 94; "Neon Lights" (novella), 94–98

capital, 25, 38, 60, 60n84, 93, 96, 167, 255, 257; relationship to patri-archal system, 106–7; return of, 93, 95, 102; transnational, 4n11, 17, 32

capitalism, 15, 78–79, 106–7, 139, 164, 219, 228–29, 236, 326, 328; China's merge with, 131–32, 137, 148, 221, 227; with Chinese char-acteristics, 28; feminists' critique of, 2, 24–26, 59; global, 21, 32, 78–79, 81, 102, 117, 173, 239, 241; neoliberal, 26, 27, 31

373